ENERGY POLICY MODELING: UNITED STATES AND CANADIAN EXPERIENCES

Volume I

Specialized Energy Policy Models

Editors

W. T. Ziemba
University of British Columbia

S. L. Schwartz
University of British Columbia

Ernest Koenigsberg
University of California, Berkeley

Martinus Nijhoff Publishing
Boston/The Hague/London

Distributors for North America:
Martinus Nijhoff Publishing
Kluwer Boston, Inc.
160 Old Derby Street
Hingham, Massachusetts 02043

Distributors outside of North America:
Kluwer Academic Publishers Group
Distribution Centre
P.O. Box 322
3300 AH Dordrecht, The Netherlands

Library of Congress Cataloging in Publication Data

Main entry under title:

Energy policy modeling.

Vol. 2: Editors, W. T. Ziemba and S. L. Schwartz.
Includes bibliographies.
CONTENTS: v. 1. Specialized energy policy models.—
v. 2. Integrative energy policy models.
1. Energy policy—Mathematical models—Congresses.
2. Energy policy—Canada—mathematical models—Congresses. 3. Energy policy—United States—Mathematical models—Congresses. I. Ziemba, W. T. II. Schwartz, Sandra L. III. Koenigsberg, Ernest.
HD9502.A2E549 333.7 79-24586

ISBN-13: 978-94-009-8750-0 e-ISBN-13: 978-94-009-8748-7
DOI: 10.1007/978-94-009-8748-7

These volumes are affectionately dedicated
to our mothers, Ruth Rosner Schwartz
and Mary Moser Ziemba.

CONTENTS

FOREWORD

Alex Cowie

As the twentieth century draws to a close, one of our greatest problems is the availability of energy. One way to study the energy problem is to resolve it into four areas: energy demand, energy sources, transportation of energy from sources to demand centers, and the optimal allocation of energy forms to demands. Each of these areas is extremely complex by itself. When efforts are made to tie them together, for example, to produce a National Policy, the complexities are compounded.

Another way to study the energy problem, because of its political and social consequences, is to resolve it into geographical areas. Individual provinces of Canada or states of the United States will have their concerns about energy within their geographical boundaries. As producer, consumer, or both, each wants to ensure an energy development program which will work to the maximum benefit of its citizens. Similarly, countries endeavor to protect their citizens and undertake energy policies that will assure either a continuation of the existing quality of life or — particularly in the case of "Third World" countries — a marked improvement in quality of life. These competing and conflicting goals call for a study which encompasses the whole world. Again, complexity is piled upon complexity. If the problem is not yet sufficiently complex, there is an equally complex question of the effect of energy production and use on the ecology.

The only way problems of this complexity can be brought within the capability of the human mind is by modeling. Global models, linear programming models, and econometric models are some of the tools required in any attempt to solve or even gain understanding of the energy problem. Models which capture the complex interactions involved, coupled with the calculating capability of computers, offer the best hope for solutions.

The study of complex problems by modeling describes the work of Operational Research. It was natural, therefore, that the 1978 Canadian Energy Policy Modeling Conference should be held in tandem with the 1978 National Conference of CORS, the Canadian Operational Research Society. Many of the conference speakers, panelists, and session chairman are also members of O.R. Societies. Operational Researchers are among the leaders in energy-related studies. These grounds alone justify CORS endorsing both the conference itself and this publication of its proceedings. However, in a larger sense, CORS is greatly concerned about any problem that faces mankind. We will always endorse undertakings, such as the 1978 Canadian Energy Policy Modeling Conference, which bring together outstanding people to communicate on the "state of the art" in the resolution of important problems and issues. Conferences like these focus public attention on problems and permit cross-pollination of ideas which promotes speedier resolution of problems.

It is a pleasure on behalf of CORS to endorse these two proceedings volumes and commend them to all who are concerned about the problem of energy availability.

CONTRIBUTORS

C. F. ARMSTRONG, CN Railways, Edmonton, Alberta T5J OK2.
EGON BALAS, Graduate School of Industrial Administration, Carnegie-Mellon University, Pittsburgh, Pennsylvania 15213.
GERALD E. BENNINGTON, Metrek Division, The Mitre Corporation, McLean, Virginia 22101.
E. R. BERNDT, Department of Economics, University of British Columbia, Vancouver, B.C. V6T 1W5.
CHRISTOPHER J. BOON, Canadian Institute for Guided Ground Transport, Queen's University, Kingston, Ontario. K7L 3N6
T. A. CAMERON, Department of Economics, Princeton University, Princeton, New Jersey 08540.
ALEX COWIE, Sun Oil of Canada, Toronto, Ontario M5S 2S4.
A. J. COX, Energy Laboratory, Massachusetts Institute of Technology, Cambridge, Massachusetts 02138.
PAUL D. CRAIG, Department of Applied Science, University of California, Davis, California 95616.
J. W. DEVANNEY III, Martingale Inc. Cambridge, Massachusetts 02139.
R. ERDMANN, Energy, Mines and Resources, Ottawa, Ontario K1A OE4.
MELVYN A. FUSS, Institute for Policy Analysis, University of Toronto, Toronto, Ontario M5S 1A1.
DAVID B. GOLDSTEIN, Department of Physics, University of California, Berkeley, California 94720.
EDWARD D. GRIFFITH, Atlantic Richfield Co., Washington, D.C. 20036.
L. B. HARSANYI, National Energy Board, Ottawa, Ontario K1A OE5.
J. F. HELLIWELL, Department of Economics, University of British Columbia, Vancouver, B.C. V6T 1W5.
RICHARD HYNDMAN, Data Resources of Canada, Toronto, Ontario M5S 2V1.
TOM L. JOHNSTON, Teknetron, Inc., Berkeley, California 94704.
M. B. KENNEDY, Martingale Inc., Cambridge, Massachusetts 02139.
J. DANIEL KHAZZOOM, Institute for Research in Energy and Economic Modeling, San Francisco, California 94116.
ERNEST KOENIGSBERG, Schools of Business Administration, University of California, Berkeley, California 94720.

Y. KOTOWITZ, Institute for Policy Analysis, University of Toronto, Toronto, Ontario M5S 1A1.

DAVID B. LARGE, Teknekron Inc., Berkeley, California 94704.

T. J. LAUGA, Swan Wooster Engineering Co. Ltd. Vancouver, B.C. V6G 1C5.

ALLEN J. LICHTENBERG, Department of Electrical Engineering, University California, Berkeley, California 94720.

F. MATHEWSON, Institute for Policy Analysis, University of Toronto, Toronto, Ontario M5S 1A1.

G. MAY, Data Metrics Ltd., Calgary, Alberta T2P 2X6.

ROBERT A. MEYER, Schools of Business Administration, University of California, Berkeley, California 94720.

MARVIN C. OTT, Office of Technology Assessment, U.S. Congress, Capitol Bldg., Washington D.C. 20510.

R. A. PREECE, National Energy Board, Ottawa, Ontario K1A OE5.

ARTHUR H. ROSENFELD, Department of Physics, University of California Berkeley, California 94720.

JOHN ROWSE, Professor of Economics, University of Calgary, Calgary, Alberta T2N 1N4 (The work reported in Professor Rowse's paper was performed while he was affiliated with the Department of Economics of Queens University, Kingston Ontario).

R. SAHI, Energy, Mines and Resources, Ottawa, Ontario K1A OE4.

S.L. SCHWARTZ, Faculty of Commerce and Business Administration, University of British Columbia, Vancouver, B.C. V6T 1W5.

ADEL S. SHALABY, National Energy Board, Ottawa, Ontario K1A OE5.

BRUCE A. SMITH, Economic Resources Associates, Kensington, California 94707.

LOWELL F. SMITH, Environmental Protection Agency, Washington, D.C. 20460.

ANDREW J. VAN HORN, Teknekron Inc., Berkeley, California 94704.

RAMESH R. WAGHMARE, National Energy Board, Ottawa, Ontario K1A OE5.

G. C. WATKINS, Data Metrics Ltd., Calgary, Alberta T2P 2X6.

H. M. WEBSTER, National Energy Board, Ottawa, Ontario K1A OE5.

F. Paul WYMAN, College of Business Administration, University of Nebraska, Lincoln, Nebraska 68588. (The work reported in Professor Wyman's paper was performed while he was affiliated with the Bechtel Corporation, San Francisco, California)

W. T. ZIEMBA, Faculty of Commerce and Business Administration, University of British Columbia, Vancouver, B.C. V6T 1W5.

PREFACE

During the period following World War II the major industrialized nations built economies that utilized and were highly dependent upon cheap and readily available energy supplies. The primary energy sources were various fossil fuels, in particular oil and natural gas that were used to produce gasoline, home heating oil, electricity from oil fired burners and myriad of other products. Oil and natural gas were in plentiful supply with much domestic production in North America and vast reserves in the OPEC (Organization of Petroleum Exporting Countries) nations. The marginal costs of production in many countries were almost negligible (about 20¢ per barrel in Saudi Arabia) and supplies virtually inexhaustible, or so it seemed. There was a decline in the real price of energy of about 30 percent over a twenty-five year period. Then, suddenly in 1973–1974, through a sequence of quick actions, the members of OPEC increased the price of oil by about 500 percent ($2.20 to $11.50). The Arab members of OPEC, namely OAPEC, saw the availability of their oil as an important political weapon. In the fall of 1973 they announced a boycott against the United States, Holland, and other nations thought to be sympathetic to the Israeli point of view in their continuing struggle with their Arab neighbors. The boycott took many forms, and lasted until the spring of 1974. It caused much dislocation in the economies of North America, Europe, Japan, and other countries. The simultaneous price rise and fear of shortages led to a period known as "the energy crisis" or "the energy-environmental crisis" or "the oil crisis." It was apparent that many economic, operations research, and scientific studies could aid in the solution and understanding of this crisis. Many energy modeling groups were formed to analyze energy-related problems from regional and economy-wide perspectives. The suddenly felt need for sound government action to alleviate the economic shock caused by these dislocations has led to increased use of quantitative modeling techniques by various government agencies. Never before has operations research and econometrics played such an important role in the preparation and execution of government actions as in the wake of the 1973–1974 energy crisis. In the ensuing four years, analyses of a multitude of energy problems were undertaken and the field of energy policy modeling became one of the fastest growing industries in the industrialized world. This has led to numerous sessions at economics, operations research, and other conferences as well as specialized conferences on various energy topics. The "Canadian Energy Policy Modeling Conference," held in North Vancouver, May 18–20, 1978, was organized to assess the state of the art in energy modeling in North America. A major aim of the conference was to determine the extent to which energy modeling had and could make a contribution to the energy policy decision-making process. The participants and speakers at the conference were a balanced mixture of industry, government, and academics from the United States and Canada.

These two volumes contain revised and updated versions of the major papers presented at the conference plus edited transcriptions of the panel discussions and several additional papers aimed at particular topics deemed worthy of further study at the conference. These include contributions by: Marcuse on why one would wish to utilize models in a world that is so uncertain; Greenberg on crash mode modeling; and Fuller and Ziemba's survey of twenty major United States and Canadian energy policy models. The coverage is broken down into eight parts, four of which appear in each volume. The first volume is concerned with "specialized" energy policy models, such as those occurring in the study of demand, supply, coal and transportation, and the problems and interactions of energy, environment, and conservation. The second volume is concerned with attempts to mesh supply and demand elements in an integrative fashion. Its major sections are concerned with the process of energy policy modeling, national and regional energy modeling concepts and methods, the Canadian-United

States gas pipeline, and the problems of financing energy development projects. This breakdown is suggestive rather than forming a strict guide to the contents of each volume. Each section is introduced with a survey of topics and related literature that interface with the papers in the section. The introductions are not meant to be definitive surveys, rather they are intended to put the papers in perspective in light of the current literature on energy policy modeling.

All the papers were refereed and they were also edited by Sandra Schwartz and me to minimize inconsistencies of style, form, and content. Thanks are due to the various authors for their contributions to these volumes and their patience and understanding regarding our red penciling of their papers. Since one of our primary goals is to assess the current state of energy modeling, the papers take many forms. Many of the papers describe the development and use of models that have been or are currently in actual use. Others are discussional in nature and are concerned with energy problem areas or model development and use. Several papers describe preliminary work concerned with the development of major energy models and indicate the direction that they expect future work to take. There are of course, many differences as well as similarities and interconnections between the energy problems of Canada and the United States. One of the primary differences borne out by the papers and panel discussions in these volumes is the more widespread use of econometric simulations in Canada and the more integrative optimizing approach of the United States' models. This is partly due to historical precedents and the expense of integrative model construction and the greater availability of large research grants in the United States.

A number of people contributed to the success of the conference and aided in the preparation of these volumes. Jack Mitten and John Roberts initially suggested that I organize a session concerned with "National Energy Policy Models" at the annual general meeting of CORS, held May 15–18, 1978, in North Vancouver. It seemed appropriate to expand this suggested session into a full conference that would begin with the CORS session linking the two conferences. The CORS council has endorsed the conference and these volumes as an activity it wishes to support, and its current president, Alex Cowie, has kindly provided the Foreword to the volumes. Herb Drechsler and Ernest Koenigsberg kindly assisted me in the organization of the conference. Ernest also organized the sessions on coal and transportation and is responsible for Section III of Volume I on this topic. While I was visiting at the Department of Industrial Engineering and Operations Research, University of California, Berkeley, in the winter and spring of 1978, Bill Jewell kindly provided much support and encouragement as well as several valuable suggestions concerning the conference. The conference was organized as an activity of the Management Science Research Centre, Faculty of Commerce and Business Administration, University of British Columbia. Thanks are due to Peter Larkin, Dean of Graduate Studies, U.B.C., and Peter Lusztig, Dean of the Faculty of Commerce and Business Administration, for their financial contributions to the conference budget. My U.B.C. colleagues Ernst Berndt, Erwin Diewert, John Helliwell, and Peter Nemetz have made a number of very helpful suggestions concerning the preparation of these volumes. Trudy Cameron and Joan Rush have aided us in our research for the volume. Trudy and Dave Fuller did masterful jobs of transcribing the panel discussions into a coherent readable form. Special thanks go to the following individuals who served as referees: E. Balas, G. E. Bennington, E. R. Berndt, T. A. Cameron, T. E. Daniel, W. E. Diewert, J. D. Fuller, M. A. Fuss, D. Granot, H. J. Greenberg, E. D. Griffith, R. C. Grinold, J. Hayward, T. Johnston, B. A. Kalymon, E. Keonigsberg, A. Kydes, A. J. Lichtenberg, W. Marcuse, F. Mathewson, J. M. Mulvey, S. C. Parikh, T. Parson, S. C. Peck, E. R. Peterson, R. A. Preece, J. Rogers, M. Rothman, R. Sahi, A. Shogan, D. G. Waddingham, and G. C. Watkins. Excellent clerical and typing assistance was received from Barbara Blancard, Monica Heinrich, Violet Jung, Jupian Leung, Helen McCann, Lillian McClanaghan, and Mabel Yee. Finally, special thanks go to Sandra Schwartz for joining me as a coeditor of these volumes.

W. T. Ziemba

I ENERGY DEMAND MODELING

S. L. Schwartz

From the end of World War II until the early 1970s there was a strong and steady increase in the demand for energy. The abundant supplies of fossil and other fuels from domestic and imported sources were sufficient to lead to an actual fall in the real price of energy of about 30 percent over a twenty-five-year period. The cheap and readily available energy supplies, particularly fossil fuels, led to industrial development in the western world of economies dependent upon these inputs. Energy was typically considered to be an intermediate good with fixed requirements to output. This is seen dramatically in plots of GNP versus energy use which are remarkably close to straight lines. Production function estimation would consider capital and labor to be the crucial inputs with energy's availability taken essentially as unlimited with its total use and cost multiples of final output. The dramatic 500 percent increase in oil prices ($2.20 to $11.50 per barrel) in 1973–1974 led to a reassessment of this approach. Oil based products and related fossil fuels such as natural gas were no longer cheaper nor did they seem to be as readily available. The period 1972–1977 witnessed a 37 percent increase in the real cost of energy. With this rise in energy prices, the projections of demand growth quickly declined. The 1973 projection for energy demand in Canada for

1975–1990 was about 5.8 percent per year reflecting past trends. By 1975 these projections were already in the 3.7–4.8 percent range, which allowed for a growth in energy per capita of 2.5 percent (Hopper, 1975). Current projections are even lower. Brooks et al. (1977) in estimating energy demand to the year 2025, found that under all scenarios the rate of increase was less than 3 percent per year, and 2 percent is perhaps the upper limit. In the United States the rate of increase of energy demand dropped to 1 percent per year, while in Europe demand actually experienced a negative growth rate. Thus, there clearly is a price responsiveness to the demand for various fuels.

This section presents seven studies of energy demand that span the spectrum of price sensitive demand analyses. Though all of the studies are for Canada, similar studies have been undertaken for the United States and other countries, and much of the methodology is directly applicable in other applications. A recent review of many of the major energy demand studies in the United States, Canada, and other countries has been given by Pindyck (1979). Reference to some of these studies will be made here. The principal approach of all the studies considered in this section is the statistical or econometric approach to energy demand. Typically an underlying economic model is postulated and optimal economic behavior then yields equations representing various economic phenomenon. A statistical model is then formed from these equations and the various parameters are estimated using past data and consistent estimation techniques. In some cases the economic model has a weak theoretical foundation, and the aim of the investigators is to determine that model that best fits the data. The models are used to understand and explain the rationale behind the absolute level and changes in the demand for the particular forms of energy under consideration and the effects of various energy prices and other inputs. Some of the models have been developed to provide a specific and hopefully reliable, subject to statistical confidence levels, mechanism to predict demands for various energy products over time in light of changes in input quantities. It is to be noted that the papers in this section do not consider the so-called engineering approach to demand estimation in which one adds up all the energy "needed" for specific industrial, consumer, residential, transportation, etc., uses to arrive at final demands. Since the engineering approach provides detail and the economic approach specifically considers price effects, combining them would be most desirable in many applications. At present little of this is done. For more on this "marriage of economic and engineering approaches," see the panel discussion in Volume II on the "Future of

National Energy Modeling,'' Hoffman and Jorgenson (1977), and Berndt and Wood (1979).

The studies included here are indicative of the wide variety of econometric demand forecasting models developed in Canada. They vary from the comprehensive highly aggregate demand study of Preece, Harsanyi, and Webster which reports on the energy demand forecasting model of the National Energy Board (NEB) and the Sahi-Erdmann model of interfuel substitution for all final use demands used in the Department of Energy, Mines and Resources (EMR), Canada; to intermediate level studies including the Cameron and Schwartz study of demand by manufacturing sector and Fuss's paper on regional manufacturing demand taking into account supply constraints; to more specific studies including the Hyndman, Kotowitz, and Mathewson study of residential demand for electricity and gas; the Berndt, May, and Watkins model of Alberta electric demand; and more disaggregated yet, the Shalaby and Waghmare study of passenger car gasoline demand.

The Preece, Harsanyi, and Webster study reports on a top-down demand model that is used by the NEB for demand projections and to analyze and formulate energy policy. The NEB is responsible for certain federal energy policy decisions such as availability of fuels for export, and their terms of reference require that they provide adequate supplies to meet domestic demand before exports are permitted. Thus the beginning of policy analysis is a projection of the domestic demand as well as the domestic supplies. Their model forecasts demand by sector and region and fuel type in terms of output Btus. It begins with a regionalized macroeconomic forecast of the economy based on the CANDIDE model and projections of energy prices. The model can be used to test sensitivity to various future developments both in terms of general economic growth and energy availability. As with all models in constant use, improvements are always being made and the model is updated in the light of new data. The methodology incorporates both the ''need'' and price-responsive demand approaches. The equations for most sectors omit price effects. For iron and steel, energy demand is a function of output in the sector. Energy demand for marine and rail transport is a function of real domestic product (RDP); for air the equation includes the relative price of air transport as well. Demand for road diesel, asphalt, and lubes and greases are functions of past consumption and RDP; while demand for other diesel includes the relative price of gas. Though energy demand in these sectors is still generally dependent on fixed proportions of energy to output and lagged demand (essentially a proxy for output), new equations have been estimated for the residential, commercial, and industrial sectors that take account of price elasticity of demand.

Demand estimation for the residential, commercial, and industrial sectors proceeds by first projecting total energy demand as a function of price and demographic and economic variables. Then market shares are obtained exogenously on the basis of past trends modified by expectations of future changes. The equation for the residential sector estimates total energy demand per single family household (space and water heating, appliances, and lights). The regional intercepts vary and it is not clear what variables are accounted for in the constant. Variables include real disposable income per household, price of energy relative to the Consumer Price Index (CPI), and degree days; all with common slopes except for the Atlantic region which has a different slope on real disposable income. For the commercial and industrial sectors, individual equations are estimated for each region. Both contain similar variables as the residential — for commercial, RDP in the service industries, real price of energy, degree days; and for industrial, RDP in forestry, mining manufacturing and construction, capital output ratio, and the relative price of energy. This is an aggregate model and as such can give a first approximation to national energy demand. Its aggregate nature is also a shortcoming. Relying as it does on broad definitions of sectors makes it difficult to forecast the impact of various policy changes on energy demand except if that policy results in regional differences. Preece, Harsanyi, and Webster assume that the output mix in each sector will remain constant. A second problem is that the fuel shares are not carefully modeled but rely on past trends and judgment and not on relative price and/or availability, again making it difficult to project changes. Other aspects not covered and that might be fruitful directions for future research include short/long run distinctions, recognition of technical change, and the incorporation of underlying production relationships. Some of these considerations are addressed in other papers in this section, and these techniques and model might be incorporated into the NEB model to make it more complete.

Sahi and Erdmann discuss a model used at EMR for medium term projections of energy demand. Their primary focus is on the substitutability among fuels. Their model is also a top-down model. They begin with useful energy demand in Btus for the residential, commercial, and industrial sectors based on energy prices, economic activity, and temperature. This is then broken down into market shares which are a function of the prices of the various fuels with some constraints including consideration of lagged shares. Modified by end use efficiency estimates, the result is an estimate of the actual energy purchased. The share analysis focuses on the three major fuels in each sector and region which account for 80–90 percent of the energy demand. For example, in the commercial and industrial sectors this would be electricity, natural gas, and fuel oil. The remaining fuels are treated as residuals.

The reported total energy demand elasticities are similar to the NEB estimates for residential, −0.40 (NEB, −0.39), and industrial, −0.48 (−0.49), but much higher for the commercial, −1.06 (−0.66). The income elasticities are below the NEB estimate for residential, 0.34 (0.51) and commercial, 0.20 (1.39), but the same for industrial, 1.00 (1.02).

The estimated market share equations resulted in lags of response to price changes of more than forty-five years, so use is made of previous studies to obtain what are considered more reasonable estimates. It appears that market share determination would be a good area for further work. Substantial substitutability among fuels is found. Own-price elasticities are negative and are elastic (absolute value greater than one) for all fuels and sectors except electricity in the industrial sector. Oil and natural gas are strong substitutes. There are a number of perverse (negative, implying complements) elasticities involving the electricity cross-elasticities — with gas in all sectors and with oil for commercial and industrial. This is not a symmetric relationship. The estimated lags are fairly long, averaging more than six years. A nice feature is the comparison of interfuel cross-elasticities presented in Table 2–5.

As with the NEB model, this model is still in the developmental stage. Several areas in which the model could be improved for use as a policy tool are: (1) elasticities might be a function of market penetration; (2) allowance could be made for new fuels having significant market shares (i.e., at present there is no method for accounting for the residual fuels); and (3) as output rather than input Btus are used, there is no apparent relationship between end use efficiency and prices, yet this has been identified as an area of potential conservation. Fuel demand can be reduced (supply increased) by increasing the efficiency of utilization of energy. A number of studies on end-use efficiency were reported recently (Roche, 1979). The average fuel used now is only 80 percent efficient. E. T. Hayes, formerly of the U.S. Bureau of Mines, predicts that by 2000 efficiency will be only 75 percent, as less accessible and less easily tapped energy sources are used. Net energy also is a function of the type of delivery system used. A. Melcher analyzed two modes of utilizing coal to heat houses: (1) generation of electricity and distribution through the utility grid; and (2) coal gasification with gas delivered to homes and burned there. The second option was more energy efficient than the first. The loss in (1) was 1 percent to mine, plus additional to transport to the plant, and fully two-thirds lost in conversion to electricity. Oil is also subject to massive depletion in transit; 2 percent is lost in drilling, 11 percent to run the refinery, and on net for every 1000 Btus of oil in the ground, only 100 Btus is usable. Even with gasohol, the new product to stretch oil supplies, it has been found that many of the sources are net energy consumers (e.g., wheat and corn), while sugar cane is only a modest net energy producer. The solar satellite also borders on being a net energy consumer.

The papers by Cameron and Schwartz and by Fuss utilize the translog methodology to estimate the demand for energy. While studies such as those previously discussed point to the existence of price responsiveness in energy demand, the Cameron and Schwartz paper investigates the differential response patterns of individual manufacturing sectors. This is important for pointing toward policy interventions that may be needed to smooth the path of adjustment of various, in the past, relatively price inelastic sectors. Another feature of the study is the adjustment of the capital price series to account for inflation.

Several previous studies have investigated the impact of various government tax policies directly on investment and indirectly on energy. Berndt (n.d.) documents how various tax policies in the United States have decreased the relative prices of capital and energy vis-à-vis labor and have led to the increased utilization of energy. As alternative production possibilities are available, conservation of energy (reduction in demand) can be achieved by a lessening of these incentives. This, of course, would also necessitate a switch in stabilization policies which often emphasize capital. Berndt suggests instead an employment tax credit. See also Jorgenson and Hudson (1974).

It is clear that if energy and investment both have prices that do not reflect true costs then the production structure will be biased toward these inputs. An additional bias that has recently been a problem is inflation. Due to the long life of capital, inflation has the impact on the investment decision of lowering the real relative cost of capital, thus inducing investment. If an adjustment is not made to accommodate this then the apparent price responsiveness will be biased and small changes in the cost of capital (related to the interest rate) will result in large changes in capital utilization. Even increases in the apparent cost of capital will result in increases in investment as the inflationary cost reduction effect is masked. If policy designed to change future factor utilization is to be effective, elements such as this must be isolated so only the true price responsiveness remains. The Cameron-Schwartz paper is an attempt to cope with this issue. The lag structure is represented by a simple three-year lag; the mode of accounting for inflation is to consider only changes in the rate of inflation as being significant. The impact of this adjustment on the relative cost of capital is large. In the original series the cost of capital in the period 1957–1974 increased more than the cost of labor, while in the corrected series it increased much less. This provides a better explanation for the increased capital intensity experienced in most sectors during that period. This correction for inflation provides a more reasonable estimate of the own elasticity of demand for capital and makes the cross-elasticities of demand among the factors interpretable. The energy elasticities range from -0.2 to -1.00, and average -0.63. Most resource pairs are substitutes which agrees with the Griffin and Gregory (1976) estimates, but not with other studies such as Berndt and Wood (1975) and Fuss (1977). This reflects the more appropriate estimate of capital costs. Sectors that would experience trouble coping with higher energy prices are discussed, as well as policy interventions to ease their adjustment.

The paper by Fuss is concerned with a regional model of energy demand with six fuel types for total manufacturing. The paper develops new methodology so that one can give specific consideration to supply constraints rather than utilizing the standard assumption of infinitely elastic supply. The model is thus a bridge to the integrative models reported in Volume II. The model recognizes that we do not just rely on the price system to allocate fuels but there are also supply constraints. In fact, though economists are more concerned with fuel prices, often the primary concern with consumers and producers is supply within fairly wide price ranges. Fuss's procedure begins by estimating shadow prices for the constrained fuels. Firms are then assumed to optimize using these "as if" prices. In the application, a basic four-region, two-level translog model is used. The production model has four factors: capital, labor, energy, and materials; and there is an energy sub-model with six energy types also of the translog form. Energy demand is measured in Btus with the sub-model providing essentially a price index of energy inputs and a means of obtaining price responsiveness of individual energy types while maintaining the same structure as the factor demand model.

Constraints are placed on natural gas and/or fuel oil and the other fuels (electricity and coal) are unconstrained. An iterative procedure is used as the model is a share, not a quantity model. Convergence is guaranteed as the own-price elasticities are negative. Projections are made for

Ontario for 1980–1985, and a number of interesting results are discussed. Differences between the constrained and unconstrained scenarios are the result of variations between short and long run adjustments. Constrained elasticities are, of course, less than unconstrained. There are both substitution and pseudo-income effects, i.e., aggregate energy demand decreases as some fuels are constrained and price rises.

The nature of the interaction among inputs varies depending upon the constraints imposed, and resources may switch from being substitutes to being complements. Hence, models estimated using data from periods when there were fuel availability constraints have elasticity estimates that are biased downward and may have inaccurate cross-elasticity estimates. Thus there should be an extension of Fuss's approach used in the estimation of the historical elasticities. Even Fuss's application is still not perfectly consistent since he utilizes past data estimated without the same supply restrictions. The results however are valid and important: long run elasticities are likely underestimated and in the long run all resources are substitutes.

Another issue is that new fuel availabilities become more crucial. For this it is important to have fully integrated supply-demand models that include energy R&D and new energy sources such as solar and cogeneration explicitly such as those discussed in Volume II. Fuss investigates the impact of constraints of two fuels that are strong substitutes (natural gas and oil). It would be interesting to see the results of an analysis with other fuel constraints such as electricity, which is widely believed to have negligible substitutability with other fuels.

The last three papers present more specific demand models. Hyndman, Kotowitz, and Mathewson investigate residential demand for electricity and natural gas. In this study of Canadian demand by region, residential energy consumption is divided into heating and appliance use. For heating, demand is a function of equipment in place. Hence, only with new construction or renovation is the option for switching available, i.e., there is a "lumpy" demand function. Appliance demand changes with the accumulation of durables and is said to be more sensitive to the price of fuels; it is a continuous demand function. Though these two demands were derived separately, they are combined and total gas and electric demands are the dependent variables. The underlying model is control theoretic in nature. Optimality conditions and approximations yield linear demand equations.

Price elasticity estimates for heating are not exact but bounds are given: the lower bound includes construction demand while the upper includes renovations and deaths as well. The heating elasticities are all very high except electricity demand with respect to oil prices. With respect to appliances, the electric own demand elasticity is very low (−0.07) and there is little impact of gas price changes (−0.006), while for natural gas the own is somewhat higher though inelastic (−0.24) and the cross with electricity is higher (0.61). In comparison with the Sahi-Erdmann paper, the elasticity of demand for heat is larger while that for appliances is lower.

Unfortunately oil was excluded as the required data were unavailable; this is a notable omission because oil is a major fuel both in terms of present use and future availability problems. Also the natural gas distribution network was expanded during the sample period, so with only two fuels some areas had no choice but to go electric if oil is excluded. Also prior to 1963 high electricity prices precluded use of electricity for heating. The model provides an interesting technique for analyzing the fuel choice but more work might be required to discover additional explanatory variables and better capture the behavior of consumers.

Another shortcoming of the heating component of the Hyndman, Kotowitz, and Mathewson model is that no methods for energy conservation are built into the model. Improving insulation is ignored as historically the standards have determined the level of insulation; however, this may no longer be valid, at least it should not be presumed valid. The various governments (provincial and federal) have instituted programs to encourage insulating houses to higher standards and it would be useful to be able to determine the effectiveness of these programs. It would be helpful to include the price of insulation as a variable. Also no provision is made for adjusting the thermostat downward in response to higher fuel prices, nor for other energy sources such as solar. The latter omission might be significant in terms of new construction and renovations. Even passive solar options might significantly reduce demand for the fuel included in the model. No explanation is provided for renovations and terminations of existing houses. Thus it is not clear if relative fuel price changes would result in a significant number of renovations, particularly of heating systems.

A comprehensive investigation of electricity demand in Alberta is presented in the paper by Berndt, May, and Watkins. This study is especially interesting due to the cheap availability of natural gas and easy access to oil. Some figures cited early in the paper make it likely that there is little price responsiveness of electricity demand: in the residential sector, electricity provides only 12 percent of the BTUs but accounts for 47 percent of the expenditures; in the commercial sector, 16 percent of the BTUs and 60 percent of the expenditures; and in the industrial, 14 percent and 50 percent respectively. Several alternative models are considered. One issue is the question of using an independent approach (i.e., estimating electric demand ignoring other fuels) or a share approach (where the category "other fuels" is included). One would expect the share approach with an estimate of the overall energy demand to work best, but given the limited substitutability between electricity and other fuels evident in past studies, a strong case can be built for the individual approach as well. Both methods are reported for residential, while the share approach alone is reported for commercial and industrial. This is surprising as the coefficient on the gas price in the independent equation for residential is insignificant, implying limited substitution (as it is reported, electricity is not used for heat). With this in mind it is not surprising that the two methods yield quite different results. Variables appear in the share model that are not significant in the independent model and vice versa (for example, the female participation rate). In the share approach, income is significant but not price. For residential demand it appears that the independent approach is preferable. For this model, the coefficient on the lagged variable is high as in the Hyndman-Kotowitz-Mathewson paper (approximately 0.68), while short run and long run price (income) elasticities are −0.23 (.71) and −0.73 (0.98) respectively in line with other studies.

Another issue important in the current energy debate concerns the appropriate definition of the price of electricity, and whether average or marginal or both should be included. This issue is discussed in Section IV of this volume under conservation as a declining block structure appears to encourage demand and many advocate use of marginal cost of capacity pricing. The question here is which price best explains demand and can be used to project future demand under alternative price schemes. This debate began with an article by Taylor (1975) who argued that in order to avoid biased elasticity estimates, both prices are necessary even though intramarginal cost is often not available and/or data are costly to collect. Berndt (1978) reviews the issue and shows empirically that a minor correction can take account of the intramarginal price effect, which is essentially an income effect. He also argues that Halvorsen's (1975) finding that use of ex post average rates yield the same elasticities as marginal rates is an artifact of the Cobb-Douglas functional form he used.

Berndt, May, and Watkins report only the share approach for the commercial and industrial sectors, i.e., electricity versus other fuels which, of course, reduces to one equation. Translog functions are estimated with six variants for each sector and technological change is included. The system of equations selected as best implies neutral technological change. The results indicate a decreasing price elasticity of energy over the sample, from −0.5 to −0.25; capital and energy are initially substitutes but become complements as energy becomes less elastic, while energy and labor are substitutes. These results for the commercial sector seem to bear out results found in the industrial sectors by Cameron and Schwartz. The own elasticity of electric energy is −0.75 (1961) increasing to −0.86 (1974) and −0.84 (1976). In this two-fuel model the own of electricity is the negative of the cross-elasticity between electricity and other fuels, assuming total energy is constant. Of course the net elasticities with the total energy use variable are not symmetric: the own elasticities for electricity are higher −0.95, −0.82, −0.84 (1961, 1970, 1976 respectively); while the cross-elasticities are lower.

For the industrial sector, the best model was one specifying non-neutral technological change that was labor saving, capital using, and energy neutral. As in the commercial sector, the own-price elasticity of energy has declined from −0.47 (1961) to −0.37 (1976). This is lower than the estimate from other studies for total Canadian manufacturing (see, for example, Fuss, 1977) but is higher than the estimate for prairie energy demand by McRae (1978) of −0.67. Capital and labor and labor and energy are substitutes, and capital and energy are complements; while in the McRae paper, all inputs are substitutes. The own elasticity of electricity is about −0.85, indicating a high degree of substitutability among fuels. This is higher than expected given the previous studies reported; for example, McRae (1977) estimated this at −0.31.

The final paper of this section is the most disaggregated. Shalaby and Waghmare investigate the passenger car demand for gasoline as a subsection of the NEB model reported by Preece, Harsanyi, and Webster. This paper indicates the complexity involved in estimating a single part of a model in detail. To estimate the demand requires estimation of: (1) new car sales, (2) stock of cars (scrappage), (3) small versus larger car shares of the market, (4) annual mileage per car, and (5) urban versus rural miles driven as well as data on many demographic and economic variables. The model has been developed for use to simulate the impact of various policies on gasoline demand. One problem with the projection methodology is that they estimate small cars are driven fewer miles than large. This is true historically, but as large cars are phased out this is likely to change, hence, the entire model may not hold. It would be preferable to estimate miles driven and then obtain a car size split. This is the approach taken in the four models compared by Sweeney (1979) as part of the Energy Modeling Forum. First, vehicle miles were estimated as a function of various demands such as distance to work, to vacation, etc. This is hard to model. Standard variables include population (elasticity of miles to population is about one), income (elasticity also about one) and cost of gas (elasticity quite small, generally about −0.15 to −0.25). The second phase requires estimating the average miles per gallon of the vehicle fleet (Fmpg). This adjusts slowly, given the large stock effect but is still a significant variable. It is the elasticity of Fmpg with respect to gas price that is of interest to policy makers who question whether gas price changes are sufficient to increase auto fuel efficiency or whether standards must be mandated. Sweeney compares the estimates based on four models. These models represent two approaches: the direct estimate type and the share approach. The estimates of the direct approach, are −0.7, while for the share approach they range from less than −.05 to about −.3. The direct approach was judged to be better for a long run estimate as it captures both the greater share of small versus large cars and the increases of fuel efficiency within that class itself. Choice of appropriate policy hinges on the proper estimate of this variable. Whether financial incentives are sufficient to induce fuel efficiency depends on whether this elasticity is high or low.

Blomqvist and Haessel (1978) are indirectly concerned with Fmpg. They have developed a disaggregate model for estimating demand for autos by type (size and age) as functions of prices of the autos and of gas. They find that auto price is more significant than gas price.

Caution must be taken in making comparisons among studies, as often they do not represent the same thing nor do they ask the same question. Pindyck (1979) provides some guidelines for making comparisons and arriving at estimates of the various demand elasticities. As there is generally little variation in a given time series and the data base is typically not large enough to capture the fuel adjustment to any price changes that do occur, time series studies often provide short run, not long run, estimates of elasticities. On the other hand, cross-country studies represent a wide range of price ratios and resources bases, and technologies are more representative of longer run elasticities.

International comparisons of energy demand and utilization exhibit the wide range of variability that is possible, as well as destroy the myth that there is an increasing relationship between energy use and GNP. Pindyck (1979) provides a chart of the Btus/GNP for six countries for 1960–1975. Canada was highest, averaging approximately 68,000 Btu/$GNP, followed by the United States at 60,000, the United Kingdom at 55,000, the Netherlands and West Germany at 50,000, and with France at the bottom with 30,000. Goen (1975), by undertaking a detailed comparison of the energy utilization patterns of the United States and West Germany, was able to recommend areas of potential energy savings. In 1972, West Germany used half the energy per capita of the United States. This ratio varies from 25 percent in transportation, 48 percent residential, 58 percent industrial, and 56 percent commercial. There are many reasons for this variation in energy utilization that reflects adaptation to higher energy costs in West Germany; these include: (1) more self-generation of electricity by industry (29 percent versus 6 percent), resulting in greater thermal efficiency; (2) point of use/heat on demand hot water heating (one-third U.S, requirements of energy for this use); (3) improved utilization of electric generation capacity with peak load pricing and pumped storage for peak demand; and (4) smaller cars and greater reliance on mass transit. See also Section IV of this volume for investigation of various energy-saving suggestions.

Pindyck (1979) provides a table with comparative elasticities of demand for energy and among fuel types. This provides a useful summary of the range of estimates. For the residential sector, the time series studies for various countries range from −0.12 to −0.56; while cross-country studies yield a range of −0.71 to −1.10. The Preece, Harsanyi, and Webster (PHW) and the Sahi and Erdmann (SE) estimates of −0.39 and −0.40 both fall within the range for short run estimates. Though income elasticities tend toward 1.0; the estimates reported here are low: 0.51 (PHW) and 0.34 (SE). With respect to the demand for individual fuels, the own elasticity of demand for oil and natural gas are approximately −1.0, indicating apparent ease of substitution. For electric demand the range of estimates is quite wide: −0.30 to −1.2. As Pindyck notes, one would expect electric demand to be less elastic than oil or natural gas, as in many uses there is no substitute for electricity. The Sahi-Erdmann paper presents higher own elasticities: natural gas and oil both greater than −1.5 and electricity almost −1.0. As Hyndman, Kotowitz, and Mathewson estimate seperate elasticities for heating and appliances, their elasticities are not comparable. Heating elasticities are quite high: electricity, −2.1 to −3.6; and natural gas, −2.0 to −2.5; while those for appliances are −0.00 and −0.24 respectively. Berndt, May, and Watkins have lower estimates of the electricity short and long run price elasticities: −0.23 and −0.73 respectively.

For the industrial sector, estimates of elasticities again differ depending on whether time series or cross-section data are used. For time series data the own-price elasticity of energy demand is approximately −0.50 and capital and energy are complements; while for cross-section analysis the value is −0.80 and greater with capital and energy being substitutes. This same split arises between the time series data and engineering studies as reported by Berndt and Wood (1977). Both the Preece-Harsanyi-Webster and the Sahi-Erdmann papers confirm the general result of an energy own elasticity of about −0.5, while Fuss estimates −0.46. The Halvorsen and Ford (1978) study of U.S. individual sectoral demand for energy found a wide range of variability with an average energy own elasticity of −0.66 and a range to −2.54. The average compares well with the Cameron-Schwartz study while the range is higher.

For this sector, Pindyck finds no consensus among the estimates of interfuel substitution except to note that possibilities exist and that demand for electricity is less elastic than demand for other fuels. This is borne out by the Sahi-Erdmann study where the own elasticities for electricity, natural gas, and oil are −0.80, −1.01, and −1.48 respectively. Their estimates are higher than those of Fuss and Waverman (1975); −0.64, −0.97, and −1.31 respectively. The Fuss paper reports unconstrained elasticities for six fuels: ranging from a low of −0.72 for electricity to a high of −1.96 for coal.

There is also no consensus with respect to the demand for motor gasoline. Estimates range from −0.2 to −0.7 depending on, among other things, whether time series or cross-section data are used. Pindyck believes that even these estimates are too low, and that long run elasticities are about −1.0 (It is not possible to make a direct comparison with the Shalaby-Waghmare paper.)

For electricity generation there is also scope for substitution among fuels, with own elasticities for oil, natural gas, and coal ranging from −1.0 to −4.0; −0.8 to −1.4 and −0.4 to −1.2 respectively (Pindyck, 1979). (It is not possible to make direct comparisons with the NEB model as the data are not reported.)

In summary, all the studies in this section as well as the studies in the literature indicate that the elasticity of demand for energy is sufficiently high that we no longer need talk about energy requirements but can inquire about energy demands under various scenarios. This increases our options in energy policy.

REFERENCES

Berndt, E. R. 1978. *The demand for electricity: Comment and further results.* UBC Department of Economics, Programme in Natural Resource Economics Working Paper 28.

Berndt, E. R. Tax policy, energy demand and economic growth. In *Full employment on a small planet,* ed. M. Gaffney. Madison: University of Wisconsin Press, forthcoming.

Berndt, E. R., and Wood, D. O. 1975. Technology, prices and the derived demand for energy. *Review of Economics and Statistics* 57:259–268.

Berndt, E. R., and Wood, D. O. 1979. Engineering and econometric interpretations of energy-capital complementarity. *American Economic Review* 69:342–354.

Brooks, D. B.; Erdmann, R.; and Winstanley, G. 1977. *Some scenarios of energy demand in Canada in the year 2025*. Report of the Demand and Conservation Task Force, Ottawa.

Blomqvist, A. G., and Haessel, W. 1978. Small cars, large cars, and the price of gasoline. *Canadian Journal of Economics* 11:470–489.

Fuss, M. A. 1977. The demand for energy in Canadian manufacturing. *Journal of Econometrics* 5:89–116.

Fuss, M., and Waverman, L. 1975. *The demand for energy in Canada*. Toronto: University of Toronto, Institute for Policy Analysis.

Goen, R. L. 1975. *Comparison of energy consumption between West Germany and the United States*. SRI EGU 3519, Menlo Park, Calif.

Griffin, J. M., and Gregory, P. R. 1976. An intercountry translog model of energy substitution responses. *American Economic Review* 66:845–857.

Halvorsen, R. 1975. Residential demand for electric energy. *Review of Economics and Statistics* 57:12–18.

Halvorsen, R., and Ford, J. 1978. Substitution among energy, capital, and labor inputs in U.S. manufacturing. In *Advances in the economics of energy and resources*, vol. I, ed. R. S. Pindyck. Greenwich, Conn.: J.A.I. Press.

Hoffman, K. C., and Jorgenson, D. W. 1977. Economic and technology models for evaluation of energy policy. *Bell Journal of Economics* 8:444–466.

Hopper, W. H. 1975. *Canadian energy policy planning*. Notes for an Address to the 13th Pacific Science Congress, E.M.R., Ottawa.

Jorgenson, D. W., and Hudson, E. A. 1974. Tax policy and energy use. In *Fiscal Policy and the Energy Crisis*, Hearings before the Subcommittee on Energy of the Committee on Finance, U.S. Senate. Washington, D.C.: U.S. Government Printing Office.

McRae, R.N. 1978. *Regional demand for energy by Canadian manufacturing industries*. University of Alberta, Canadian Energy Research Institute, Working Paper 78-7.

Pindyck, R. S. 1979. "The Characteristics of the Demand for Energy." In *Energy Conservation and Public Policy*, ed. W. Sawhill. Englewood Cliffs, N.J.: Prentice Hall Inc.

Roche, P. B. 1979. Energy-costly energy is wasting resources, some analysts worry. *Wall Street Journal*, May 3, p. 1.

Sweeney, J. L. 1979. *Structural econometric modeling of gasoline consumption*. Energy Modeling Forum, mimeo.

Taylor, L. D. 1975. The demand for electricity: A survey. *Bell Journal of Economics* 6:74–110.

1 THE ENERGY DEMAND FORECASTING SYSTEM OF THE NATIONAL ENERGY BOARD*

R. A. Preece, L. B. Harsanyi, and H. M. Webster

This paper presents the National Energy Board's long term energy demand forecasting model in its present state of development. The orientation is to first provide a general overview of the structure of the model. This is followed by a discussion of some of the more important elements of the model, with emphasis on the results of recent research at the NEB. Energy demand forecasts developed with the aid of this forecasting system, and earlier versions of it, are contained in several NEB published reports (1977a, 1977b, 1978).

1.1 OVERVIEW OF THE MODEL

1.1.1 General

The model is used to forecast energy demand by sector, energy type, and region. A central characteristic of the methodology is that a total energy

*Much of the general structure of the model originates from work done at the Department of Energy, Mines and Resources (Gorbet, 1974). With regard to the research and development carried out at the National Energy Board, special acknowledgments are extended to M. McKee, A. Shalaby, and R. Waghmare.

approach is employed. The basic unit of analysis is the market sector and for each sector, total energy demand and the fuel selection process are analyzed separately. This approach has several advantages, but perhaps the most important is that in forecasting the demand for one energy type, other energy types have to be explicitly taken into account. Another advantage of the total energy approach is that it is more likely that energy demand forecasts for individual energy types will add up to a reasonable total than when each energy type is forecast separately.

The forecasts are prepared on an "effective energy" or output Btu basis, whereby input (or reported) Btus for each energy type and sector are adjusted by an estimate of the utilization efficiency associated with that energy type and sector. A desirable characteristic of this approach is that, when aggregating across energy types, it enables the analysis of total energy behavior in the absence of changes due to shifts in the market shares of energy types with different utilization efficiencies (Harsanyi, 1971; Gorbet, 1974a).

The energy demand forecasts for each market sector are obtained through a combination of econometric modeling and "judgment." The sum of the market sector forecasts yields a forecast of secondary energy demand; from this, a forecast of primary energy demand is derived. A flowchart of the model is presented in Figure 1-1.

1.1.2 Exogenous Variables

Two basic sets of exogenous variables are required as input to the model: economic growth assumptions and price assumptions. National forecasts of the various economic and demographic variables used to obtain energy demand forecasts are from the 1.2M version of the CANDIDE model.* Regional economic-demographic projections are obtained through judgmental projections of "regional spreading ratios." In general, the historical trends in these ratios have been very gradual and steady, indicating that the errors that may be introduced through the use of this methodology are probably not very great.

*CANDIDE is a large computerized econometric model of the Canadian economy which has been developed by the Economic Council of Canada with the assistance of several departments of the federal government and private consulting firms. The development of the model has been proceeding since 1970, and the current version, CANDIDE 1.2M, was developed in 1976. The model being used at the Board is the 1.2M version with further modifications made by the Board staff.

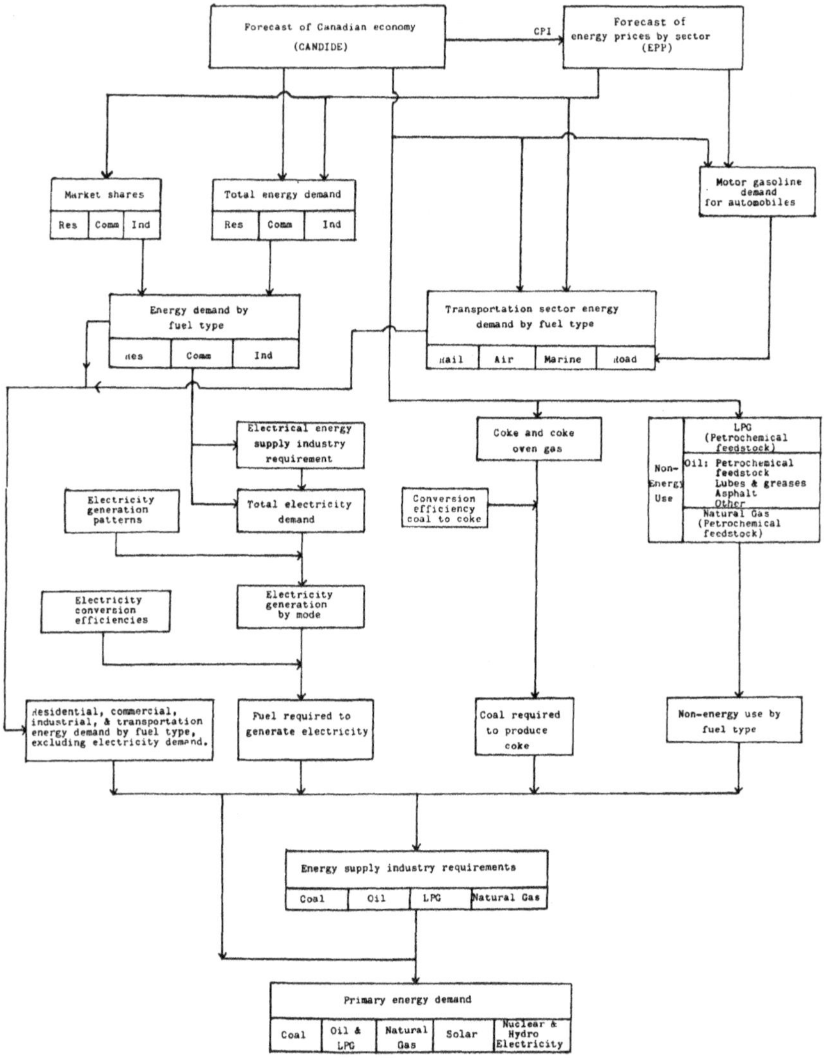

FIGURE 1-1. Flowchart of total energy demand module

With regard to energy prices, a new model, the Energy Price Program (EPP), has recently been developed at the Board to provide the relevant price projections. This model is used to project burner tip prices by region, sector, and major energy type. These prices are then used to make market share projections and to form weighted average energy price projections which are used for forecasting total energy demands. The projected market shares provide the weights in the calculations.

The general method or flow of the Energy Price Program is as follows: The starting point for obtaining burner tip price projections for oil and gas is an assumption regarding the international price of crude oil landed in Montreal. From this, Toronto refinery gate and city gate price projections of domestic crude and natural gas are derived, via decision rules with respect to the price of domestic crude relative to international crude and domestic gas relative to domestic crude. Refinery and city gate prices for other regions are then derived from projections of relevant "transportation" margins. An exception is British Columbia, where the starting point is the international price of crude "landed" in Vancouver. The approach to obtaining the refinery and city gate prices is the same as for Toronto. Given regional projections of refinery and city gate prices for oil and gas, burner tip prices are derived through the application of projected refining and/or distribution margins, which of course vary by fuel type, market sector, and region. The various transportation, refining and distribution margins are projected judgmentally, taking into account appropriate historical trends.

Burner tip equivalent electricity price projections are based, in large part, on appropriate historical trends, electric utility plans, and expectations regarding rate increases.

1.1.3 The Residential, Commercial, and Industrial Sectors

The methodologies used in forecasting energy demands in the residential, commercial, and industrial sectors are essentially the same. First, forecasts of total energy are obtained, by region, based on estimated equations linking energy demands to their major determinants: economic and demographic variables and energy prices. Given the various total energy projections, forecasts of the demand for each energy type by sector and region are then obtained via market share analysis. These projections are developed exogenously, based on the analysis of historical trends, on expectations regarding probable effects of projected relative energy prices, and on market intelligence. A discussion of our recent research regarding total energy equations in these three sectors is given in Section 2.

The industrial sector is defined to exclude the petrochemical industry and the iron and steel industry as it relates to coke and coke-oven gas demand. Both of these industries are analyzed separately. The approach used to forecast energy demands for the petrochemical industry follows. Total Canada coke and coke-oven gas demands are projected through the use of a relatively simple econometric equation linking demand to real domestic product

TABLE 1-1. Energy demand equations for the iron and steel industry, and the transportation and non-energy use sectors

1. Iron and Steel Industry—Demand for Coke and Coke-Oven Gas

$$\ell n\ \text{CKEDEM} = \underset{(4.41)}{1.31} + \underset{(12.46)}{.57}\ \text{RDPIS}$$

$\bar{R}^2 = .90$, COV (%) = 1.13, D.W. = 1.21, Est. period: 1958–1975.

2. Transportation Sector

Rail

$$\text{RLDISDEM} = \underset{(11.99)}{29836.03} + \underset{(15.97)}{2.17}\ \text{RDPMMA}$$

$\bar{R}^2 = .94$, AAPE = 3.1, D.W. = 1.91, Est. period 1958–1975.

Air

$$\text{AVFUEL/POP} = \underset{(2.56)}{-1.06} + \underset{(20.47)}{.78}\ (\text{GNP/POP}) - \underset{(.90)}{.03}\ (\text{AIR/CPI})$$

$\bar{R}^2 = .96$, COV = 7.2, D.W. = .72, Est. period: 1958–1975.

Marine

$$\ell n\ \text{DEMMAR} = \underset{(7.46)}{3.39} + \underset{(13.08)}{.60}\ \ell n\ \text{RDPMMA} - \underset{(5.99)}{.333}\ \text{DUM}$$

$\bar{R}^2 = .91$, COV = .47, D.W. = 1.42, Est. period: 1959–1975.

Road

Road diesel

$$\ell n\ \text{RDC} = \underset{(3.31)}{-3.18}\ \text{ATLDUM} - \underset{(3.38)}{3.84}\ \text{QUEDUM} - \underset{(3.40)}{4.09}\ \text{ONTDUM} - \underset{(3.28)}{3.46}\ \text{PRADUM} - \underset{(3.27)}{3.29}\ \text{BCDUM} + \underset{(4.07)}{.79}\ \ell n\ \text{RDP} + \underset{(10.4)}{.74}\ \ell n\ \text{RDC}_{-1}$$

$\bar{R}^2 = .98$, AAPE = .77, D.W. = 1.60, Est. period: 1961–1975.

"Other" motor gasoline

$$\ell n\ \text{OMOGAS} = \underset{(2.77)}{6.40}\ \text{ATLDUM} + \underset{(2.48)}{5.89}\ \text{QUEDUM} + \underset{(2.48)}{5.89}\ \text{ONTDUM} + \underset{(2.66)}{5.90}\ \text{MANDUM} + \underset{(2.82)}{6.40}\ \text{SASKDUM} + \underset{(2.73)}{6.27}\ \text{ALTADUM} + \underset{(2.64)}{6.06}\ \text{BCDUM} + \underset{(3.21)}{.42}\ \ell n\ \text{RDP} - \underset{(2.83)}{1.34}\ \ell n\ \text{RGAS} + \underset{(3.02)}{.42}\ \ell n\ \text{OMOGAS}_{-1}$$

$\bar{R}^2 = .95$, AAPE = 1.04, D.W. = 2.58, Est. period: 1966–1975.

3. Non-Energy Use Sector

Asphalt

$$\ell n\ \text{DEMASH} = \underset{(3.82)}{2.78}\ \text{ATLA} + \underset{(3.42)}{2.49}\ \text{QUE} + \underset{(3.19)}{2.29}\ \text{ONT} + \underset{(3.62)}{2.72}\ \text{PRAR} + \underset{(3.55)}{2.47}\ \text{BC} + \underset{(5.17)}{.56}\ \ell n\ \text{RDP} + .48\ \ell n\ \text{DEMASH}_{-1}$$

$\bar{R}^2 = .98$, COV = .59, D.W. = 1.90, Est. period: 1961–1974.

TABLE 1-1. *Continued*

Lubes and Greases

$$\ell n \text{ DEMLUBG} = \underset{(4.81)}{2.70 \text{ ATLA}} + \underset{(4.68)}{2.61 \text{ QUE}} + \underset{(4.71)}{2.76 \text{ ONT}}$$
$$\underset{(4.73)}{2.77 \text{ PRAR}} + \underset{(4.80)}{2.69 \text{ B.C.}} + \underset{(1.96)}{.07 \text{ DUMNWT}}$$
$$+ \underset{(4.44)}{.37 \ \ell n \text{ RDP}} + .56 \ \ell n \text{ DEMLUBG}_{-1}$$

$\bar{R}^2 = .99$, COV = .4, D.W. = 2.13, Est. period: 1961–1974.

Definitions:

CKEDEM	= The demand for coke and coke-oven gas in trillions of input BTUs; all Canada.
RDPIS	= Real Domestic Product in the iron and steel industry expressed in millions of 1961 dollars.
RLDISDEM	= Demand for diesel in the rail sector, total Canada, billions of BTUs.
RDPMMA	= Real domestic product in mining, manufacturing, and agriculture; millions of 1961 dollars.
AVFUEL	= Consumption of aviation gasoline and aviation turbo fuel, total Canada, billions of output BTUs.
POP	= Population; thousands of persons.
GNP	= Gross national product; millions of 1961 dollars.
AIR	= Index of airfares; 1961 = 1.0.
CPI	= Consumer price index; 1961 = 1.0.
DEMMAR	= Consumption of energy in the marine sector, total Canada; billions of output BTUs.
DUM	= Dummy variable; equals 1 in 1975, 0 before 1975.
RDC	= Road consumption of diesel; billions of output BTUs.
RDP	= Real domestic product; millions of 1961 dollars.
OMOGAS	= Total gasoline minus gasoline used by passenger automobiles.
RGAS	= The price of gasoline deflated by the RDP deflator.
DEMASH	= Demand for asphalt; thousands of barrels.
RDP	= Real domestic product; millions of 1961 dollars.
DEMLUBG	= Demand for lubes and greases; thousands of barrels.
DUMNWT	= Dummy variable; equals 1 in 1961 and 1962, 0 otherwise.

Numbers in brackets are t statistics.

in the iron and steel industry (see Table 1-1). The regional split is obtained exogenously.

1.1.4 The Transportation Sector

The transportation sector consists of four subsectors: road, rail, air, and marine, each of which is analyzed separately. For each of the rail, air, and marine subsectors, econometric equations are used to project (essentially all of) total energy demand in Canada. For both rail and marine, demands are assumed to be a function of real domestic product in manufacturing, mining, and agriculture. The variables affecting energy demand in the air subsector are per capita GNP and an air fare index. The equations for these three subsectors have been recently estimated at the NEB, and are presented in Table 1-1. Once total energy projections are obtained for each of these subsectors, demands by energy type and/or region are obtained judgmentally.

The road transportation sector is broken down into three components: road diesel, motor gasoline for vehicles other than passenger cars, and motor gasoline for passenger cars. Simple econometric models are used to project demands for road diesel and "other" motor gasoline. Specifically, road diesel is estimated as a function of real domestic product and a lagged dependent variable. "Other" motor gasoline is estimated as a function of real domestic product, the real price of motor gasoline, and a lagged dependent variable. Both equations were estimated using regional cross-section time series data. The sample period was 1961–1974 for the road diesel equation and 1968–1974 for "other" motor gasoline. The equations are presented in Table 1-1.

A fairly elaborate model is used to project motor gasoline demand for passenger cars. The model, which takes into consideration new car sales of large and small cars, fuel efficiencies, scrappage rates, etc., is described in chapter 7.

1.1.5 Non-Energy Use

For each component of non-energy use, except petrochemical feedstocks, demand is forecast via simple econometric equations or by judgmental projections of historical trends. The equations for asphalt and lubricating oils and greases have as exogenous variables total real domestic product and a lagged dependent variable (see Table 1-1). Both equations were estimated using pooled regional cross-section and time series data.

Forecasts of petrochemical feedstock requirements are developed within a total energy context. The general methodology is to first develop forecasts of the production of primary petrochemicals (e.g., ethylene) in Canada, which are then translated into forecasts of energy requirements for that production. For the earlier years of the forecast period, the forecasts of petrochemical production are based on an evaluation of information regarding company plans and proposals in this area. For the later years, the production forecasts are based in large part on forecasts of Canadian demand for primary petrochemicals. The geographical distribution of forecast primary petrochemical production (plant location) and the type of feedstock to be used — oil, gas, or LPGs — are determined through utilization of information from various sources.

1.1.6 Energy Supply Industries Including Electricity Generation

Demand by the energy supply industries for oil, LPG, coal, natural gas, and electricity is forecast by applying projected factors or proportions to forecast total market sector demand for each energy type. The relevant proportions, which vary by region and over time, are developed exogenously, drawing upon appropriate historical data, market intelligence, and engineering studies.

The starting point for forecasting energy requirements for the generation of electricity is an electricity demand forecast, which is the sum of demand in the residential, commercial, and industrial sectors and requirements by energy supply industries. Given the demand forecast, a forecast is prepared regarding the quantities of electricity to be produced by each energy type by region. Within each region separate analyses are carried out regarding major utilities, minor utilities, and industrial self-generation of electricity. The analysis is based on the examination and evaluation of utility system expansion plans, historical data, and miscellaneous market intelligence.

Energy supply industry requirements of electricity consists of transmission losses resulting from the supplying of electricity to domestic and export markets. Conversion losses associated with the generation of electricity are included in total energy demand by forecasting demand for the fuels required to generate electricity, including that electricity used in the energy supply industries.

1.2 RECENT RESEARCH IN THE RESIDENTIAL, COMMERCIAL, AND INDUSTRIAL SECTORS

New total energy equations have recently been developed at NEB to aid in forecasting energy demands in the residential, commercial, and industrial sectors. These equations replace those developed at EMR several years ago (Gorbet, 1974). In all three sectors, the estimated equations are static, with the result that the various estimated elasticities approximate long term elasticities. Since the dependency of energy demands on investment decisions is not adequately taken into account, direct use of these equations for forecasting is hazardous, particularly in light of recent and expected large energy price increases. Specifically, it is expected that the response of energy demands to changes in energy prices will not be instantaneous but rather will take place over a number of years. This problem is presently overcome by imposing judgmentally determined price lag structures on the equations before using them for forecasting. It would be preferable to estimate dynamic equations, but given existing time series availability, "dynamic" specifications generally take the form of the use of lagged dependent variables, which have a number of limitations. These include the nature of the response mechanism imposed, the econometric problems introduced (Johnston, 1960), and the possibility that errors will tend to multiply over time when such specifications are used for forecasting. Further, our recent experimentation for the market sectors suggests that the empirical results are often poorer when a lagged dependent variable is included in the specification, particularly for time series estimation.

1.2.1 The Residential Sector

The total energy equation developed for the residential sector (see Table 1-2) derives from well-developed consumer demand theory, whereby energy demand is postulated to be a function of income and the price of energy relative to other goods and services. The dependent variable is total energy demand (excluding coke and coke-oven gas) in the residential sector, in output BTUs, divided by the stock of single dwelling households. The exogenous variables are real disposable income per household, the weighted average price of energy in the residential sector divided by the consumer price index, and normalized degree days. The equation has a double log form and is estimated using ordinary least squares, from pooled regional cross-section and time series data to exploit the extra degrees of freedom gained and the additional variation of the pooled sample. The estimation period was 1962–1975, across six regions, resulting in ninety-eight observations.

Regional intercepts were allowed to vary, but in general, common regional slopes were employed assuming that consumers in various regions would change their energy consumption patterns in the same manner, as changes in incomes and prices occurred. The exception was the Atlantic, where a slope dummy for income was incorporated. This significantly improved the results for that region, indicating that Atlantic consumers appear to be more sensitive to changes in income than are other consumers.

TABLE 1–2. The total energy equation in the residential sector

Dependent Variable	Intercepts							$\ell n \frac{YDP}{(CPI)(HOHO)}$		$\ell n \frac{PENR}{CPI}$	ℓn (DD)	$\bar{R}^2$
	ATL	QUE	ONT	MAN	SASK	ALTA	B.C.	*Common Slope*	*ATL. Difference*			
$\ell n \frac{TE}{STS}$	3.30	4.78	4.29	4.27	4.27	4.24	4.14	.51	.58	−.39	.57	.96
	(24.2)	(55.3)	(49.3)	(55.4)	(56.4)	(62.1)	(43.8)	(15.4)	(7.0)	(5.3)	(5.5)	
	Residual Analysis											
Statistic	ATL	QUE	ONT	MAN	SASK	ALTA	B.C.					
AAPE	5.1	2.9	2.3	3.4	2.8	3.5	4.5					
D.W.	.85	2.39	1.01	1.56	1.75	1.52	.56					

Definitions:

TE = Total energy, billions of output BTUs.
STS = Number of single dwelling households; thousands.
YDP = Personal disposable income; millions of dollars.
CPI = Consumer price index; 1961 = 1.0.
HOHO = Number of households; thousands.
PENR = Weighted average price of light fuel oil, natural gas and electricity in the residential sector; dollars per million output BTUs.
DD = Normalized degree days.

Numbers in brackets are t statistics.

While most of the data were readily available from Statistics Canada publications, the exceptions should be noted. The energy quantity data for the individual Prairie provinces were developed at NEB (for this and all other sectors), as were regional consumer price indexes. The degree day data were compiled at NEB and EMR. The light fuel oil prices entering into the weighted average price of energy are from an unpublished Statistics Canada survey. The electricity price consists of a weighted average of the cost of the first 500 Kwh consumed per month and the average cost of 1000 to 5000 Kwh per month. The weights used were estimates of electricity used for electric appliances and electricity used for space heating. Natural gas prices were based on average revenue calculations.

Although problems associated with demand modeling when the consumer faces a declining block rate structure are well known, it is felt that the use of electricity prices based on electricity bills data goes part way toward eliminating this problem (Taylor, 1975). Moreover, the prices actually faced by space-heating customers versus those faced by consumers for appliance use are taken into account through the weighting scheme. With regard to natural gas, most residential customers use natural gas for space-heating, for which the marginal price is relatively constant. Hence, the use of average revenue is not a significant problem (Berndt and Watkins, 1977).

The results, summarized in Table 1-2, are quite good. All variables have the theoretically correct sign and are highly significant. The adjusted $\bar{R}^2$ is very high at .96. Further, the magnitudes of the various elasticities appear to be quite reasonable. In addition, the average absolute percentage errors (AAPEs) are 5 percent or less for every region, based on the transformed results. Generally the equations do not exhibit autocorrelation, although the Atlantic and British Columbia are of some concern. Ideally the problem should be corrected through reestimation of the equation, but with a pooled equation in double log form this is not a simple task. What is required is the application of a time series autocorrelation model involving estimation of the regional first order autocorrelation coefficients, and the application of generalized differencing of the original model with subsequent reestimation on a pooled basis (Pindyck and Rubinfeld, 1976). It is not clear, however, that a reasonable error specification for the transformed variables will result, and further analysis is required. In terms of using the equation for forecasting, the problem is probably not serious. The effect will be to produce a larger variance in the forecast error than might otherwise be the case. This can be corrected in the short term by making slight adjustments to the forecast in light of analysis of the trends in the error term. Over the longer term the forecast will still be correct on average, since the coefficients remain unbiased.

1.2.2 The Commercial Sector

As is widely recognized, it is difficult to model energy demand in the commercial sector due to its heterogeneous "catch-all" nature (Department of Energy, Mines and Resources, 1977). The results are given in Table 1-3. The equations are estimated in double log form. The dependent variable is total energy demand in the commercial sector, in output Btus. The independent variables are real domestic product in the commercial sector, the weighted average price of energy divided by the CPI, normalized degree days, and, for several regions, a dummy variable to capture a data reclassification problem for heavy fuel oil between the industrial and commercial sectors. Real domestic product in the commercial sector is defined as the sum of real domestic products in the following subsectors: energy utilities, wholesale and retail trade, finance, insurance and real estate, service industries, and public administration and defense. The price of energy consists of the prices of natural gas, light fuel oil, heavy fuel oil, and electricity in the commercial sector weighted by the market shares of these energy types in this sector. For each energy type, the energy price is an average price, i.e., total revenue received by the supplier divided by quantity sold.

Separate equations have been estimated for each of the seven regions of Canada, for the period 1962-1974. The rationale for using time series estimation rather than pooled cross-section time series is that the commercial sector consists of a number of heterogenous subsectors, each with different relative importance depending on the region. Thus, for the total sector, one would not expect the same response to changes in exogenous variables in different regions.

Data (obtained from EMR) on real domestic product in the commercial sector, by region, are available only through 1970. For the period 1971-1974, the data were estimated. The procedure was to use an estimated equation for each region which related real domestic product in the commercial sector to gross provincial product, total Canada real commercial product and a trend term, based on the period 1962-1970.

The results for the commercial sector energy demand equations generally seem fairly reasonable. All variables have the theoretically correct sign, and very high $\bar{R}^2$s, with the exception of Saskatchewan. The average absolute percentage errors are less than 5 percent, again with the exception of Saskatchewan. The Durbin Watson statistics indicate that no autocorrelation is present.

The estimated price coefficients are statistically insignificant in several regions and the coefficients on degree days are insignificant in almost all regions. In both cases there are strong a priori grounds for including these

TABLE 1-3. The total energy equation in the commercial sector

Region	*Intercept*	ℓn (YCP)	ℓn (PENC/CPI)	ℓn (DD)	DUMHFO	$\bar{R}^2$	AAPE	D.W.
Atlantic	−.62	1.53	−.50	.17	−.34	.96	4.25	1.37
	(.33)	(6.36)	(1.64)	(.36)	(2.25)			
Quebec	−7.67	2.28	−.88	.12	−.18	.99	2.59	3.06
	(8.12)	(21.15)	(6.25)	(.32)	(3.83)			
Ontario	−3.09	1.39	−.85	.09	−.08	.99	2.78	1.57
	(.2)	(8.44)	(3.27)	(.18)	(1.17)			
Manitoba	−.15	1.49	−.74	.47		.95	4.17	2.22
	(.09)	(6.62)	(1.23)	(.91)				
Saskatchewan	4.57	.73	−.49	1.12		.61	8.41	1.50
	(2.02)	(2.21)	(.99)	(1.29)				
Alberta	3.16	1.02	−.88	.02		.98	3.12	1.43
	(5.0)	(12.66)	(5.01)	(.06)				
B.C., Yukon,	−2.49	1.68	−.31	.73		.98	3.82	2.04
N.W.T.	(1.38)	(8.32)	(.96)	(1.97)				

Definitions:

YCP = Real domestic product in energy utilities, wholesale and retail trade, finance, insurance and real estate, service industries, and public administration and defense; millions of 1961 dollars.

PENC = Weighted average price of heavy fuel oil, light fuel oil, natural gas and electricity; dollars per million output Btus.

CPI = Consumer price index; 1961 = 1.

DD = Normalized degree days.

DUMHFO = Dummy variable; equals 1 in 1973 and 1974.

Bracketed figures under coefficients indicate t statistics.

variables. Regarding degree days, the rationale is that space-heating forms a considerable portion of the use of energy in the commercial sector. At least part of the reason for the statistical insignificance of these variables is that there is often strong collinearity between these and the other exogenous variables in the equations. Experimentation revealed that the error terms were more satisfactory when these variables were left in, both in terms of their average size and their randomness. Thus, these variables have been retained in the equations. Multicollinearity is not a serious problem when an equation is used for forecasting, as long as one expects the collinearity to remain in the future.

Several economic activity variables, including real commercial product, retail trade, personal disposable income, and commercial sector employment, were analyzed as driving variables in the commercial sector. Real commercial product provided the best results, presumably since it constitutes a more comprehensive description of activity in this sector.

Further experimentation was carried out using pooled cross-section and time series data rather than time series per se. As expected, the results were better using time series. This was particularly apparent upon examining the regional error terms. The interregional differences in coefficients also suggest the inappropriateness of using a pooled equation for regional forecasts of energy demand in the commercial sector.

1.2.3 The Industrial Sector

The total energy equations developed for the industrial sector are presented in Table 1-4. Individual equations were estimated for each of the seven regions of Canada, using ordinary least squares. For each region the dependent variable is total energy consumed in the industrial sector (as previously defined), in output Btus. The independent variables are real domestic product in the industrial sector, the ratio of net capital stock in the manufacturing sector to real domestic product in the industrial sector, which is a convenient measure of capital intensity of production, and the ratio of the weighted average price of energy in the industrial sector to the gross domestic product price deflator for the industrial sector. Real domestic product is defined to include output of the forestry, mining, manufacturing, and construction sectors. The fuels covered in the weighted average price of energy are natural gas, heavy fuel oil, light fuel oil, coal, and electricity. The equations are again estimated in double log form.

TABLE 1-4. The total energy equation in the industrial sector

Region	*Intercept*	ℓn RDPI	ℓn (KN/RDPI)	ℓn (PENI/POI)	$\bar{R}^2$	AAPE	D.W.
Atlantic	3.09	.53	.32	−.53	.96	3.89	2.29
	(3.89)	(6.72)	(1.67)	(3.65)			
Quebec	1.17	.85	.62	−.68	.95	2.78	1.61
	(.47)	(11.36)	(1.96)	(3.98)			
Ontario	.71	.88	.58	−.64	.99	1.64	2.44
	(.37)	(20.49)	(2.50)	(2.10)			
Manitoba	.64	.91	.56	−.45	.98	1.73	1.49
	(.40)	(9.12)	(3.11)	(2.84)			
Saskatchewan	−10.46	2.03	1.28	−.90	.96	1.67	2.01
	(2.68)	(5.29)	(4.42)	(3.91)			
Alberta	4.75	.79	.08	−.07	.99	1.67	2.45
	(2.86)	(7.75)	(.47)	(.30)			
B.C., Yukon,	−2.44	1.18	.72	−.16	.98	2.73	2.24
N.W.T.	(.89)	(9.54)	(2.60)	(1.02)			

Definitions:

RDPI = Real domestic product in forestry, mining, manufacturing, and construction; millions of 1961 dollars.
KN = Net capital stock in the manufacturing sector; thousands of 1961 dollars.
PENI = Weighted average price of coal, light fuel oil, heavy fuel oil, natural gas, and electricity in the industrial sector; dollars per million output Btus.
POI = Gross domestic product in the industrial sector divided by real domestic product in the industrial sector; 1961 = 1.

Bracketed figures under coefficients indicate t statistics.

For the Atlantic region, Quebec, Ontario, and British Columbia, the estimation period was 1961–1974; for Manitoba, Saskatchewan, and Alberta, it was 1962–1974. Much of the data utilized is from readily available Statistics Canada publications. Regional real domestic product data and capital stock data were developed at EMR as were the oil price data. The overall explanatory powers of the equations, as measured by $\bar{R}^2$, are very good with the lowest value being .95. Examination of the error terms is also quite encouraging. The average absolute percentage errors are less than 5 percent in every region, and often considerably less. Another characteristic of the errors for any given region is that deviations from the AAPE are generally quite small, and even the largest error in the period is usually not much more than twice the AAPE. Finally, causal examination of the error terms revealed that they are generally quite random. Certainly there is no strong trend in any region. Tests performed on the Durbin Watson statistic confirmed these observations. Specifically, in three regions there is no autocorrelation, and in the other four the tests were inconclusive, i.e., the D.W. fell in the indeterminate range. Thus, to the extent there is some dependency between the residuals, it is minor and would not cause any significant problem in using the equations for forecasting.

Examination of the coefficients themselves also points to the reasonableness of these equations. All the coefficients have the theoretically correct signs, and their magnitudes are generally in line with a priori expectations. Further, an examination of the "t" statistics reveals that, with few exceptions, all coefficients are highly significant. In the few cases where they were not, at least part of the problem would appear to be collinearity between the variables in question and other variables in the equation. Thus, these variables were retained. Finally, the coefficients appear to be reasonably stable as changes in the estimation period generally did not change the values of the coefficients appreciably. The coefficients of the capital output ratio suggest a complementarity between energy and capital, which is consistent with other recent work (Canadian Energy Research Institute, 1978; also chapter 2 of this volume).

A word might be said regarding the use of time series versus pooled time series cross-section data in estimating regional total energy equations in the industrial sector. Although there are costs and benefits of both approaches, time series would appear to be preferable for several reasons. First, on a priori grounds, one would not expect the same response to changes in a given exogenous variable in different regions because the composition of the industrial sector is so different between regions. Second, empirical examination suggests that time series is more satisfactory for regional forecasts of energy demand. Examination of Table 1-4 suggests that there often are significant interregional differences in the coefficients. Further, a comparison of AAPEs from pooled equations that were estimated versus the reported time series equations (both sets of equations having the same specifications) revealed that the average errors were consistently lower with time series, sometimes substantially so. Finally, casual observation suggested that the error terms were generally more random when generated from time series analysis. On the cost side of using time series is the fact that a necessarily small number of observations have to be used in estimation, reducing the available degrees of freedom.

1.3 APPLICATIONS OF THE MODEL

The current version of the Board's energy demand forecasting model, as previously discussed, has been in use at the Board since April, 1978. It was with the aid of this model that forecasts contained in a recently published Board report were prepared (National Energy Board, 1978). It is expected that the model will continue to be used in its current form for the development of energy demand forecasts, with further model improvements being incorporated as time permits.

In general, the model is employed to determine the expected Canadian energy requirements, based on a most likely forecast of economic and demographic growth, as well as energy prices. Given the uncertainties in forecasting energy demands, the model is also used to derive high and low demand forecasts, based on alternative economic and price inputs. Such forecasts are required by the Board in order to assess the need for additional natural gas pipelines or oil port facilities in Canada, for example, or to determine exportable surpluses of indigenous crude oil and natural gas.

REFERENCES

Berndt, E. R., and Watkins, G. C. 1977. Demand for natural gas: Residential and commercial markets in Ontario and British Columbia. *Canadian Journal of Economics* 10:97–111.

Canadian Energy Research Institute. 1978. *The industrial demand for oil and gas in Ontario*. Study No. 2, ISBN-0-920522-01-7, pp. 32–39.

Department of Energy, Mines and Resources. 1977. *Energy demand projections — A total energy approach*. Report ER77-4, pp. 33–34.

Gorbet, F. W. 1974a. Energy demand projections: Input BTUs and output BTUs. Department of Energy, Mines and Resources, unpublished.

Gorbet, F. W. 1974b. Energy demand model: An analytical framework. Department of Energy, Mines and Resources, unpublished.

Harsanyi, L. B. 1971. Energy demand estimates and international comparisons. *Public Utilities Fortnightly.*

Johnston, J. 1960. *Econometric methods.* New York: McGraw-Hill Book Company, pp. 211–221.

National Energy Board. 1977a. *Canadian oil: Supply and requirements.*

National Energy Board. 1977b. *Reasons for decision: Northern pipelines.*

National Energy Board. 1978. *Canadian oil: Supply and requirements.*

Pindyck, R. S., and Rubinfeld, D. L. 1976. *Econometric models and economic forecasts.* New York: McGraw-Hill Book Company.

Sahi, R. K. and Erdmann, R. W. Chapter 2, this volume. "A Canadian interfuel substitution demand model."

Taylor, L. D. 1975. The demand for electricity: A survey. *Bell Journal of Economics* 6:74–110.

Waghmare, R., and Shalaby, A. Chapter 7, this volume. "A model for forecasting passenger car gasoline demand."

2 A POLICY MODEL OF CANADIAN INTERFUEL SUBSTITUTION DEMANDS

R. K. Sahi and R. W. Erdmann

We describe the structure and estimation of an interfuel substitution demand model that is under development at the Department of Energy, Mines and Resources. This econometric simulation model is being used to project annual energy demands by fuels, sectors, and regions over a medium term horizon under alternative assumptions of economic growth, energy prices, and conservation measures. The paper emphasizes the estimation of a system of nonlinear market share equations whose parameters were constrained to be consistent with economic theory. The estimated long run fuel own-price elasticities are in the range of -1 or greater. Although cross-price elasticities vary substantially from region to region, they are strong and positive at the national level, suggesting a high potential for interfuel substitution in the long run.

2.1 INTRODUCTION

This paper is a progress report on an interfuel substitution demand (IFSD) model being developed at the Department of Energy, Mines and Resources. The model is an extension of an earlier EMR total energy demand model (Department of Energy, Mines and Resources, 1977; Erdmann and Gorbet,

1978), with a greater emphasis on the problems and determinants of fuel choice by energy consumers. It is a substantial improvement on previous interfuel substitution analysis at EMR (Erdmann, 1977a).

The main differences between our current and previous work on interfuel substitution relate to the specification and estimation of the market share relationships. Instead of a single unconstrained weighted competing price term in the equation for each fuel, we have introduced separate price terms for each competing fuel, constrained to satisfy a set of conditions derived from economic theory. In the total demand equations, instead of using the average cost of energy, we have turned to a price index as a better measure of *price* change. The net result of these changes is a set of regional fuel price elasticities, both own and competing, which are much more plausible and which should lead to more reasonable projections of future energy demands.

The problems of making projections of individual fuel demands are numerous and serious. They include: the existence of fixed stocks of energy using capital equipment with relatively long economic life spans; differences in the costs of energy using capital equipment; differences in the availability of individual fuels; regional differences in consumers' attitudes toward the advantages of different fuels; and the effects of the introduction of new technologies and products. Our work attempts to come to grips with some of these problems in order to make projections of future fuel consumption under different policy assumptions (e.g., relative energy prices) and different assumptions about regional economic activity. The interfuel substitution projections are embedded in a comprehensive framework of total energy demand designed to project Canadian primary energy demands on a regional basis over a ten- to fifteen-year time horizon.

Following is an outline of the analytic approach used to make the projections of individual fuel demands. The specification of the equations and variables used to estimate the total demand and market share relationships is then described. This is followed by a discussion of the econometric problems that need to be taken into account in estimating these demand relationships. The preferred estimation results are then summarized. The final section of this chapter gives some conclusions about the policy applications of this type of analysis and the need for further work.

2.2 APPROACH

Like the earlier EMR total energy demand model, the IFSD model uses a top-down approach. This involves starting with a projection of total "useful'' energy demands (also described as tertiary demands and measured in terms of ''output'' Btus) in each end-use market, based on such factors as energy prices, economic activity, and temperature. The market shares of the principal fuels used to meet these total energy demands are then estimated, primarily on the basis of relative energy prices. Total demands are multiplied by market shares to arrive at an estimate of individual tertiary fuel demands. These tertiary fuel demands are then divided by their end-use efficiencies to provide a projection of secondary fuel demands, or the volumes of energy actually purchased.

This represents the behavioural core of the interfuel substitution demand model. Other assumptions and equations are used to provide estimates of transportation energy demands and non-energy demands. Total end-use demands for energy by fuel type are then used to provide an estimate of the total demand for primary fuels (coal, oil, natural gas, and primary electricity) according to assumptions about the method by which intermediate fuels (e.g., electricity) are generated and the efficiencies with which it is done. Energy supply industry requirements are also included in the final calculation.

2.3 MODEL SPECIFICATIONS

2.3.1 Total Energy Demands

The current specifications follow the line of earlier work at EMR and the National Energy Board (1977a, 1977b; also chapter 1 of this volume) to relate total tertiary energy demand in ''output'' Btus for each end-use sector to energy prices, economic activity, weather, and other appropriate energy-related variables. The adequacy of our energy model specification continues to be constrained, however, by the unavailability of appropriate activity variables, particularly on a regional basis, and the data classification problems for energy consumption.

One significant improvement here is the use of energy price indices instead of average costs as the measure of the price of total energy. The use of an index avoids the problem of apparent price changes induced by shifts in consumption from one fuel to another over time. In generating the energy price indices for each sector, we have adopted the Divisia indexing procedure (Berndt and Wood, 1975). The indices were normalized to the 1971 regional average energy cost in order to help reflect the differences in prices between regions as well as within regions.

For the weather variable, which we have attempted to include in each sector, a nonlinear specification was adopted in order to avoid a lagged effect of current temperature fluctuations on future years' energy consumption (i.e., a cold year should not have effects on energy consumption in succeeding years). The weather variable is normalized to reflect intertemporal temperature changes within each region.

All total energy demand equations were specified in double-log form. For the *residential* sector, energy demand was specified as a function of the number of households, disposable income per household, weather, a lagged dependent variable, and a variable that measures the ratio of the number of households living in single dwellings to the total number of households (single dwelling ratio). *Commercial* demand was specified as a function of personal disposable income per capita, regional population, energy prices, weather, a lagged dependent variable, the proportion of households living in multiple dwellings, and a dummy variable for 1972 to overcome an apparently serious data classification problem. The basic components of the *industrial* demand equation include the price of energy, industrial value added, capital stock, employment, temperature, and a lagged dependent variable.

2.3.2 Market Shares

The analysis of market shares has focused primarily on the three major fuels in each end-use sector which, together, account for at least 80 percent and usually above 90 percent of the energy consumption in those sectors in each region. In the residential sector, the three fuels selected are electricity, natural gas, and a combined category of light fuel oil and kerosene. In both the commercial and industrial sectors, the three major fuels selected were electricity, natural gas, and heavy fuel oil. The remaining fuels not explicitly analyzed were treated as a residual.

In our earlier interfuel substitution work (Erdmann, 1977a), we used the logit functional form of equation for each of the major fuels, and included only a single price term (own price relative to the average price of competing fuels) in each equation. The results were generally unsatisfactory. The market share relationships were not constrained to be consistent with economic theory other than the constraint inherent to the logit specification itself, which maintains the share of each fuel within the range of 0 to 1. In projections using the results of that work, the sum of all market shares frequently exceeded unity, with the result that the share of other fuels became negative.

A related difficulty was the inequality of cross-price effects. A price increase for natural gas, for example, might have a completely different effect on the demand for electricity than an increase in the price of electricity would have on the demand for natural gas. This problem was the result of the single price term in each equation, with the average cost of all competing fuels in the denominator. (This form of relative price term is used in the U.S. Department of Energy demand model [United States Federal Energy Administration, 1975].) Because of the weighting scheme used to derive average competing costs, a fuel would have the largest cross-price elasticity with respect to price of the competing fuel with the largest share of the market. In the residential sector, for example, in those regions where electricity has a larger market share than natural gas, electricity had a larger cross-price elasticity than gas with respect to oil (i.e., in the oil equation). This was an implausible situation.

The present approach has attempted to overcome many of these earlier difficulties. Constraints on the estimated coefficients have been imposed so that: (1) the market shares always sum to 1; (2) there is an equality of cross-price effects between each pair of competing fuels; and (3) for any change in any of the independent variables other than price there will be no net change in the sum of market shares. In order to impose these constraints satisfactorily, it was necessary to abandon the logit form of specification in favor of a semi-log form because of the complex nonlinearities the former specification requires to maintain the above constraints. Although the semi-log equations can be constrained to satisfy the conditions previously outlined, it does not offer the advantage of the logit function in constraining individual market shares to lie between 0 and 1. It is hoped that this will turn out to be a minor problem that can be readily overcome with nonlinear constraints and pro-rata adjustments in the simulation model.

The market share equations are:

$$M_i' = a_i + c_i \ell n X + e_i M_i'(-1) + b_{i1} \ell n(P_i/P_1) + b_{i2} \ell n(P_i/P_2)$$

$$M_i = M_i' + d_i \mathrm{DD}$$

$$M_i = a_i + c_i \ell n X + e_i M_i(-1) + b_{i1} \ell n(P_i/P_1) + b_{i2} \ell n(P_i/P_2) + d_i(\mathrm{DD} - e\mathrm{DD}(-1))$$

where M_i' = market share of fuel i, without taking account of temperature; M_i = market share of fuel i, after adjusting for temperature effects; P_i = price of fuel i, in $ per million output Btus; X = a set of independent variables other than prices and degree days; DD = degree days, normalized around 1 within each region; a_i, b_{i1}, b_{i2}, c_i, d_i, and e_i are coefficients to be estimated.

For the *price* variables, there are two sets of constraints that economic theory suggests:

1. The market share of each fuel should remain unchanged when all fuel prices change by the same proportion (i.e., homogeneity of degree zero). This price homogeneity condition is satisfied for fuel prices specified as the ratio of logarithms as they are here.
2. The change in the market share on one fuel with respect to a percentage change in the price of another should be equal to the change in the market share of the other fuel with respect to the same percentage change in the price of the first fuel. This symmetrical effect of price changes is satisfied by the restrictions $b_{ij} = b_{ji}$.

These two conditions ensure that, if the market shares sum to one before any change in prices, they will continue to sum to one after any price changes. Where some *nonprice* independent variables (such as income or capacity constraints) are also included in the market share equations, it is necessary to ensure that any net impacts on total market shares of changes in these variables should also sum to zero. This is achieved by:

3. For a change in any independent, nonprice variable, the sum of changes in the market shares of all fuels should be zero. This Cournot aggregation condition is satisfied by the restriction $\sum_i c_i = 0$.
4. The inclusion of a *temperature* variable in the market share equations makes estimation more complex. Assuming that the effect of a change in temperature from its normal value is a change in the level of the current year's desired market shares by a fixed amount rather than a proportional amount, and that the effect of a deviation in temperature from its normal level does not persist for longer than one year, the constraints that must be imposed on the coefficients for degree days are identical with those for the other independent variables $\sum_i d_i = 0$.
Attempts to isolate the influence of degree days on markets were made in each sector. Given the relative importance of space-heating requirements, we would expect temperature to exert a significant effect on total energy demand and its fuel composition only in the residential and commercial sectors.
5. Any change in one fuel's market share caused by a change in an independent variable must be exactly offset by changes to the market shares of other fuels *in every time period.* When there is only a single lagged adjustment term for each fuel share, its coefficient must be

identical in each equation, i.e., all $e_i = e$. A more complex adjustment structure would require a more elaborate matrix of adjustment coefficients. Such an approach has not been attempted here.

6. For any given level of independent variables, including prices, the market shares must sum to one. This means that the intercept terms for each of the four fuel equations must be constrained to force their market shares to sum to unity when the coefficients of all of the independent variables are set equal to zero. The following intercept constraints satisfy the Engel aggregation condition in the presence of the lagged adjustment term whose coefficient is e: $1 = e + \sum_i a_i$. Without a lagged dependent variable, e would not be part of the above constraint.

2.4 ECONOMETRIC CONSIDERATIONS

Given the data difficulties, there is no "best" way of estimating the energy demand and market share relationships. Individual equations for each region may result in better estimates of the parameters as they apply to that region, but there is such a small number of historical observations and such a narrow range of variation within each region that the parameter estimates tend to be insignificant and unstable. Pooling the data in a combined time series cross-sectional form provides a greater number of observations and a greater degree of variation for the estimation of the average regional level of all parameters. The primary disadvantage with this "pooled" method, however, is that it is more difficult to track the actual historical experience of each of the regions within the pooled sample.

This analytic technique is also fraught with theoretical problems that have not been fully resolved. The first problem is whether or not regional intercepts should be included in the regressions. The use of a common intercept forces the coefficients of the independent variables to explain all interregional as well as intraregional variation. It assumes a common market structure across all regions. Inclusion of regional intercepts can have a major impact on the coefficients of both the independent variables and the lagged dependent term. A study prepared by Datametrics for the Canadian Energy Research Institute also refers to these problems with pooled cross-sectional techniques (Datametrics Limited, 1978). The essence of Datametrics' criticism is that where a large portion of the variation is accounted for by the regional intercept terms, the model may fail to track much of the variation over time within particular regions.

In estimating total energy demand relationships, a specification in terms of total demand is to be preferred to a ratio specification, such as demand per household, because of the inherent weighting of the total form. Before estimating the market share equations, all variables were *weighted* (by the average regional energy consumption from 1963–1974) in order to give more importance in the regression results to the largest energy consuming areas. Although the results were marginally better at the national level, the parameters were nearly identical and the approach was not actively pursued.

2.5 ESTIMATION RESULTS

All total demand and market share equations have been estimated over the period 1963–1974, pooling time series for seven regions, for a total of eighty-four observations. A nonlinear system estimation technique that allows constraints on the model's parameters was used. The following presentation provides details of the preferred results for the market share equations together with a general description of the results from some other specifications examined.

2.5.1 Total Demand

Of the three sectors for which total demand equations were estimated, the results for the residential sector are the most encouraging. The preferred equations are presented in Table 2-1. The long run price elasticities are estimated to be −.40, −1.06, and −.48 for the residential, commercial, and industrial sectors, respectively. The commercial elasticity seems to be unreasonably high and probably requires downward adjustment. The long run income elasticities are .34 for the residential and .20 for the commercial sectors. For the industrial sector, the income elasticity is specified to be one and the capital-output ratio elasticity is estimated to be .67, indicating a strong complementarity between capital and energy.

2.5.2 Market Shares

Zellner's seemingly unrelated regressions method was used to estimate a system of three nonlinear market share equations (electricity, natural gas, and oil) for each sector. The coefficients for the "other fuels" equations were derived from the estimated coefficients of these three equations on the basis of the parameter restrictions previously discussed. Simultaneous system estimation of all four market share equations is not recommended because it results in a singular matrix.

TABLE 2-1. Total energy demand estimation results

Variable	*Residential*		*Commercial*		*Industrial*	
Income/Household						
(1971 $10⁶)	.0927	(0.34)				
Single Dwellings/						
Households						
Ont.	.1276	(.036)				
Man.	.2337	(.066)				
Households (10³)	1.0					
Lagged	– .7279					
Income/Capita						
(1971 $10⁶)			.0711	(0.52)		
Multiple Dwellings/						
Households			.0614	(0.18)		
Population (10³)			1.0			
Lagged			– .6076			
Dummy for 1972			.0388	(.027)		
1971			– 0.236			
Dummy for Alberta						
1972			.1065	(.061)		
1971			– .0647			
Industrial RDP						
(1971 $10⁹)					1.0	
Lagged					– .7006	
Capital/Output Ratio					.1997	(.084)
Lagged Demand						
(10^{12} OBTUS)	.7279	(.076)	.6076	(0.72)	.7006	(0.77)
Energy Price						
($/MMOBTUs)	– .1077	(.050)	– .4160	(.091)	– .1450	(.067)
Normalized Degree Days	.5282	(.068)	.5547	(.165)	.1255	(.131)
Lagged	– .3845		– .3370		– .0879	
Intercept	*R*		– .6015	(.267)	*R*	
R^2	.998		.995		.996	
Theil's U (Canada)	.006		.011		.009	
Coefficient of						
Variation (%)	0.8		1.7		1.4	

Note: All variables are expressed in logarithms. The dependent variable for each sector is the total energy demand in trillions of output BTUs. R indicates regional intercepts. For the capital/output ratio, capital is taken as the net capital stock for the manufacturing sector only and the output is the industrial RDP. The numbers in parentheses are the standard errors for the individual coefficients.

Sector/ Fuel	Intercept Common	Intercept Atlantic (incremental)	ℓn(PE/PG)	ℓn(PE/PO)	ℓn(PG/PO)	ℓn(GC)	DD	Lagged Dependent	R^2	Coefficient of Variation %
Residential										
Electricity	.04386		−.002394	−.018289			−.05828	.90	.98	4.77
	(.0028)		(.0016)	(.0030)			(.0156)			
Natural Gas	.024430		.002394		−.036947		.055781	.90	.99	5.33
	(.0034)		(.0016)		(.0024)		(.0271)			
Oil	.020189			.018289	.036947		.043776	.90	.99	3.77
	(.0035)			(.0030)	(.0024)		(.02487)			
Others	.011521						−.041277			
Commerical										
Electricity	.122532		−.021015	−.009662		.003874	−.123978	.85	.88	9.07
	(.0099)		(.0042)			(.0018)	(.0420)			
Natural Gas	.049294		.021015		−.031245	.007167	−.011929	.85	.99	7.95
	(.0121)		(.0042)		(.0081)	(.0025)	(.0482)			
Oil	−027969			.009662	.031245	−.005201	.08337	.85	.90	23.56
	(.0140)				(.0081)	(.0037)	(.0819)			
Others	.006142					−.00584	.052537			
Industrial										
Electricity	.107096	−.007588	−.019842	−.010348		−.001944		.80	.97	7.32
	(.0070)	(.0229)	(.0036)			(.0054)				
Natural Gas	.043795	.140679	.019842		−.048841	.026404		.80	.99	7.51
	(.0069)	(.0288)	(.0036)		(.0053)	(.0067)				
Oil	.025828	−.079745		.010348	.048841	−.011099		.80	.97	15.93
	(.0038)	(.0336)			(.0053)	(.0077)				
Others	.023281	−.053346				−.013361		.80		

Definitions:

PE = Price of electricity.
PG = Price of natural gas.
PO = Price of oil.
GC = Gas pipeline capacity, (mcf).

Bracketed numbers below coefficients are standard errors.

The estimated equations for each sector are presented in Table 2-2. The coefficients of the lagged dependent variables were judgmentally set at .90, .85, and .80 for the residential, commercial, and industrial sectors, respectively. The reason for this arbitrary procedure was the instability of each equation, particularly the coefficient of the lagged dependent variable, for a change in the specification of the intercept term. With one intercept term, the estimated lag coefficient was in the range of .93 to .98 (depending upon the sector and specification of the model), while with separate regional intercepts, the coefficient fell in the range of .78 to .80. The price coefficients also became insignificant or had the wrong sign when regional intercept terms were used, whereas they were much more reasonable with a common intercept. Since our purpose in pooling regional data is to exploit the interregional variations in fuel prices and market shares, a common intercept was used for the estimation of market share equations.

To avoid the long adjustment period implied by lag coefficients in the .95 range (i.e., forty-five years to achieve 90 percent of the long run price effects), it was necessary to impose more reasonable lags. The coefficient of .90 imposed in the residential sector is similar to the level (.916) estimated by Berndt and Watkins (1977). The coefficients for the commercial and industrial sectors were specified at .85 and .80 based on the technical and institutional knowledge of the sectors.

All equations have satisfactory statistical properties: the R^2s are .88 or higher, and the signs of the coefficients are consistent with prior expectations. In a preliminary estimation, the electricity-oil price coefficient turned out to be positive but insignificant for the commercial and industrial sectors, probably because of multicollinearity. Coefficients based on long-term cross-price elasticities of .24 and .25 estimated for the respective sector by Fuss and Waverman (1975) were imposed.

2.5.3 Summary of Elasticities

The preferred equations previously presented provide, for the most part, reasonable estimates of the effects on interfuel substitution of changes in relative energy prices and economic activity. This section summarizes those results, with an emphasis on the effects of price changes, on the basis of the quantities and prices which prevailed on average across Canada in 1974. These results should be treated with caution at a regional level because of substantial interregional differences in market shares and prices.

Given the price elasticities derived from the total demand and market share equations previously outlined, Table 2-3 provides a detailed summary

TABLE 2-3. Estimated long term energy price elasticities, Canada (1974)

	1% Price Increase For:			
	Total Energy	*Electricity*	*Natural Gas*	*Oil*
Residential				
Total demand	−.396	−.131	−.060	−.205
Market shares				
Electricity		−.857	.099	.758
Gas		.091	−1.502	1.410
Oil		.456	.921	−1.376
Quantities				
Electricity	−.396	−.988	.039	.553
Gas	−.396	−.040	−1.562	1.205
Oil	−.396	.326	.861	−1.581
Commercial				
Total demand	−1.060	−.786	−.155	−.119
Market shares				
Electricity		−.602	.412	.190
Gas		.401	−.996	.596
Oil		.335	1.083	−1.418
Quantities				
Electricity	−1.060	−1.388	.257	.071
Gas	−1.060	−.385	−1.151	.477
Oil	−1.060	−.451	.928	−1.537
Industrial				
Total demand	−.484	−.304	−.095	−.085
Market shares				
Electricity		−.495	.325	.170
Gas		.265	−.916	.652
Oil		.245	1.155	−1.399
Quantities				
Electricity	−.484	−.799	.230	.085
Gas	−.484	−.039	−1.011	.567
Oil	−.484	−.059	1.060	−1.484

Note: The percentage impact of a 1 percent increase in the price of the specified fuel. The *total demand elasticity* is drawn directly from the relevant equation. The effect of a price change for one fuel equals the total demand elasticity times that fuel's expenditure share. Given the semi-log form of our market share equations, the *own-price market share elasticity* for fuel *i* is equal to its own-price coefficient (the sum of the two price coefficients) divided by its own market share. The *cross-price market share elasticity* is equal to the competing price coefficient again divided by the market share for fuel *i*. The *fuel quantity elasticities* are the algebraic sum of the total demand and relevant market share price elasticities.

of the own and cross-price elasticities for each of the major fuels in each end-use sector. The own-price elasticities are strongly negative as expected, and are usually in the range of −1 or greater. Except in the commercial sector, electricity tends to have the lowest own-price elasticity while oil has the highest, again consistent with prior expectations.

Most cross-price elasticities have the expected sign. The exceptions are the cross-price elasticities of almost every fuel in all sectors with respect to electricity prices. The magnitude of the negative cross-price elasticities in the commercial sector, however, is completely unacceptable. Despite the fairly strong positive cross-price elasticities for *market shares* in that sector, the enormous total demand elasticity with respect to electricity prices tends to swamp the market share elasticities.

Table 2–3 also indicates the strength of the cross-price elasticities between oil and natural gas across all sectors. While this pattern would obviously vary from region to region, it is rather significant at the national level and appears promising for the possibility of replacing imported oil with domestic natural gas. In the residential sector, the results indicate that oil and electricity are strong substitutes but that electricity and natural gas are not. This is surprising in light of the historical battles for new markets between natural gas and electric utilities. Also surprising, although the evidence is not entirely clear, is that natural gas appears to be a stronger substitute for electricity than heavy fuel oil, in the commercial and industrial markets.

Table 2–4 summarizes our current estimates of the lag response times for total energy and the assumptions for market shares. Table 2–5 compares

TABLE 2–4. Time required to achieve 90 percent of the long run price and activity effects (years)

	Residential	*Commercial*	*Industrial*
Total Energy			
IFSD - 1978	7.3	4.6	6.5
- 1977	2.0	3.9	4.9
Demand Report - 1977	12.0	9.0	6.4
Market Shares			
IFSD - 1978	22	14	10
IFSD - 1977			
Oil	13.1	1.1	5.1
Gas	14.8	5.0	4.2
Electricity	5.1	11.3	15.2

Note: Years = $\ell n\ (1 - .9)/\ell n\ (LC)$ where LC = lag coefficient.

TABLE 2–5. A comparison of long-run price elasticities

Changes in Prices of:	*Electricity*			*Natural Gas*			*Oil*		
Changes in Quantities of:	*Electricity*	*Natural Gas*	*Oil*	*Electricity*	*Natural Gas*	*Oil*	*Electricity*	*Natural Gas*	*Oil*
Residential									
1. EMR (1978)	–.988	–.040	.326	.039	–1.562	.861	.553	1.205	–1.581
2. EMR (Oct., 1977)	–1.245	.210	.245	.432	–.888	.332	.525	.360	–.890
3. PIES, F.E.A.[1,2] (1976)	–.510	.260	.252	.075	–.721	.063	.054	.024	–.750
Commercial									
1. EMR[3] (1978)	–1.388	–.385	–.451	.257	–1.151	.928	.071	.477	–1.537
2. EMR[3] (Oct., 1977)	–.968	–.439	–.405	.164	–.278	.039	.094	–.023	–.374
3. Fuss & Waverman[4] (1975)	–.71	.50	.91	.16	–.86	.18	.56	.36	–1.09
Industrial									
1. EMR (1978)	–.799	–.039	–.059	.230	–1.011	1.060	.085	.567	–1.484
2. EMR (Oct., 1977)	–.734	–.310	–.284	.122	–.204	–.022	.032	–.066	–.272
3. Fuss & Waverman[5] (1975)	–.536	–.096	–.044	.092	–.968	.072	.714	.284	–1.306
4. PIES, F.E.A.[1] (1976)	–.469	.119	.075	.064	–.392	.049	.049	.007	–.416

Notes:

[1]Numerically calculated "long run" price elasticities for the United States in 1985. Since the equilibrium is not reached by 1985, these elasticities are less than the final long run elasticities.

[2]Residential and commercial sectors combined.

[3]Calculated on the basis of the estimated total demand elasticities of –1.060 for the 1978 study and –.74 for the 1977 study. In forecast simulations, however, the 1977 elasticity was reduced to –.37.

[4]Elasticities for Ontario calculated using 1970 market shares and prices.

[5]Calculated from the market share and total demand elasticities reported in the publication.

our *current* results with three other interfuel substitution studies: (1) Erdmann (1977a), which this work is designed to replace; (2) Fuss and Waverman (1975); and (3) the PIES demand model (United States Federal Energy Administration, 1975). In general, the own-price elasticities in our recent results are usually at least as great as in the other studies. Our cross-price elasticities, particularly between oil and gas, also tend to be higher.

2.6 CONCLUSIONS

When completed, the EMR interfuel substitution demand model will be a useful tool for assessing the impacts on energy demand and its components of a variety of energy policy measures. The list of policies suitable for analysis include the whole spectrum of federal and provincial pricing policies (including subsidies), the additional effects (i.e., nonprice) of conservation programs, and gas pipeline extension programs.

The main strength of the model may also be its chief limitation. It is oriented to the responses of energy consumers to price and market signals. It is not intended to serve as an indicator of optimal consumption, nor even to estimate the maximum potential for interfuel substitution. The model is oriented strictly to the demand portion of the overall energy system and it attempts to make conditional projections of what *could* happen as opposed to what *should* happen. In the context of the broader energy system, there is a need to recognize the feedbacks between demands and supplies—feedbacks which this model largely ignores. At EMR we have made a start in closing this loop between energy supplies and demands in the development of an energy integration model. This is a large regionalized linear programming model of the Canadian energy system which treats the refining, electrical generation, and energy production processes in more detail than is possible in an econometric model.

REFERENCES

Berndt, E. R. 1978. Energy, efficiency and productivity measurement. *Annual Review of Energy* 3.

Berndt, E. R., and Watkins, G. C. 1977. "Demand for natural gas: Residential and commercial markets in Ontario and British Columbia." *Canadian Journal of Economics* 10:97–111.

Berndt, E. R., and Wood, D. O. 1977. *Engineering and econometric approaches to industrial energy conservation and capital formation: A reconciliation.* University of British Columbia, Resources Paper No. 16.

Berndt, E. R., and Wood, D. O. 1975. Technology, prices and the derived demand for energy. *Review of Economics and Statistics* 57:259–268.

Coombs, J. A. 1969. *A cross-section study of energy demand in Canadian manufacturing industries, 1964.* Unpublished Master's Thesis, Queen's University, Kingston, Ontario.

Datametrics Limited. 1978. *The industrial demand for oil and gas in Ontario.* Study No. 2 of the Canadian Energy Research Institute, Calgary.

Datametrics Limited. 1977. *Projections of Alberta aggregate energy demand in the industrial and commercial sectors, 1977–1990.* Prepared for the Alberta Gas Trunkline Company Ltd.

Department of Energy, Mines and Resources. 1976. *An energy strategy for Canada, policies for self-reliance.* Ottawa.

Department of Energy, Mines and Resources. 1977. *Energy demand projections — A total energy approach.* Report ER77-4, Ottawa.

Erdmann, R. W. 1977a. *Interfuel substitution — Demand projections using the EMR interfuel substitution demand model.* EMR Mimeo.

Erdmann, R. W. 1977b. *Estimation of interfuel substitution elasticities.* EMR Mimeo.

Erdmann, R. W., and Gorbet, F. W. 1978. Energy demand projections for Canada — An integrated approach. In *International Studies of the Demand for Energy,* ed. W. Nordhaus. Amsterdam: North Holland Publishing Company.

Fuss, M., and Waverman, L. 1975. *The demand for energy in Canada.* Toronto: Institute for Policy Analysis, University of Toronto.

Hudson, E. A., and Jorgensen, D. W. 1974. U.S. energy policy and economic growth, 1975–2000. *Bell Journal of Economics and Management Science* 5:461–514.

McRae, R. N. 1977. *A quantitative analysis of some policy alternatives affecting Canadian natural gas and crude oil demand and supply.* Ph.D. Thesis at University of British Columbia.

National Energy Board. 1977a. *Canadian oil supply and requirements.* Ottawa, pp. 26–55.

National Energy Board. 1977b. *Reasons for decision — Northern pipelines.* Ottawa, pp. 2-2 to 2-48.

Phlips, L. 1974. *Applied consumption analysis.* Amsterdam: North Holland Publishing Co., pp. 32–56.

Preece, R. A.; Harsanyi, L. B.; and Webster, H. M. "The energy demand forecasting system of the National Energy Board." Chapter 1, this volume.

Sahi, R. K., and Erdmann, R. W. 1978. *Parameter restrictions on market share equations.* EMR Mimeo.

Theil, H. 1971. *Principles of econometrics.* New York: John Wiley and Son.

Theil, H. 1965. *Economic forecasts and policy.* Amsterdam: North Holland Publishing Co., pp. 31–42.

United States Federal Energy Administration. 1975. The project independence evaluation system econometric demand model. *National Energy Outlook,* Appendix C, Washington.

3 INFLATIONARY EXPECTATIONS AND THE DEMAND FOR CAPITAL, LABOR, AND ENERGY IN CANADIAN MANUFACTURING INDUSTRIES*

T. A. Cameron and S. L. Schwartz

This study investigates the impact of inflationary expectations on the demand for capital, labor, and energy in Canadian manufacturing industries using translog cost functions. After adjusting the price of capital services for inflationary expectations, the primary focus is placed on the elasticities of demand for energy and the cross-elasticities between energy and capital and labor services. This enables us to pinpoint sectors that will have the most difficulty adapting to high energy prices and to predict how they will cope (e.g., by increasing capital or labor).

3.1 INTRODUCTION

This study evolved from previous work (Cameron and Schwartz, 1977, 1979) that attempted to fill a void in energy demand analysis. Previous studies (Berndt and Wood, 1975; Fuss, 1977; Galbraith, 1973) had investigated

*This research was partially supported by the Imperial Oil Company of Canada, Ltd., and by the Humanities and Social Sciences Grants Committee of the University of British Columbia. Thanks go to Professors W. E. Diewert and W. T. Ziemba for helpful discussions as this research evolved.

the impact of energy price changes on demand for energy in aggregate manufacturing. However, it is unlikely that subsectors of manufacturing would exhibit identical response patterns to changes in relative factor prices. Some, of course, will be better able to cope with increased energy prices by changing to production processes that use less energy per unit output, while others do not have this flexibility. Our study (Cameron and Schwartz, 1979) demonstrated the existence of this differential response pattern. However, one shortcoming was the existence of perverse capital own elasticities. Economic theory suggests that if the price of an input increases, the use of that input will fall; that is, the own elasticity is negative. In many sectors we uncovered positive own elasticities of capital. There are a number of explanations for this phenomenon. A prime reason is that with the expectation of continuing and growing inflation, the value of machinery is also expected to increase in the future. Thus, firms are induced to buy machinery now rather than wait to purchase it at a higher cost later. Inflation and inflationary expectations thus serve to lower the *real* cost of capital and our original estimates of the cost of capital services were biased upward. In this paper we correct for this bias by reestimating the cost of capital services; we then derive the factor demands on the basis of these adjusted costs.

3.2 INCORPORATION OF INFLATIONARY EXPECTATIONS

Two elements are involved in adjusting for the real cost of capital: (1) the impact of inflation on the real interest rate, and (2) the calculation of the expected rate of inflation. (For a general discussion of these two issues, see an intermediate macroeconomics textbook such as Dornbusch and Fischer, 1978.) With respect to the first concern, an increase in inflation leads to: (a) an increase in the nominal price of goods, including capital, providing an inducement to buy now versus later; (b) an increase in the future cost of raising equity capital (i.e., decrease in share price and increase in number of shares that must be issued) leads to a motivation to sell equity now versus later; and (c) a decrease in the value of future dollars leading to an inducement to borrow now and pay later. The simple economic adjustment to these impacts is to define real interest as nominal interest minus the expected rate of inflation. This may lead to a negative interest rate (and in fact would have over our sample period), a negative cost of capital, and no real limit on capital intensity.

The debate concerning the proper adjustment of nominal interest for inflation to derive the real rate of interest began with Fisher (1930) who stated that a rise in prices results in an increase in the nominal interest but not by the full amount of the price increase. Since that time many researchers have attempted to make this relationship precise. Fama (1975) has noted that although the market does not do well in predicting inflation, there is a relationship between current interest rates and past rates of inflation. Sargent (1969, 1972) found a very long adjustment period. The adjustment took the form of a long humped distributed lag peaking at eight years, and not fully incorporated for eighteen. Lahiri's (1976) work indicates that since 1960 people have been forming price expectations more consciously and relating these to nominal interest rates. This supports the work of Yohe and Karnosky (1969) who found a stronger impact of past prices on expected inflation in the period 1961–1969 than in 1952–1960. Thus as inflation becomes more common and the image of the depression of the thirties fades, the time lag for adjustment appears to be shortening.

A study by Bassie (1976) suggests that the classical equation — nominal interest equals real interest plus the rate of inflation — is an overstatement of the impact of inflation on the nominal interest rate. He suggests that the correct formulation is nominal interest equals real interest multiplied by one plus the rate of inflation. This is consistent with the long lags that have been observed. This paper follows in the spirit of Bassie. We hypothesize that it is *changes* in the rate of inflation that impact on the real interest rate. This behavioral assumption is related to the concept of indexing as a tool for adjusting inflation. The value of indexing is that all *relative* prices are kept equal; the impact should be similar to a price freeze except for lags in adjustment. A constant expected rate of inflation then yields a constant real rate of interest (ceteris paribus). However, if the expected rate of inflation increases (decreases) the real interest rate decreases (increases) and there is a *change* in relative prices, with a movement toward increasing purchases of long-lived goods now (later) before their prices go up (down). Therefore real interest is defined as nominal bond interest minus the expected change in the rate of inflation.

The next step is to calculate the expected change in the rate of inflation. Given the lags involved with investment decisions (see Galbraith, 1973) as well as the observation that expectations adjust with a lag as above, it has been determined that a three-year moving average of changes in the inflation rate is the proper adjustment factor. Interest is not affected by a constant rate of inflation; only *changes* in inflation give rise to changes in interest.

3.3 METHODOLOGY AND DATA

This study investigates the price elasticities of demand in nineteen two-digit SIC (standard industrial classification) sectors of Canadian manufacturing for the period 1957–1975. The general methodology follows Berndt and Wood (1975), Fuss (1977), Griffin and Gregory (1976), and Cameron and Schwartz (1979). Translog cost functions are defined for each sector, input demand equations are estimated, and from these, the price elasticities of demand for each of the inputs are generated.

The input demand equations are

$$s_i = \alpha_i + \sum_j \gamma_{ij} \ell n p_j + c_i \ell n y$$

where input demand, s_i, is a function of prices and scale of output, γ_{ij} is the change in share i resulting from one percent change in the price p_j (the γ_{ij} are not strictly measures of substitution as shares can decrease though input use increases), c_i is the change in share i resulting from one percent change in scale, y is output measured as a Törnqvist index of inputs, i = labor, capital and energy.

The Allen partial elasticities of substitution are

$$\sigma_{ij} = \frac{\gamma_{ij} + s_i^2 - s_i}{s_i^2} \qquad \text{for } i = j,$$

$$\sigma_{ij} = \frac{\gamma_{ij} + s_i^2 - s_i}{s_i s_j} \qquad \text{for } i \neq j,$$

and the price elasticities are $PE_{ij} = \sigma_{ij} s_j$. See Cameron and Schwartz (1977) for details.

The data requirements for the translog model include cost shares and price indices for each input. Total costs were readily available for labor and energy. For capital, current service flows were estimated, adjusting for inflationary expectations as in section 3.2. Törnqvist price indices are estimated, since these reflect both price changes and the resulting changes in the share of the input and are the most appropriate indices for the translog model (Diewert, 1976). Details concerning data construction appear in Cameron and Schwartz (1977).

Input price indices are given in Table 3–1. There has been a sharp drop in the *relative* price of energy in the sample period. The *nominal* price of energy dropped in the early sixties and did not regain its 1957 level until 1971. Although energy prices rose sharply in 1974 and 1975, the average increase over the entire period was only 60 percent. Meanwhile, the price of

TABLE 3-1. Price indices for capital, labor, and energy, average for all sectors (base year 1957)

Year	Capital (uncorrected)	Capital (corrected)	Labor	Energy
1957	1.000	1.000	1.000	1.000
1958	.974	.887	1.049	.970
1959	1.072	.907	1.096	.935
1960	1.110	.845	1.134	.902
1961	1.121	.904	1.191	.926
1962	1.182	1.016	1.236	.899
1963	1.176	1.046	1.278	.895
1964	1.266	1.110	1.333	.895
1965	1.361	1.170	1.396	.918
1966	1.513	1.277	1.482	.891
1967	1.613	1.338	1.572	.911
1968	1.734	1.389	1.692	.911
1969	1.972	1.508	1.818	.923
1970	2.126	1.582	1.945	.950
1971	2.106	1.476	2.087	1.016
1972	2.140	1.549	2.250	1.058
1973	2.281	1.705	2.433	1.145
1974	3.091	2.475	2.746	1.394
1975	unavailable	2.636	3.100	1.643

Note: Source for columns 1, 3, and 4, except 1975, is T. A. Cameron and S. L. Schwartz, "An Analysis of Sectoral Energy Demand: The Manufacturing Industries of Canada." Vancouver: University of British Columbia, Faculty of Commerce Working Paper No. 475, 1977.

labor tripled, and the price of capital increased 160 percent. Note the impact of correcting the cost of capital for inflationary expectations. Uncorrected, the price of capital would have increased more than that of labor, while the corrected capital price change was less. This adjustment has been especially significant toward the end of the sixties and the early seventies.

3.4 RESULTS AND POLICY IMPLICATIONS

3.4.1 Overview

The parameter estimates from the regressions are reported in Table 3-2. (Sector 2 results are not reported due to nonconvergence.) For the machinery sector the original specification was not valid so the model was redefined,

TABLE 3-2. Regression results

Sectors	Parameter Estimates (standard derivatives in parenthesis)							Regression Statistics	
	α_L	γ_{LL}	γ_{LK}	C_L	α_K	γ_{KK}	C_K	R_L^2	R_K^2
1. Food and Beverages	.76	.16	−.13	−.21	.17	.12	.25	.52	.71
	(.006)	(.042)	(.041)	(.040)	(.006)	(.041)	(.040)		
3. Rubber	.30	.10	−.09	−.28	.15	.10	.28	.67	.71
	(.013)	(.087)*	(.086)*	(.051)	(.012)	(.084)*	(.050)		
4. Leather	.92	.12	−.11	.21	.05	.11	−.21	.91	.88
	(.002)	(.012)	(.013)	(.017)	(.003)	(.016)	(.020)		
5. Textiles	.75	.10	−.10	−.12	.20	.11	.11	.41	.55
	(.081)	(.061)*	(.053)*	(.054)	(.007)	(.047)	(.049)		
6. Knitting Mills	.84	.07	−.07	−.11	.13	.07	.09	.29	.36
	(.003)	(.034)	(.029)	(.050)	(.003)	(.026)	(.043)		
7. Clothing	.96	.04	−.04	.00	.04	.04	−.01	.58	.62
	(.001)	(.011)	(.009)	(.02)*	(.001)	(.008)	(.02)*		
8. Wood	.81	.09	−.10	−.15	.13	.12	.17	.57	.56
	(.008)	(.048)*	(.051)*	(.042)	(.009)	(.056)	(.044)		
9. Furniture and Fixtures	.90	.09	−.08	−.04	.07	.07	.05	.57	.64
	(.003)	(.020)	(.019)	(.012)	(.003)	(.019)	(.011)		
10. Paper	.60	.18	−.14	−.18	.25	.13	.21	.88	.93
	(.005)	(.030)	(.028)	(.018)	(.005)	(.035)	(.018)		

Note: All coefficients are significant at the .05 level except those marked by *. ** indicates original model was not valid and regression was run without scale. R_i^2 refer to the R^2 for the labor ($i = L$) and capital ($i = K$) equations.

continued

TABLE 3-2. *Continued*

Sectors	Parameter Estimates (standard derivatives in parenthesis)							Regression Statistics	
	α_L	γ_{LL}	γ_{LK}	C_L	α_K	γ_{KK}	C_K	R_L^2	R_K^2
11. Printing and Publishing	.88 (.001)	.09 (.007)	−.09 (.008)	−.09 (.007)	.11 (.001)	.09 (.009)	.11 (.008)	.94	.94
12. Primary Metals	.63 (.005)	.11 (.031)	.09 (.034)	−.13 (.018)	.26 (.006)	.11 (.038)	.11 (.020)	.75	.79
13. Metal Fabricating	.85 (.005)	.06 (.028)	−.05 (.028)*	−.04 (.013)	.12 (.005)	.05 (.029)*	.05 (.017)	.31	.44
14. Machinery	.87 (.0031)	.05 (.029)*	−.04 (.023)	**	.11 (.003)	.05 (.019)	**	.16	.36
15. Transportation Equipment	.85 (.008)	.03 (.039)*	−.03 (.037)*	−.071 (.022)	.12 (.008)	.04 (.035)*	.06 (.021)	.43	.53
16. Electrical Products	.88 (.006)	.08 (.040)*	−.08 (.040)*	−.03 (.021)*	.10 (.006)	.07 (.039)*	.05 (.021)	.35	.45
17. Nonmetallic Minerals	.61 (.008)	.24 (.059)	−.13 (.043)	−.16 (.044)	.22 (.008)	.11 (.042)	.17 (.034)	.50	.74
18. Petroleum and Coal	.46 (.005)	.17 (.039)	−.19 (.038)	−.25 (.028)	.48 (.004)	.20 (.038)	.25 (.027)	.86	.87
19. Chemicals	.63 (.008)	.19 (.054)	−.16 (.047)	−.15 (.039)	.26 (.009)	.19 (.054)	.12 (.038)	.65	.72

eliminating scale of production. The own elasticities are appropriately negative except in the case of capital and labor in the leather sector. This sector appears to be an anomaly. It has been a declining sector: its real output index decreased 15 percent from 1961, and employment in the sector declined about 20 percent, although there has been a trend toward greater capital utilization, with capital stock increasing 35 percent from 1957 to 1975.

Correcting for inflation, and hence eliminating the perverse own elasticities, represents an improvement over (Cameron and Schwartz, 1979) where almost 75 percent of the sectors had theoretically incorrect own elasticities for capital and/or labor. This reflects the more appropriate consideration of inflationary expectations in analyzing the combination of capital and labor.

3.4.2 Estimated Cost Shares

The sectors have been ranked according to increasing capital, decreasing labor, and increasing energy shares in Table 3–3. For convenience, the sectors have been grouped into secondary (low capital, high labor) and primary (high capital, lower labor). The labor and capital rankings are extremely close (only two cases of rank reversal). With respect to energy shares there is also a distinction between the primary and secondary groups: the order within the groups varies although the elements in each group are the same. Energy shares range from a low of about 1 percent in clothing (high labor, low capital) to 14 percent in nonmetallic minerals. These groups and rankings are very similar to those reported in Cameron and Schwartz (1979). The anomalous energy ranking of the petroleum and coal sector (12th) relative to its capital and labor rankings (18th) appears again. As explained in Cameron and Schwartz (1979), this is due to the fact that only "purchased fuels and electricity" are measured. The option of using its own output as a fuel input, biases upward the energy elasticity estimates for this sector.

3.4.3 Energy Price Elasticities

The own-price elasticity for energy is greater than that for labor and capital in all sectors except machinery, transportation equipment, and nonmetallic minerals where the capital own elasticities are slightly higher. This means that of these three inputs, energy input utilization is the most sensitive to price changes. In the case of the labor input, this probably reflects the

TABLE 3-3. Ranking of sectors by increasing capital shares, decreasing labor shares, and increasing energy shares

Sector	Ranking by Share of		
	Capital (1)	Labor (2)	Energy (3)
Secondary $\begin{pmatrix} S_K \leq 15\% \\ S_L \geq 80\% \end{pmatrix}$			
7 Clothing	1	1	1
4 Leather	2	2	3
9 Furniture	3	3	7
16 Electrical products	4	5	4
14 Machinery	5	4	5
11 Printing and publishing	6	6	2
13 Metal fabricating	7	7	9
6 Knitting	8	8	6
15 Transportation equipment	9	9	8
Primary $\begin{pmatrix} 16 < S_K < 30\% \\ 80 > S_L > 55\% \end{pmatrix}$			
8 Wood	10	10	13
1 Food and beverages	11	12	14
3 Rubber	12	11	10
5 Textiles	13	13	11
17 Nonmetallic minerals	14	14	18
12 Primary metals	15	15	16
19 Chemicals	16	16	15
10 Paper and allied products	17	17	17
18 Petroleum and coal $\begin{pmatrix} S_K \sim 50\% \\ S_L \sim 47\% \end{pmatrix}$	18	18	12

inpact of unionization and labor contracts plus increasing use of skilled labor working to make labor more of a "fixed" input.

The demand for energy is moderately "price inelastic" in all sectors (i.e., price elasticity of absolute value less than one). In many sectors, these elasticities have been declining, especially in the early part of the sample period. See Table 3-4 and Figure 3-1.

In comparison with Cameron and Schwartz (1979), these elasticities range slightly higher and there have been some changes in the rank ordering of sectors. The two sectors with the least elastic energy demand are the same in both studies, as are the four most elastic. However, in the middle range

TABLE 3-4. Elasticities, selected years

Sector	*Year*	*Energy (own)*	*Labor/Energy (cross)*	*Capital/Energy (cross)*
1. Food and Beverages	1957	−.654	.050	.119
	1963	−.613	.031	.104
	1968	−.575	.021	.090
	1974	−.540	.014	.082
	Average	−.591	.027	.099
3. Rubber	1957	−.585	.037	−.010
	1963	−.558	.033	−.008
	1968	−.519	.029	−.007
	1974	−.489	.025	.004
	Average	−.539	.031	−.009
4. Leather	1957	−.606	*	*
	1963	−.568		
	1968	−.527		
	1974	−.545		
	Average	−.553		
5. Textiles	1957	−.662	.050	.004
	1963	−.627	.042	−.001
	1968	−.613	.040	−.001
	1974	−.597	.037	.001
	Average	−.624	.042	.000
6. Knitting Mills	1957	−.607	.024	−.014
	1963	−.548	.020	−.019
	1968	−.546	.020	−.019
	1974	−.544	.020	−.015
	Average	−.564	0.21	−.018
7. Clothing	1957	−.613	0.10	−.017
	1963	−.558	.008	−.023
	1968	−.510	.007	−.024
	1974	−.462	.006	−.022
	Average	−.530	.007	−.024
8. Wood	1957	−.974	.072	−.041
	1963	−.968	.076	−.049
	1968	−.968	.076	−.043
	1974	−.972	.075	−.025
	Average	−.968	.076	−.043
9. Furniture and Fixtures	1957	−.799	.021	.080
	1963	−.785	.018	.085
	1968	−.764	.015	.075
	1974	−.749	.013	.066
	Average	−.772	.016	.080

TABLE 3-4. *Continued*

Sector	Year	Energy (own)	Labor/Energy (cross)	Capital/Energy (cross)
10. Paper	1957	−.671	.095	.192
	1963	−.669	.084	.180
	1968	−.663	.065	.159
	1974	−.662	.057	.153
	Average	−.666	.074	.168
11. Printing and Publishing	1957	−.915	.016	.025
	1963	−.909	.014	.023
	1968	−.901	.012	.020
	1974	−.893	.010	.018
	Average	−.904	.013	.022
12. Primary Metals	1957	−.525	.088	.033
	1963	−.504	.079	.024
	1968	−.491	.072	.029
	1974	−.492	.072	.033
	Average	−.503	.078	.028
13. Metal Fabricating	1957	−.770	.026	.064
	1963	−.754	.022	.061
	1968	−.727	.018	.054
	1974	−.710	.015	.050
	Average	−.738	.020	.057
14. Machinery	1957	−.458	.021	−.050
	1963	−.435	.020	−.058
	1968	−.320	.016	−.060
	1974	−.238	.013	−.061
	Average	−.364	.018	−.059
15. Transportation Equipment	1957	−.596	.032	−.039
	1963	−.527	.027	−.054
	1968	−.508	.025	−.043
	1974	−.509	.025	−.036
	Average	−.536	.027	−.046
16. Electrical Products	1957	−.908	.022	.044
	1963	−.903	.020	.043
	1968	−.893	.016	.037
	1974	−.890	.015	.033
	Average	−.899	.018	.041
17. Nonmetallic Minerals	1957	−.309	−.008	.254
	1963	−.251	−.025	.230
	1968	−.184	−.047	.202
	1974	−.190	−.059	.194
	Average	−.217	−.036	.217

18. Petroleum and Coal	1957	−.998	.077	.029
	1963	−.972	.079	.032
	1968	−.971	.080	.032
	1974	−.974	.087	.034
	Average	−.972	.081	.032
19. Chemicals	1957	−.390	.069	.006
	1963	−.371	.065	−.004
	1968	−.362	.060	.009
	1974	−.376	.061	.018
	Average	−.373	.064	.003

there is much variation in rank ordering between the two studies. The most elastic sectors have shown the least variation over the sample period, while those most inelastic have become increasingly inelastic. Note especially the ranking of sectors 8 and 18 (wood and petroleum and coal). The high elasticity they display is consistent with their ability to revert from purchased fuel to internal energy from their own outputs or by-products. Other sectors exhibiting strongly elastic energy demand are 16 and 11 (electrical products and printing and publishing).

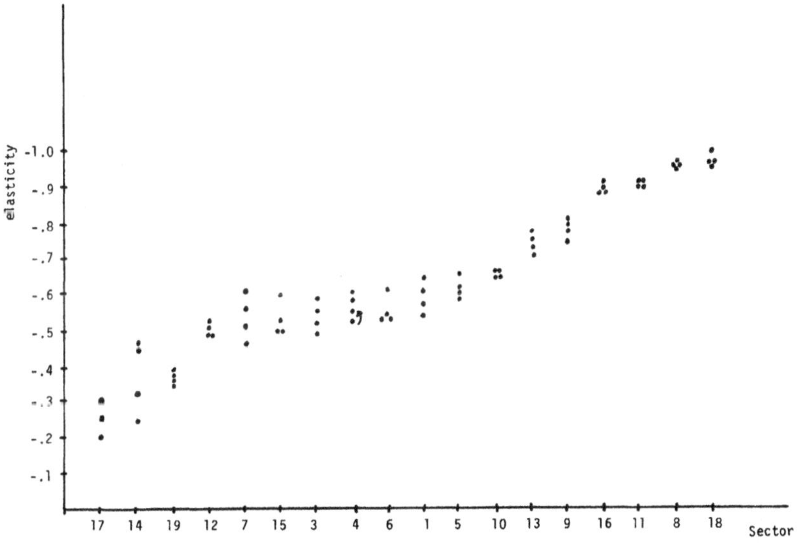

FIGURE 3-1. Estimated own-price elasticities of energy (in 1957, 1963, 1968, 1974); elasticities decrease over the four observations, except sector 4

The least elastic sectors are 17, 14, and 19 (nonmetallic minerals, machinery, and chemicals). Machinery does have a low share of energy, but nonmetallic minerals and chemicals rank very high in energy use (at 18th and 15th, respectively). These latter two sectors should be expected to experience the most difficulty in adjusting to high energy price.

Other sectors that are likely to experience problems adpating to energy price changes are those with high energy shares, but only moderately elastic energy demand. Paper and allied products (ranking 17th) has the option of shifting out of the energy market and relying on wood wastes (see Cox and Helliwell, chapter 9 of this volume), so that although it uses large amounts of energy, its energy demand elasticity is moderately high. Primary metals (ranking 16th) has also exhibited energy demand that is relatively elastic. Considering all these points, we can summarize that concern about the impact of changing energy prices should be focused on sectors 17 and 19, nonmetallic minerals and chemicals.

3.4.4 Cross-Price Elasticities

The cross-price elasticities between energy, capital, and labor enable us to predict how individual sectors will adapt to higher energy prices. Table 3–4 reports these cross-elasticities for four benchmark years as well as the averages over the period. Observe first that all the elasticities are very small. This is due to the substantially smaller share of energy relative to capital and labor. Note also that positive cross-elasticities imply substitutability (increases in the price of energy yield increases in the quantity of labor or capital) while negative signs indicate complementarity. All resource pairs are substitutes except capital and energy in sectors 3, 6, 7, 8, 14, 15, and labor and energy in sector 17. (Labor and capital are substitutes in all sectors except 9 [furniture] where they were weak complements, −0.002.) Taking into account both the cross-elasticities and the relative shares of capital and labor, a rise in the price of energy will lead to more labor intensive production in ten sectors (3, 5, 6, 7, 8, 12, 14, 15, 18, 19) and to more capital intensive production in seven sectors (1, 9, 10, 11, 13, 16, and 17).

For the sectors that will experience difficulty coping with energy prices (17 and 19), the input adjustments that would need to be accommodated are quite different. In nonmetallic minerals, capital and energy have been substitutes but the cross-elasticity is quite high (0.217) so that higher energy prices would create demand for a large amount of additional capital in a sector that is already capital intensive. Labor and energy are complements (−.036), so increases in the price of energy will make this relatively capital intensive sector even more capital intensive. In order to adapt to the higher energy prices, this sector might need help in raising capital, perhaps by way of guaranteed loans or special tax write-offs.

In the chemicals sector, energy is substitutable with both capital (0.005) and labor (0.064). Thus increased energy prices would make this very capital intensive sector relatively less capital intensive. Here, a bottleneck might arise in filling requirements for skilled labor. Assistance to this sector could be by way of scholarships and special training programs.

The average capital/energy cross-elasticity is 0.038 while that of labor/energy is 0.033. In comparison with other studies: Berndt and Wood (1975) find that capital and energy display substantial complementarity, their estimated cross-price elasticity is about -0.15. Fuss (1977), on the other hand, finds that energy and capital exhibit only very slight complementarity. His estimate is -0.004. Griffin and Gregory (1976) arrive at estimates more consistent with those of this study: PE_{KE} ranges from 0.08 in Denmark to 0.17 in Belgium and Norway. In their study, then, capital and energy are substitutes. Berndt and Wood (1975) find that energy and labor are slightly substitutable, with an estimated PE_{LE} very close to 0.03. Fuss's (1977) estimate is 0.043. (Due to the perverse own elasticities in Cameron and Schwartz [1979], the cross price elasticities were not valid.)

3.5 CONCLUSIONS

The sectors that are predicted to have the most difficulty in coping with higher energy prices are nonmetallic minerals and chemicals. Other sectors have elasticities in the range of -0.5 to -1.0 and would appear to be in a position to cope with the changing price structure. For the most part the means of adaptation will be the substitution of both labor and capital for energy, although there are some sectors where the shift will be toward more labor but less capital and energy, and others when the shift is toward more capital but less labor and energy. Given these cross-elasticities, suggestions were made for helping these two most sensitive sectors to cope. Now that the own elasticities and cross-elasticities have been calculated, further research should investigate the implications of various price scenarios for resource demand and the structure of production.

REFERENCES

Bassie, V. L. 1976. The real rate of interest: A thesis in pseudoscience. *Quarterly Review of Economics and Business* 16:7–18.

Berndt, E. R. and Wood, D. O. 1975. Technology, prices and the derived demand for energy. *Review of Economics and Statistics* 57:259–268.

Cameron, T. A. and Schwartz, S. L. 1977. An analysis of sectoral energy demand: The manufacturing industries of Canada. Vancouver: University of British Columbia, Faculty of Commerce Working Paper No. 475.

Cameron, T. A. and Schwartz, S. L. 1979. Sectoral energy demand in Canadian manufacturing industries. *Energy Economics* 1:112–118.

Cox, A. J. and Helliwell, J. F. Economic modeling of energy supply from burning wood wastes at British Columbia pulp and paper mills. Chapter 9, this volume.

Diewert, W. E. 1976. Exact and superlative index numbers. *Journal of Econometrics* 4:115–147.

Dornbusch, R. and Fischer, S. 1978. *Macro-Economics.* New York: McGraw-Hill.

Fama, E. F. 1975. Short term interest rates as predictors of inflation. *American Economic Review* 65:269–282.

Fisher, I. 1930. *The theory of interest.* New York: MacMillan.

Fuss, M. A. 1977. The demand for energy in Canadian manufacturing: An example of the estimation of production functions with many inputs. *Journal of Econometrics* 5:89–116.

Galbraith, J. K. 1973. *Economics and the public purpose.* Boston: Houghton Mifflin.

Griffin, J. M. and Gregory, P. R. 1976. An intercountry translog model of energy substitution response. *American Economic Review* 65:845–857.

Lahiri, K. 1976. Inflationary expectation: Their formation and interest rate effects. *American Economic Review* 66:124–131.

Sargent, T. J. 1969. Commodity price expectations and the interest rate. *Quarterly Journal of Economics* 83:123–140.

Sargent, T. J. 1972. Anticipated inflation and the nominal rate of interest. *Quarterly Journal of Economics* 86:212–225.

Statistics Canada. 1957–1975. Annual Industry Reviews, Ottawa.

Yohe, W. P. and Karnosky, D. S. 1969. Interest rates and price level changes, 1952–69. *Federal Reserve Bank of St. Louis Review* 51:19–36.

4 THE DERIVED DEMAND FOR ENERGY IN THE PRESENCE OF SUPPLY CONSTRAINTS

Melvyn A. Fuss*

The purpose of this paper is to introduce a procedure for utilizing, in forecasting and policy simulation, existing econometric models of industrial energy demand during a period of supply constraints. These existing models (e.g., Berndt-Wood and Hudson-Jorgenson) were estimated assuming infinitely elastic supply curves for energy components. However, we demonstrate that such models can still be used in a supply constraint regime if we assume that the producer continues to optimize subject to the constrained opportunities and the production technology. In essence, market prices for constrained inputs are replaced by shadow prices and the duality relationships between cost (or profit) and production are retained. The procedure is illustrated using a model previously estimated by the author for Canadian manufacturing. Constrained forecasts and price elasticities for 1985 are presented, assuming natural gas and fuel oil supplies are constrained to the 1980 demand level. Significant differences occur in the pattern of demands for other energy components such as coal and electricity between the unconstrained and constrained regimes.

*The author wishes to thank Charles Cohen for extensive programming assistance and Michael Denny and Leonard Waverman for helpful comments on an earlier draft. Thanks are also due to W. E. Diewert and W. T. Ziemba for their help in preparing the paper for this volume.

4.1 INTRODUCTION

Many government policies directed toward energy conservation in Canada and the United States are based on the assumption that the supplies of non-renewable energy resources will be insufficient in the near future to satisfy demand at politically feasible energy price levels. If the price system is not used as the ultimate allocative mechanism, some form of supply restriction will be required. This is likely to be true in particular with respect to the industrial use of natural gas and refined petroleum products.

The current generation of industrial demand models are long run equilibrium models, usually using the translog functional form (Berndt, Fuss, and Waverman, 1977; Fuss, 1977; Griffin and Gregory, 1976; Hudson and Jorgenson, 1974). These models were estimated assuming infinitely elastic supply curves for energy components. It is models of this type which are likely to be available for forecasting and policy simulation in the near future. However, any supply constraints which become important will affect the estimated price elasticities of demand and must be taken into account when evaluating the responsiveness of demand to government policies. The purpose of this paper is to introduce a procedure for utilizing these estimated structures in the changed environment of energy supply constraints. As an illustration of the proposed technique, we explore the effects of constraining the supply of natural gas and fuel oil on the demand for other factors of production in Canadian manufacturing. We are particularly interested in the effect of constrained supplies on the demand for other energy types, such as electricity and coal.

This paper will show that supply constraints can be incorporated into a model of cost-minimizing behavior in which the producer behaves as if he faced shadow prices for the constrained inputs, rather than market prices. The duality between cost and production is retained, and provides a link between the unconstrained and the constrained production structures. An estimated unconstrained structure is also presented (Fuss, 1977). We demonstrate how this structure can be utilized to analyze constrained demand. Also presented is an empirical analysis of the structure of demand in 1985 for energy inputs in Ontario manufacturing, assuming binding supply constraints with respect to natural gas and heavy fuel oil. Suggestions for additional applications concludes this paper. One of the more important applications discussed is the use of the model to distinguish between the short run and long run responses to changes in energy prices. This application is made possible by the fact that the difference between the short and long run response is essentially the difference between constrained and unconstrained demand.

4.2 A MODEL OF PRODUCER BEHAVIOR SUBJECT TO SUPPLY CONSTRAINTS

Suppose a producer of manufacturing output chooses inputs to minimize the cost of producing a given output. Faced with supply restrictions with respect to some factors of production, the producer continues to minimize cost subject to the constrained opportunities and the production technology. Let the production function be

$$Q = f(x_1, \ldots, x_n) \tag{4.1}$$

where Q is output and $x_i \geq 0$, $i = 1, \ldots, n$ are inputs.

Let $x_1, \ldots, x_r$ be unconstrained (from above) inputs and $x_{r+1}, \ldots, x_n$ be constrained inputs such that

$$x_j \leq x_j^* \qquad j = r + 1, \ldots, n. \tag{4.2}$$

Then the producer's optimization problem is to minimize

$$\sum_{i=1}^{n} p_i x_i$$

where p_i is the service price of the ith input, subject to $Q \leq f(x_1, \ldots, x_n)$ and $x_i \leq x_i^*$ for $i = r + 1, \ldots, n$.

The natural Lagrangian is

$$L = \sum_{i=1}^{n} p_i x_i + \mu[Q - f(x_1, \ldots, x_n)] + \sum_{i=r+1}^{n} \lambda_i[x_i - x_i^*]. \tag{4.3}$$

The Kuhn-Tucker necessary conditions for an optimum are:

$$\frac{\partial L}{\partial x_i} = p_i - \mu\frac{\partial f}{\partial x_i} \geq 0 \qquad i = 1, \ldots, r \tag{4.4}$$

$$\frac{\partial L}{\partial x_i} = p_i - \mu\frac{\partial f}{\partial x_i} + \lambda_i \geq 0 \quad i = r + 1, \ldots, n \tag{4.5}$$

$$\frac{\partial L}{\partial \mu} = Q - f(x_1, \ldots, x_n) \leq 0 \tag{4.6}$$

$$\frac{\partial L}{\partial \lambda_i} = x_i - x_i^* \leq 0 \qquad i = r + 1, \ldots, n \tag{4.7}$$

$$\sum_{i=1}^{r} x_i \cdot \left[p_i - \mu\frac{\partial f}{\partial x_i}\right] + \sum_{i=r+1}^{n} x_i \left[p_i - \mu\frac{\partial f}{\partial x_i} + \lambda_i\right] = 0 \tag{4.8}$$

$$\mu \cdot [Q - f(x_1, \ldots, x_n)] + \sum_{i=r+1}^{n} \lambda_i [x_i - x_i^*] = 0 \tag{4.9}$$

$$x_i \geq 0, i = 1, \ldots, n; \lambda_i \geq 0, i = r + 1, \ldots, n, \mu \geq 0.$$

Assuming that f is a quasi-concave function, the Kuhn-Tucker necessary conditions for an optimum are also sufficient (Arrow and Enthoven, 1961). If production is technically efficient, then $Q = f(x_1, \ldots, x_n)$ in (4.6); therefore, $\mu > 0$ will satisfy (4.9) since the constraint *qualification* is trivial given that f is a production function. If we also assume that the producer employs all inputs considered at nonzero levels, *then* (4.4) and (4.5) hold *with* equality. In that case, $\mu > 0$, and (4.4) and (4.5) together imply that the producer's constrained cost minimization solution is to set the marginal rate of technical substitution (MRTS) equal to the price ratio, where the prices relevant for the constrained inputs are the *shadow* prices. For example,

$$\text{MRTS}_{i,j} = \frac{\partial f}{\partial x_i} / \frac{\partial f}{\partial x_j} = \frac{p_i}{p_j + \lambda_j} = \frac{p_i}{p_j^*} \quad \begin{array}{l} i = 1, \ldots, r \\ j = r + 1, \ldots, n \end{array} \tag{4.10}$$

(where $p_j + \lambda_j$ is the shadow price of a constrained input) is part of the description of the optimal marginal conditions. Note from (4.9) that when $x_j < x_j^*$, $\lambda_j = 0$ implying that market and shadow prices coincide.

In equation (4.10) we have just reproduced the usual cost minimization solution except for the fact that some prices are shadow prices rather than market prices. Solving equations (4.4) through (4.9) yields the producer's constrained cost function

$$C = C(p_1, \ldots, p_r, p_{r+1}^*, \ldots, p_n^*, Q). \tag{4.11}$$

Alternatively, utilizing the theory of duality between production and cost, we can start with the cost function (4.11) and assume that the producer acts *as if* he minimizes cost subject to the mix of market and shadow prices appearing in (4.11). We know from the marginal conditions (4.10) that this basic duality property is not affected by the use of shadow prices for some of the inputs. Of course if $p_j^* \neq p_j$, then p_j^* will be endogenous. However, the point of the above analysis is to demonstrate that we can treat the producer as behaving as if p_j^* were exogenous. The endogenous nature of p_j^* will be taken into account below.

Utilizing Shephard's Lemma (see Diewert, 1971) we have

$$\frac{\partial C}{\partial p_i} = x_i \qquad i = 1 \ldots r \tag{4.12}$$

$$\frac{\partial C}{\partial p_i^*} = \begin{cases} \dfrac{\partial C}{\partial p_i} = x_i & \text{for } \lambda_i = 0 \qquad (4.13) \\ & i = r+1, \ldots, n. \\ x_i^* & \text{for } \lambda_i \neq 0 \qquad (4.14) \end{cases}$$

For any input $i \in \{r + 1, \ldots, n\}$ for which the supply constraint is not binding, equation (4.13) which generates the cost-minimizing input demand functions, is equivalent to that specified by (4.12) and can be lumped with (4.12). For simplicity, we assume that $\lambda_i \neq 0$ for all $i \in \{r + 1, \ldots, n\}$.

Let

$$p^1 \equiv (p_1, \ldots, p_r);\ p^2 \equiv (p_{r+1}, \ldots, p_n);\ p^* \equiv (p^*_{r+1}, \ldots, p^*_n)$$

$$x^1 \equiv (x_1, \ldots, x_r);\ x^2 \equiv (x_{r+1}, \ldots, x_n);\ \text{and } x^* \equiv (x^*_{r+1}, \ldots, x^*_n).$$

Then the cost function (4.11) is

$$C = C(p^1, p^*, Q) \qquad (4.15)$$

and the derived demand equations (4.12) through (4.14) are

$$\nabla C_{p^1} = x^1(p^1, p^*, Q) \qquad (4.16)$$

$$\nabla C_{p^*} = x^*. \qquad (4.17)$$

Solving (4.17) for p^* yields the *inverse* demand functions

$$p^* = h(x^*, p^1, Q) \qquad (4.18)$$

which can be used to compute the shadow price vector p^*.[1]

When there are no binding supply constraints

$$p^* = p^2 \text{ and } \nabla C_p = \binom{x^1}{x^2}$$

is a system of direct derived demand functions for *all* inputs which can be estimated in the usual manner. Assuming no change in the underlying production possibility set, (i.e., no technical change induced by the supply constraints) the behavior of the producer during the constrained regime can be obtained by setting $x^2 = x^*$ and $p^2 = p^*$ in the estimated structure.[2]

1. In this case we know that a solution to (4.18) exists since C is monotone and strictly concave in p^* and only one sector is involved.

2. The assumption that induced technical change which conserves the constrained inputs does not occur is probably valid in the short-run but not in the long-run. For a model of energy demand which incorporates this form of induced technical change, see Berndt, Fuss, and Waverman (1977).

4.3 AN ESTIMATED PRODUCTION STRUCTURE FOR CANADIAN MANUFACTURING

In this section we summarize a model of production technology, estimated by the author, using a time series cross-section data set drawn from Canadian manufacturing 1961–1971. Details of the derivation and estimation of the model can be found in Fuss (1977). It is assumed that during this time period there were no significant supply constraints involving the postulated factors of production.

4.3.1 The Model

We assume that a production function exists of the form

$$Q = F(E, L, M, K) \tag{4.19}$$

where Q is gross output and E, L, M, and K are inputs of energy, labor, materials, and capital respectively.

If we assume cost minimizing behavior and exogenous factor prices and output levels, the theory of duality implies that there exists a unique representation of the underlying technology in the form of a cost function.

$$C = g(p_{\mathrm{E}}, p_{\mathrm{L}}, p_{\mathrm{M}}, p_{\mathrm{K}}, Q) \tag{4.20}$$

where C is total cost and p_i are the factor prices.

A translog function which provides a second order approximation to (4.20) and does not impose homotheticity on the production structure is

$$\begin{aligned} \ell n C = {} & \alpha_0 + \sum \alpha_i \ell n p_i + \alpha_Q \ell n Q + \tfrac{1}{2}\sum_i \sum_j \gamma_{ij} \ell n p_i \ell n p_j \\ & + \sum_i \gamma_{iQ} \ell n Q \ell n p_i + \tfrac{1}{2}\gamma_{QQ}(\ell n Q)^2. \end{aligned} \tag{4.21}$$

Cost minimization with optimization errors implies

$$S_{ikt} = \alpha_i + \sum_j \gamma_{jk} \ell n p_{jkt} + \gamma_{iQ} \ell n Q_{ikt} + u_{ikt} \tag{4.22}$$

where i or j indexes the factor of production, k indexes the region, and t indexes time. S_{ikt} is the cost share of the ith factor in the kth region in the total cost of production.

Imposition of the adding up criterion and the properties of neoclassical production theory leads to the following constraints being imposed on the system of equations (4.22):

$$\begin{aligned} & \sum_i \gamma_{ij} = \sum_i \gamma_{iQ} = \sum_i \alpha_i = 0 \qquad \text{(adding up)} \\ & \sum_j \gamma_{ij} = 0 \qquad \text{(homogeneity of degree zero in prices) and} \\ & \gamma_{ij} = \gamma_{ji} \qquad \text{(symmetry).} \end{aligned} \tag{4.23}$$

The error term (u_{ikt}) in (4.22) is not likely to be randomly distributed. We hypothesize that it consists of two additive components: λ_{ik}, which is constant over time but differs between regions and factors, and ϵ_{ikt}, which is random with zero expectation. In addition, we assume that the random components of error terms from different factor demand equations are contemporaneously correlated, but uncorrelated over time, that is

$$E(\epsilon_{ikt}\ \epsilon_{iks}) = \begin{cases} \sigma_{ik} \text{ when } t = s \\ 0 \text{ when } t \neq s \end{cases} \tag{4.24}$$

Equation (4.22) then takes the form:

$$S_{ikt} = (\alpha_i + \lambda_{ik}) + \sum_j \gamma_{jk} \ln p_{jkt} + \gamma_{iQ} \ln Q_{ikt} + \epsilon_{ikt} \tag{4.25}$$

which is estimated by an iterative Zellner efficient procedure (to correct for heteroskedasticity across equations) with individual factor, region constant terms. Note that the additional constraint, $\sum_i \lambda_{ik} = 0$ must be added to (4.23). Equation (4.25), estimated subject to (4.23) and (4.24), provides the demand structure for the four aggregate inputs: capital, labor, materials, and energy.

In addition, a subaggregate energy model is developed (to provide the demand structure for individual energy types) in the following way. Assume that (4.19) is separable in energy:

$$Q = Q[E(E_1, \ldots, E_N), L, M, K] \tag{4.26}$$

where E_i is the ith energy type $i = 1, \ldots, N$ and E is homogeneous in the E_i. Then the cost function (4.20) takes the form

$$C = C[p_E(p_{E_1}, \ldots, p_{E_N}), p_L, p_M, p_K, Q]. \tag{4.27}$$

The price of aggregate energy P_E can be approximated by an index obtained from:

$$\ln p_E = \beta_0 + \sum_i \beta_i \ln p_{E_i} + \tfrac{1}{2} \sum_i \sum_j \beta_{ij} \ln p_{E_i} \ln p_{E_j} \tag{4.28}$$

where (4.28) is a unit cost function of the translog form. The parameters of (4.28) can be estimated up to an arbitrary scaling factor β_0 by applying Zellner's (1962) seemingly unrelated regressions technique to the system of share equations

$$S_{E_i} = \beta_i + \sum_j \beta_{ij} \ln p_{E_j} \tag{4.29}$$

The constraints

$$\sum_i \beta_i = 1, \sum_j \beta_{ij} = 0, \beta_{ij} = \beta_{ji} \text{ (all } i, j, i \neq j)$$

are imposed in the estimation. Substituting parameter estimates from (4.29) into (4.28) yields $\hat{p}_E$, which is used as an instrumental variable in (4.25) (see

Fuss [1977] for details). Estimation of the system of equations (4.29) provides a means of obtaining the price responsiveness of the demand for individual energy types. The estimation procedure used in the aggregate model was also used in the subaggregate energy model (see Fuss [1977]).

4.3.2 The Estimated Structure

The model previously described was estimated for total Canadian manufacturing. Four regions were included in the combined time series — cross-section data set: Quebec, Ontario, the Prairies, and British Columbia and the Yukon for the period 1961–1971. The Maritimes region was excluded due to the lack of appropriate data on natural gas. Inputs into the production process were specified to be labor, capital, materials, and the energy types — coal, liquid petroleum gas, fuel oil, natural gas, electricity, and motor gasoline.

4.3.3 The Interfuel Substitution Model

The energy submodel provides empirical estimates of the parameters of an aggregator function for the six energy types and an aggregate price index for "total energy" consistent with the underlying technological constraints on interfuel substitution. The estimated equations are presented in Table 4–1. See Fuss (1977) for more details.

4.3.4 The Aggregate Inputs Model

The aggregate model provides empirical estimates of the parameters of the underlying production technology involving aggregate capital, labor, energy, and materials. The estimated parameters are presented in Table 4–2. These estimates are obtained by estimating the system (4.25) subject to the constraints (4.23) and (4.24); replacing p_E by its instrumental variable $\hat{p}_E$, obtained from the energy sub-model by replacing the parameters in equation (4.28) by their estimates. The reader will note that several of the parameters in Tables 4–1 and 4–2 are not significantly different from zero. Of more importance is the fact that the price elasticities which summarize the production technology are significant. See Tables 2 and 4 in Fuss (1977).

TABLE 4–1. Total manufacturing energy sub-model, parameter estimates

Exogenous Variables *Shares*	DQUE	DONT	DPR	DBCY	LPCOAL	LPLPG	LPFOIL	LPNG	LPELEC	LPGAS	R^2*
SCOAL	.132 (.051)	.197 (.050)	.197 (.044)	.102 (.044)	−.0830 (.0323)	00128 (.00158)	0242 (.0299)	.100 (.022)	−.0256 (.0197)	−.0168 (.0282)	.752
SLPG	.0072 (.0045)	.0081 (.0041)	.0077 (.0043)	.0065 (.0039)	.00128 (.00158)	−.00913 (.00097)	−.00074 (.00217)	.00237 (.00147)	−.00246 (.00260)	.00867 (.00341)	.772
SFOIL	.157 (.094)	.119 (.088)	.028 (.079)	.124 (.081)	.0242 (.0299)	−.00074 (.00217)	−.0576 (.0593)	.00302 (.0250)	.0499 (.0283)	−.0188 (.0514)	.740
SNG	.045 (.043)	.231 (.041)	.278 (.041)	.075 (.037)	.100 (.022)	.00237 (.00147)	.00302 (.0250)	−.0686 (.0207)	−.0715 (.0173)	.0349 (.0250)	.966
SELEC	.592 (.053)	.372 (.051)	.347 (.051)	.629 (.046)	−.0256 (.0197)	−.00246 (.00260)	.0499 (.0283)	−.0715 (.0173)	.0151 (.0342)	.0347 (.0363)	.978
SGAS	.067 (.100)	.072 (.090)	.142 (.087)	.063 (.086)	−.0168 (.0282)	.00867 (.00341)	−.0188 (.0514)	.0349 (.0250)	.0347 (.0368)	−.0427 (.0655)	e) −.092

Definitions:

SCOAL = Share of coal in the total cost of energy.
SLPG = Share of liquid petroleum gas.
SFOIL = Share of fuel oil.
SNG = Share of natural gas.
SELEC = Share of electricity.
SGAS = Share of motor gasoline.
LPCOAL = Logarithm of the price of coal (thousands of dollars per 10^6 Btus).

LPLPG = Price of LPG.
LPFOIL = Price of fuel oil.
LPNG = Price of natural gas.
LPELEC = Price of electricity.
LPGAS = Price of motor gasoline.
} in logarithmic form
DQUE = Dummy variable for Quebec.
DONT = Dummy variable for Ontario.
DPR = Dummy variable for the Prairies.
DBCY = Dummy variable for British Columbia and the Yukon.

The numbers in parentheses are asymptotic standard errors.

*The negative R^2 is due to the presence of constrained parameters. Unconstrained OLS estimation resulted in an R^2 of .19 for the gasoline equation. In the context of share equations a low R^2 is not necessarily a result of misspecification but may be an indication of approximately constant shares with respect to price and regional variation.

TABLE 4-2. Total manufacturing—aggregate energy model, parameter estimates

Exogenous Variables *Shares*	DQUE	DONT	DPR	DBCY	$L\hat{P}_E$	LP_L	LP_M	LP_K	LQ	R^2
S_E	.169 (.047)	.164 (.048)	.150 (.043)	.166 (.043)	.00881 (.00362)	.00577 (.00500)	−.00962 (.00557)	−.00497 (.00411)	−.00926 (.00302)	.974
S_L	.564 (.130)	.557 (.135)	.483 (.120)	.515 (.120)	.00577 (.00500)	.0641 (.0162)	−.0626 (.0121)	−.00724 (.0158)	−.0238 (.0084)	.945
S_M	−.134 (.120)	−.153 (.124)	−.005 (.110)	−.060 (.109)	−.00962 (.00557)	−.0626 (.0121)	.0618 (.0140)	.0104 (.0119)	.0446 (.0078)	.985
S_K	.401 (.169)	.432 (.176)	.372 (.156)	.379 (.158)	−.00497 (.00411)	−.00724 (.0158)	.0104 (.0119)	.00180 (.0232)	−.0116 (.0104)	.792

Definitions:

S_E = Share of energy in the value of gross ouput.
S_L = Share of labor.
S_M = Share of materials.
S_K = Share of capital.
$L\hat{P}_E$ = Logarithm of the instrumental variable for the price of energy.
LP_L = Price of labor services.
LP_M = Price of materials.
LP_k = Price of capital services.
LQ = Gross output in constant dollars.
(LP_L through LQ:) in logarithmic form

The notation for the dummy variables is the same as that used in Table 4-1.

The numbers in parentheses are asymptotic standard errors.

Note: The negative intercepts do not imply that monotonicity is violated. A rescaling of the exogenous variables would make these coefficients positive without affecting the other parameter estimates. Fitted shares are positive for all observations.

4.4 CONSTRAINED DEMAND AND TWO-STAGE TRANSLOG MODEL

The unconstrained translog structure presented in section 4.3 has cost shares rather than quantities as derived dependent variables. This fact, characteristic of translog models, creates problems when one is attempting to solve for the shadow prices during the period of constraints, since the constrained quantities appear implicitly rather than explicitly (as is suggested by equation (4.18). In fact, the shadow prices have to be obtained by iteration. We begin this section by outlining the solution concept.

Assume that the last s energy components are subject to binding supply constraints. Let $S^*_{\mathrm{E}_j}$ represent the cost share of the constrained energy input, where shadow prices p^*_j are used to value the constrained inputs, i.e.,

$$S^*_{\mathrm{E}_j} = \frac{p^*_j E^*_j}{\sum_{j=1}^{r} p_j E_j + \sum_{j=r+1}^{n} p^*_j E^*_j} \quad j = r+1, \ldots, n. \tag{4.30}$$

Then the subset of equation (4.29) corresponding to the constrained energy types can be written

$$S^*_{\mathrm{E}_j} = \beta_j + \sum_{j=1}^{r} \beta_{ij} \ln p_{\mathrm{E}_j} + \sum_{j=r+1}^{n} \beta_{ij} \ln p^*_{\mathrm{E}_j}. \tag{4.31}$$

In addition, the aggregator function (4.28) is then

$$\begin{aligned} \ln p^*_{\mathrm{E}} = {} & \beta_o + \sum_{j=1}^{r} \beta_j \ln p_{\mathrm{E}_j} + \sum_{j=r+1}^{n} \beta_j \ln p^*_{\mathrm{E}_j} \\ & + \tfrac{1}{2} \sum_{j=1}^{r} \sum_{i=1}^{r} \beta_{ij} \ln p_{E_j} \ln p_{\mathrm{E}_i} + \tfrac{1}{2} \sum_{j=r+1}^{n} \sum_{i=r+1}^{n} \beta_{ij} \ln p^*_{\mathrm{E}_j} \ln p^*_{\mathrm{E}_i} \\ & + \tfrac{1}{2} \sum_{j=1}^{r} \sum_{i=r+1}^{n} \beta_{ij} \ln p_{E_j} \ln p^*_{\mathrm{E}_i}. \end{aligned} \tag{4.32}$$

Finally, the aggregate energy share equation from (4.22) becomes

$$S^*_{\mathrm{E}} = \alpha_E + \sum_{j \neq E} \gamma_{jE} \ln p_j + \gamma_{EE} \ln p^*_{\mathrm{E}} + \gamma_{EQ} \ln Q. \tag{4.33}$$

Since the share equations of the model other than those specified in (4.31) and (4.33) do not involve the constrained energy quantities, they can be ignored in the solution process. The problem is to find $p^*_{\mathrm{E}_j}$ which satisfy

(4.31) through (4.33) and the constraints $E_j = E_j^*$, $j = r + 1, \ldots, n$ (which have been substituted in (4.31) through (4.33) using (4.30)).

To obtain a solution algorithm, note that

$$p_{E_j}^* \equiv \frac{1}{E_j^*}(S_{E_j}^* \cdot S_E^* \cdot C^*) \qquad j = r + 1, \ldots, n \tag{4.34}$$

where C^* is the constrained total cost of production, obtained from (4.21) by replacing p_E by p_E^*.[3] Therefore, we need to add to the system (4.31) through (4.33) the identity (4.34) and the equation[4]

$$\begin{aligned} \ell n\, C^* &= \alpha_0 + \sum_{i \neq E} \alpha_i \ell n\, p_i + \alpha_E \ell n\, p_E^* + \alpha_Q \ell n\, Q \\ &+ \tfrac{1}{2} \sum_{\substack{i, \\ \neq E}} \sum_{j} \gamma_{ij} \ell n\, p_i \ell n\, p_j + \tfrac{1}{2} \sum_i \gamma_{iE} \ell n\, p_i \ell n\, p_E^* \\ &+ \sum_{i \neq E} \gamma_{iQ} \ell n\, p_i \ell n\, Q + \gamma_{EQ} \ell n\, p_E^* \ell n\, Q + \tfrac{1}{2} \gamma_{QQ} (\ell n\, Q)^2. \end{aligned} \tag{4.35}$$

Equations (4.31) through (4.35) provide all the information necessary for an iterative solution to obtain $p_{E_j}^*$. We begin with arbitrary prices $p_{E_j}^1$ for the constrained inputs. Substituting the $p_{E_j}^1$ and the actual p_{E_i}, $i = 1, \ldots, r$ into equations (4.31) through (4.33) and (4.35) yields estimated shares $S_{E_j}^1$, S_E^1 and total cost (value of gross output) C^1.

From (34) we can obtain an alternative estimate $p_{E_j}^2$ of $p_{E_j}^*$,

$$p_{E_j}^2 = \frac{1}{E_j^*} (S_{E_j}^1 \cdot S_E^1 \cdot C^1). \tag{4.36}$$

Let

$$p_{E_j}^3 \equiv \Theta p_{E_j}^1 + (1 - \Theta) p_{E_j}^2,$$

where $0 < \Theta < 1$ is a damping factor, and use $p_{E_j}^3$ as the new estimate of $\overset{*}{}_{E_j}$ in the next interation. Convergence is achieved when

$$p_{E_j}^{n+1} = \frac{1}{E_j^*} [S_{E_j}^n \cdot S_E^n \cdot C^n] = p_{E_j}^n \text{ for } j = r + 1, \ldots, n.$$

3. The reader will note that in Table 4-2 we defined S_E as the share of the value of gross output. For a justification of the use of the value of output in place of total cost see Fuss (1977) pp. 106-107.

4. The cost function with Hicks-neutral technical change was estimated as

$$\begin{aligned} \ell n\, C/Q = &-.042 \text{ DQUE } -.047 \text{ DONT } -.022 \text{ DPR } -.017 \text{ DBCY } -.0174\, T \\ &+ \sum \alpha_i \ell n p_i + \sum\sum \gamma_{ij} \ell n p_i \ell n p_j + \sum \gamma_{iQ} \ell n Q \ell n p_i \end{aligned}$$

where T is time and the estimates of α_i, γ_{ij}, γ_{iQ} appear in Table 4-2.

The estimated production structure presented in section 4.3 corresponds to a strictly quasi-concave, differentiable production function (see Fuss [1977]). Therefore, there exist unique shadow prices p^*_{Ej}. Does the iterative process described above converge to p^*_{Ej}? The answer is yes, and we can demonstrate this fact in the following way. Since the underlying production function is strictly quasi-concave, factor own-price elasticities are negative,[5] so that an *over*estimate of the equilibrium shadow price implies an *under*estimate of quantity demanded. Suppose $p^1_{Ej} > p^*_{Ej}$, then $E^1_j < E^*_j$ and the constraint is not binding, which implies $p^2_{Ej} = p_{Ej}$ (the market price) $< p^*_{Ej}$ and $p^2_{Ej} < p^3_{Ej} < p^1_{Ej}$. Two cases can occur. If $p^3_{Ej} < p^*_{Ej}$ then $E^3_j > E^*_j$. In this case a shadow price greater than p^*_{Ej} is needed to "clear" the market, so that $p^4_{Ej} > p^*_{Ej}$. If $p^5_{Ej} < p^*_{Ej} < p^6_{Ej}$, etc., the estimated shadow price exhibits damped[6] oscillatory behavior around p^*_{Ej} until convergence is achieved. The second possibility is that $p^3_{Ej} > p^*_{Ej}$. Then $p^4_{Ej} = p_{Ej}$ and $p^4_{Ej} < p^5_{Ej} < p^3_{Ej}$. Either damped monotone convergence occurs, or at some point $p^n_{Ej} < p^*_{Ej}$ in which case damped oscillatory behavior prevails. A similar analysis can be constructed to demonstrate convergence when $p^1_{Ej} < p^*_{Ej}$.

4.5 AN EMPIRICAL EXAMPLE

This section explores the effect of supply constraints on the 1985 demand for energy in Ontario manufacturing. Initially, we assume that natural gas supply in 1985 is constrained to the level demanded in 1980. As a second example we assume that both natural gas and heavy fuel oil 1985 supplies are constrained to their respective 1980 demand levels.

We require forecasts of the exogenous variables in 1980 and 1985. Energy price forecasts were obtained from private sources and are similar to those used by Fuss, Hyndman, and Waverman (1977) in their unconstrained forecasts. The remaining exogenous variables were obtained from the University of Toronto's TRACE annual econometric model projections. They are also similar to those used in Fuss, Hyndman, and Waverman (1977). The predicted values of the exogenous variables used are presented in Table 4-3.

5. For a verification that the estimated elasticities are indeed negative, see Tables 4 and 5 in Fuss (1977).

6. This is why the weight Θ is called a damping factor.

TABLE 4–3. Exogenous variables used in forecasts (Ontario)

Variable	*Units*	*1980*	*1985*
PCOAL	\$ per 10^6 Btus	3.21	4.38
PLPG	"	7.22	8.95
PFOIL	"	2.46	3.05
PNG	"	2.04	2.29
PELEC	"	7.67	10.47
PGAS	"	10.76	13.35
P_L	\$ per hour	7.88	11.27
P_M	index, 1962 = 1.0	2.56	3.10
P_K	index, 1962 = 1.0	2.90	3.95
Q	millions of constant 1961 dollars	32.63	39.12

Table 4–4 presents the comparative forecasts of demand, with and without supply constraints, for the various components of energy and for labor services. The labor input is included because of the interest of policy makers in the effect of supply constraints on employment. In general, the effect of supply constraints is as expected. When natural gas supply alone is constrained below the unconstrained demand, the effect is to increase the demand for substitutes, especially coal and fuel oil. There is a reduction in the aggregate demand for energy, reflecting the fact that supply restrictions have increased the cost of the energy input. There is a small increase in the demand for labor, a result of the fact that energy and labor are long run substitutes in production. Constraining natural gas and fuel oil leads to

TABLE 4–4. The effect of supply constraints on forecasts

			1985		
Input	*Units*	*1980*	*Uncon-strained*	*Natural Gas Constrained*	*Natural Gas & Fuel Oil Constrained*
Coal	10^{12} Btus	41.2	32.5	41.0	42.8
LPG	"	4.1	4.2	4.4	4.4
Fuel Oil	"	79.6	89.9	91.5	79.6*
Natural Gas	"	151.9	188.5	151.9*	151.9*
Electricity	"	74.0	73.7	73.6	75.1
Motor Gasoline	"	5.6	5.8	6.8	6.6
Total Energy	"	356.4	394.6	369.2	360.4
Labor	10^8 man hr.	20.55	20.76	20.79	20.80

*Supply constrained to 1980 level of demand.

similar results. The demand for substitute energy sources is increased while the aggregate demand for energy declines. The demand for labor is also increased over what it would be without supply constraints. Equilibrium shadow prices and cost shares are presented in Table 4–5.

4.5.1 The Structure of Demand in 1985

An alternative and probably more informative way of analyzing the effects of supply constraints is to compare price elasticities of demand with and without constraints. This can easily be done within our framework. For any input x_i the own price elasticity when no supply constraints are present is

$$\epsilon_{ii} = \frac{\partial \ell n x_i}{\partial \ell n p_i} \qquad i = 1, \ldots, n \tag{4.37}$$

where we assume $p_j, j \neq i$ and Q are held constant.

It can be shown (Fuss, 1977) for the two-stage translog model the own price elasticities of demand are given, for the aggregate inputs, by

$$\epsilon_{ii} = \frac{\gamma_{ii} + S_i^2 - S_i}{S_i} \tag{4.38}$$

where S_i is the cost share of the ith aggregate input; and, for the energy sub-aggregate inputs, by

$$\epsilon_{ii} = \frac{\beta_{ii} + S_{E_i}^2 - S_{E_i}}{S_{E_i}} + S_{E_i} \cdot \epsilon_{EE} \tag{4.39}$$

where S_{E_i} is the ith energy component's share of total energy cost, and ϵ_{EE} is the own price elasticity of demand for aggregate energy. When the supply constraints $x_j = x_j^*$ are present, the own price elasticity is

$$\epsilon_{ii}^* = \frac{\partial \ell n x_i(p^1, p^*)}{\partial \ell n p_i} \tag{4.40}$$

where p_j, $j \neq i$, $j = 1, \ldots, r$, and Q are held constant and $x_j = x_j^*$, $j = r + 1, \ldots, n$, or

$$\epsilon_{ii}^* = \frac{\partial \ell n x_i}{\partial \ell n p_i} (p^* \text{ constant}) + \frac{\partial \ell n x_i}{\partial \ell n p^*} \cdot \frac{\partial \ell n p^*}{\partial \ell n p_i} . \tag{4.41}$$

The first term in (4.41) and $\partial \ell n x_i / \partial \ell n p^*$ can be obtained from (4.38) or (4.39) when the shares are evaluated at the shadow prices. However, $\partial \ell n p^* /$

TABLE 4–5. Prices and cost shares (Ontario 1985)

Input	Market Price ($/10⁶ Btus)	Shadow Price ②[1]	Shadow Price ③	Cost Share at Market Prices[2] ①	Cost Share at Market Prices[2] ②	Cost Share at Market Prices[2] ③	Cost Share at Shadow Prices[2] ②	Cost Share at Shadow Prices[2] ③
Coal	4.38			.083	.105	.111	.102	.105
LPG	8.95			.022	.023	.023	.022	.022
Fuel Oil	3.05		3.44	.160	.163	.143	.160	.154
Natural Gas	2.29	2.77	2.80	.252	.205	.207	.238	.237
Electricity	10.47			.450	.451	.464	.437	.442
Motor Gasoline	13.35			.045	.053	.052	.051	.050
Aggregate Energy	7.97 (index 1962 = 1.0)	8.4	8.55	.0167	n.c.	n.c.	.0171	.0173
Labor	11.27 ($ per man-hour)			.227	n.c.	n.c.	.228	.228
Materials	3.10 (index)			.559	n.c.	n.c.	.559	.559
Capital	3.95 (index)			.216	n.c.	n.c.	.215	.215

1. ① = unconstrained demand
② = natural gas constrained to 1980 demand level
③ = natural gas and fuel oil constrained to 1980 demand levels
n.c. = not calculated

2. For energy components, cost share is share of total energy cost. For aggregate inputs, cost share is share of total production cost.

$\partial \ell n p_i$ cannot be obtained without explicit solution of the inverse demand functions. Therefore, instead of calculating the elasticities analytically, we utilize the results of section 4.4 to obtain a numerical solution. The procedure is to re-solve the constrained optimization problem using an increased p_i, $i = 1, \ldots, r$ and compute the percentage change in x_i. However, a computation of (4.41) for a small change in p_i could be strongly influenced by round-off errors. To avoid this problem, and to provide a sharp contrast between the constrained and unconstrained demand structures, we present in Table 4–6 the comparative arc elasticities obtained from a doubling of p_i. The arc elasticities (for example, see p. 30 of Asimakopulos (1978)) are defined as

$$A_{ii} = \frac{x_{2i} - x_{1i}}{\bar{x}_i} \bigg/ \frac{p_{2i} - p_{1i}}{\bar{p}_i} \tag{4.42}$$

where x_{1i}, x_{2i} are the quantities demanded before and after the price change respectively;

$$\bar{x}_i = \frac{x_{1i} + x_{2i}}{2}, \bar{p}_i = \frac{p_{1i} + p_{2i}}{2}. \tag{4.43}$$

We also present the unconstrained point elasticities in order to put the arc elasticities in perspective. Clearly the switch to arc elasticities does not affect the analysis.

Table 4–6 demonstrates the Le Chatelier Principle (Samuelson, 1947) that constrained price elasticities will not exceed the unconstrained ones, and will decline as more constraints are imposed.[7] Consider coal for example. The unconstrained arc elasticitiy is −2.19. It declines to −1.36 and then to −1.27 as first one and then two constraints are imposed. In fact, it can be shown that if all energy inputs except coal are constrained to the 1980 demand levels (five constraints), the 1985 own-price elasticity of coal falls to −0.06.

Table 4–7 provides a detailed empirical example of the effects of supply constraints on the structure of demand.[8] In comparing the constrained and

7. Since we are dealing with arc elasticities and energy has a borderline complementarity relationship with capital and materials, it is possible, as Samuelson (1960) has shown, for the Le Chatelier Principle to be violated. However, no violation occurred as can be seen from Table 4–6.

8. The cross-price point elasticity for energy component i with respect to the price of energy component j can be calculated (Fuss, 1977) as

$$\frac{1}{S_{E_i}}[\beta_{ij} + S_{E_i} S_{E_j}] + \epsilon_{EE} \cdot S_{E_j}.$$

The arc elasticity is calculated in a manner analogous to equation (4.42).

TABLE 4-6. Constrained and unconstrained own-price elasticities (Ontario 1985)

Input	*Point Elasticity Unconstrained*	*Arc Elasticity Unconstrained*	*Arc Elasticity Natural Gas Constrained*	*Arc Elasticity Natural Gas and Fuel Oil Constrained*
Coal	−1.96	−2.19	−1.36	−1.27
LPG	−1.41	−1.42	−1.41	−1.41
Fuel Oil	−1.27	−1.31	−1.31	n.r.
Natural Gas	−1.13	−1.13	n.r.	n.r.
Electricity	−0.72	−0.75	−0.75	−0.68
Motor Gasoline	−1.92	−2.12	−1.81	−1.81
Aggregate Energy	−0.46	n.c.	n.r.	n.r.

n.r. = not relevant since associated price is an endogenous shadow price
n.c. = not calculated

unconstrained structures, we need to recognize that there are two effects operating, a substitution effect and an aggregate energy "output" expansion effect. Consider the natural gas constraint case. Constraining natural gas increases the implicit (shadow) price of energy and reduces the demand for aggregate energy. Therefore, the expansion effect results in a reduction in the demand for energy components. However, the increase in the implicit price of natural gas leads to an increase in the demand for component substitutes and a reduction in the demand for component complements, "aggregate energy" held constant. Gross substitutability or complementarity can arise, depending on the net sum of the substitution and expansion effects.

Table 4-7 illustrates the result of these complex interactions. For example, for an increase in the price of coal, coal and electricity are gross complements in the unconstrained and single constraint case, but become gross substitutes in the double constraint case. Similarly, when the price of fuel oil is changed, fuel oil and LPG are unconstrained gross complements, but become gross substitutes when the supply of natural gas is constrained. As a final example, when the price of coal is changed, motor gasoline and coal are complements in the unconstrained case, become substitutes in the single constraint case, and then revert again to complements in the double constraint case. The fact that energy components can switch between substitutability and complementarity in the presence of supply constraints demonstrates the considerable effect that these supply constraints can have on the structure of demand and, hence, on the results of forecasts and policy simulations.

TABLE 4–7. The structure of demand (arc elasticities resulting from doubling of price, Ontario 1985)

(a) *Unconstrained*

	Coal	*LPG*	*Fuel Oil*	*Natural Gas*	*Electricity*	*Motor Gasoline*
Coal	−2.19	−0.03	0.18	0.39	−0.03	−0.42
LPG	0.03	−1.42	0.004	0.02	0.004	0.20
Fuel Oil	0.34	−0.22	−1.31	0.08	0.18	−0.44
Natural Gas	1.01	0.24	0.15	−1.13	−0.04	0.76
Electricity	−0.12	0.12	0.53	−0.09	−0.75	0.86
Motor Gasoline	−0.23	0.36	−0.13	0.14	0.08	−2.12

(b) *Natural Gas Constrained*

	Coal	*LPG*	*Fuel Oil*	*Natural Gas*	*Electricity*	*Motor Gasoline*
Coal	−1.36	0.09	0.23	n.r.	−0.03	0.03
LPG	0.04	−1.41	0.01	n.r.	0.004	0.19
Fuel Oil	0.36	0.05	−1.31	n.r.	0.18	−0.30
Natural Gas	n.r.	n.r.	n.r.	n.r.	n.r.	n.r.
Electricity	−0.17	0.09	0.52	n.r.	−0.75	0.74
Motor Gasoline	−0.01	0.39	−0.11	n.r.	0.08	−1.81

(c) *Natural Gas and Fuel Oil Constrained*

	Coal	*LPG*	*Fuel Oil*	*Natural Gas*	*Electricity*	*Motor Gasoline*
Coal	−1.27	0.10	n.r.	n.r.	0.01	−0.02
LPG	0.04	−1.41	n.r.	n.r.	0.004	0.19
Fuel Oil	n.r.	n.r.	n.r.	n.r.	n.r.	n.r.
Natural Gas	n.r.	n.r.	n.r.	n.r.	n.r.	n.r.
Electricity	0.03	0.11	n.r.	n.r.	−0.68	0.69
Motor Gasoline	−0.04	0.39	n.r.	n.r.	0.06	−1.81

Note: In order to interpret the numbers, the reader should apply the convention that the effect of a change in the price of coal on each of the components is contained in the first row; the effect of a change in the price of LPG is contained in the second row, etc. Thus the first row consists of eleasticities of the form

$$\frac{\partial \ell n\, x_i}{\partial \ell n\ \mathrm{PCOAL}},\ i = 1, \ldots 6$$

where x_i is the demand for the ith component.

n.r. = not relevant since associated price is an endogenous shadow price

4.6 FURTHER EXTENSIONS AND APPLICATIONS

In the preceding analysis we have assumed an unconstrained estimation period and a constrained simulation (or forecast) period. However, the methods developed in this paper are applicable if the reverse is true. For example, regulation of natural gas prices in the United States during the 1960s and 1970s is generally thought to have resulted in supply constraints. If deregulation occurs, then structures estimated during a period of supply constraints will need to be used to analyze an unconstrained market. To deal with this case, the correct procedure is to estimate for the constrained period a restricted cost (or profit) function, treating constrained quantities as exogenous.[9] Differentiating the restricted function with respect to the constrained quantities yields expressions for the market clearing shadow prices. Setting these expressions equal to the actual prices during the period of deregulation, and solving for the implied quantities will result in the appropriate unconstrained quantities demanded.

A second application of our analysis is to the distinction between long run and short run demand structures. We could interpret the constrained quantities as demand rather than supply constrained in the sense that price increases of a particular energy component do not lead to increases in demand for "constrained" substitutes in the short run. For example, suppose we define the short run as the period in which the fuel oil-output ratio and the natural gas-output ratio cannot be increased due to energy type specific capital equipment. Then Table 4-5 demonstrates that the short run own-price arc elasticity of demand for electricity resulting from a doubling of the price of electricity is −0.68. The long run elasticity results from the unconstrained case and is −0.75. It can be shown that if the short run is defined as the period in which the energy intensity of production of all energy components other than electricity must remain unchanged, the short run own-price arc elasticity of demand for electricity falls to −0.20. While this analysis cannot replace a properly specified dynamic adjustment model, it does allow short run simulation and forecasting using the existing estimated long run structures of energy demand. This fact is important since estimated dynamic models with theoretical validity are not available currently to aid in the formation of economic policy.[10]

9. For analyses of the properties of restricted (variable) cost and profit functions see Diewert (1974); Lau (1976); or McFadden (1978).

10. For an initial exploration of an econometric model derived explicitly from economic theory which incorporates dynamic adjustments in energy demand markets, see Berndt, Fuss, and Waverman (1977).

REFERENCES

Arrow, K. and Enthoven, A. 1961. Quasi-concave programming. *Econometrica* 29:779–800.

Asimakopulos, A. 1978. *An introduction to economic theory: Microeconomics.* Oxford: Oxford University Press.

Berndt, E.; Fuss, M.; and Waverman, L. 1977. *Dynamic models of the industrial demand for energy.* Palo Alto, Calif.: Electric Power Research Institute Research Report EA-580.

Berndt, E., and Wood, D. 1975. Technology, prices and the derived demand for energy. *The Review of Economics and Statistics* 57:259–68.

Diewert, W. E. 1971. An application of the Shephard duality theorem: A generalized Leontief production function. *Journal of Political Economy* 79:481–507.

Diewert, W. E. 1974. Applications of duality theory. In *Frontiers of quantitative economics,* vol. II, eds. M. D. Intrilligator and D. A. Kendrick. Amsterdam: North-Holland Publishing Co.

Fuss, M. A. 1977. The demand for energy in Canadian manufacturing: An example of the estimation of production structures with many inputs. *Journal of Econometrics* 5:89–116.

Fuss, M. A.; Hyndman, R.; and Waverman, L. 1977. Residential, commercial and industrial demand for energy in Canada: Projections to 1985 with three alternative models. In *International studies of the demand for energy,* Contributions to Economic Analysis, vol. 120, ed. W. D. Nordhaus. Amsterdam: North-Holland Publishing Co., Chapter 9.

Griffin, J., and Gregory, P. 1976. An intercountry translog model of energy substitution responses. *American Economic Review* 66:845–857.

Hudson, E., and Jorgenson, D. 1974. U.S. energy policy and economic growth, 1973–2000. *The Bell Journal of Economics and Management Science* 5:461–514.

Lau, L. J. 1976. A characterization of the normalized restricted profit function. *Journal of Economic Theory* 12:131–163.

McFadden, D. 1978. Cost, revenue and profit functions. In *Production economics: A dual approach to theory and applications,* eds. M. A. Fuss and D. McFadden. Amsterdam: North-Holland Publishing Co., Chapter I.1.

Samuelson, P. A. 1947. *Foundations of economic analysis.* Cambridge: Harvard University Press.

Samuelson, P. A. 1960. An extension of Le Chatelier principle. *Econometrica* 28:368–379.

Zellner, A. 1962. An efficient method of estimating seemingly unrelated regressions and tests for aggregation bias. *Journal of the American Statistical Association* 57:348–368.

5 THE RESIDENTIAL DEMAND FOR ELECTRIC ENERGY AND NATURAL GAS IN CANADA

R. Hyndman, Y. Kotowitz, and F. Mathewson*

Residential demand for energy comprises household demand for heating and applicance use. For heating use, the type of energy and the energy requirements are determined at the time of dwelling construction or major renovation. For energy consumption in appliance use, there is a continuous choice of energy type with on-going accumulation of durable goods. The model of residential energy demand developed here incorporates the different nature of household energy demand associated with heating and appliance use as well as the changing availability of natural gas during the sample period. Using data for four Canadian regions (Quebec, Ontario, the Prairies, and British Columbia), the estimated model of electricity and natural gas reveals that price and income elasticities at the decision time for lumpy heating decisions are much greater than those associated with continuous appliance decisions.

*The authors wish to thank Ontario Hydro for financial support for this work and L. T. Higgins for valuable comments and suggestions.

5.1 INTRODUCTION

This study builds a residential demand model for electricity and natural gas.[1] The features of this model differentiating it from other models surveyed recently by Taylor (1975) are: (1) a separation of household decisions into heating decisions, characterized as discrete lumpy investments, and appliance decisions, characterized as continuous investments; (2) a corresponding empirical finding that price and income elasticities are much greater at the decision time for lumpy heating decisions than for continuous appliance decisions; and (3) an aggregation of households over regions facing different supply constraints on natural gas at any moment of time.

A recent study by Berndt and Watkins (1974) estimates a combined residential and commercial demand model for natural gas for Ontario and British Columbia. Although our study has similarities with their model, there are important specification differences between our two approaches which yield differences in interpertation and results. Both papers stress the distinction between more and less flexible consumer decisions on energy demand. As heating demands constitute lumpy and major decisions in energy demands, changes in the heating plant represent flexible and significant expenditures for most households that occur only periodically. We stress the flexibility associated with those households who have the option of making these major changes in their heating equipment — households purchasing new dwelling units or households undertaking major renovations to existing houses. Associated with these changes in the stocks of heating equipment are changes in energy demand.

Aside from energy demands for heating, households demand energy to operate appliances. Underdeveloped secondary markets for appliances mean that it is costly to replace the appliance before it is fully depreciated. This is an inflexible element in the demand for a particular fuel. However, net growth in the demand for durable stocks represents a flexible component of energy demand. Therefore, we would expect appliance energy demands to demonstrate some price elasticity where these durable demands are increasing. We develop a simple capital accumulation model to explain changes in this appliance stock and adjustments in the complementary energy demand.

1. Initially, this study included a model for the residential demand for oil heating. However, the oil data in the Canadian sample are extremely deficient (Sahi and Erdmann, Chapter 2, this volume). For example, a simple regression between residential oil demand and degree days found no relationship. Consequently, residential oil demand for heating is an excluded equation in our model. However, oil prices are still included in the demand equations for the substitute fuels.

By focusing on end uses and heating-appliance decisions in particular, we permit fuels to have different elasticities by use both in the short and the long run. For example, our estimated equations indicate that heating elasticities are high in the long run and adjustment is slow, whereas appliance elasticities are low and adjustment is fast.

We estimate the residential demand for both electricity and natural gas using aggregated Canadian cross-sectional data for four regions (Quebec, Ontario, the Prairies, and British Columbia) for 1958 to 1971. As estimated elasticities are useful for forecasting demand, observations for 1972 and 1973 are reserved to test the forecasting ability and thus overall consistency of our model through time.

5.2 THE MODEL

Since there are basic differences between the nature of heating and appliance decisions, we differentiate between heating demands and appliance demands into which we place all residential nonheating demands. At the expense of some descriptive reality, we adopt the more tractible assumption of separability in the sense of additively separable utilities on the part of households between decisions for heating and nonheating objectives. The provincially aggregated Canadian data base places restrictions on the specification right at the outset. First, the aggregation of the data across heating and nonheating end uses means that although the nature of the household capital decision suggests separate models for heating and nonheating uses, these models cannot be estimated separately but must be aggregated. Second, the poor quality of the oil quantity data means that oil demand is excluded from this model. This has the price of excluding beneficial econometric restrictions, for example, the guarantee that the sum of all fuel shares is one.

If we define G as aggregate household demand for units of natural gas, E as aggregate household demand for units of electricity (units are Btu's) and subscripts h and a to represent heating and appliance use respectively, then our assumptions mean that $E(t) \equiv E_{\mathrm{h}}(t) + E_{\mathrm{a}}(t)$ and $G(t) \equiv G_{\mathrm{h}}(t) + G_{\mathrm{a}}(t)$, where heating and appliance demands are independent of each other.

Taking differentials yields:

$$\Delta E \equiv \Delta E_{\mathrm{h}} + \Delta E_{\mathrm{a}} \quad (5.1)$$

$$\Delta E \equiv \Delta G_{\mathrm{h}} + \Delta G_{\mathrm{a}} \quad (5.2)$$

This paper develops structural models to explain each of these separate components of demand.

5.2.1 Heating Energy Demand

We assume that households choose one fuel exclusively from the possible alternatives to heat their homes. Weather conditions influence individual heating requirements and we assume that weather affects heating demand in a linear fashion. Weather in our model is measured as $D(t)$, degree days below 65 °F. Therefore, for both electricity and natural gas, heating demand is the sum of individual household demand plus a weather component,

$$G_h \equiv H \cdot g_h + \gamma^g H \cdot D \tag{5.3}$$

$$E_h \equiv H \cdot e_h + \gamma^e H \cdot D \tag{5.4}$$

where g_h and e_h define the heating demand for natural gas and electricity (respectively) for normal weather conditions by a typical household multiplied by the proportion of households using natural gas or electricity (respectively); H defines the number of households; γ^g and γ^e (assumed constant over all households) are the marginal effects of weather on gas and electricity demand for heating.

Taking a total differential of (5.3) and (5.4) yields:

$$\Delta G_h \equiv H\Delta g_h + g_h \Delta H + \gamma^g \Delta(H \cdot D) \tag{5.5}$$

$$\Delta E_h \equiv H\Delta e_h + e_h \Delta H + \gamma^e \Delta(H \cdot D). \tag{5.6}$$

We need to take into account the nature of household decisions about changes in the heating plant. As furnaces are durable goods that are available only in large and discrete sizes, and as there are no rental markets for these durables nor well-developed secondary markets for the sale of used furnaces, households purchase furnaces only infrequently and then in lumpy amounts. Households that have the flexibility to make heating adjustments appear to be those contemplating some major change in their housing stock. For ΔH we may identify three classes of such households as: (1) those purchasing newly completed residential dwellings, defined as c; (2) those undertaking major housing renovations, defined as r; and (3) those who tear down their existing dwelling units, defined as d. We associate with each of these households an average or typical heating demand component defined as g_{hc}, g_{hr}, or g_{hd} for gas, and e_{hc}, e_{hr}, or e_{hd} for electricity. These terms represent the probability of selecting natural gas or electricity demand for space-heating times the gas or electricity demand for that household. The product of these vectors defines $g_h \Delta H$ and $e_h \Delta H$.

The aggregate nature of the data dictates that we assume that existing households not moving or renovating to maintain their previous demands for electricity or gas net of any changes in weather conditions, i.e.,

$H\Delta e_h = H\Delta g_h = 0$. While this assumption excludes the effect of lower thermostats on heating demands, it only makes explicit what most models assume implicitly.

This permits us to write (5.5) and (5.6) as

$$\Delta G_h = g_{hc}c + g_{hr}r - g_{hd}d + \gamma^g\Delta(H \bullet D) \tag{5.7}$$

$$\Delta E_h = e_{hc}c + e_{hr}r - e_{hd}d + \gamma^e\Delta(H \bullet D). \tag{5.8}$$

We consider group c at first. The choice of the type of heating system for new completions is characterized as a modal choice subject to the availability of the fuel options. The choice is assumed to depend on the prices of the three fuels.

The price of insulation should enter the choice of heating fuels as well. However, it appears that historically most new houses have been insulated at the standards of existing building codes. This suggests that these codes, rather than the price of insulation, were the controlling factors.

It is useful to sketch the heating decision process for consumers in new houses. Let gas, electricity, and oil demand for the relevant subset of houses be g_h, e_h, or o_h, respectively. The decision is then one of exclusive choice amongst the three candidate fuels:

$$\max U^i = U(\beta^i_g g_h + \beta^i_e e_h + \beta^i_o o_h) + Z$$

subject to

$$g_h, e_h, o_h \geq 0$$

$$p_g g_h + p_e e_h + p_o o_h + Z = M^i$$

where Z is an all-purpose numeraire commodity whose price is set equal to one; p_g, p_e and p_o are the real per unit prices of the respective fuels; M^i is the household's income; the β^i's are the household's perception of the relative quality attributes of each fuel type. With a distribution of β's across relevant consumers (and ignoring oil demand for reasons of data quality), our decision process permits us to identify the gas and electricity heating demands for these households as

$$g_{hc} \equiv \alpha^g(p_e, p_o, p_g)$$

and

$$e_{hc} \equiv \alpha^e(p_e, p_o, p_g).$$

For estimation purposes, in linearized form these become

$$g_{hc} \cong \tilde{\alpha}^g + \alpha^g_e p_e + \alpha^g_o p_o + \alpha^g_g p_g$$

and

$$e_{hc} \cong \tilde{\alpha}^e + \alpha^e_e p_e + \alpha^e_o p_o + \alpha^e_g p_g.$$

While our data measure c, the number of newly completed residential dwellings, we have no direct measure of renovations (r) or terminations of existing houses (d). Experimentation suggests that there is no apparent satisfactory method of indirectly specifying the model to capture these effects. Consequently, we assume that these demands are a constant proportion of the stock of households so that

$$g_{\mathrm{hr}} r - g_{\mathrm{hd}} d \cong \phi^g H(-1)$$

and

$$e_{\mathrm{hr}} r - e_{\mathrm{hd}} d \cong \phi^e H(-1)$$

where ϕ^e, ϕ^g are constants of unknown sign.

Substituting these heating specifications into (5.7) and (5.8) yields

$$\Delta G_{\mathrm{h}} \cong (\tilde{\alpha}^g + \alpha_{\mathrm{e}}^g p_{\mathrm{e}} + \alpha_{\mathrm{o}}^g p_{\mathrm{o}} + \alpha_{\mathrm{g}}^g p_{\mathrm{g}})c + \phi^g H(-1) + \gamma^g \Delta(H \cdot D)$$

and

$$\Delta E_{\mathrm{h}} \cong (\tilde{\alpha}^e + \alpha_{\mathrm{e}}^e p_{\mathrm{e}} + \alpha_{\mathrm{o}}^e p_{\mathrm{o}} + \alpha_{\mathrm{g}}^e p_{\mathrm{g}})c + \phi^e H(-1) + \gamma^e \Delta(H \cdot D).$$

There is a further adjustment due to changes in gas availability during the sample period which affects the number of households with access to natural gas between 1958 and 1973. In 1956, the Trans-Canada Pipeline, a major East-West transmission line, was completed. This, together with expanding natural gas distribution networks, means that there was a dramatic expansion in gas availability for households during this period. Our model needs to account for these changes by adopting an appropriate aggregation procedure. To do this, we define ξ as the portion of households with access to natural gas at time t. Assume new housing completions have access to natural gas at the same rate as existing households. Define $\mathrm{HG} \equiv \xi H$. The equation for the demand for natural gas for heating uses corrected for natural gas availability is then:

$$\Delta G_{\mathrm{h}} = (\tilde{\alpha}^g + \alpha_{\mathrm{e}}^g p_{\mathrm{e}} + \alpha_{\mathrm{o}}^g p_{\mathrm{o}} + \alpha_{\mathrm{g}}^g p_{\mathrm{g}})\xi c + \phi^g \mathrm{HG}(-1) + \gamma^g \Delta(\mathrm{HG} \cdot D). \quad (5.9)$$

Consistent aggregation requires that we distinguish between electricity demand for households that do and do not have access to natural gas. Experimentation suggests that such a distinction yields a highly collinear explanatory variable set. Thus we do not make this distinction, but we do reorganize the resulting downward bias to our own-elasticity and gas cross-elasticity estimates for households with access to natural gas. Consequently, the equation for changes in the residential demand for electricity for heating purposes is:

$$\Delta E_{\mathrm{h}} = (\tilde{\alpha}^e + \alpha_{\mathrm{e}}^e p_{\mathrm{e}} + \alpha_{\mathrm{o}}^e p_{\mathrm{o}} + \alpha_{\mathrm{g}}^e p_{\mathrm{g}})c + \phi^e H(-1) + \gamma^e \Delta(H \cdot D). \quad (5.10)$$

5.2.2 Appliances Energy Demand

Unlike heating systems, multiple appliance stocks using both natural gas and electricity may be held by consumers. Therefore, the choice of appliance is characterized as a continuous variable model. Here, the choice is between gas and electric equipment, with oil excluded, as oil is used only to a small extent in hot water heating and less elsewhere.

The household decision model used in this section is the typical partial adjustment model. It is useful to sketch the consumer process which generates such a model.

In the production of household services from energy and appliances by households, we assume technological coefficients fixed at any moment of time. Under this assumption, we may aggregate units of durables in units of energy. If S_e measures units of electric durables and S_g measures units of gas durables, the associated energy packages are:

$$e_a = \Theta S_e \quad \text{and} \quad g_a = \pi S_g \tag{5.11}$$

where Θ, π are technologically optimal Btus per unit of electric or gas appliance respectively.

The total stock of durables may be defined through the appropriate selection of units as $S \equiv S_e + S_g$. Net additions to the stock are gross investment (I) (whose price per unit is defined as P_I) minus depreciation (δS) or $\dot{S} \equiv I - \delta S$.

In any period, dollars from a given income, M, not spent on additions to the stock of durables or energy payments, are spent on an all-purpose good whose price is set equal to one and whose utility is assumed additively separable from "energy" utility.

The typical household decision process may be characterized as:

$$\underset{I,\, S_e \geq 0}{\text{Max J}} = \int_0^{\infty} e^{-pt}\{U(S_e, S\text{-}S_e) + \phi(M - \phi p_e S_e + \pi p_g(S\text{-}S_e) - pI)\}dt$$

$$s.t.\ \dot{S} = I - \delta S,$$

where U and ϕ are strictly concave.

This straight-forward optimal control problem's solution is characterized by the usual marginal conditions on the controls and the equations describing the evolution of S and the adjoint variable through time. The optimal path is stable and the long run steady-state solution is unique.

To generate the equations to be estimated, our procedure at this point follows Rasmussen (1973). We focus on e_a and g_a, the two variables of interest for our empirical demand interests. Corresponding to the long run steady-state levels of the stocks of appliances using each fuel, given our assumptions on technology, (5.11) defines long run steady-state levels of demands for electricity and natural gas. Such values depend on the price and income parameters of the model denoted as $v \equiv (p_e, p_g, p_o, p_I(\rho + \delta), M)$. If long run steady-state values are denoted by an asterisk, then we may write $e_a^* = e_a^*(v)$ and $g_a^* = g_a^*(v)$.

We may define discrete linear approximations to the stable trajectory for electricity and natural gas demand around the steady-state values as the conventional partial adjustment model: $\Delta e_a = \mu(e_a(-1) - e_a^*)$ and $\Delta g_a = \mu(g_a^* - 1) - g_a^*$ where μ (<0) is the stable root.

Rearranging the first difference term and differencing the resulting equation with respect to changes in the price and income parameters yields:

$$\begin{bmatrix} \Delta e_a \\ \\ \Delta g_a \end{bmatrix} = \begin{bmatrix} (1+\eta(1-\delta))(1+\eta^e) & 0 & -\eta\dfrac{\partial e_a^*}{\partial v} \\ \\ 0 & (1+\eta(1-\delta)(1+\eta^g) & -\eta\dfrac{\partial g_a^*}{\partial v} \end{bmatrix} \begin{bmatrix} \Delta e_a(-1) \\ \Delta g_a(-1) \\ \Delta v' \end{bmatrix} \quad (5.12)$$

where $\eta^e \equiv \Delta\Theta/\Theta(-1)$, $\eta^g \equiv \Delta\pi/\pi(-1)$, technological change parameters.

These technological change parameters are exogeneous and represent changes in appliance design over the sample period.

Again, consistent aggregation procedures require a distinction between households serviced and not serviced by natural gas. Using ϵ, previously defined for the purposes of aggregating heating demands as the proportion of households with access to natural gas, we may differentiate three cohorts of households, each of which has its own distinct energy demand:

1. $HG(-1) \equiv \xi(-1) \cdot H(-1)$. These are households that existed last period and continue to exist in an area currently and previously serviced by natural gas.
2. $HG'(-1) \equiv (\xi - \xi(-1)) \cdot H(-1)$. These are households that existed last period and continue to exist in an area serviced only currently but not previously by natural gas.
3. $HG'' \equiv \xi(H - H(-1))$. These are new households that exist currently in areas serviced by natural gas.

Total consumers with access to natural gas is then:

$$\xi H \equiv \xi(-1) \cdot H(-1) + (\xi - \xi(-1)) \cdot H(-1) + \xi(H - H(-1)).$$

For cohorts (1) and (3), natural gas demand is given by Δg_a along the optimal trajectory given by (5.12). For cohort (2), natural gas demand is assumed to be $-\mu^s g_a^*$ where $-\mu^s(>0)$ is an adjustment rate for newly-serviced existing households: g_a^* is measured as the sum of (1) the long run steady-state level of consumption that would have been used by these consumers in the previous year if gas had been available, plus (2) changes in this long run gas consumption due to changes in price and incomes included in the vector of exogenous variables $(\partial g_a^*/\partial v \Delta v)$. These assumptions have advantages for aggregating demand.

Defining $g_a^*(-1) \equiv k_g G_a(-1)/\mathrm{HG}(-1)$ and $G_a^* \equiv \mathrm{H}g_a^*$ and adding natural gas demands across cohorts yields:

$$\Delta G_a \equiv [1 + \mu(1 - \delta)][1 + \eta^g]\Delta G_a(-1) - \mu^s k_g G_a(-1) \cdot \mathrm{HG}'(-1)/\mathrm{HG}(-1) - \mu \frac{\partial g_a^*}{\partial v} \mathrm{HG}\Delta V. \tag{5.13}$$

Similar considerations yield a demand equation for electricity to service the accumulated stock of durables using electricity. Again, consistent aggregation dictates a distinction between electricity demand for appliances by households with and without access to natural gas. However, the same result persists. Under such a distinction, some experimentation indicates that the explanatory variable set is highly collinear. Therefore, this distinction is not made. This biases downward our estimates of own elasticity and cross-elasticity of gas price.

The resulting demand equation for electricity for appliance use is:

$$\Delta E_a \equiv [1 + \mu(1 - \delta)][1 + \eta^e]\Delta E_a(-1) - \mu \frac{\partial e^*_a}{\partial v} H\Delta v \tag{5.14}$$

The final demand model for the change in the residential demand for electricity and natural gas to be estimated is obtained by substituting (5.14) and (5.10) into (5.1), and (5.13) and (5.9) into (5.2), and adding stochastic error terms to yield:

$$\Delta E = (\widetilde{\alpha}^e + \alpha_e^e p_e + \alpha_o^e p_o + \alpha_g^e p_g)c + \phi^e H(-1) + \gamma^e \Delta(H \cdot D) + [1 + \mu(1 - \delta)][1 + \eta^e]\xi E_a(-1) - \mu \frac{\partial e_a^*}{\partial v} H\Delta v + u_e, \tag{5.15}$$

and

$$\Delta G = (\widetilde{\alpha}^g + \alpha_e^g p_e + \alpha_o^g p_o + \alpha_g^g p_g)\xi c + \phi^g \mathrm{HG}(-1) + \gamma^g \Delta(\mathrm{HG} \cdot D) + [1 + \mu(1 - \delta)[1 + \eta^g]\Delta G_a(-1) - \mu^s k_g G_a(-1) \cdot \mathrm{HG}'(-1)/\mathrm{HG}(-1) - \frac{\partial g_a^*}{\partial v} \mathrm{HG}\Delta v + u_g. \tag{5.16}$$

Equations (5.15) and (5.16) represent consistently aggregated residential demand equations for electricity and natural gas that can be estimated with our data. The variables in these equations are defined in Table 5-1.

TABLE 5-1. Variables

Δ	—indicates a one-year change in the respective variable
$E(G)$	—total residential electricity (natural gas) consumption
$E_h(E_a)$	—residential electricity consumption for heating (appliances)
$G_h(G_a)$	—residential gas consumption for heating (appliances)
H	—number of households
$e_h(g_h)$	—"typical" electricity (natural gas) heating demand by a household
D	—degree days below 65 °F in the months of January–May and September–December
c	—housing completions measured as a two-year moving average of single family, semi-detached, and row housing completions weighted by an index of size for heating requirements
r	—housing renovations
d	—terminations of existing housing stock
g_{hi}	—"typical" gas heating demand for housing change i = c,r,d
p_e	—the marginal price of electricity for residential consumers between 500 kwh and 1000 kwh per month, deflated by the consumer price index (CPI), lagged one year
P_g	—the marginal price of gas to a typical residential heating customer deflated by the CPI, lagged one year
P_o	—the retail price of home heating oil, deflated by the CPI, lagged one year
ξ	—proportion of households with access to natural gas
$e_a(g_a)$	—"typical" electric (natural gas) appliance load by a household
$S_e(S_g)$	—the stock of durable appliances using electricity (natural gas)
S	—the total stock of durables
P_I	—Canadian consumer price index for consumer durables, deflated by CPI; $p_I(\rho + \delta)$, a user cost for durables, lagged one year
ρ	—real discount rate, estimated as the ninety-day rate on commercial paper minus a correction for anticipated inflation
δ	—a depreciation rate on consumer durables, assumed to be .10
ϕ, π	—technologically optimal BTUs per unit of electric or gas appliance respectively
μ^e, μ^g	—the annual rates of change in energy inputs per unit of service produced by durables and energy for electricity and natural gas respectively, assumed to be −.01.
M	—personal disposable income per household, deflated by the CPI, lagged one year
HG	—an estimate of the number of households in an area serviced by gas

continued

TABLE 5-1. *Continued*

HG′	—an estimate of the number of old households in areas newly serviced by natural gas
HG″	—an estimate of the number of new households in areas serviced by gas
k_g	—the ratio between long run desired natural gas consumption and actual average natural gas consumption
ζ	—a dummy variable equal to 0 prior to 1963, equal to 1 otherwise
$-\mu$	—the annual rate of adjustment for households towards their target stock of appliances
$-\mu^s$	—the rate of adjustment towards a target stock of gas appliances for existing households in the first year of newly established natural gas service

5.3 ESTIMATION

Our demand equations are estimated using Canadian data aggregated into four regions (Quebec, Ontario, the Prairie Provinces, and British Columbia) over the period 1958 to 1971.[2] The pooling of time series data for the different regions is required because there are too few observations to estimate the models for each region individually. Such pooling implicitly assumes that the demand relationship is stable across regions and over time.

The measurement of certain variables in these demand equations requires explanation. First, all housing completions are not homogeneous with respect to heating demands. As data on completions by type of dwelling are not available, and to smooth the timing of completions, c is measured as a two-year moving average of $\tilde{c}$:

$$\tilde{c} \equiv (\text{completion of dwellings}) \times \left[\sum_j \frac{\text{dwelling starts type } (j)}{\text{dwelling starts}} \times f_j \right]$$

where j is the type of dwelling units—single family, semi-detached, and row; f_j is a set of "heating weights" from a provincial utility to reflect typical heating demand based on average size for each housing type: $f_{\text{single}} = 1, f_{\text{semi}} = 0.8, f_{\text{row}} = 0.6$.

2. The energy consumption data are from Statistics Canada *Detailed Energy Supply and Demand in Canada* (1958–1969, 1970–1972, 1972–1974); energy price data are from Statistics Canada *Electricity BTU's for Domestic, Commercial and Small Power Service;* other data are from *Canadian Housing Statistics, Census of Canada, Canada Year Book, Gas Utilities, Household Facilities and Equipment* and *National Income and Expenditure Accounts* where appropriate for appropriate years.

As residential demand excludes apartments charged at bulk rates for electricity and gas, "number of households" has to be corrected for households in multiple family dwellings. To accomplish this, H is measured as the number of households times the proportion of single family dwellings in all dwellings.

Prior to 1963, due to high electricity prices relative to oil and natural gas, there was virtually no use of electricity for heating. A simple way to correct for this discontinuous adjustment in demand is to define a dummy variable $\zeta = 0$ prior to 1963 and $\zeta = 1$ otherwise, and to modify the change in total residential electric demand to: $\Delta E_e = \zeta \Delta E^e_h + \Delta E^e_a$.

The price and income levels and changes entering the demand equations should be expected price and income levels and changes. Based on a naive expectations hypothesis, realized levels and changes from the previous period are used for the expectations of these variables.

Degree days are those below 65 °F. There is no recorded measure for degree days above 75 °F, so cooling degree days remain a left-out variable in this model.

The lagged endogenous variables in our model are $\Delta E_a(-1)$ and $\Delta G_a(-1)$, the previous change in residential consumption of electricity and natural gas for the operation of household appliances, respectively. These variables are not directly measurable and are replaced by $\Delta E(-1)$ and $\Delta G(-1)$, the previous respective change in total residential consumption, a substitution which biases downward the estimate[3] of $[1 + \mu(1 - \delta)](1 + \mu^i)$.

Estimation of the residential demand model for natural gas requires a series for $\mathrm{HG} \equiv \xi H$ and $\mathrm{HG}'(-1) \equiv (\xi - \xi(-1))H(-1)$. Neither of these nor ξ is available as published data, but both are estimated through an ξ series estimated using data on miles of gas distribution pipelines (details of this may be obtained from the authors). To compensate for a faster introduction of natural gas into newly completed subdivisions, the availability factor multiplying completions is measued as $\xi + (1 - \xi)/2$, which represents upward adjustment of the ξ series.

To facilitate the interpretation of coefficients and forecasting, 1971 values in Ontario are selected arbitrarily as a base, and variables are measured in units relative to those values.

3. This is tantamount to including in the regression a variable $\Delta E_h(-1)$ or $\Delta G_h(-1)$ which should be omitted. This variable should have a zero coefficient but it is constrained by the specification to have the coefficient $[1 + \mu(1 - \delta)][1 + \eta^i]$, $i = e,g$. If $\Delta E_h(-1)$ or $\Delta G_h(-1)$ are uncorrelated with the other exogenous variables, their inclusion in their respective equations should bias downward the estimate of $[1 + \mu(1 - \delta)][1 + \eta^i]$, $i = e,g$, the magnitude of the bias depending on the relative magnitudes of the variance of $\Delta E_h(-1)$ to $\Delta E_a(-1)$ and $\Delta G_h(-1)$ to $\Delta G_a(-1)$.

5.4 RESULTS AND INTERPRETATION

Estimation results for residential electricity and natural gas are presented in Table 5–2. For natural gas, the lagged coefficient is not significantly different from zero and is dropped from the reported equation. This result indicates, measurement bias aside, that households in their continuous accumulation of gas appliance durables adjust very quickly to steady-state levels. As a portion of natural gas demand arises from rental hot water units, and as only a limited number of basic appliances are potentially fuelled by natural gas, this result is reasonable. Neither of these potential uses in these circumstances involve stock adjustment problems.

For electricity, the lagged coefficient is significantly different from zero as expected, given the number of end uses for electricity and the lack of rental markets for most of these durables. The presence of the lagged term raises one additional estimation issue. Ordinary least squares (OLS) estimates of models that include endogenous variables in the presence of any autocorrelation in the error term yield inconsistent estimates of the parameters. To correct for any such autocorrelation, a Hildreth-Lu iterative (HILU) estimate on transformed variables is calculated and presented together with OLS estimates in Table 5–2.

In general, the estimated equations "perform reasonably well" in terms of explained variance and the sign and significance of coefficients. The use of the HILU technique yields significant negative autocorrelation signs.[4]

Generally, the coefficients have expected signs; some perverse signs do appear in coefficients in the estimated equations although in most cases these coefficients are not significantly different from zero. Thus, although the signs on the price of oil in the electric heating model and the price of gas in the electric appliance model are both negative when we would expect electricity and these fuels to be substitutes for these end uses, they are insignificant.

However, natural gas demand for appliance use appears to be an inferior good. One explanation for this result rests with the assumption of the universal separability in the heating and appliance decision. Households making major changes in their heating plants frequently make simultaneous changes in appliances. This is because of the block structure of prices which reduces the marginal price of energy to consumers whose appliances use the same fuel for heating. Therefore the negative sign on income for natural gas appliance demand may reflect a downward adjustment for appliances if the

4. In our case, $\rho < 0$. The rationality for this result depends on what ρ represents. For example, if the error structure of the levels is $u_t = \rho u_{t-1} + (1 - \rho)u_{t-2} + \lambda$ where λ has the usual properties and $1 > \rho > 0$, then for first differences the estimated ρ should be negative.

TABLE 5-2. Estimation of residential electricity and natural gas demand

	Variables												
	C	p_{ec}	P_{oc}	P_{gc}	$H(-1)$	$\Delta(H \cdot D)$	$\Delta E(-1)$	$H\Delta p_e$	$H\Delta p_g$	$H\Delta p_I$ $(\rho+\delta)$	$H\Delta Y$	R^2	ρ
1. Electricity (OLS)	.095 (.053)	−.081 (.023)	−.047 (.076)	.048 (.018)	.022 (.006)	.125 (.029)	.337 (.141)	−.002 (.045)	−.035 (.050)	−.022 (.013)	.052 (.080)	.915	
2. Electricity (HILU)	.047 (.046)	−.051 (.016)	−.01[illegible] (.053)	.029 (.013)	.010 (.005)	.140 (.029)	.556 (.110)	−.034 (.037)	−.003 (.042)	−.045 (.021)	.008 (.081)	.941	−.55 (.13)
	C	p_{ec}	p_{oc}	p_{gc}	$HG(-1)$	$\Delta(HG \cdot D)$	$(G \cdot HG'/HG)(-1)$	$HG\Delta p_e$	$HG\Delta p_g$	$HG\Delta p_I$ $(\rho+\delta)$	$HG\Delta Y$	R^2	$D.W.$
3. Natural Gas (OLS)	−.376 (.166)	.328 (.103)	.333 (.221)	−.191 (−.070)	−.019 (.040)	.327 (.084)	.177 (.160)	.611 (.264)	−.238 (.452)	−.098 (.066)	−.743 (.356)	.770	2.46

Forecasting (% Change)

Equation	*Region*																
	Quebec				Ontario				Prairies				B.C.				
	72(P)	72(A)	73(P)	73(A)	72(P)	72(A)	73(P)	73(A)	72(P)	72(A)	73(P)	73(A)	72(P)	72(A)	73(P)	73(A)	C
1. Electricity (OLS)	5.7	6.8	4.2	8.3	7.5	5.5	4.9	5.4	3.7	3.0	1.9	1.9	2.6	1.9	1.9	2.8	.676
2. Electricity (HILU)	6.1	6.8	4.6	8.3	8.2	5.5	4.6	5.4	4.3	3.0	1.8	1.9	2.9	1.9	1.8	2.8	.649
3. Natural Gas (OLS)	2.9	2.1	−2.3	−.6	9.2	11.4	−.1	−5.0	4.1	11.0	−1.1	−4.2	2.6	4.2	−.4	.9	.859

Definitions

A = Actual

P = Predicted

C = Correlation coefficient between actual and predicted

Standard errors are reported in parenthesis.

income effect in the heating model has captured some appliance demand in housing completions.

Corresponding to each of the estimated equations in Table 5-2, Table 5-3 reports the corresponding elasticities evaluated for Ontario in 1971, given our normalization on the data. For new housing completions in our model, the change in electricity demand for heating due to a change in the price of electricity may be written as: $\partial E_{\mathrm{h}}^{e}/\partial p_{\mathrm{e}} = \alpha_{\mathrm{e}}^{e}c$. As p_{e} for Ontario in 1971 equals one, then the corresponding price elasticity becomes: $E_{\mathrm{hc}}^{e} = \alpha_{\mathrm{e}}^{e}/e_{\mathrm{hc}}$.

Although α_e is estimated in our equation, e_{hc} is not measurable from the data. We attempt to bound e_{hc} with two estimates. One estimate may be obtained by substituting values of prices for one year in the relevant part of the estimated equation. If we do this for the HILU estimate for Ontario in 1971 where $p_{\mathrm{e}} - p_{\mathrm{o}} = p_{\mathrm{g}} = 1$ (because all variables are normalized for Ontario 1971), we obtain an estimate $\hat{\epsilon}_{\mathrm{hc}} = -3.64$. Alternatively, we may

TABLE 5-3. Elasticity estimates* and adjustment speeds

	Elasticities						*Adjustment Speed*
	p_{e}	p_{o}	p_{g}	$p_{\mathrm{I}}(\rho+\delta)$	C	Y	μ
1. Electricity (OLS)							
Heating (upper)	−5.78	−3.36	3.43	—	1	—	—
Heating (lower)	−2.25	−1.31	1.33	—	1	—	—
Appliance (long-run)	− .003	—	− .05	.03	—	.07	−.73
2. Electricity (HILU)							
Heating (upper)	−3.64	− .79	2.07	—	1	—	—
Heating (lower)	−2.13	− .46	1.21	—	1	—	—
Appliance (long-run)	− .07	—	− .006	−.09	—	.18	−.48
3. Natural Gas (OLS)							
Heating (upper)	4.37	4.44	−2.54	—	1	—	—
Heating (lower)	3.48	3.54	−2.03	—	1	—	—
Appliance (long-run)	.61	—	− .24	−.10	—	.74	1

*Evaluated for each respective fuel relative to each respective variable for prices normalized for Ontario in 1971

measure the price elasticity of heating demand by including renovations and deaths of houses; then our estimates become $\tilde{e}_{\mathrm{hc}} = .024$ and $\tilde{\epsilon}_{\mathrm{h}}^{e} = -2.13$.

Consequently, heating elasticities appear to lie between two extremes if our allocation of the load is correct. Table 5–3 reports these bounds for all heating elasticities from both estimated equations for electricity and the single estimated equation for natural gas, as well as reporting a single estimate of the appliance elasticity for existing households.

Table 5–3 reveals that for residential heating decisions, both own- and cross-elasticities are generally high. In fact, all elasticities, with the exception of the cross-price elasticity of electrical heating demand with respect to the price of oil, exceed one, even at the estimated lower limit. Conventional wisdom ranks electricity, gas, and oil in descending order of cleanliness and price per Btu as candidates for home-heating fuels. Our results are consistent with this ranking. From the estimated electricity and gas demand equations, electricity and gas are clearly substitutes for heating. From the estimated electricity demand equation, oil is not a good substitute for electricity. However, from the estimated gas demand equation, oil does appear to be a substitute for gas for home heating.

One feature of the appliance elasticities for electricity deserves comment. To the extent that the estimate of the coefficient on the lagged endogenous term is biased downward, the speed of adjustment on the appliance stock is biased upward. This, together with our inability to distinguish electrical customers who do and do not have access to gas, biases downward estimates of the long run price and income elasticities of the appliance demand for residential electricity. In fact, these estimates appear to be unduly low.

As the elasticity of the electricity and natural gas demand with respect to new completions is one by construction, the income elasticity of electricity for new completions depends directly on the income elasticity of housing demand.[5]

Estimates of the income elasticity of housing demand in Canadian and U.S. studies range from .35 to 2.3, with the majority of them between 0.6 and 1.0 (Smith, 1974, pp. 29–30). Thus, the income elasticity of electricity and natural gas demand for heating should fall within this same range.

Forecasts for 1972 and 1973 are reported in Table 5–2 for each of the four regions. Inspection reveals that the model forecasts the growth rates reasonably well for the two years.

5. Define $R \equiv \sum_{o}^{t} c(j)$. Then, for electricity, given our specification of heating demand in equation (5.11) adding over new completions yields $E_{\mathrm{h}} = \alpha^{e}(p_{\mathrm{e}},p_{\mathrm{o}},p_{\mathrm{g}})R$. Therefore, if income changes, we have $\Delta E_{\mathrm{h}}\, Y/(\Delta Y \cdot E) \equiv \alpha^{e} c Y/(\Delta Y \alpha^{e} R) \equiv \Delta R Y/(\Delta Y R) \equiv \eta$. We measure η by the income elasticity of the demand for housing services.

Direct comparisons between our results and other models are not possible as other models do not break down energy consumption by end use. A comparison with Sahi and Erdmann (Chapter 2, this volume) reveals the expected result that our estmates of residential heating elasticities are higher and residential appliance elasticities are lower than both theirs and other overall elasticities.

5.5 CONCLUSIONS

The model of residential electricity and natural gas demand developed in this paper is composed of two parts: (1) a modal choice model to explain the exclusive selection of one of the available choices of fuels for home heating (electricity, natural gas, oil); and (2) a continuous choice model of durable appliance demand and consequently energy demand for appliances.

The empirical estimates indicate that major changes in the heating system of houses are very price and income responsive, whereas appliance decisions of a more continuous nature are much less price and income responsive with stocks adjusting fairly quickly towards their long run levels. This breakdown by end use is important for utilities that anticipate a changing composition to their residential load.

As judged by the correlation coefficient between the actual and predicted values, both the electricity and natural gas models forecast changes in demand fairly accurately.

REFERENCES

Berndt, E. R. and Watkins, G. C. 1974. Demand for natural gas: Residential and commercial markets in Ontario and British Columbia. *Canadian Journal of Economics* 10:97–111.

Rasmussen, J. A. 1973. Applications of a model of endogenous technical change to U.S. industry data. *Review of Economic Studies* 40:225–238.

Sahi, R. K. and Erdmann, R. W. A policy model of Canadian interfuel substitution demands. Chapter 2, this volume.

Smith, L. 1974. The post war Canadian housing and residential mortgage markets and the role of government. Toronto: University of Toronto Press.

Statistics Canada. 1958–1974. *Detailed energy supply and demands in Canada.*

Statistics Canada. 1958–1974. *Electricity bills for domestic, commercial and small power service.*

Taylor, L. D. 1975. The demand for electricity: A survey. *Bell Journal of Economics* 6:74–110.

6 AN ECONOMETRIC MODEL OF ALBERTA ELECTRICITY DEMAND*

E. R. Berndt, G. May, and G. C. Watkins

Econometric models of Alberta electricity demand are estimated for the residential, commercial, and industrial sectors. Two approaches are utilized according to whether electricity is treated as an implicit component of overall energy demand or on an individual basis. Attention is directed toward estimating elasticities employing average electricity prices or by accounting for declining block tariffs, but the distinction is not found to be empirically important. The estimated price elasticity of electricity demand (ignoring effects on total energy demand) is around −0.3 in the residential sector, −0.6 in the commercial sector, and −0.9 in the industrial sector.

6.1 INTRODUCTION

This paper concerns an econometric model of the demand for electricity in Alberta. The results presented here relate to the residential, commercial, and industrial sectors. Attention is also directed toward data computation, especially in terms of alternative definitions of electricity prices.

*We wish to acknowledge financial support for this research from The Electric Utility Planning Council of Alberta.

To begin, we outline a few salient points about electricity consumption in Alberta. Over the period 1961–1976, electricity consumption grew at an average annual rate of 10.1 percent, Alberta real GDP grew by 7 percent, and population by 2.2 percent. However, declining annual growth rates of electricity have been evident in recent years. Of total energy demand (measured in input Btus) in the residential sector, the share of electricity has doubled since 1961, reaching 12 percent by 1976. The predominant fuel in this sector is natural gas, accounting for some 80 percent. In terms of expenditures, electricity accounts for 47 percent in 1976, while gas is 43 percent. In the commercial sector, electricity's Btu share has again doubled, 1961–1976, from 8 to 16 percent. The principal fuel is natural gas (73 percent of consumption in 1976). Similar to the residential sector, the share of electricity in expenditures is much greater — approaching 60 percent in 1976, compared with some 30 percent on gas. In the industrial sector, the volume share of electricity doubled from about 7 percent in 1961 to 14 percent in 1976. However, electricity's share of expenditures in the industrial sector has been quite stable at around 50 percent; recently the share of gas has risen to about 25 percent.

In general, two approaches were attempted in each demand sector. Given the apparent relatively limited substitutability between electricity and other energy sources, the independent approach treated electricity consumption without explicit reference to overall energy demand. The share approach treats electricity as a component of overall energy demand. This involves estimation of equations for total energy demand and an associated expenditure share equation for electricity. The results for the residential sector embrace both approaches; the commercial and industrial results are confined to the share approach.

The following section of this paper discusses the question of the appropriate definition of electricity prices. The next three sections discuss the most promising results for the residential, commercial, and industrial sectors. The final section summarizes our conclusions.

6.2 ELECTRICITY PRICES

A distinguishing feature between this and other Canadian studies of energy demand is the treatment of electricity price. We follow U.S. researchers (Halvorsen, 1973; Houthakker and Taylor, 1970) who have considered the inclusion of marginal price, in addition to an average price, in the estimating equations. The distinction between marginal and average price is important for several reasons. Traditional declining block price schedules for electricity imply the supply curve to an individual customer is downward-sloping — average price declines with rising consumption. When ex post average price is used as the price variable in the regression equation, there may be a problem of proper identification of the demand curve. Estimated price elasticities of demand might be highly significant statistically, yet could actually be a mixture of supply and demand effects. While the inclusion of certain other variables could perhaps resolve this problem, ideally prices should be obtained exogenously, directly from the rate structure. The question of which price to include from the rate structure is equally important, at least theoretically.

Accepted theory since Houthakker (1951) stressed the use of marginal price since it is theorized the consumer equates costs and benefits "at the margin." Taylor (1975) has shown that both marginal price and average price, or expenditure up to the marginal block, ought to be included in the demand equation. If average price were excluded, the estimated elasticity on marginal price would be biased. In Taylor's framework, the coefficient on marginal price captures the so-called price effect, while the intramarginal expenditure (average price up to the marginal block) variable represents a type of income effect. In other words, changes in the front-end of the rate structure do not affect consumption at the margin, but they do reduce or increase disposable income. The coefficient on the intramarginal expenditure variable should be opposite in sign to the income variable. However, the construction of marginal price data involves extensive effort. Fortunately, the Alberta data available to us have allowed very detailed examination of the pricing issue, particularly in the residential sector. Some problems of consistent data availability and methodological difficulties make the approach more tenuous in the commercial and especially the industrial sector.

We have identified marginal price by matching historical rate schedules with bill frequency distributions. By locating the number of bills ending in each block of a given rate schedule, a weighted-average marginal price can be computed. Using a procedure suggested by Taylor, intramarginal expenditure is defined as the difference between expenditure on electricity, had marginal price applied to each *kwh* sold, and the actual total expenditure on electricity.

6.3 RESIDENTIAL SECTOR

Initial notions about the principal influences on electricity consumption in the residential sector suggested the following variables would be worthy of consideration: prices (of electricity, other fuels, and electrical appliances); real income per household; weather fluctuations; apartment densities; household densities; and the female labor force participation rate.

6.3.1 Independent Approach

Our point of departure is a Houthakker-Taylor (H-T) type model (Houthakker and Taylor, 1970) which relates energy consumption to prices, income, and lagged consumption. The following result was obtained (*t* values in parentheses) in the linear equation form, based on 1961–1976 annual data.

$$\begin{aligned} \text{QELEC} = {} & \underset{(2.4)}{3.742} - \underset{(-2.3)}{0.006^{*}\text{MPELEC}} - \underset{(-0.3)}{0.0002^{*}\text{IMEXHH}} \\ & + \underset{(1.4)}{0.408^{*}\text{YPDHH}} + \underset{(3.8)}{0.685^{*}\text{QELEC}(-1)} \\ R^2 = {} & 0.996, \end{aligned} \qquad (6.1)$$

where QELEC is electricity consumption per household, MMBTU; MPELEC is real marginal price of electricity from residential rate structure, ¢/MMBTU; IMEXHH is real intramarginal expenditure on electricity per household; and YPDHH is real personal disposable income per household.

This equation yields short run elasticities at the mean of -0.23 (marginal price) and $+0.31$ (real income); the corresponding long run elasticities are -0.73 (price) and $+0.98$ (income). While real intramarginal expenditure (IMEXHH) has the "correct" sign, it is insignificant. The adjustment coefficient attaching to lagged consumption is relatively low in the residential context, implying quite a high rate of "depreciation" or speed of adjustment. The implication is an average three-year turnover rate, which suggests the predominant use of appliances is relatively short lived.

In the corresponding log form equation, the long run price elasticity is the same as for the linear model, but the income term is insignificant; the intramarginal expenditure variable is insignificant and of the "wrong" sign.

Berndt (1978) has shown analytically that econometric results excluding the IMEXHH variable should be virtually identical to results obtained when that variable is included in the regression equation. Moreover, in small samples sparse degrees of freedom may in fact justify excluding the IMEXHH variable. When IMEXHH is excluded from the linear equation (6.1), we obtain short run elasticities for marginal price and income of -0.23 and 0.26 respectively, while the associated long run elasticities are -0.82 and 0.94. Inclusion of the price of a potential energy substitute — natural gas — in the basic H-T model yielded a positive but insignificant estimate of the cross-price elasticity. Especially in Alberta, substitutability between gas and electricity in the residential sector is restricted, since virtually no electricity is used for space heating and electric water heaters are quite rare.

The use of ex post average electricity price rather than marginal electricity price in the basic H-T type equation increased the elasticities marginally in the short run, but the long run elasticities were much the same. Specifically, the short run elasticities for price and income were −0.24 and 0.37 respectively; the corresponding long run elasticities were −0.6 and 0.95, much the same order of magnitude as when marginal price was employed.

Other variables that did not prove significant when added to the basic H-T formulation were degree days,[1] the female participation rate,[2] the ratio of apartments to total households, the real price of appliances, and nominal household income deflated by the price of electrical appliances.

6.3.2 Share Approach

There are two components to the share approach: the total demand for residential energy (excluding transportation uses) and the expenditure share of electricity in this total. We deal with each in turn.

6.3.2.1 Total demand for residential energy. Our initial equation involved relating the quantity of residential energy consumption per household to real income per household, degree days, and a Divisia price index of total energy, based on the Btu prices and market shares of the individual fuels earlier identified. The result in log form was:

$$\begin{aligned} \ell n\mathrm{QENER} &= \underset{(54.1)}{7.78} - \underset{(4.0)}{0.28^{*}}\ell n\mathrm{PDIV} + \underset{(13.3)}{0.81^{*}}\ell n\mathrm{YPDHH} \\ &\quad + \underset{(5.5)}{0.57^{*}}\ell n\mathrm{DDS16} \\ R^2 &= 0.987, \qquad \mathrm{DW} = 1.88, \end{aligned} \tag{6.2}$$

where QENER is total energy consumption per household, MMBTU; PDIV is Divisia price index for total energy using the average price of electricity; and DDS16 is ratio of actual heating-season degree-days to sixteen-year (1961–1976) normal. The elasticities are −0.28 for price, 0.81 for income, and 0.57 for degree days.

Other variables tested as additions to this basic equation but dropped as insignificant were lagged consumption, the female labor force participation rate, and the intramarginal electricity expenditure variable. The introduc-

1. Our earlier comment about lack of space heating use of electricity is relevant here.

2. The *a priori* sign of this is ambiguous. Increasing female participation rates could be associated with increased reliance on electrical appliances and with increased income per household; alternatively, less time spent at home could entail less appliance and lighting consumption.

tion of average persons per household (POPHH) was significant and negative in sign, indicating that greater household "density" decreases energy requirements per household in the residential sector.

6.3.2.2 Share of electricity demand in total energy demand. Conventional share equation analysis using a generalized function such as the translog (Berndt, Darrough, and Diewert, 1977) suggests treating shares as a function of prices of fuel inputs. Implicitly we have two cost or expenditure share equations, one for the share of electricity, one for the share of other fuels. Since the shares sum to unity we have $M_E = 1 - M_O$ if the electricity cost share is M_E and the other energy cost share is M_O. Thus, least squares estimation of M_E share equation provides implicit estimates of parameters in the M_O share equation. The econometric results are equivalent regardless of which equation is chosen for estimation. Also, the price elasticity of fuel i with respect to fuel j is the negative of the own-price elasticity of fuel i (see Berndt and Wood, (1979). Note that individual fuel price elasticities are "relative" rather than "total" elasticities, since total energy consumption rather than total overall consumption of all goods and services is held constant. We will return to this point later.

The best results for the share specification were obtained with the following equation:

$$\begin{aligned} \text{SHELEC} = {} & \underset{(0.2)}{0.051} + \underset{(2.72)}{0.0118^* \ell\text{n PRATEO}} + \underset{(6.6)}{0.368^* \ell\text{n FPART}} \\ & - \underset{(-3.3)}{0.0935^* \ell\text{n DDS16}}, \\ R^2 = {} & 0.946, \quad \text{DW} = 1.60, \end{aligned} \tag{6.3}$$

where SHELEC is expenditure share of electricity in total energy expenditures in the residential sector. This yielded the following estimate for the relative price elasticity of electricity: $\epsilon_{EE} = -0.28$. The sign of the female participation rate variable is important. It suggests a shift toward electricity expenditures as the female labor force expands, indicating perhaps greater appliance demand, including the "second income" effect.

Inclusion of a lagged cost share in the cost share equation was not significant. Real income per household was significant of itself, but rendered the price coefficient insignificant. If real income were excluded, it is implicitly being assumed that income elasticities are unity (shares are not a function of income). When the income coefficient for the M_E equation is negative (positive), the implied income elasticity is less than (greater than) unity. See Berndt, Darrough, and Diewert (1977) for further discussion. Although the variable degree days was insignificant, it was of the "right" sign, in that it suggested that the higher the degree days, the lesser the cost share of electricity. This reflects the relative importance of heating requirements in the non-electric sector.

6.4 COMMERCIAL SECTOR

In the commercial sector, we report on the share approach only. Only very simple equations proved useful in the independent approach.

6.4.1 Total Commercial Energy Demand

Our approach in the share analysis involved the use of a production-cost function procedure, where output in the commercial sector is treated as a function of three inputs: capital (K), labor (L), and energy (E). Our specification allows for the possibility of non-neutral technical change among inputs. Thus we do not necessarily assume technical progress proceeds independently of the mix of inputs required to produce a given level of output. Provision is made for different rates of technical change to apply to each factor of production, capital (K), labor (L), or energy (E). The methodology involves the specification of a translog cost function and associated cost share equations for each input — capital, labor, and energy. See Berndt and Wood (1975) and Berndt (1978).

Estimation of the translog cost model can proceed in a number of ways. For example, the share equations can be estimated as a system by itself, or the unit cost equation along with the share equations can be estimated as a combined system of equations. In addition to testing whether technological progress is accelerating, linear, or decelerating, we can also test for Hicks-neutrality. Under Hicks-neutrality, cost shares are independent of time, in that each of the inputs is affected in the same, neutral manner.

Using the method of maximum likelihood, six translog models were estimated for the commercial sector:

1. Cost share equations only — neutral technical change
2. Cost share equations plus unit cost equation — neutral technical change
3. Cost share equations only — non-neutral technical change
4. Cost share equations plus unit cost equation — non-neutral technical change
5. Cost share equations plus unit cost equation — linear neutral technical change

6. Cost share equations plus unit cost equation — linear non-neutral technical change.

In the estimation process, the energy share equation was treated as the residual, since the three share equations always sum to unity. Parameter and elasticity estimates are numerically invariant to the choice of share equation treated as the residual.

Best results were achieved for equation set 5. Although the degree of fit on the capital (K) and labor (L) share equations was relatively modest (R^2 of 0.6 to 0.7), the fit on the unit cost equation was good (better than .90), as was the fit on the entire system. The implication of the results is that non-neutral technical change in the commercial sector is not a useful specification, and that accelerated technical change is not required when a unit cost equation is included for estimation purposes. Estimates of elasticities for Model 5 are shown in Table 6-1. The own-price elasticity of energy shows a declining trend over time, falling from around −0.5 in 1961 to −0.25 in 1976. The relationship between capital and energy is initially substitutable, but reverses to become complementary. However, the magnitude of the effect of energy prices on the demand for capital is very small, while the effect of the price of capital on the demand for energy is more appreciable. The asymmetry of these elasticities reflects the differences in cost shares.[3] Energy and labor are substitutes, with energy demand increasing by about one-third of any increase in the relative price of labor. Capital and labor are substitutable inputs. The rate of technical change (cost diminution) is about 2.2 percent per year.

6.4.2 Share of Electricity in Total Commercial Energy Demand

We have outlined the specification, interpretation, and estimation of a translog cost function model. Assuming that commercial firms attempt to minimize costs, we obtained cost share equations for capital, labor, and total energy, along with the associated price elasticities. We now focus

3. This can be more readily understood by visualizing an industry with a large share of capital and a small share of energy cost. Having established complementarity between capital and energy, an increase (decrease) in the price of either input will induce a reduction (increase) in the quantity employed of both inputs. However, given the relatively large capital cost share and small energy cost share, any change in the price of energy will impact on the employment of capital to a lesser extent than a proportionate change in the price of capital would on the employment of energy.

TABLE 6-1. Selected price elasticities, Alberta commercial sector

Price Elasticity	*Model 5*		
	1961	*1970*	*1976*
ϵ_{KK}	-0.26	-0.28	-0.27
ϵ_{LL}	-0.29	-0.27	-0.27
ϵ_{EE}	-0.48	-0.36	-0.25
ϵ_{KL}	0.26	0.29	0.28
ϵ_{LK}	0.27	0.25	0.26
ϵ_{KE}	0.002	-0.006	-0.008
ϵ_{EK}	0.03	-0.13	-0.22
ϵ_{LE}	0.02	0.02	0.02
ϵ_{EL}	0.45	0.49	0.47
Estimated Annual Rate of Neutral Technical Progress	2.16%	2.16%	2.16%

Definitions:
K = capital
L = labor
E = energy
ϵ_{ii} = own price elasticity of ith input
ϵ_{ij} = elasticity of ith input with respect to the price of jth input

attention on the additional decomposition of total energy services into electricity (denoted S) and other energy (denoted O). The important separability assumption made is that although the optimal derived demand for total energy depends on the prices of total energy, capital and labor, the choice between electricity and other fuels within the total energy service demanded is not affected by the price of capital or the price of labor. Rather, choice between S and O depends only on their relative prices. Therefore we specify and estimate a share equation in which the cost share of electricity in total energy expenditure is regressed on a constant term and on the logarithm of the price ratio P_S/P_O (PRATEO). The following econometric results were obtained:

$$\begin{aligned} \text{SHELEC} &= \underset{(5.8)}{1.27} - \underset{(-3.2)}{0.114^{*}} \ell n\text{PRATEO}, \\ R^2 &= 0.446, \qquad \text{DW} = 1.66, \end{aligned} \tag{6.4}$$

where SHELEC is expenditure share of electricity in total energy expenditures in the commercial sector. The implied relative price elasticity estimates for electricity are $\epsilon_{OO} = -\epsilon_{OS} = -0.75$, -0.86 and -0.84 for 1961, 1970, and 1976, respectively. These relative price elasticities hold total energy consumption constant and since any electricity price increase affects not only the electricity-other split, but also the total amount of energy demanded, it is important that we also calculate total elasticities ϵ^*_{ij}. These are calculated as follows:

$$\epsilon^*_{SS} = \epsilon_{SS} + \text{SHELEC}\epsilon_{EE}$$
$$\epsilon^*_{SO} = \epsilon_{SO} + \text{SHOTHER}\epsilon_{EE}$$
$$\epsilon^*_{OS} = \epsilon_{OS} + \text{SHELEC}_{EE}$$
$$\epsilon^*_{OO} = \epsilon_{OO} + \text{SHOTHER}\epsilon_{EE}$$

where SHOTHER is the cost share of non-electric energy in total energy costs and ϵ_{EE} is the price elasticity of demand for total energy.

Inserting estimates of ϵ_{EE} from Table 6–1 as well as the relative elasticity estimates from the previous paragraph, yields the total elasticity estimates given in Table 6–2. The electricity total own-price elasticity ϵ^*_{SS} in the commercial sector is estimated at -0.84 in 1976. Such an estimate appears rather large (in absolute value) a priori; nonetheless this compares favorably to other published estimates of long run electricity elasticities in the commercial sector.

6.5 INDUSTRIAL SECTOR

The discussion of the industrial sector parallels the commercial sector. Thus, only the share approach results are reported.

6.5.1 Total Industrial Energy Demand

Total energy and electricity share equations were estimated using the production-cost function approach described in the preceding Commercial section. We again specified a translog cost function and cost share equations for capital (K), labor (L), and energy (E). Six alternative models, which vary in their treatment of technical change and whether the share equations are treated alone or together with the unit cost function, were estimated by maximum likelihood.

The results obtained were especially attractive when technical progress was specified as linear.[4] Our preferred model, called Model 6, employs a

4. The null hypothesis of linear technical progress (as opposed to quadratic technical change) was not rejected by the data at the 95-percent significance level.

TABLE 6–2. Selected net price elasticity among electricity (*S*) and other energy (*O*) in the commercial sector

Net Elasticity	*1961*	*1970*	*1976*
ϵ^*_{SS}	−0.95	−0.82	−0.84
ϵ^*_{SO}	0.47	0.46	0.49
ϵ^*_{OS}	0.50	0.65	0.70
ϵ^*_{OO}	−0.98	−1.01	−0.95

non-neutral specification of technical change. The R^2 for the energy share equation was 0.9 and the overall system R^2 was 0.99. The null hypothesis of overall neutrality of technical change against non-neutrality is decisively rejected. Technical change seems to have proceeded in a way that has been labor saving, capital using, and energy neutral.

Own- and cross-price elasticity estimates for the capital, labor, and total energy inputs in Model 6 are presented in Table 6–3 for selected years. The own-price elasticity for total energy falls from about −0.5 in 1961 to about −0.4 in 1976. Similar to the commercial sector, capital and labor are substitutable, as are labor and energy; capital and energy tend to be complemen-

TABLE 6–3. Selected price elasticities, Alberta industrial sector

Price Elasticity	*Model 6*		
	1961	*1970*	*1976*
ϵ_{KK}	−0.15	−0.15	−0.15
ϵ_{LL}	−0.18	−0.18	−0.19
ϵ_{EE}	−0.47	−0.36	−0.37
ϵ_{KL}	0.15	0.16	0.15
ϵ_{LK}	0.15	0.15	0.16
ϵ_{KE}	0.0006	−0.006	−0.004
ϵ_{EK}	0.006	−0.09	−0.06
ϵ_{LE}	0.04	0.03	0.03
ϵ_{EL}	0.46	0.45	0.43
Estimated Rate of Annual Technical Progress (%)	2.07	2.10	2.09

tary. These elasticity estimates provide a partial explanation of why the Alberta industrial sector has become more energy intensive. Because of rising real wages and investment tax incentives, industry in Alberta has substituted toward capital and energy and away from labor. In addition, although technical progress has conserved on the use of all inputs, it has saved labor inputs considerably more than capital inputs, and has only marginally affected energy. Technical progress is estimated to have occurred at the rate of 2.1 percent per year.

6.5.2 Share of Electricity in Total Industrial Energy Demand

We now focus attention on factors affecting the split of total energy into electricity (S) and other non-electric energy inputs (O). Following the logic developed in the commercial sector, we specify a cost share equation for electricity which is a function of the logarithm of the electricity/other energy price ratio (ℓnPRATEO) and a constant term. When other energy prices are expressed by a Divisia price, we obtain the equation:

$$\begin{aligned} \text{SHELEC} &= \underset{(4.05)}{1.44} - \underset{(-2.65)}{.164} \ell n \text{PRATEO} \\ R^2 &= .350, \qquad \text{DW} = 0.56. \end{aligned} \tag{6.5}$$

The degree of fit is not appreciable but the results are sensible.

The relative and total price elasticities are presented in Table 6–4. The relative elasticities (holding total energy consumption constant) display substantial interfuel substitutability between electricity and other non-electric energy, larger than we expected; the relative own-price elasticity for electricity is about −0.87 to −0.83 in 1976, while the relative cross price elasticity estimates for ϵ_{SO} are 0.83 to 0.87. The results displayed in Table 6–4 suggest that demand for electricity is almost unit elastic in the Alberta indus-

TABLE 6–4. Price elasticities among electric (S) and other non-electric (O) energy inputs, Alberta industrial sector

	Relative			*Total*		
	1961	*1970*	*1976*	*1961*	*1970*	*1976*
ϵ_{SS}	−0.95	−0.78	−0.87	−1.15	−0.97	−1.04
ϵ_{SO}	0.95	0.78	0.87	0.68	0.61	0.67
ϵ_{OS}	0.72	0.88	0.78	0.52	0.69	0.61
ϵ_{OO}	−0.72	−0.88	−0.78	−0.99	−1.05	−0.98

trial sector; these total elasticity estimates compare favorably to published longrun electricity price elasticity estimates from other studies in various parts of North America. The total elasticities are greater than relative price elasticities in absolute value, since price increases for electricity affect not only the split between electricity and non-electric energy, but also the total amount of energy demanded.

6.6 CONCLUSION

It is feasible to construct useful econometric models for simulating electricity demand in Alberta. We have utilized two approaches. Given relatively limited substitutability between electricity and other energy sources, electricity consumption could be treated without explicit reference to overall energy demand. This is called the independent approach. The second approach treats electricity as a component of overall energy demand, involving estimation of equations for total energy demand and associated share equations for electricity, and is called the share approach.

While the appropriate treatment of electricity prices is potentially critical, analysis of the results between using marginal and average prices discloses only modest differences. The intramarginal expenditure variable is generally insignificant.The overall conclusion is that the the distinction between estimating elasticities by using average electricity prices or by accounting for declining-block electricity rate tariffs is not empirically important. Theoretical considerations also support this finding.

In the residential sector, the preferred individual approach model provided estimation of short run price and income elasticities of -0.24 and 0.37 respectively; the corresponding long run elasticities are -0.6 and 0.95. In the share approach, elasticities for total energy demand were -0.28 for price, 0.81 for income, and 0.57 for heating degree days. The short run-long run distinction was not applicable in estimating total energy demand. The share of electricity in total energy demand was dependent on price of electricity relative to other fuels, degree days, and the female participation rate in the labor force. The price elasticity of electricity, ignoring the effect on total energy demand, is -0.28 (by coincidence). If the impact of higher electricity prices on total energy demand were also included, the price elasticity becomes -0.41.

Results in the commercial sector are confined to the share approach. A production-cost function equation identifying capital, labor, and energy as inputs yielded an own-price elasticity of energy which declined from around -0.5 in 1961 to -0.25 in 1976. The relationship between capital and energy is initially substitutable, but later complementary. The rate of technical change of about 2.2 percent per year is found not to affect the mix of inputs (neutral). The relative price elasticity of electricity derived from the share equation was around −0.7 in 1961, declining to −0.6 in 1976. If price-induced energy demand effects were included, the total price elasticity of electricity is −0.95 in 1961 declining to −0.84 in 1976.

Similarly to the commercial sector, reported results in the industrial sector relate only to the share approach. The production-cost function equation again employing capital, labor, and energy as inputs disclosed an own-price elasticity for energy of −0.5 in 1961 falling to −0.4 in 1976. Capital and energy tend to be complementary. Technical progress is estimated to have occurred at a rate of about 2.1 percent per year, but to have proceeded in a way that is labor saving and capital using, rather than neutral as in the commercial sector. The relative price elasticity of electricity derived was −0.95 in 1961 declining to −0.87 in 1976; the corresponding elasticities including the impact of electricity prices on total energy consumption are −1.15 in 1961 and −1.04 in 1976.

REFERENCES

Berndt, E. R.; Darrough, M. N.; and Diewert, W. E. 1977. Flexible functional forms and expenditure distributions: An application to Canadian consumer demand functions. *International Economic Review* 18:651–676.

Berndt, E. R., and Wood, D. O. 1975. Technology, prices and the derived demand for energy. *Review of Economics and Statistics* 57:259–268.

Berndt, E. R., and Wood, D. O. 1979. Engineering and econometric interpretation of energy-capital complementarity. *American Economic Review* 69:342–354.

Berndt, E. R. 1978. The demand for electricity: A comment and further results. University of British Columbia, Programme in Natural Resource Economics, Resources Paper No. 28.

DataMetrics Limited. 1977. Projections of Alberta aggregate energy demand in the industrial and commercial sector, 1977 to 1990.

Halvorsen, R. 1973. Demand for electric power in the United States. University of Washington, Institute for Economic Research. Discussion Paper No. 73-13.

Houthakker, H. S. 1951. Some calculations of electricity consumption in Great Britain. *Journal of the Royal Statistical Society (A),* Vol. 114, Part III: 351–371.

Houthhakker, H. S., and Taylor, L. D. 1970. *Consumer demand in the United States,* 2nd ed. Cambridge: Harvard University Press.

Taylor, L. D. 1975. The demand for electricity: A survey. *Bell Journal of Economics* 6:74–110.

7 A MODEL FOR FORECASTING PASSENGER CAR GASOLINE DEMAND*

Adel S. Shalaby and Ramesh R. Waghmare

This paper presents the National Energy Board's model to forecast gasoline consumption by passenger automobiles. This model is part of NEB's energy forecasting system (Preece, Harsanyi, and Webster, this volume), and it has also been used by the Alberta Energy Resources Conservation Board. The model consists of behavioral equations for per capita new car sales, the market share intermediate and standard cars, scrappage rates, and the average annual mileage per car. The exogenous variables in the model include fuel economies, car prices, gasoline prices, the proportions of miles traveled on urban and non-urban roads, the average and maximum life of cars, and other demographic and macroeconomic variables. The model may be used to forecast gasoline consumption and to simulate the effects on gasoline consumption of changes in the exogenous variables which may reflect economic conditions such as increasing incomes; technical changes such as those which affect vehicle life; or policy changes such as the setting of fuel economy standards.

*This reserach was supervised by Dr. Peter Eglington and Mr. Les Harsanyi. We are thankful to Dr. Munir Sheikh for several helpful hints.

7.1 INTRODUCTION

This paper presents a model for forecasting passenger car gasoline demand in Canada, by region, which was developed in the Forecasts and Market Intelligence Division of the National Energy Board. The model is based on data for the period 1966–1975 for seven regions: the Atlantic provinces, Quebec, Ontario, Manitoba, Saskatchewan, Alberta, and British Columbia, including the Yukon and the Northwest Territories. It can be used to forecast, through simulation, the expected change in gasoline consumption from policies such as tax increases on heavy automobiles, changes in gasoline taxes, legislation prescribing fuel efficiencies in new autos, etc., or behavioral changes such as changes in the average miles traveled per car.

Passenger car gasoline consumption in each region is estimated by summing the results obtained by multiplying the number of cars of each size and age by the appropriate distances traveled in urban and rural areas divided by the appropriate fuel economy. The estimation of the number of cars of each size and age is derived from estimates of new car sales, estimates of the market shares of large and small cars, and estimates of scrappage rates (discussed in later sections). Estimates of total miles traveled are also discussed, as are the estimated proportions of these miles spent in urban and non-urban driving and the associated fuel economies. This paper concludes with remarks on the uses to which the model may be put.

7.2 NEW CAR SALES

New car sales are estimated using an equation relating per capita car sales to the ratio of automobile price to disposable income, the unemployment rate, the real gasoline price, and the lagged stock of cars per driver-age population. The implication of using the ratio variable; i.e., automobile price relative to disposable income, is that the elasticity of demand for new car sales with respect to car price varies inversely with income. The estimated equation is:

$$\begin{aligned}\frac{\text{NCS}}{\text{POP}} = &\underset{(3.37)}{0.0341}\ \text{ATL} + \underset{(3.56)}{0.0347}\ \text{QUE} + \underset{(2.96)}{0.0298}\ \text{ONT}\\ &+ \underset{(2.44)}{0.0248}\ \text{MAN} + \underset{(2.33)}{0.0215}\ \text{SAS} + \underset{(2.23)}{0.0244}\ \text{ALTA}\\ &+ \underset{(1.73)}{0.0179}\ \text{BCY} - \underset{(1.75)}{0.00413}\ \frac{\text{RAP}}{\text{PCRY}} - \underset{(3.10)}{0.00938}\ U\end{aligned}$$

$$
\begin{aligned}
&- \underset{(2.10)}{0.000422}\ \text{RGAS} - \underset{(5.45)}{0.0799} \left(\frac{\text{STK}}{\text{DAP}_{-1}}\right) - (10)^{-9} \times \underset{(5.73)}{275}\ \text{SDLMV} \\
&- \underset{(3.58)}{0.00609}\ \ \text{DATL (69–70)} - \underset{(4.30)}{0.000938}\ \ \text{DSAS (69–71)},
\end{aligned}
$$

$$F = 42.28, \bar{R}^2 = .908, \text{DW} = 2.09, \text{AAPE} = 4.32\%, \qquad (7.1)$$

where values in parentheses are t statistics; a value greater than 1.67 indicates significance at the 95 percent level; AAPE = average absolute percentage error of the estimate; NCS = new car sales in the region (in millions); POP = regional population (in millions); ATL, QUE, ONT, MAN, SAS, ALTA and BCY = intercept dummies for the Atlantic provinces, Quebec, Ontario, Manitoba, Saskatchewan, Alberta and British Columbia (including the Yukon and the Northwest Territories); RAP = real automobile price in the region (1961 Toronto dollars); PCRY = regional per capita real disposable income (1961 Toronto dollars); U = the regional unemployment rate; RGAS = real gasoline price in the region (1961 Toronto dollars); STK = regional stock of passenger cars outstanding at the beginning of the year; DAP = driver age population in the region defined to include persons sixteen years old and above; SDLMV = man-days lost in strikes in the Canadian automobile industry; DATL and DSAS = dummies for some erratic observations for the Atlantic Provinces and Saskatchewan, for years 1969–1970 and 1969–1971, respectively.

Equation (7.1) indicates that a rise in the price of new cars or in gasoline prices, ceteris paribus, would lead to a decrease in the sales of new cars. At higher levels of income or lower levels of unemployment, new car sales increase. The unemployment rate has been included as a cyclical indicator of economic conditions. It provides information about the phase of the cycle and expected income which would not be provided by the inclusion of only the disposable income variable since it is affected by built-in stabilizers such as transfer payments. New car sales could be regarded partly as net addition to stock and partly as replacement for scrapped vehicles, the number of which will depend on the existing stock. Therefore the stock of existing cars has been included as a determinant of new car sales. The variable "man-days lost in strikes" (SDLMV) represents a supply constraint on the availability of new cars.

Generally, short run elasticities are derived from linear equations by multiplying the coefficient of the regressor times the ratio of the historical mean of that regressor to the historical mean of regressand. For $Y = \alpha + \beta X$, the elasticity of Y with respect to X is $\beta\ (\bar{x}/\bar{y})$ where $\bar{x}$ and $\bar{y}$ denote the average values for the observed x's and y's over the sample period. Thus elasticities of new car sales with respect to real automobile prices (RAP), the unemployment rate (*U*), and the real gasoline price (RGAS) are then: RAP = −.163, *U* = −.136, RGAS = −.49, using the mean values of the relevant variables over the sample period 1966–1975.

7.3 MARKET SHARE EQUATIONS

The rising gasoline prices since 1973 and the conservation ethic have led to a fundamental change in the automobile industry. For example, full-size models (over 4,000 pounds) which accounted for 40 percent of new car sales during 1966–1975 (subcompact, compact, and intermediate models accounted for 20 percent each) were made up to about 700 pounds lighter beginning in 1977. According to some industry analysts, even these lighter full-size models may be extinct by 1980 as further weight reductions have been planned by General Motors for the 1980 model year. We wanted our gasoline consumption model to be able to simulate changes due to shifts in the sizes of cars purchased. Since there has been a blurring of sizes, the model includes only two classes: small (subcompact and compact) and large (intermediate and standard). We have estimated an equation for the market share of large models, and use it with the new car sales equation (7.1) to obtain the share of small models residually.

Our equation postulates that the share of large models in new car sales increases with a rise in the relative price of small models (relative to the price of large models), and decreases with an increase in the real gasoline price, the ratio of fuel economy of small models to large models, the unemployment rate, and the proportion of females in the labor force. The last variable reflects our hypothesis that, generally, smaller cars are preferred by working women. Also, if second car ownership is considered by a family in response to the woman joining the working population, it would likely be a small car. The estimated equation is:

$$
\begin{aligned}
\left(\frac{\mathrm{I + STD}}{\mathrm{NCS}}\right) = {} & \underset{(1.77)}{0.419}\ \mathrm{ATL} + \underset{(1.90)}{0.418}\ \mathrm{QUE} + \underset{(1.78)}{0.325}\ \mathrm{ONT} \\
& + \underset{(1.98)}{0.368}\ \mathrm{MAN} + \underset{(2.18)}{0.384}\ \mathrm{SAS} + \underset{(1.95)}{0.356}\ \mathrm{ALTA} \\
& + \underset{(1.35)}{0.258}\ \mathrm{BCY} - \underset{(3.35)}{0.0163}\ U - \underset{(1.00)}{0.429}\ \frac{\mathrm{FEM}}{\mathrm{TLF}} \\
& + \underset{(3.96)}{0.460}\ \frac{\mathrm{WTARPS}}{\mathrm{WTARPL}} - \underset{(.77)}{0.000826}\ \frac{\mathrm{WTAFES}}{\mathrm{WTAFEL}}\ \mathrm{RGAS}
\end{aligned}
$$

$$+ \underset{(3.28)}{0.285} \left(\frac{\text{I} + \text{STD}}{\text{NCS}}\right)_{-1} \tag{7.2}$$

$$F = 142.5, \bar{R}^2 = .968, \text{DW} = 2.25, \text{AAPE} = 3.1\%,$$

where I = sales of intermediate models; STD = sales of standard models; NCS = total new car sales; ALT, QUE, etc., = provincial dummies; U = unemployment rate; FEM/TLF = the proportion of females (FEM) in total labor force (TLF); WTARPS/WTARPL = the ratio of weighted average real price of small models (WTARPS) to the weighted average real price of large models (WTARPL); WTAFES/WTAFEL = the ratio of the weighted average city fuel economy of small models (WTAFES) to the weighted average city fuel economy of large models (WTAFEL); and RGAS = the real gasoline price.

Two points about equation (7.2) above may be noted. First, the coefficients of relative fuel economy (WTAFES/WTAFEL) and the female proportion of the labor force (FEM/TLF) are not significant at a 5-percent level in a one-tailed test. Since in a forecasting framework, a score of 1.00 is generally considered acceptable, we have included the female proportion of the labor force. The t value of relative fuel economy is only 0.77 in this equation, and if the variable "proportion of female labor force" were omitted from the equation, it would be even lower at 0.32. However, as cars continue to be downsized in the future, changes in the ratio of fuel economies will probably occur. Relative fuel economy must be included as an independent variable in order that the equation may be used to simulate these changes, even though its t value is low.

Second, gasoline price was included in a multiplicative form (the product of the gasoline price with the ratio of fuel economies) because attempts to include it separately were unsuccessful. This formulation implies that the elasticity of the market share of large cars with respect to the ratio of fuel economies varies directly with gasoline price. Thus, the higher the gasoline price, the higher is the percentage reduction in the market share of large models in response to a given percentage improvement in the relative fuel economy of small models.

Short run elasticities of the market share of large models with respect to the independent variables in (7.2) calculated from the parameters and the mean value of the regressand over the estimation period are: unemployment rate, −0.10; proportion of female labor force, −0.25; relative prices, +.60; and gasoline price, −0.10.

To estimate long run elasticities from short run elasticities, multiply by (1 − coefficient of the lagged dependent variable)$^{-1}$. This is an approximation based upon holding the value of the lagged dependent variable equal to the dependent variable, and summing the resulting geometric progression. Since the coefficient of $(I + STD)/NCS)_{-1}$ is .285; the long run elasticities are 1.40 = 1/1.285) times the short run elasticities.

7.4 PROBABILITIES OF SURVIVAL

We have not been successful in estimating equations relating scrappage rates to variables such as income, unemployment, gasoline price, and fuel economies. The main problem is lack of data. Estimates of new car sales on a provincial basis start only in 1961 and some data such as provincial unemployment rates and fuel economies start only in 1966. After surveying work in this field we borrowed from International Research and Technology Corporation (1976) the following equation that relates probability of survival of a vehicle to the median life and age of the vehicle:

$$P(j) = \left[1 + \left(\frac{j}{t}\right)^{4.7}\right]^{-1} \tag{7.3}$$

where $P(j)$ is the probability of survival of cars of age j, and t is the median or "half life" of the car. (For example, a half life of twelve years implies that 50 percent of the new cars, bought during year $(t - 12)$, are still on the road at the end of year twelve.)

There were wide differences in scrappage rates across provinces. Scrappage, expressed as a percentage of last year's stock, was lowest in British Columbia, followed by the Prairie provinces, Quebec, and Ontario. We experimented with this equation assuming various values for the half life of cars (t) and maximum year of survival (j) to obtain values for j and t for each province which lead to acceptable forecasts of stocks for the period 1972–1975. To facilitate this experimentation, the series on new car sales on a provincial basis was extrapolated to 1946 by applying provincial proportions for 1961 to pre-1961 data on sales in Canada as a whole.

For Ontario and Quebec, we arrived at a half life of ten years and maximum survival of sixteen years; and for the Atlantic provinces, a half life of nine years and maximum survival of sixteen years. For each of the Prairie provinces, a half life of twelve years was used. Minor differences were, however, estimated for the maximum year of survival;. for Alberta, Saskatchewan, and Manitoba these were twenty-two, twenty, and twenty-one years, respectively. Probabilities of survival for the British Columbia region were the most difficult to estimate. After experimenting with several values, it was found that assuming a half life of eighteen years with a maximum survival of twenty-nine years forecasted stocks in 1974 and 1975 reasonably well. (The average absolute forecasting error was 5 percent during the two years.)

The probability of survival declines at a faster rate once the half life of the car is reached. Thus, while for Alberta, 50 percent of the cars are on the road at the end of twelve years, only 16 percent are on the road at the end of seventeen years. The probabilities of passenger car survival for each region are given in Table 7-1.

TABLE 7-1. Probability of auto survival

AUTO AGE	ATL.	QUE.	ONT.	MAN.	SASK.	ALTA.	B.C.+
1	1.0000	1.0000	1.0000	1.0000	1.0000	1.0000	1.0000
2	.9992	.9995	.9995	.9998	.9998	.9998	1.0000
3	.9943	.9965	.9965	.9985	.9985	.9985	.9998
4	.9784	.9867	.9867	.9943	.9943	.9943	.9991
5	.9406	.9630	.9630	.9839	.9839	.9839	.9976
6	.8705	.9169	.9169	.9630	.9630	.9630	.9943
7	.7652	.8424	.8424	.9264	.9264	.9264	.9883
8	.6350	.7405	.7405	.8705	.8705	.8705	.9784
9	.5000	.6213	.6213	.7945	.7945	.7945	.9630
10	.3787	.5000	.5000	.7020	.7020	.7020	.9406
11	.3103	.3898	.3898	.6008	.6008	.6008	.9101
12	.2355	.2980	.2980	.5000	.5000	.5000	.8705
13	.1808	.2256	.2256	.4070	.4070	.4070	.8219
14	.1414	.1706	.1706	.3264	.3264	.3264	.7652
15	.1131	.0900	.1295	.2595	.2595	.2595	.7020
16	.0628	.0200	.0500	.2055	.1855	.2055	.6350
17				.1629	.1429	.1629	.5668
18				.1295	.1034	.1295	.5000
19				.1034	.0500	.1034	.4368
20				.0500	.0200	.0831	.3787
21				.0270		.0700	.3264
22						.0600	.2803
23							.2401
24							.2055
25							.1760
26							.1508
27							.1295
28							.0800

+ = Inclusive of Territories.

7.5 ESTIMATION OF MILEAGE TRAVELED

Mileage equations for large amd small cars were adapted from an unpublished study by Environment Canada, which analyzed data collected from a survey of 5,857 drivers on the type of vehicle (subcompact, compact, intermediate, or full-sized), age of the vehicle, miles traveled per year, urban/nonurban mileage split, fuel economies (city/highway), and province of residence of the driver. Their estimates were:

1. Subcompact:
$$\text{Annual mileage per car} = 12{,}036 - 723\ (\text{age of car})$$
$$R^2 = 0.77,$$
2. Compact:
$$\text{Annual mileage per car} = 10{,}033 - 445\ (\text{age of car})$$
$$R^2 = 0.65,$$
3. Intermediate:
$$\text{Annual mileage per car} = 11{,}434 - 484\ (\text{age of car})$$
$$R^2 = 0.57, \text{ and}$$
4. Standard:
$$\text{Annual mileage per car} = 12{,}829 - 610\ (\text{age of car})$$
$$R^2 = 0.80.$$

We adapted these equations to obtain equations for the two car types included in our model by incorporating recent information that large size models (intermediate and standard) travel on the average 14,000 miles during the first year, while small models (subcompact and compact) travel 13,000 miles. The effect of the age of the car on annual mileage was derived for our two model types by averaging the slopes in the appropriate Environment Canada equations. Thus, the slope in the annual mileage equation for small models is the average of slopes in (1) and (2), and for large models the average of slopes in (3) and (4). This yields:

$$\text{Small Cars: Annual mileage per car} = 13{,}000 - 584\ (\text{age of car})$$
$$\text{Large Cars: Annual mileage per car} = 14{,}000 - 547\ (\text{age of car})$$

7.6 FUEL ECONOMIES AND URBAN/NONURBAN TRAVEL SPLIT

Estimates of fuel economies (Table 7-2 provides the average values for Canada) for the historical period are based on the Environment Canada survey

TABLE 7-2. Automobile fuel economies—by class and purpose 1966–1975 (miles per imperial gallon)

	SUB-COMPACT		*COMPACT*		*INTER-MEDIATE*		*STANDARD*	
YEAR	*City*	*Hwy*	*City*	*Hwy*	*City*	*Hwy*	*City*	*Hwy*
1966	21	27	18	22	15	18	12	17
1967	21	26	18	21	15	19	13	18
1968	20	25	18	22	15	19	14	18
1969	23	28	18	22	14	18	13	18
1970	25	32	19	23	14	18	12	17
1971	22	28	20	25	14	19	12	17
1972	22	28	19	23	14	18	12	16
1973	21	27	18	23	13	18	11	15
1974	21	26	19	24	14	18	10	14
1975	23	28	20	25	15	19	11	15

Source: "Canadian Automobile Driver Survey," Economic and Technical Review Report EPS 3-AP-73-10, Environment Canada.

previously discussed. For purposes of estimating market share equations, small car fuel economies for each region were defined as a weighted average of the fuel economies of subcompact and compact models, the weights used being the share for each region of each of these subtypes in total sales of small cars. Similarly, fuel economies of large cars were defined as the weighted average of the fuel economies of intermediate and full size models.

The Federal Department of Transport (1978) assumes a 55:45 split between urban and nonurban travel. In the United States, the proportion of travel on urban roads by personal passenger vehicles (autos and motor cycles) is estimated at 58 percent (Energy and Environment Analysis Inc., 1975). The Environment Canada survey which we follow gives somewhat higher estimates of the proportion of urban travel and provides a disaggregation for subcompact, compact, intermediate, and standard cars. Averaging estimates for subtypes comprising large and small categories yields estimates for the proportion of urban travel. See Table 7-3.

7.7 APPLICATIONS OF THE MODEL

Applications of this model include forecasting and simulation. The model was used by the Alberta Energy Resources Conservation Board (1978) to forecast automobile consumption of gasoline in Alberta. At the National Energy Board, forecasts of passenger car gasoline consumption from the

TABLE 7-3. The proportion of urban travel by small and large cars in various provinces

Province	*Small*	*Large*
Atlantic	60.0	60.5
Quebec	60.0	60.5
Ontario	60.0	60.5
Manitoba	60.0	61.5
Saskatchewan	60.0	61.5
Alberta	60.0	61.5
British Columbia	67.0	68.0

model are combined with forecast gasoline consumption by vehicles other than automobiles (mainly trucks) to yield projections of total road consumption of gasoline (NEB, 1978). The model can be used to simulate the effects on automobile gasoline consumption of policy measures such as imposing excise taxes on heavier cars, changing excise taxes on gasoline, or introducing mandatory levels of fuel economy.

For example, the model predicts that the imposition of an excise tax on large automobiles would reduce gasoline consumption by reducing new car sales and by increasing the share of small cars in total new car sales. Excise taxes levied on large automobiles would increase the average automobile price, leading to a reduction in automobile sales according to equation (7.1), and hence a reduction in gasoline consumption. Second, the rise in the relative price of large automobiles would reduce the share of large cars in new car sales as implied by equation (7.2). Since small cars are not only more fuel efficient than large cars, but are also estimated to be driven fewer miles on the average, the increase in the share of small cars in new car sales will further lower automobile gasoline consumption over time.

This model can also be used, at least on a judgmental basis, to simulate the effects on gasoline consumption of technological innovations in the automobile industry or changes in consumer behavior. For example, an increase in diesel-powered automobiles could be modeled by a downward adjustment to the intercept terms in the equation for new car sales, which historically were all gasoline powered. Adjustments could also be incorporated to model the view of some industry analysts who believe that once the ratio of two persons per car is reached, new car sales will increase at a rate just sufficient to maintain the ratio at about that level. Similarly, an increase in car usage due to an increase in leisure time could be accounted for by adjustments in the two mileage equations.

REFERENCES

Davies, G. W. 1976. The demand for automobiles in Canada. *Gasoline price increases and the Canadian automobile industry,* J. R. Melvin, ed., London, Canada, mimeographed.

Energy and Environment Analysis Inc. 1975. *Gasoline consumption model.* Arlington, Va.

Energy Resources Conservation Board. 1978. *Energy requirements in Alberta 1977–2006,* ERCB Report 78-I.

Environment Canada. *Canadian automobile driver survey.* Economic and Technical Review Report EPS 3-AP-73-10.

International Research and Technology Corporation. 1976. *Automobile demand model.* Washington, D.C.

Jack Faucett Associates Inc. 1976. *Fuel economy policies and their effects on automobile ownership, use, and fuel consumption.* Federal Energy Administration, Washington, D.C.

N. D. Lea and Associates. 1976. *A study of measures to encourage the adoption of more energy efficient automobiles, volumes 1 and 2.* Prepared for the Transportation Development Agency, Ministry of Transport.

National Energy Board. 1978. *Canadian oil: Supply and requirements.*

Preece, R. A.; Harsanyi, L. B.; and Webster, H. M. *The energy demand forecasting system of the National Energy Board.* Chapter 1, this volume.

Transport Canada. 1978. *1978 fuel economy guide.*

II ENERGY SUPPLY MODELING

W. T. Ziemba

This section of the volume contains five papers concerned with various aspects of the economics of energy supply. The papers treat quite diverse topics: Balas presents a game theoretic model to determine the optimal size of the United States' strategic petroleum reserve; Cox and Helliwell investigate the possible use of wood wastes in British Columbia pulp and paper mills; Wyman describes a simulation model helpful in the operating design of the Syncrude tar sands plant in Alberta; and Rowse and Khazzoom present linear programming supply models for western Canada and the United States, respectively. The first three studies present basically completed work while the final two papers give progress reports related to ongoing studies.

In the early 1970s, members of OPEC (the Organization of Petroleum Exporting Countries) realized that the major industrial powers not only based their economies and life styles on cheap fuel, primarily petroleum products, but were extremely vulnerable to a shortage of energy. Besides their 500 percent increase in the price of oil in 1973–1974 they also realized that oil was now a substantial political weapon. This culminated in a boycott against countries such as the United States and Holland that were favorable to Israel in its continual tension and conflicts with their

Arab neighbors. The boycott by the OAPEC (the Arab members of OPEC) lasted from mid-October 1973 to mid-March 1974. The embargo led to an extreme shortage of gasoline and fuel oil in the United States and to an era that became termed the "energy crisis." Besides the substantial loss in GNP output, the whole idea of the United States being held up for ransom runs counter to the American ego and way of life. Hence, avoidance of future embargoes was a prime objective of government policy. An effective way to avoid future embargoes would seem to be provided by a huge stockpile of reserves located in the United States that could be drawn upon when needed. Such a Strategic Petroleum Reserve (SPR) would diminish the United States' vulnerability and offer protection against possible future oil embargoes. It would also provide a source of oil that could be used to smooth out price effects in periods when world demand for inputs exceeded supply of available exports. In December 1975 the creation of the SPR became law in the form of the "Energy Policy and Conservation Act" (Public Law 94-163). The law provided for a reserve of 150 million barrels (MMB) by December 1978, about 500 MMB by December 1982 (equal to three months 1974-1975 supply) with an ultimate SPC of up to 1000 MMB. The reserve was to be stored in salt caverns on the Gulf Coast.

Although the sizes stipulated were based on economic analysis they were largely determined in an ad hoc fashion. The real question is: how large should the reserve be to provide an adequate deterrent against possible embargoes? Balas addresses this question in his paper. His approach is to view the problem as a game with two actors: the United States and OAPEC. The OAPEC strategies consist of embargoes of varying intensities and lengths including the no embargo option. The United States strategies consist of the various ways the SPR might be utilized. The size of the SPR is a parameter in both players' payoff function. The two-person nonconstant sum game approach provides a novel investigation of the problem since it specifically analyzes the size of the SPR as an embargo deterrent. The United States' objective is that of minimizing total costs of the SPR (interest charges plus storage and removal costs) plus the GNP loss caused by a possible OAPEC embargo. The OAPEC objective has political and economic components. The purpose of any embargo is to put political pressure on the United States (and, of course any other countries involved in the embargo). This portion of the objective may be represented as a function of the GNP loss inflicted by the embargo. The second term in the objective is a function of the economic loss suffered by OAPEC due to the cutback in petroleum production during the embargo. The solution yields an optimal size of the SPR and also a probability distribution function of embargoes of varying intensities and lengths for each stockpile considered. Parametric analysis using the quite reasonable functions assumed by Balas yields the following conclusions: (1) a larger United States SPR is an incentive for reducing rather than increasing the length of an embargo; (2) a small SPR yields intense embargoes of long lengths with high costs; (3) SPR sizes of at least 500 MBB in 1981 and 1100 MBB in 1985 lead to no embargoes; and (4) an SPR equivalent of seven to eight months supply of imports from OAPEC leads to optimality of the no embargo option.

Balas' findings formed part of the debate concerning the appropriate size of the SPR (Balas, 1976). Progress on the formation of the SPR has been slower than planned. Although the SPR was supposed to be of size 150 MMB by December 1978, it was in fact only 80 MBB in March 1979 when the crisis in Iran was at its peak. The shortage to the United States then became one-half MMB per day. The SPR was not used at this time. A prime reason was that the equipment designed to pump the oil out of the caverns was not scheduled to be put in place until the fall of 1979 (Mossberg, 1979). (Moreover, a plan to distribute the oil when it is pumped out was not available at that time.) This crisis led to a temporary pumping system at an extra cost of $5 million. The Iran crisis, in many ways a defacto embargo, lead to a worldwide supply shortage and a resulting steep jump in the price of oil to its present cost of about $19 per barrel. The costs of placing oil in the caverns has risen to about $3 per barrel from the originally projected $1.50, as assumed in Balas' calculations. Despite the parameter changes, many of which change in proportion to the price rise, Balas' conclusions still appear reasonable. A difficulty that remains is that the current shortage of supply renders it difficult for the United States to purchase extra oil for the SPR at reasonable prices.

Balas (1979) recently completed the final report concerning his study of the SPR. Among other things it contains the results of over one-hundred scenarios and there is little change in his basic conclusions. See the postscript to his paper.

Kinberg, Shakun, and Sudit (1978, 1976) have developed a series of models related to but different in character from Balas' for the strategic oil reserve problem. The game players are the coalition of major oil importing countries and OPEC. The models are based on the premise that the major function of strategic buffer stocks is to smooth increases in oil prices by gradually releasing the buffers during an embargo, thereby cushioning the shock effects on consumer economies. Their general model is a control theoretic formulation of the buffer-embargo game where each coalition attempts to maximize its discounted expected utility over the horizon chosen. The respective decision variables are the change in size of the reserve in each period and the rate of reduction in oil production in each period. There is a price generating mechanism dependent upon the values of these parameters. They make the (dubious) assumption that the costs of building, maintaining, and utilizing the required reservoirs are negligible in comparison to the magnitude of the welfare losses. The general model is difficult to analyze and solve, so the authors concentrate their attention on simplified models. The objective of the oil consuming countries is to minimize the disutility associated with oil price increases while that of the producers consists of a political gain term, an economic-political interdependence term, plus revenue loss and gain terms. If one assumes that there is a single build-up period followed by a permanent embargo of constant size throughout the following two periods, then closed form solutions for the buffer level and embargo rates are obtainable. Using representative data, the authors conclude that: (1) a sufficiently high buffer level (about 62 percent of the build-up period usage) will avert an embargo; (2) consumers can alter producers' disutility of foregone revenues resulting from an embargo by making investment opportunities more attractive and thus eliminate or reduce the size of the embargo; and (3) the buffer stock will smooth out the shock effects on consuming economies if an embargo does take place.

Further applications of game theory to the analysis of energy modeling problems appear in Becker, Owen, and Thrall (1978) and Carbone et al. (1978).

During the coming decades the high costs and shortages of conventional fossil fuel will require curtailment of their use. This reduction will take many forms such as various conservation measures and substitution into alternative fuels including synthetic fossil fuels. This substitution is likely to be most dramatic in industrial and consumer uses that are very energy intensive. The pulp and paper industry provides a notable example. (Recall the Cameron-Schwartz paper in the previous section which pointed out the sectors that were likely to have trouble coping with high energy prices. The study indicated that pulp and paper though energy intensive, is a very energy price elastic sector.) The paper by Cox and Helliwell investigates the use of wood wastes to replace oil and natural gas consumption and to produce electricity in this industry in British Columbia. The pulp and paper industry is a heavy consumer of energy. It uses 42 percent of the natural gas and 80 percent of the heavy fuel oil used by industry in the province and also purchases 16 percent of all the electrical energy sold by the province's major electric utility, B.C. Hydro (Farrow, 1979). The wood waste energy source consists of slashed and broken branches found in the forest stocks and bark, shavings, slabs, edgings, sawdust, etc., left over in the lumber and pulp mills. A "hog" machine pulverizes the wood waste into usable fuel that is termed "hog fuel." The standard unit of measurement is the GPU or gravity packed unit (200 ft^3) of wood waste. Cox and Helliwell investigated two basic substitution possibilities at nineteen pulp and paper mills: (1) the replacement of all fossil-fueled burners by burners using 85 percent hog fuel and 15 percent oil or natural gas; these burners are attached to steam-producing boilers at 600 pounds per square inch (psi); and (2) the possibility of constructing high pressure 1250 psi burners to utilize a large pressure drop for the production of electricity by "noncondensing" turbines. A discussion of the engineering features of these and related technologies for recovering energy from wood waste and a technical evaluation of the merits of the various systems available in British Columbia appears in Levelton (1978).

The Cox-Helliwell model predicts: (1) the maximum amount of steam required per hour including the extent to which the maximum capacity will be used; (2) the size of boiler required; (3) the amount of electrical capacity that can be maintained from steam from a 1250 psi boiler; and (4) the total steam flow to provide process heat and electricity. The model compares the operation of hog and fossil fuel burners of equivalent capacity. Calculations are made from a private (industry) point of view using actual price estimates and a social (economy-wide) point of view using world prices for oil and gas. The simulations estimate that: the pulp and paper industry has already reduced yearly fossil fuel consumption by 15.6 bcf (billion cubic feet) of natural gas and 3.5 MMB of oil with hog fuel substitution; and that a further savings of 19.9 bcf of gas and 4 MMB of oil is possible with new capital investment of $248.4 million in 1978 dollars. Since gas has historically been cheaper for equivalent btu value than oil, one would expect that higher savings would be obtained at the oil-fired burner mills. This is indeed the case. It is estimated that the cash value per GPU delivered to the plant is $13.40 for gas mills and $24.08 for oil mills. When natural gas and oil are valued at their export prices in the fall of 1978, $2.40 Cdn. per mcf (thousand cubic feet) and $15 Cdn. per barrel landed in Montreal the value of the GPU becomes $22.29 and $24.34, respectively. (At the July 1979 prices of $2.80 US per mcf and about $19 US per barrel these values become about $30 Cdn. and $35 Cdn., respectively.) Conversion to the hog fuel burners is clearly very desirable; using the fall 1978 data result in average value per GPU of $4.17–$7.79 at gas mills and $3.79–$18.65 at oil mills after deduction of capital cost charges for the new burners (see Cox (1978) for precise statement of interest and other assumptions). Recently three of the mills (Crofton, Elk Falls, and Port Alberni) have increased their use of hog fuel.

The analysis also indicates that at ten of the nineteen mills it is profitable to produce electricity, and each GPU is estimated to have a value of $14.67 at the coastal mills and $11.50 at the interior mills. Thus, athough hog fuel is most economically employed as a replacement for fossil fuels, especially oil, it is profitable to use it to produce electricity. Cox and Helliwell estimate that the pulp and paper industry could increase its electrical generating capacity from 219.8 to 543.7 Megawatts and its energy production from 2.51 to 4.32 billion kwh. With full conversion there would be shortages of wood wastes on the coast and surpluses in the interior. Cox and Helliwell have calculated the distances by which excess hog fuel could be profitably shipped by truck, rail, or barge. With current prices it would be advantageous to produce electricity at those mills where there is excess supply of hog fuel and not at the other mills.

The paper by Cox and Helliwell describes part of a large study concerned with various aspects of the economic analysis of wood waste use in British Columbia's pulp and paper industry. The central paper providing the equations of the model and the description of the technical process being modelled is Cox (1978). Helliwell and Cox (1979a) consider some of the broader economic implications and institutional barriers with particular reference to such issues as the potential financial problems for natural gas pipelines and distribution systems that rely heavily on their sales to pulp and paper mills. The effects of electricity pricing schedules on the economics of electricity generation by pulp and paper mills are discussed in Helliwell and Cox (1979b). They show how a flexible simulation model can be used to optimally choose projects from both social and private points of view, and to evaluate policies that have the potential for removing divergence between the two types of decision (1978).

In their report on "Energy Futures for Canadians," the Federal Department of Energy, Mines and Resources has projected that even with a greatly reduced rate of increase in energy demand, the total demand is likely to double by the year 2000 and increase by a further 25 percent by 2025. While substitutions such as those discussed by Cox and Helliwell will be very important and helpful, the sheer growth in total demand by population growth and other factors will require that Canada substantially increase its available energy resources. It is government policy to achieve a "sustainable self-reliance in energy." For example one target is for oil imports to not exceed a third of oil usage in 1985. (Whether or not the Clark government will change this policy is not yet known.) Gander and Belaire's (1978) projections for energy usage are:

	1975	*2000*	*2025*	*Increase 1975–2025 %/year*
Oil ('000 bbls/day)	1780	2400	2500	0.7
Natural Gas (BCF/yr)	2500	3200	3600	0.7
Coal (million tons)	30	120	200	3.7
Renewables (excluding conventional hydro; '000 bbb/day oil equivalent)	—	400	1000	—
Electricity (GWe of capacity)	60	210	275	3.1
Total (quads)	8	16	20	1.8

Thus it is expected that there will be substantial increases in the use of oil (in the early stages), coal, renewables, and electricity, and a moderate increase in the use of natural gas. If anything like this scenario occurs, and the self-reliance goal is taken seriously, there will need to be substantial increases in Canadian energy resources. The increased oil production is assumed to come from oil sands and heavy oil deposits in Alberta and Saskatchewan, and possibly from frontier sources. The main heavy oil deposits are in the Lloydminster and Cold Lake areas. Present EMR (1977) estimates are that the Lloydminister area has 6–30 billion barrels (of bitumen) in place of which 1–5 billion barrels is ultimately recoverable, and the Cold Lake area has about 165 billion barrels in place and about 55 billion barrels is ultimately recoverable. Current production at Cold Lake is about 5000 bls/day of crude. The investment and operating costs associated with the coming large scale development of these regions are enormous; about $4000–6000 per barrel of daily production for Lloydminster and about $2.6–3 billion (in 1976 dollars) for a 100,000 bbl/day plant at Cold Lake with a twenty-five-year lifetime (EMR, 1977). For an assessment of the current situation regarding oil and natural gas supplies and demands, see the National Energy Board reports (1978, 1979).

There will also be discoveries of new reservoirs in existing and new areas. Uhler (1979) has observed that these new discoveries seem to arrive in bunches as "oil plays" and not in a continuous stream from year to year. The actual costs of these new oil and gas resources is hard to determine and the estimates available are unreliable. Uhler has attempted to estimate these costs by specifying and estimating translog production functions that relate drilling effort, land holdings for exploratory purposes, and geophysical activity to oil and gas discoveries. Finding costs can then be estimated using the production function along with the prices of these three inputs. One observation is that finding costs, especially for oils, have risen sharply and often tend to approach or even exceed current well head prices.

The largest deposits consist of the Tar Sands formations in the Athabasca, Peace River, Wabasca, and Buffalo Hills regions of northern Alberta. These deposits have bitumen-impregnated sands that occur either on the surface (with an overburden of 10–100 feet) in veins of ore 120–300 feet thick or at depths of about 2000 feet. There are about 789 billion barrels in place of which about 74 billion is surface mineable and 553 billion is in situ mineable in the Athabasca region. The ultimately recoverable resources at Athabasca are estimated by EMR to be about 38 billion barrels of surface mineable bitumen (which would yield about 26.5 billion barrels of synthetic crude) and 40–140 billion barrels of in situ mineable bitumen. Estimates vary but a scenario such as that described by The Honorable W. J. Yurko, Alberta's Minister of the Environment is indicative of the possible future development of the Tar Sands (Thierman, 1974). Yurko estimates that there will be one new plant (of capacity 100–150,000 bbl/day) every one and a half to two years in the late 1970s and early 1980s, escalating to a plant every year in the late 1980s. In the 1990s there will be one second-generation plant of capacity 200–300,000 bbl/day each year so that by the year 2000 there will be about twenty plants with a combined capacity of 3 MBB/day.

Whether or not all these plants will be built depends upon a number of factors, not the least important being the cost of and demand for alternative crude oil. The total costs of a Tar Sands plant are enormous: the $2 billion or more cost for a 100,000 bbls/day plant works out to over $20,000 per daily barrel of product. Operating costs are $5–$7 per barrel and there are royalty and income tax costs to consider as well. The recent OPEC price increase to about $19 US per barrel certainly strengthens the case for additional Tar Sands plants, however, the costs and risks involved are staggering. A good source for information on various economic, engineering, political, environmental, geological, financial, manpower, etc., aspects of the Athabasca Tar Sands is

Thierman (1974). The continuing political and economic discussions concerning a just and equitable sharing of Alberta's fossil fuel wealth is discussed in Scott (1976).

The first Tar Sands plant began operation in 1967 and has a current capability of 50,000 bbls/day although its operators, the Great Canadian Oil Sands Ltd. (GCOS), had planned for a capacity of 65,000. A plant with a capacity of 125,000 bbls/day operated by the Syncrude Canada Ltd. consortium (of governments and oil companies) is now under construction near Fort McMurray with an estimated cost of $2.1 billion and is expected to be operational in about 1981. Two additional tar sands plants to be built by the Allsands consortium at Fort McMurray and the Esso consortium at Cold Lake were recently approved by the Alberta Energy Conservation Board. Both call for plants with capacities of approximately 140,000 bbls/day. Construction will begin in the early 1980s and be completed in about five years. The projected costs are $5 billion for Allsands, and $6 billion for Esso which yields daily barrel of product investment costs well over $30,000.

There are many difficult problems associated with bringing a Tar Sands plant on line. Besides the tremendous cost there are a variety of engineering, environmental, and social aspects of the project. A key aspect is the design of the mining operation. The paper by Wyman describes a simulation of the operations of Syncrude. A key point at issue was the feasibility and relative advantages and disadvantages of five possible mining schemes. Four were based on so called "bucket wheel excavators" as used at the GCOS plant and the fifth was a "dragline" system.

The simulation considered the entire operations of Syncrude in five models: mining, transportation, storage, extraction, and weather. Over each year the model traced each event that changed the rate of material flow through each piece of equipment. The discrete event/continuous flow was modeled in GPSS V (General Purpose System Simulation model 5), by defining the transactions entities in the simulation languages SIMSCRIPT or GASP to be changes in flow rate such as plant breakdowns, changes in mining geology, weather interruptions, scheduled maintenance, conveyor moves, and full or empty storage-pile events. In mid-1973 pressure was growing to make a final decision regarding the actual proceeding of the project and to order the mining and other equipment. There was an intense seven-week period to develop, test, and utilize the final simulation model. A team of five analysts worked in shifts so program development could be made twenty-four hours a day. There was intense interaction between engineers and modelers, as the modelers attempted to respond to differing data and engineering modifications. (For more on such "crash mode" modeling efforts see Greenberg's paper in Volume II.) The final recommendation was for the dragline system. The entire process provides an excellent example of model development with interaction between the relevant affected parties and its eventual implementation and use. Wyman's paper is reprinted here from the November 1977 issue of *Interfaces.* It won the first prize in the 1977 Practice of Management Science Competition.

A similar simulation model to that described by Wyman for Syncrude is in operation at GCOS. It is described by Professor A. A. Cunningham (1978) as follows:

> MINEX is a simulation model of Great Canadian Oil Sands Ltd's Athabasca tarsand mining, upgrading, and refining process. The overall production process is technologically and logistically a very complex one. It involves surface mining operations to remove muskeg, overburden and tarsand, conveyor systems to move tarsand to the extraction plant followed by some ten further processes with various in-process storages, and finally a pipeline to deliver crude to Edmonton. The model represents the interactions of all these subprocesses taking account of their differing reliabilities and production rates as well as the interdependencies introduced by operating rules for scheduling activities such as maintenance of process components and start-ups.
>
> Being a complicated system it is difficult to predict with confidence the effect of major changes in operating procedures and equipment on total throughput. Upper management, therefore, commissioned the development of a model suitable for investigating such impacts. The work on the model began in February, 1977. Later, in May of 1977 it was revealed that the Company was to commence a major comprehensive study of the feasibility, technically and economically, of expanding the process to deliver up to 50 percent more crude. The O.R. project to develop the model then became a key element of the Expansion Study.
>
> The MINEX model went through several evolutionary phases, and different people contributed in different ways at different times to its development. J. Swirles led the project, provided general advice and guidance in formulating the model and, most importantly, acted as a mediator to interpret and reach agreement regarding various issues of process and mining engineering and of modeling. The basic modeling work was done by A. A. Cunningham of the Department of Industrial Engineering, University of Toronto, with the vital conceptual and programming assistance of Karen Elliot of SUNOCO Inc.'s Department of Decision Support Services (SUNOCO Inc. is a sister company of GCOS, both owned by SUN Co.). Later software and modeling development was carried out by Dan Johnston in collaboration with A. A. Cunningham and Peter Gillies. In addition, many engineers, managers, and operating personnel helped with their critical evaluations of model logic and data.

The final version of the model, used then extensively throughout the following six months of the Expansion Study, was completed by the end of September, 1977.

The project meets all the usual criteria of success. The model was verified to accurately predict past performance using historical parameter values. Also, having adapted it in response to the many serious criticisms of earlier versions, it predicted future performance with changed mine and plant configurations in a way that the operating and design engineers found plausible. Consequently, the Expansion Study team made extensive use of the model and credited it with a major role in choosing the final $180 million expansion program. Further, steps have already been taken to use the model for routine planning and budgeting purposes, as well as to continue its development as a tool to aid analysis of subsequent major capital proposals.

Corresponding to the immense Tar Sands in Canada are the vast reserves of oil shale in Colorado, Utah, and Wyoming. The reserves have been estimated to contain 1.8 trillion barrels of bitumen, of which about 129 billion are ultimately recoverable. There are no plants presently in operation to convert the oil shale into synthetic crude and none are yet in construction. Ericsson and Morgan (1978) have developed an activity analysis model to investigate the question concerning how much shale oil could be profitably produced at varying replacement costs.

The model is based on the current state of technology with existing resource and environmental constraints. The results indicate that it would be profitable to produce 2 MMB/day at a price of $12 per barrel in 1975 prices. A key constraint is water availability. At $18 a barrel (in 1975 prices), it is profitable to pump Mississippi River water to these sites to produce 15 million barrels per day, which is about 80 percent of present United States consumption. Although OPEC prices have not and may never achieve this latter level, it seems that oil shale may well become an important source of synthetic oil in the not too distant future.

The final two papers present progress reports by Rowse and Khazzoom on the development of major linear programming supply models. Rowse has developed a static supply model for the four western provinces of Canada: British Columbia, Alberta, Saskatchewan, and Manitoba for the Economic Council of Canada. The model is designed to minimize extraction, conversion, and transportation costs while meeting specified demands at representative supply points in Canada and the United States (for exports). The static model is intended to form the basis for a dynamic national energy model that will be able to estimate and analyze regional and intertemporal adjustments to wealth accrual, natural resource rents, labor requirements, and economic growth potentials associated with alternative energy resource utilization scenarios. Rowse provides some illustrative results obtained with the static model using base case and low price scenarios for the year 1974, and compares the models results with the actual values of some key energy quantities.

Khazzoom describes progress on the development of a large scale linear programming supply model of the United States economy. It is a disequilibrium model in the sense that demands are not necessarily met, and in fact will not be, unless the corresponding resource prices are sufficient to yield a return deemed adequate by the producer. The objective is to maximize total discounted profits by the energy sector over the horizon. Only profitable technologies will be used and the model specifically considers the possible use of new and advanced technologies. The model utilizes the 1967 U.S. input-output table and incorporates detailed engineering supply data concerning alternative technologies. The output is a schedule of energy availability as a function of energy resource prices and a schedule of associated investment requirements in energy technologies over the same horizon. To test the model, Khazzoom presents some preliminary results for the years 1967–1969.

DeBuen (1979) has developed an energy supply model for the Province of British Columbia for the B.C. Hydro Company. The linear programming model is designed to minimize the total discounted operating and capital costs involved in the production, conversion, transportation, distribution, and utilization of the different resources available to meet demands for energy in the residential, commercial, industrial, and transportation sectors of the provincial economy. The major fuels considered in the model are hydroelectric, oil, natural gas, coal, hog fuel, and various synthetic fuels. The model is run on a yearly average cost basis, i.e., total costs are the discounted sum of the average yearly costs over horizons of ten to thirty years. This approach provides an effective method for handling end effects since projects may be begun in periods prior to the end of the model's horizon and extend past this horizon. (For a discussion of several alternative ways to mitigate the impact of end effects in energy planning models see the paper by Grinold in Volume II.) Various annual and biannual model variants have been run to investigate the results of alternative scenarios, data sensitivity, etc. Model size varies from 1700 to 3500 rows and requires about 2000–5000 simplex iterations.

The output of the model is the determination of: (1) the electric plant capacity to be built in each possible site, on a year-by-year basis. This includes hydro, conventional thermal, future advanced thermal, pumped storage, and other nonconventional such as geothermal, tidal, wind, solar, or fuel cells; (2) the electric transmission systems associated with the generating facilities, and those that correspond to general expansion of the system which are necessary to carry increasing generation as the system grows; (3) the electric distribution expenditures required to get the energy to the consuming centers; (4) the running costs involved in the operation of the electric system, on an annual basis (fixed charges, fuel, and maintenance); (5) the amounts of natural gas, petroleum derivatives, coal, hog fuel, and synthetic fuels to be supplied on an annual basis; and (6) the end-use equipment required, as a result of additions to meet incremental system growth and replacement of retired units or conversion.

Some of the major conclusions are that there should be: (1) continuing development of hydroelectric resources for the next twenty years; (2) increased utilization of natural gas, especially in the heating markets; (3) accelerated reduction in the consumption of petroleum derivatives; (4) continued use, in limited amounts, of hog fuel, and limited development of geothermal power; (5) increased use of coal; (6) a delay in use of advanced technologies for generation of electric power until after the turn of the century; (7) delay of the nuclear option until at least the first decade of the next century; and (8) no development of large scale solar, tidal, wind, or other "exotic" sources.

None of the papers in this section are specifically concerned with the possible use of nuclear power, although such an option is inherent in the models described by Rowse and Khazzoom. A more thorough treatment of nuclear power's possible contribution to the energy future in North America is contained in the papers in Volume II concerned with integrative models. Information on the current state of nuclear technology and available fuel is contained in the CIM Bulletin (1978) and in Mining Engineering (1978). Dissenting views concerning the dangers and possibly enormously expensive costs of nuclear energy appear in Knelman (1976) and Lovins (1976). Another important energy source in North America's future is coal. Various aspects of coal supply and demand and its transportation are considered in the next section of this volume. Useful sources of information concerning various energy supply technologies are Abelson and Hammond (1978), Dorf (1978), and McMullan, Morgan, and Murray (1976).

REFERENCES

Abelson, P. H. 1974. *Energy: Use, conservation and supply.* Washington, D.C.: American Association for the Advancement of Science.

Abelson, P. H., and Hammond, A. L. 1978. *Energy II: Uses, conservation and supply.* Washington, D.C.: American Association for the Advancement of Science.

Balas, E. 1976. Recommendation for the overall size of SPR. FEA memo, October 28. Published in *Hearing before the Committee on Interior and Insular Affairs.* U.S. Senate, 95th Congress, February 4, 1977.

Balas, E. 1979. The strategic petroleum reserve: How large should it be? MSRR No. 436, Carnegie-Mellon University.

Becker, J.; Owen, G.; and Thrall, R. M. 1978. A game theoretic analysis of alternative source development. In *Energy policy,* eds. J. S. Aronofsky; A. G. Rao; and M. F. Shakun. *Studies in the Management Sciences* 10:95–108.

Carbone, R.; Garr, W. L.; Gusfafson, S. A.; Kortanek, K. O.; and Sweigart, J. R. 1978. A bargaining resolution of the efficiency versus equity conflict in energy and air pollution regulation. In *Energy policy,* eds. J. S. Aronofsky; A. G. Rao; and M. F. Shakun. *Studies in the Management Sciences* 10:95–108.

CIM Bulletin. 1978. Uranium: Deposits and exploration. December, pp. 61–68.

Conservation and Utilization Committee. 1972. Fort McMurray Athabasca Tar Sands development strategy. Edmonton.

Cox, A. J. 1978. An economic evaluation of the use of wood wastes to generate heat and electricity at pulp and paper mills in British Columbia. Resources Paper No. 20, Programme in Natural Resource Economics, University of British Columbia.

Cox, A. J. and Helliwell, J. F. 1978. Economic modeling of energy supply from burning wood waste at B.C. pulp and paper mills, Resources Paper No. 21, Programme in Natural Resource Economics, University of British Columbia.

Cunningham, A. A. December 13, 1978. Private communication.

De Buen, V. 1979. An energy model of British Columbia. *IEEE Transactions,* 79CH1458-9-PWR Paper No. A79-523-2.

Dorf, R. C. 1978. *Energy, resources and policy.* Reading, Mass.: Addison-Wesley.

Energy, Mines and Resources, Canada. 1977. Oil sands and heavy oils: The prospects. Report EP77-2, Ottawa.

Ericsson, N. R., and Morgan, P. 1978. The economic feasibility of shale oil: An activity analysis. *The Bell Journal of Economics* 9:457–487.

Farrow, M. 1979. Vast energy source "growing" in woods, mills. *The Vancouver Sun,* July 10, 1979.

Gander, J. E., and Belaire, F. W. 1978. *Energy futures for Canada.* Energy, Mines and Resources, Canada, Report EP78-1, Ottawa.

Helliwell, J. F., and Cox, A. J. 1979a. Wood waste as an energy source for the British Columbia pulp and paper industry: Economic implications and institutional barriers. In *Energy policy: The global challenge,* ed. P. N. Nemetz. Montreal: Institute for Research in Public Policy, pp. 245–263.

Helliwell, J. F. and Cox, A. J. 1979b. Electricity pricing and electricity supply: The influence of utility pricing on electricity production by pulp and paper mills. *Resources and Energy* 1: No. 3.

Helliwell, J. F. and Cox, A. J. 1978b. Simulation analysis of energy production in the British Columbia pulp and paper industry. Proceedings of *Simulation, modelling and decision in energy systems,* sponsored by the International Association of Science and Technology for Development, Acta Press, Calgary.

Kinberg, Y.; Shakun, M. F.; and Sudit, E. F. 1976. The energy crisis from a game theory viewpoint. *SCIMA: Journal of Management Science and Applied Cybernetics* 5.

Kinberg, Y.; Shakun, M. F.; and Sudit, E. F. 1978. Energy buffer stock decisions in game situations. In *Energy policy,* eds. J. S. Aronofsky; A. G. Rao; and M. F. Shakun. *Studies in the Management Sciences* 10:109–127.

Knelman, F. H. 1976. *Nuclear energy: The unforgiving technology.* Edmonton: Hurtig Publishers.

Levelton, B. H., and Associates Ltd. 1978. An evaluation of wood waste energy conversion systems. Report to the British Columbia Wood Wastes Energy Coordinating Committee, March 31.

Lovins, A. B. 1976. Energy strategy: The road not taken. *Foreign Affairs:* 65–96.

McMullan, J. T.; Morgan, R.; and Murray, R. B. 1976. *Energy resources and supply.* London: John Wiley.

Meyer, R. F., ed. 1977. *The future supply of nature-made petroleum and gas.* New York: Pergamon Press.

Mining Engineering. 1978. Special issue: Uranium. Vol. 30, October.

Mossberg, W. S. 1979. When U.S. set up that oil reserve, it left one thing out. *Wall Street Journal,* March 15, 1979.

National Energy Board. 1978. *Canadian oil: Supply and requirements.* Ottawa, September.

National Energy Board. 1979. *Canadian natural gas: Supply and requirements.* Ottawa, February.

Scott, A., ed. 1976. *Natural resource revenues: A test of federalism.* Vancouver: University of British Columbia Press, 1976.

Thierman, V. D., ed. 1974. *The Athabasca oil sands.* Montreal, Quebec: The Engineering Institute of Canada.

Uhler, R. S. 1979. Oil and gas finding costs. Mimeo, Department of Economics, University of British Columbia.

8 CHOOSING THE OVERALL SIZE OF THE STRATEGIC PETROLEUM RESERVE

Egon Balas

The purpose of the Strategic Petroleum Reserve (SPR) is to diminish U.S. vulnerability to, as well as to offer protection against, possible future oil embargoes. This paper formulates the problem of determining the optimal size of SPR as a parametric bimatrix game between the United States and its potential opponent. The strategies of the opponent are embargoes of various intensities and lengths, including of course the no embargo option. The strategies of the United States are various ways of using the reserve. The size of the reserve itself is a parameter present in both payoff functions. Solving the game for the relevant reserve sizes yields interesting conclusions on the desirable size of the reserve, as well as on U.S. drawdown policies in case of an embargo. The crucial element in the game-theoretic approach is that, unlike the traditional cost-benefit analysis, it fully captures the embargo-deterrent effect of an appropriate Strategic Petroleum Reserve.

8.1 INTRODUCTION AND BACKGROUND

In 1976 I spent the fall semester on leave from my University, as a visiting operations research analyst with the Federal Energy Administration (FEA) in Washington.* I first got interested in the Strategic Petroleum Reserve (SPR) because the optimal location of storage sites seemed to be a problem where my skills could be helpful. I very soon discovered, however, that the concern for the location of storage facilities was entirely overshadowed by the more basic preoccupation with the pending decision on the overall size of the reserve, and so I decided to work on the problem of choosing the optimal size of the SPR. My findings were summarized in a memorandum dated October 28, 1976, published later in the Congressional Hearings. This paper is a slightly modified and expanded version of that memorandum.

From mid-October 1973 until mid-March 1974, the United States was the object of an oil embargo on the part of the OAPEC (Organization of Arab Petroleum Exporting Countries, a grouping within OPEC). Right before the embargo, U.S. petroleum consumption was about 17 MMB/day (million barrels per day), of which about 6.2 MMB/day was being covered by imports. Roughly 22 percent of these imports, or about 1.4 MMB/day, were coming from the OAPEC countries. This supply interruption and the subsequent quadrupling of the price of oil had a severe impact on the U.S. and world economy. In the United States, the GNP loss directly ascribed to the embargo was officially estimated to have been between $10–20 billion (Project Independence Report, Appendix A V). Other estimates are much higher.

The embargo has alerted U.S. policy makers and the public at large to the vulnerability that our high degree of dependence on oil imports entails. As a result, in December 1975, Congress passed the Energy Policy and Conservation Act (Public Law 94–163), which provided for the creation of a Strategic Petroleum Reserve, meant to reduce the vulnerability of the United States to petroleum supply interruptions and to alleviate the impact of such disruptions, should they occur. The law called for an Early Storage Reserve of at least 150 MMB to be put in place by December 1978, and for a total Strategic Petroleum Reserve of up to 1,000 MMB. It further specified that by December 1982 the reserve should reach a level corresponding to the volume of imports during the three consecutive highest import months of 1974–1975, subsequently determined to be about 500 MMB. Finally, it called on the Administration to submit a SPR Plan by December 1976.

Several alternative technologies for storing oil were studied in 1974–1975, and storage in underground salt domes was found to be by far

*I wish to thank Harvey Greenberg for inviting me to the Federal Energy Administration, David Nissen for making my visit possible, and both of them for creating the excellent conditions under which I worked. I had many useful discussions on the subject of this paper with Phil Childress, Fred Murphy, and others. Last, but not least, my thanks go to Marc Sheinberg, whose help was crucial in bringing my project to completion.

the most convenient solution economically, environmentally, as well as from the standpoint of security. The vast salt formations in the southern states offer more than sufficient potential storage sites. Creating an underground storage facility in a salt dome (leaching the cavity and building the connecting pipeline network) costs about \$1.5/barrel of oil, a modest amount in comparison with the cost of the oil itself (about \$13/barrel), where both costs are expressed in 1975 dollars.

In order to make a recommendation on the overall size of the reserve as part of the SPR Plan that it was preparing for Congress, the Federal Energy Administration has conducted several studies of the efficiency of various reserve sizes. The basic approach used was cost-benefit analysis.

8.2 THE LIMITATIONS OF COST-BENEFIT ANALYSIS

If we assume that an embargo will take place some time during the next fifteen years, a good measure of the efficiency of SPR is the total cost to the United States of the embargo, as a function of the reserve size. This total cost can be measured by the sum of (1) the cost of the reserve, and (2) the GNP loss caused by the petroleum shortfall that the reserve cannot replace. The cost of the reserve is an increasing linear function of the size of the reserve, whereas the GNP loss can be approximated by a quadratic function of the percentage petroleum shortfall, where the latter decreases linearly with the reserve size. As a result, the total cost is a convex function of the reserve size, which has a minimum. Figure 8–1 illustrates a case where the minimum total cost occurs for a SPR of 500 MMB.

This kind of analysis yields a perfectly adequate measure of the usefulness of the reserve in its impact-reducing capacity; but it fails to assess its value as an embargo deterrent, since it assumes the occurrence of the embargo independently of the existence and size of SPR.

Furthermore, since the history of the last thirty years in the Middle East has produced at least one embargo-prone conflict every seven years, assuming two embargoes during the next fifteen years is at least as justified as assuming one. Making this assumption doubles the size of the GNP loss used in the calculation, while it leaves unchanged the total cost of the stockpile. The outcome for the example of Figure 8–1 is that the point of minimum total cost shifts from a stockpile of 500 MMB to one of 750 MMB, as shown in Figure 8–2.

8.3 A PARAMETRIC BIMATRIX GAME

Since any embargo is the result of a conflict, and since conflict situations are best analyzed by the mathematical discipline called game theory, the

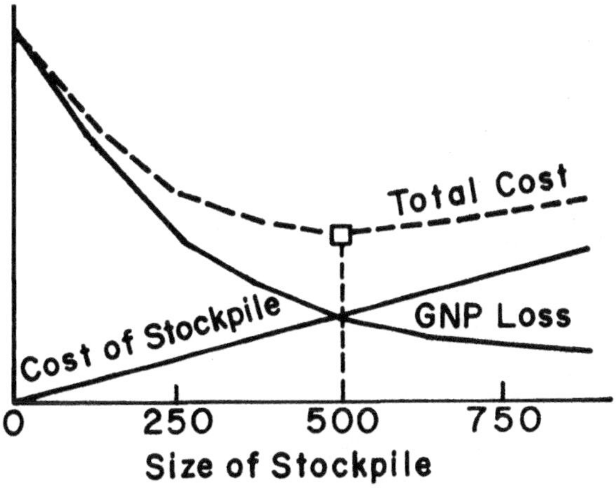

FIGURE 8-1. One embargo during 1977-1990

proper analytical tool that suggests itself for determining the optimal size of the SPR is a game theoretical model, namely a parametric bimatrix game. Such an approach, unlike the traditional cost-benefit analysis, addresses simultaneously both aspects of the SPR, i.e., its embargo-deterrent as well as its impact-reducing aspects. Rather than assuming the occurrence of an embargo to be an event independent of the existence and size of the SPR, this approach treats the embargoes of various lengths and intensities as possible outcomes of the game, whose probability of occurrence is a function of, among other things, the size of the U.S. petroleum reserve.

In a bimatrix game there are two players, each of whom has several strategies at his disposal. The objectives pursued by the two players are expressed by their respective payoff functions, given by two $m \times n$ matrices, $A = (a_{ij})$ and $B = (b_{ij})$. The interpretation of the latter is that if player 1 uses strategy i and player 2 uses strategy j, then player 1 gains a_{ij} units and player 2 gains b_{ij} units (here "gain" means loss whenever a_{ij} or b_{ij} is negative). A mixed strategy x for player 1 is a non-negative m-vector whose components sum to one, and whose interpretation is that player 1 uses strategy i with probability x_i. A mixed strategy y for player 2 is a n-vector defined and interpreted in an analogous fashion. An equilibrium point is a pair of mixed strategies $(\bar{x},\bar{y})$, such that $\bar{x}A\bar{y} \geq xA\bar{y}$ for all strategies x available to player 1, and $\bar{x}B\bar{y} \geq \bar{x}By$ for all strategies y available to player 2. The essential characteristic of an equilibrium point is that it maximizes each player's gain (minimizes each player's loss), under the assumption that his opponent plays the game in a best possible way. This concept is

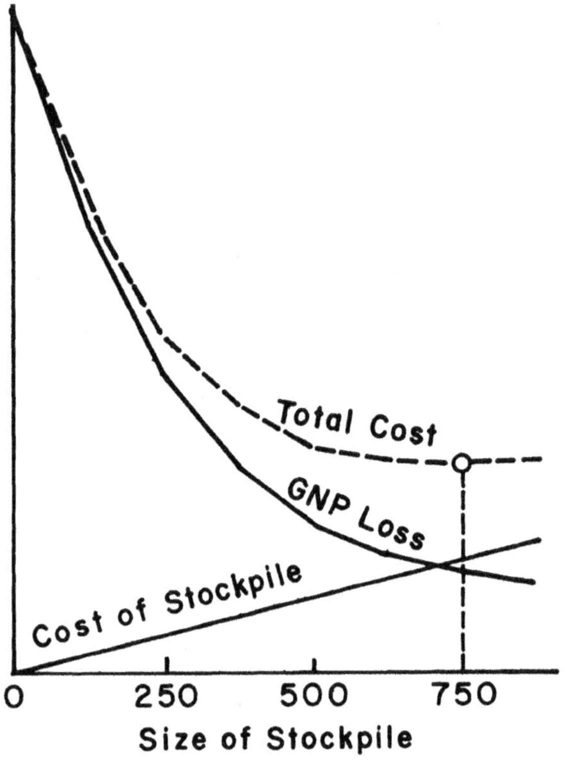

FIGURE 8-2. Two embargoes during 1977-1990

due to Nash (1951), who also showed that every bimatrix game has an equilibrium point. An efficient method for finding such a point was given by Lemke and Howson (1964).

To formulate the problem of the optimal size of the SPR as a parametric bimatrix game, we assume, based on the experience of the past thirty years, that during the next fifteen years there will be two conflict situations in the Middle East. A conflict situation is defined as one in which the OAPEC countries, or some of them, wish to pressure the United States into some action alien to its political goals. Such a situation may, but need not, lead to an embargo. Note that this is a considerably weaker assumption than the one used earlier. For each conflict situation, we formulate a bimatrix game in which the two players are the OAPEC and the United States. The United States has a petroleum stockpile whose size is a parameter in the game, i.e., we wish to solve the game for all relevant stockpile sizes, and determine that range of stockpile sizes, for which the outcomes are most convenient. The strategies available to the OAPEC are the embargoes of varying length and intensity, including, of course, the "no embargo" option. At some point one may also wish to consider strategies of a different type, e.g., a politically motivated price-hike. The strategies available to the United States are the various possible drawdown policies (uniform, exponential with different rates, etc.).

The objective of the United States is to minimize the total cost, i.e., the sum of the GNP loss caused by the OAPEC action, and the cost of the stockpile over the whole period considered. Hence, the U.S. payoff function (to be maximized) is the negative of this sum. It depends, of course, on the value of the parameter expressing the size of the stockpile.

The objective of the OAPEC is more difficult to assess and to quantify in a way that makes sense. Since this is the most delicate part of formulating the game, it will be discussed in some detail. A conflict situation was earlier defined as one in which the OAPEC wants to blackmail the United States into some action contrary to U.S. policies. Thus, the objective of the OAPEC is to exert pressure on the United States. It seems reasonable to assume that the pressure exerted by some OAPEC action increases with the damage caused to the United States. On the other hand, actions of the type considered here also carry some cost to the OAPEC. We will, therefore, assume that the payoff function of the OAPEC is of the form $f = g - h$, where g is a function of the GNP loss inflicted upon the United States via the embargo, and h is a function of the cutback in petroleum production which accompanies the embargo. As to the shape of these functions, since conflict situations are triggered by, and related to, events which usually have a rather rapid course, it is natural to perceive an embargo as a blackmailing device whose objective is to obtain some action of considerable urgency. It, therefore, seems reasonable to assume that the function g, while increasing with the size of the U.S. GNP loss, decreases with the length of the period over which the loss is spread. In other words, we assume that a GNP loss inflicted upon the United States in the first quarter of the embargo is of "full value" to the OAPEC, a loss of the same magnitude inflicted in the second quarter is of somewhat lesser value, etc.; and losses suffered by the United States a year later are of little if any value.

On the other hand, the loss suffered by the OPEC as a consequence of a given petroleum production cutback (and of possible retaliatory action on the part of the United States and its allies) may be easy to bear at the beginning, in view of the sizeable surplus that these countries possess. As time goes by and the surplus is consumed, the loss becomes felt. It seems, therefore, reasonable to assume that the function *h* starts at a level close to 0 and increases slowly with both the size of the percentage cutback in petroleum production, and the length of time over which the cutback is imposed.

The functions *f*, *g*, and *h* are illustrated in Figure 8-3, which represents them as functions of time (number of days) for a given stockpile size and daily petroleum cutback (both the cutback in daily petroleum imports and the resulting daily GNP loss are assumed to be constant over time). The function *g* is equal to the cumulative GNP loss function in the first quarter, then asymptotically approaches the horizontal line. The function *h* is almost horizontal in the first quarter, then asymptotically approaches a line paral-

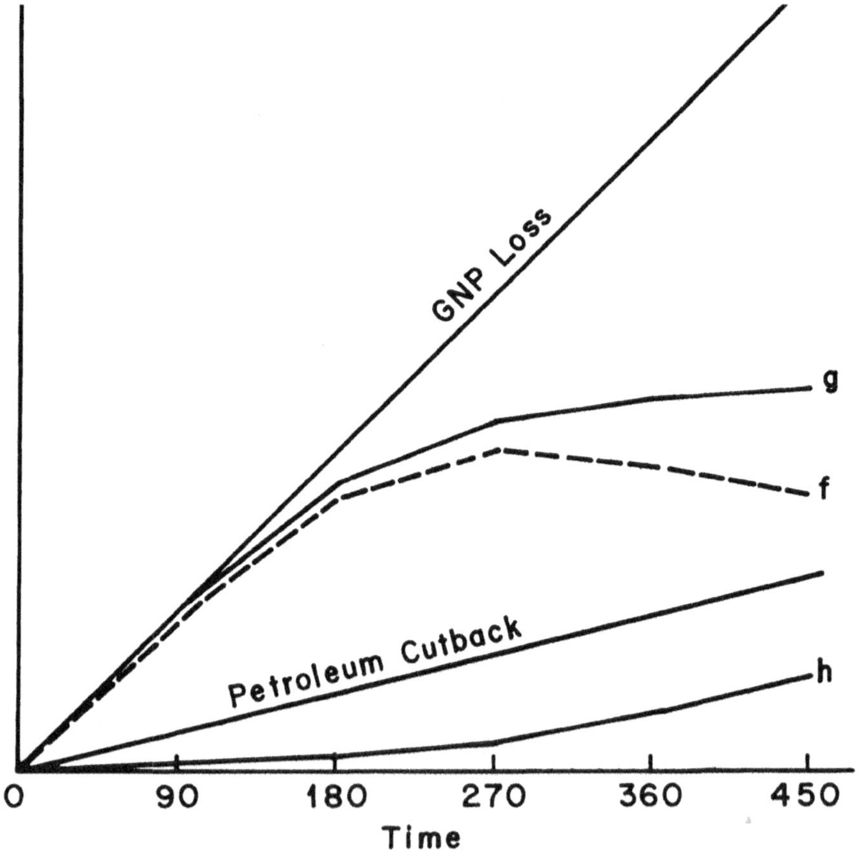

FIGURE 8-3. Payoff function of OAPEC

lel to the cumulative petroleum cutback function. The resulting function $f = g - h$ is first increasing, then decreasing; and its maximum corresponds to the optimal (for the OAPEC) length of the embargo, given its assumed intensity and the size of the U.S. stockpile.

One can, of course, argue about the correct numerical values for the coefficients defining the functions g and h, but it seems that there is little room for argument about the general shape of f, g, and h, which reflects the basic features of the type of conflict situation considered here.

This model has several advantages. It takes a global view of the problem, i.e., it incorporates into the analysis all major aspects, including the embargo-deterrent effect of the stockpile. If solved for all relevant stockpile sizes, it yields not only an optimal size for the stockpile, but also valuable information on the probability distribution of the embargoes of varying length and intensity for each stockpile size considered. Further, it produces optimal drawndown strategies for the various stockpile sizes.

The major difficulty with the model is that the outcomes depend on the coefficients of the payoff function f, about which little is known. The way to cope with this difficulty is to parametrize the coefficients of f and solve the game for the relevant range of values rather than for a single set of numerical values of these coefficients.

8.4 RESERVE SIZE AND EMBARGO LENGTH

As it so often happens with mathematical models, the process of formulating the model itself yields insights which may be as important as the ones obtained by solving the model numerically. We discuss one such example.

Sometimes the argument is voiced that a U.S. petroleum stockpile sufficiently large to match the shortfall from an embargo of six months might be an incentive for the OAPEC to impose an embargo longer than six months. This argument rests upon the naive assumption attributed to the OAPEC that we would use up our six months' stockpile in six months rather than spread it over a longer period and use some conservation measures. Beyond this straightforward refutation of the argument, it can actually be shown that to the extent that OAPEC objectives are adequately expressed by a function of the general form shown in Figure 8-3, a larger U.S. stockpile is an incentive for reducing rather than increasing the length of an embargo. Consider two situations, one with a smaller stockpile (#1) and one with a larger stockpile (#2), and assume that an embargo of a given intensity accompanied by a fixed daily cutback in OAPEC petroleum production is instituted. Both situations are represented in Figure 8-4. Naturally, in situa-

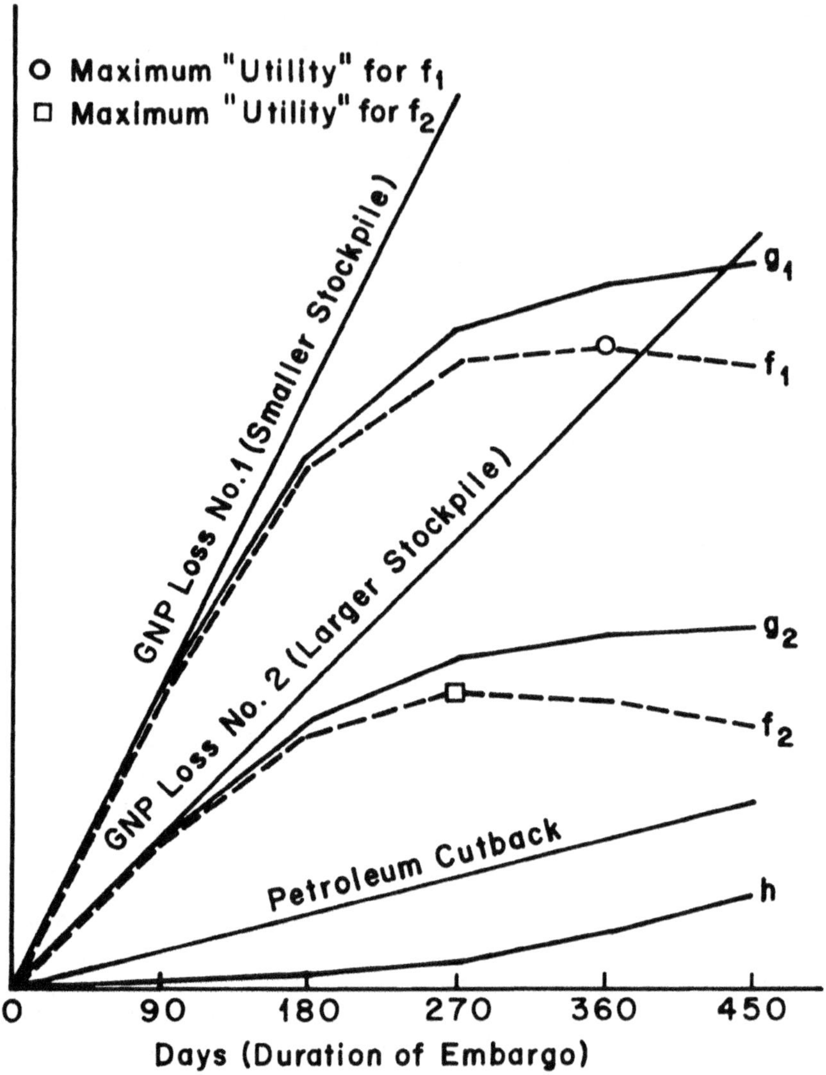

FIGURE 8–4. "Utility" of embargo to OAPEC: $f = g - h$

tion 1 the export cutback is accompanied by a greater GNP loss, because of the smaller stockpile; this is expressed in the fact that the slope of the GNP loss curve #1 is sharper than that of the GNP loss curve #2. Accordingly, the function g_1 corresponding to situation 1 takes on higher values than the function g_2 corresponding to situation 2, though both functions are in exactly the same position relative to the corresponding GNP loss functions. Since the cutback in OAPEC petroleum production is not affected by our stockpile, the function h is the same in both cases. Comparing now the two payoff functions for the two situations, $f_1 = g_1 - h$ and $f_2 = g_2 - h$, we see that the maximum of f_2 is to the left of the maximum of f_1.

8.5 SOME NUMERICAL RESULTS

In order to make full use of the model discussed here, one has to solve the game for all plausible scenarios and all relevant reserve sizes, as well as for all justifiable payoff functions of the two players. In most cases the game has equilibrium points in pure strategies. When it does not, we use an integer programming formulation (to be discussed elsewhere) to find all stable equilibrium points in mixed strategies. This work is currently in progress. Here we illustrate the kind of answers that one can obtain from this model by analyzing the outcome of the game for some typical cases.

Two conflict situations are considered, in 1981 and 1985 respectively. The OAPEC strategies considered (shown in Table 8-1) are potential

TABLE 8-1. OAPEC strategies considered

OAPEC Strategy	*OAPEC Export Cutback (%)*	*U.S. Daily Shortfall (MMB)*	*Duration (days)*
1981 case			
1	0 (no embargo)	0	0
2	25	2.5	180
3	25	2.5	360
4	50	3.5	180
5	50	3.5	360
1985 case			
1	0 (no embargo)	0	0
2	25	4.3	180
3	25	4.3	360
4	50	5.5	180
5	50	5.5	360

embargoes of varying length and intensity, corresponding to some of the supply interruption scenarios developed at FEA. For these as well as for other information on the subject, see Strategic Petroleum Reserve Plan (1976).

The U.S. strategies are the drawdown policies for the case of an embargo. It is asumed that 3 percent of the daily petroleum shortfall is taken care of by conservation measures. The remaining supply gap (termed net shortfall) is to be replaced according to the following four strategies.

1. Replace the entire net shortfall for as long as the reserve lasts.
2. Replace the entire net shortfall until the reserve gets depleted to the level of forty-five days' net shortfall; thereafter use up 1/45 of the current reserve daily.
3. Same as 2, with a critical level of ninety days.
4. Same as 2, with a critical level of 135 days.

Strategies 2–4 are called exponential drawdown policies. If α_j is the critical level (in days) defining the jth strategy, strategy 1 can also be represented as an exponential drawdown policy, with $\alpha_1 = 1$.

To generate the OAPEC payoff function $f = g - h$, the quarterly U.S. GNP loss was calculated for each OAPEC strategy and each reserve size by using an estimator developed by R. Holcombe in his revised study of the economic impact of a petroleum supply interruption (Holcombe, 1976). Denoting by L_i the GNP loss in the ith quarter of the embargo, the function g was taken to be $g = L_1 + .8L_2 + .5L_3 + .2L_4$. Further, denoting by V the value of one quarter's OAPEC petroleum exports and by p_i the percentage cutback in the ith quarter of the embargo, the function h was taken to be of the form $h = .5V[.25(p_1/50)^2 + .5(p_2/50)^2 + .75(p_3/50)^2 + (p_4/50)^2]$. Naturally, g and h were expressed in the same units (millions of 1975 dollars, but this is immaterial; the only relevant thing is the relative size of the values of f corresponding to a given stockpile size).

As to the U.S. payoff function, this is the negative of the total cost p (reserve cost plus GNP loss) to the United States of the OAPEC action corresponding to each strategy and to each reserve size. The cost of the stockpile was calculated on the basis of a build-up program which starts in 1977 and adds every year up to 200 MMB storage capacity until the target size is reached. The cost of stockpiling consists of \$1.5/B for creating and maintaining the storage facility, and an opportunity cost of \$1.3/B/year (10 percent of the purchase price of \$13/B) for the money tied up in the stockpile, all in 1975 dollars. It is assumed that if the stockpile is used up in an embargo, it is replenished in the year following the embargo. The GNP loss was calculated by using the previously mentioned estimator.

The basic difference between the 1981 and the 1985 cases is in the level of the U.S. imports from the OAPEC countries, which puts a limit on the intensity of the embargoes that the OAPEC can impose.

Tables 8-2 and 8-3 summarize the outcome of the game for several relevant reserve sizes in 1981 and 1985 respectively. The most salient feature of Tables 8-2 and 8-3 is that in the presence of only a small stockpile, the optimal OAPEC strategy is the heaviest kind of embargo; whereas, in the presence of a large U.S. stockpile, the optimal OAPEC strategy is to have no embargo at all. This expresses the embargo-deterrent effect of a stockpile. The relevant question, of course, is what size of stockpile is sufficient to make an embargo an unlikely strategy to be chosen in case of a conflict situation. In terms of the game, this question reduces to finding the smallest value of the parameter (stockpile size) for which strategy 1 becomes optimal for the OAPEC. In Table 8-2 this value is 500 MMB, whereas in Table 8-3 it is 1,100 MMB. The main difference between the two situations represented in these tables is in the volume of OAPEC exports to the United States, assumed to be considerably higher (and thus make possible considerably heavier embargoes) in 1985 than in 1981. Obviously, the larger the volume of U.S. imports from the OAPEC countries, the larger the size of the stockpile needed to deter an embargo.

TABLE 8-2. Game outcome (1981 case)

Reserve size	350	475	500
Solutions of the game (equilibrium points)	(5,4)	(3,2)	(1,1),(1,2)
Interpretation:			
Optimal OAPEC strategies	50% cutback 3.5 MMB/day 360 days	25% cutback 2.5 MMB/day 180 days	no embargo
Optimal U.S. strategies	α_4 = 135 days	α_2 = 45 days	$\alpha_{1,2}$ = 1–45 days
Total cost to the U.S. (billions of 1975 dollars, present valued for 1975)	38.63	11.90	2.24

TABLE 8-3. Game outcome (1985 case)

Reserve size	500	750	1,000	1,100
Solutions of the game (equilibrium points)	(5,4)	(5,4)	(3,2)	(1,1),(1,2) (1,3),(1,4)
Interpretation:				
Optimal OAPEC strategies	50% cutback 5.5 MMB/day 360 days	50% cutback 5.5 MMB/day 360 days	25% cutback 4.3 MMB/day 180 days	no embargo
Optimal U.S. strategies	$\alpha_4 = 135$	$\alpha_4 = 135$	$\alpha_2 = 45$	any
Total cost to the U.S. (billions of 1975 dollars, present valued for 1975)	61.58	49.00	15.54	3.24

8.6 CONCLUSIONS

Solving the game for several different sets of assumptions and the range of relevant reserve sizes yields the following tentative information on the deterrent effect of the SPR:

Volume of U.S. Imports from OAPEC	*Approximate Stockpile Size for Which Embargo Becomes Unattractive*
MMB/Day	MMB
2.5–3.5	500–750
3.5–4.5	750–1,000
4.5–6.0	1,000–1,300

The conclusion emerging from this analysis is that *the overall size of the Strategic Petroleum Reserve should be the equivalent of seven to eight months' U.S. petroleum imports from the OAPEC countries.* If we assume that the total volume of U.S. imports of petroleum products by 1985 will be around 10 MMB per day, and that approximately 45 percent of this amount (i.e., 4.5 MMB/day) will originate with the OAPEC countries, then the optimal size of the Strategic Petroleum Reserve is in the vicinity of the 1,000 million barrels put forward by the Energy Conservation and Policy Act of 1975. If, however, the volume of OAPEC imports will be higher than this amount (a possibility not to be lightly dismissed), then the optimum stockpile size is proportionally larger. Any recommendation for a smaller stockpile size needs to be accompanied by some realistic proposal for keeping the OAPEC imports at a correspondingly lower level.

Further, given the uncertainty surrounding the future level of U.S. imports from the OAPEC countries on the one hand, and the relatively low cost of the storage facilities on the other (salt mine leaching plus connecting facilities cost about $1.5 per barrel), it seems desirable to create a storage capacity well in excess of the contemplated size of the SPR, so as to keep open the possibility for future upward adjustments of the size of SPR in case of an unexpected increase in U.S. imports from the OAPEC.

8.7 POST SCRIPTUM

As this paper goes to press, the computational study outlined at the beginning of section 8.5 has just been completed (see Balas (1979)). The game was solved for over one hundred scenarios involving all plausible combinations of assumptions. The conclusions of this paper were essentially confirmed, with an upward shift of about 15 percent in the recommended SPR size for every prospective import level, due to a reassessment of the GNP loss function by the Department of Energy.

The analysis carried out in Balas (1979) has also shown that the sensitivity of our conclusions to changes in the various assumptions is well within the limits of reasonableness. Thus, changing the cost of storage facilities from $1.5/barrel to $3/barrel hardly at all affects the outcome. Assuming a frequency of conflicts of ten or twenty years, instead of seven years, reduces the optimal reserve size by at most 5 percent. On the other hand, changes in the parameter defining the OAPEC's payoff function affect the outcome more seriously. A strong reduction of the rate at which the OAPEC's perceived gain from the loss inflicted upon the United States decreases with time, or a drastic increase in the OAPEC's assumed capacity to absorb its own losses may cause an increase of as much as one-third in the optimal reserve size.

The single most important parameter determining the optimal size of the SPR remains the level of U.S. oil imports from OAPEC at the time of a potential conflict; and for most of the plausible scenarios, the optimum size of the reserve falls between the equivalent of 250 and 300 days of U.S. imports from the OAPEC.

REFERENCES

Balas, E. 1977. Recommendation for the overall size of SPR. FEA Memorandum, October 28, 1976. Published in *Hearing Before the Committee on Interior and Insular Affairs,* U.S. Senate, 95th Congress, February 4, 1977.

Balas, E. 1979. The strategic petroleum reserve: How large should it be? M.S.R.R. No. 436, June, Carnegie-Mellon University.

Holcombe, R. G. 1976. A model to estimate the economic impact of an interruption in U.S. petroleum imports, final report. Department of Economics, Texas A. and M. University.

Lemke, C. E., and Howson, J. T. 1964. Equilibrium points of bimatrix games. *SIAM Journal of Applied Mathematics* 12:413–423.

Nash, J. 1951. Non-cooperative games. *Annals of Mathematics* 54:286–295.

Project Independence Report. 1974. Federal Energy Administration, November.

Strategic Petroleum Reserve Plan, (Public Law 94–163, Section 154). 1976. Federal Energy Administration, December.

9 ECONOMIC MODELING OF ENERGY SUPPLY FROM BURNING WOOD WASTES AT BRITISH COLUMBIA PULP AND PAPER MILLS*

A. J. Cox and J. F. Helliwell

This paper analyzes the use of wood wastes to replace the extensive fossil-fuel consumption at nineteen pulp and paper mills in British Columbia, and the further use of wood wastes to produce electricity at these mills. The evaluation, which is based on simulation models of energy consumption at each of the mills, is done from the points of view of both the firms involved and of the economy as a whole. The latter evaluation is carried out using world prices for fossil fuels and the cost of electricity from new British Columbia Hydro projects. The private returns are found to depend primarily on the price paid for fossil fuel and electricity. Some predictions can be made as to the amount that the mill managers would be willing to pay for hauling wood waste (to overcome apparent shortages in some locations) and still earn a positive return on the investment in wood waste-burning facilities.

*This paper is condensed from Cox, A. J., and Helliwell, J. F., "Economic Modeling of Energy Supply from Burning Wood Waste at B.C. Pulp and Paper Mills," Resources Paper No. 21, Programme in Natural Resource Economics, University of British Columbia, 1978. This work has been supported by U.B.C's Programme in Natural Resource Economics which is financed by the Social Sciences and Humanities Research Council of Canada.

9.1 INTRODUCTION

The authors have been working on the economics of energy production and energy use in the British Columbia pulp and paper industry. The primary concern is with the possibilities for increased use of wood wastes (usually referred to as "hog fuel") to replace fossil fuels and to generate electricity. This has involved building simulation models for nineteen of British Columbia's major pulp and paper mills (though this paper presents results from eighteen simulations, since two mills will be building a common steam plant). We have written a series of related papers describing various aspects of our research (Cox, 1978; Helliwell and Cox, 1978, 1979a, 1979b). This paper discusses the potential energy production from wood wastes in the context of the total British Columbia energy supply situation, analyzes the likely supply of wood wastes in the various regions of the province, and considers the economics of transporting wood wastes from one region to another.

An important component of Canada's energy strategy is the use of the price mechanism to control energy demand and increase energy supply. Such a policy, already partially implemented for crude oil and natural gas, is intended to provide appropriate economic incentives for consumers to use energy more efficiently, while on the supply side encouraging producers to search for and develop higher-cost deposits of these fuels. See Department of Energy, Mines and Resources (1976).

There is an additional effect of increased prices on the supply side; as the price of traditional energy sources increase, alternative fuels appear as potentially significant elements of energy supply. The establishment of the quantitative importance of these alternative energy sources requires a detailed analysis of various industries that are in a position to develop them.

Another reason to undertake detailed, industry-by-industry analysis of energy-use patterns is to analyze the degree to which the industrial sector is able to substitute away from increasing-cost energy sources, thus insulating itself from price increases, relieving the downward pressure on production levels and employment, and maintaining export markets.

The use of wood wastes to replace the extensive fossil-fuel consumption at pulp and paper mills in British Columbia, and the further use of wood wastes to produce electricity at these mills, affords the opportunity to do just such an analysis. The potential importance of hog fuel is underlined by considering the proportion of the province's total energy consumption by this one industry. The latest figures available to us indicate that this industry consumes about 50 percent of all the natural gas consumed by the province's industrial sector and 85 percent of the heavy fuel oil; purchases 15 percent of electric energy sold by the British Columbia Hydro and Power

Authority, the province's largest electric utility; and has an installed electric capacity that is 11 percent of the total generating capacity of B.C. Hydro.

9.2 DESCRIPTION OF THE MODEL

The model simulates, as comprehensively as possible, energy requirements at individual pulp and paper mills in the province. This paper discusses application of the model to two uses of hog fuel as a substitute for traditional sources of energy. The first is the replacement of all fossil-fueled burners with burners fueled 85 percent by hog fuel and 15 percent by oil or natural gas. These burners are attached to steam-producing boilers at conventional (600 psi) pressures. The second possibility evaluated is that of constructing a higher pressure (1250 psi) boiler in order to utilize a larger pressure drop for the production of electricity by "noncondensing" turbines (also known as "topping" or "back-pressure" turbines).

The model predicts, from average production figures for each mill, the maximum amount of steam required per hour during the winter, and the usual electrical capacity requirements. The process heat requirements (minus steam available from previously constructed hog-fueled boilers and chemical recovery boilers) dictate the size of the 600-psi boiler required. The model predicts the amount of electrical capacity that can be maintained from the required flow of steam coming from a 1250-psi boiler, and the total steam flow required to provide (1) process heat and (2) the energy required to produce the amount of electricity that the mill chooses to generate.

While the model predicts the necessary size of a boiler built to meet peak winter requirements and the size of electricity generating facilities that utilize this peak, it also predicts the extent to which this maximum capacity will be used. The higher the peaking requirement, the lower is the average return to these investments (Helliwell and Cox, 1979b).

Since the model produces separate accounts of the costs and benefits due to fossil fuel replacement and those due to electricity generation, we can discuss them separately.

9.3 EVALUATING THE ECONOMICS OF FOSSIL FUEL REPLACEMENT

From the size of the 600-psi boiler necessary for the provision of process heat, and large enough to replace as much fossil fuel as possible, we compute the capital cost of a hog-fueled boiler and of a fossil-fueled boiler of equivalent capacity. These figures are used to generate operating and maintenance costs for these boiler and burner types.

The present value (or total net return) of the fossil fuel displacement project is computed by depreciating the capital stock of the hog fuel burner over the life of the project and computing the total rental cost to the firm of holding this capital stock, adding the operating and maintenance costs, all discounted to 1978. From these costs are subtracted equivalent costs of building and operating a fossil-fueled burner of the same capacity. This net cost is subtracted, each year, from the discounted private revenue due to savings in fossil fuel not consumed. (Our assumptions concerning future prices of oil and gas and of the inflation rate are discussed in Cox (1978).)

To compute the total value of the project to the economy as a whole we use a similar method, but use world prices for oil and gas and social opportunity costs for capital.

The "value" of a Gravity Packed Unit of wood waste (a GPU or Unit = 200 cubic feet) is computed by discounting and summing the total amount of hog fuel used over the life of the project and dividing that figure into the present value of the returns from the project. This value per unit of hog fuel represents the amount individual pulp and paper plants should be willing to pay for hog fuel delivered to the plant, including the costs of gathering and transporting wood waste. Ultimately, as fuel prices continue to rise, this value may cover the costs of yarding and hauling otherwise unmarketable timber from logging sites. Transportation costs covered by this private value of wood wastes will give us some idea of the potential supply of hog fuel in different locations.

While there are several categories of mills that could be used to facilitate a discussion of the results, we concentrate on two categories: (1) gas-consuming mills, located primarily in the interior and, therefore subject to wide seasonal oscillations in heat requirements; and (2) oil-consuming mills, all located on the milder southern coast. Our results are listed more comprehensively in Cox and Helliwell (1978).

The simulations indicate that the pulp and paper mills we have modeled have already reduced their fossil fuel consumption by about 15.6 billion cubic feet (bcf) of natural gas and 3.5 million barrels of oil each year, through the combustion of wood waste. We estimate that a further 19.9 bcf of natural gas could be saved each year through increased use of wood waste. Oil-consuming mills could save an additional 4.0 million barrels of heavy fuel oil each year. The total capital cost of the additional 600-psi hog-fuel-fired boilers necessary to displace as much fossil fuel as possible would be 248.4 million 1978 dollars.

The private, imputed value of a Unit of hog fuel burnt to displace natural gas, averaged over all gas-consuming mills, is $13.40. The equivalent value for oil-consuming mills is \$24.08. This large difference is, of course, due to the far lower price currently paid by the mills for a Btu from natural gas, compared to a Btu from oil. When natural gas is valued at its current export price of \$2.16 (US), or \$2.40 (Cdn.), per thousand cubic feet (mcf), hog fuel used to displace this fossil fuel is valued at \$22.29/Unit. Reduced oil consumption, valued at a Montreal landed price of \$15.00 (Cdn.) per barrel, results in an average value for wood waste of \$24.34/Unit.

We have examined the consequences of changing some of our assumptions. The effect of the two-year tax deduction for these projects as opposed to the conventional 20 percent declining balance write-off added only \$1.40 per Unit to the value of wood waste used to displace oil or natural gas. A recent undertaking by the federal government to cover 20 percent of the capital costs of certain hog fuel projects adds an additional \$1.80 to the value of wood waste.

Of much greater consequence is the deduction of the capital cost of an equivalent fossil-fueled burner from the capital costs of the hog fuel project. In making this deduction we implicitly assume that the mills require a new boiler to make up their full process heat requirements, and are free to choose between a hog fuel burner and a fossil fuel burner. Most mills are not faced with such a favorable situation. They already have, in addition to some stock of hog-fueled boiler equipment (at most mills), a functioning stock of fossil-fueled boilers which, in total, provide an adequate amount of heat for production requirements. The reduction in value of wood waste resulting from the introduction of the constraint on investment choices, represents the costs of investments made in response to the low prices of energy in the early years of this decade.

Removing the off-setting cost of a new fossil-fueled boiler reduces the weighted average value of wood waste at gas-consuming mills by \$4.17, to \$7.79 per Unit. For oil-consuming mills the reduction is \$3.79, to \$18.65 per Unit.

Our results do suggest, however, that only one mill may incur a loss due to the construction of an additional wood waste-fired boiler, even if no allowance is made for the cost of a fossil-fueled boiler. All other mills would receive a return greater than their cost of capital, provided that the total cost of collecting hog fuel did not exceed the present value of the project.

9.4 EVALUATING THE ECONOMICS OF ELECTRICITY GENERATION

In producing steam for their process heat requirements, pulp and paper mills can utilize the drop in pressure from the boiler to the production site to generate electricity. The greater the drop in pressure, the greater the amount of electricity that can be produced per pound of steam passed through the turbine on the way to the production site. Since the heat lost in condensation is attributed to the production process, the only thermal cost to generating electricity is that lost in the turbine itself, about 4,000 Btu per kilowatt hour (kwh). This follows the thermal cost indicated in Simons (1974). The amount of electricity that can be produced from a given boiler will depend upon the amount of steam required and, therefore, can vary over the course of a year, and from hour to hour.

In this section we evaluate the returns to the mills from purchasing 1250-psi boilers in order to increase the amount of electricity that the mill can produce. These higher pressure boilers will only be constructed as part of fossil fuel displacement projects; no new boilers will be built to upgrade lower pressure hog-fueled or chemical recovery boilers.

The private savings due to electricity not purchased are based on B.C. Hydro's projected industrial rates. By 1980 these rates will average about 1.5 cents per kwh in 1980 cents. These rates have already been announced since B.C. Hydro must set its bulk rates at least two years in advance. In addition to reduced purchases, revenue to the firm may also include, for the ten mills with at least occasional excess generating capacity, sales to the utility at its recently announced purchasing price of 0.8 cents per kwh in 1979.[1] The social value of electricity is based upon B.C. Hydro's cost of producing electricity from new projects, as estimated in Osler (1977) with some modifications. Here it is assumed that the utility's own estimates of the capital costs of future projects are accurate, and that it will not suffer the sorts of cost overruns that it has experienced in the recent past.

The weighted average cost of producing electricity from the remaining noncondensing capacity is 1.09 cents per kwh. Some mills, however, experience much higher than average costs of producing electricity. These mills already have large stocks of electricity generating facilities and of hog fuel-burning facilities assumed to be attached to 600-psi boilers. Such a configuration results in only small economies of scale being captured in generating equipment. Again, seasonal oscillations affect the profitability of this investment. For a discussion of the optimal investment strategy for these mills, see Helliwell and Cox (1979b). That paper also discusses, in a more exact manner, mill characteristics that affect the returns to electricity gener-

1. Reported in "Cost of 'Hog Fuel' Hydro to Increase," *Vancouver Sun*, April 4, 1978. Mills that produce large amounts of kraft pulp will often have large amounts of surplus electricity to sell, since kraft pulp requires relatively large amounts of heat and small amounts of electricity in its production. The relatively low price that B.C. Hydro has offered to pay for this electricity will result in smaller returns to the production of excess electricity.

ation. Eight mills cannot, under the current electricity pricing stucture, achieve a positive return to further investment in electricity generation projects.

Assuming only the choice between the 600- and 1250-psi boilers, and that firms choose the alternative with the highest present value (which, in eight cases, is doing nothing at all), we estimate that the pulp and paper industry could more than double its current electric generation capacity from 219.8 Megawatts to 543.7 Megawatts. With this additional capacity the mills could increase their energy production by 2.51 billion kwh to 4.32 billion kwh. The increase in capacity represents 4.5 percent of B.C. Hydro's installed capacity in the fiscal year 1977–1978. The increase in energy production represents 10.4 percent of the utility's total sales in British Columbia in that year, or about 40 percent of their bulk sales to industrial customers.

Of the ten mills that would find it profitable to produce electricity, the coastal mills would place an average value of $14.67 per Unit for wood waste used to generate electricity. Interior mills would obtain, on average, a value of $11.50 per Unit.

The weighted average value of hog fuel used to generate electricity from all eighteen possible projects is about $7.40 per Unit. However, if we compute the benefits to these projects based on the replacement cost of electricity, the value of a Unit of wood waste rises to $32.00. If the mills actually bought and sold electricity at this price, all but two would find it profitable to add to their cogeneration capability. Six previously uninterested mills would add 105 Megawatts of generating capacity, and three other mills would choose higher pressure boilers. This would bring the total, profitable, generating capacity, restricted only by the continued existence of some lower pressure chemical recovery boilers, to almost 650 Megawatts.

We have estimated the effect of the current two-year tax write-off for noncondensing generators as well as some other programs designed to overcome the discouraging effect that the current price structure has on investment in cogeneration projects. Accelerated tax write-offs and 20 percent capital cost subsidies for new boilers increased the value of wood waste, in this use, by almost $8.00, resulting in a per Unit value of hog fuel that is almost four times greater than if no such subsidies or accelerated tax write-offs existed. The value of wood waste used in this manner, however, never rises above one-third of what it would be if mills paid the replacement value of the electricity that they consumed, and received that price for the surplus electricity that they sold.

There are possibilities for increasing electricity production still further, although we do not evaluate them here. These possibilities include the conversion of recovery boilers to 1250 psi, or the upgrading of all boilers to still higher pressures from which more noncondensing electricity can be produced per thousand pounds of process steam.

9.5 ENERGY PRICING AND WOOD WASTE SUPPLY

Any estimate of the potential for fossil fuel and electricity savings depends on the available supply of wood waste. The supply of wood waste in British Columbia has been characterized by shortages on the coast and surpluses in the interior of the province.[2] Table 9–1 lists, for seven regions, hog fuel production in 1980 as predicted in Reid, Collins, and Associates (1978), and our estimates of the hog fuel required to displace fossil fuel and to produce the maximum noncondensing electricity available at pulp and paper mills in these regions. Figure 9–1 shows the location of these regions. For each region, we also indicate the surpluses (or deficits) of hog fuel. This computation takes account of only the demand for hog fuel from the pulp and paper mills if they were to displace as much fossil fuel as possible, and generate as much electricity as could be obtained from noncondensing turbines and 1250-psi boilers.

The next step is to analyze the scope for shipping hog fuel between regions. Tables 9–2 and 9–3 present, for each region in the province, the distances that hog fuel could be transported at a cost equal to various imputed private values of wood waste used for fossil fuel displacement or electricity generation. Each of the columns represents one of four modes of transport: a truck averaging twenty-five mph, a truck averaging forty mph, rail, or barge. Costs of transportation by truck are computed assuming an hourly rental cost in 1978 of $31.00 per hour. Rail transport charges are computed assuming a cost of $0.05 per ton per mile. Trucking and rail prices are those quoted by companies involved. Barging costs assume a fixed loading and unloading cost of $5.00 per Unit and a transportation cost of $0.04 per Unit per mile. This is based on charges quoted by barging companies in Vancouver and by one pulp and paper mill owner. These costs are considerably higher than the 0.6 cents per ton-mile estimated as the average cost of barging in the U.S. (Case and Lave, 1970).

2. Two reports by Reid, Collins, and Associates (1974, 1978) list hog fuel production in various regions of the province. In the latter report, the estimated hog fuel production for 1976 was over 28 percent greater than production in 1973, as reported in the earlier report. The projection of supplies in 1980 in the Southern Coast Region doubled, apparently because in the earlier report the authors overestimated the amount of sawdust and shavings that would be used in the production of pulp.

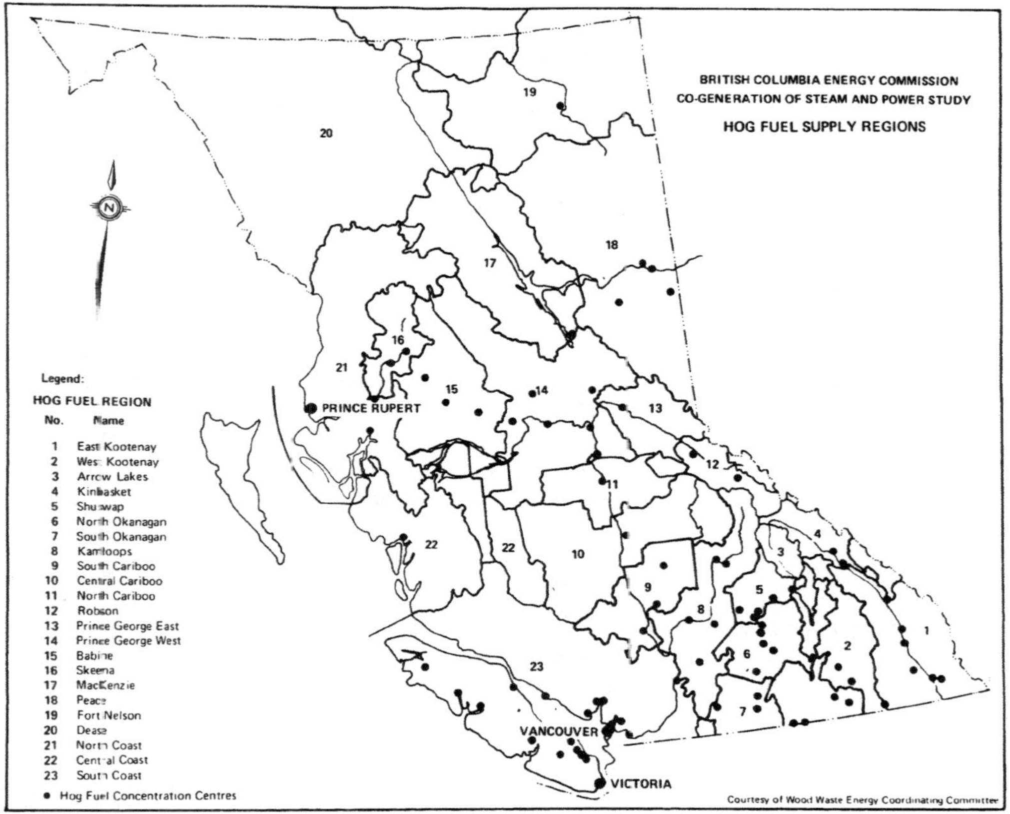

FIGURE 9-1. Hog fuel supply regions

TABLE 9–1. Wood waste supply and demand in seven regions of British Columbia

Zones	(1) Mills	(2) Current use of Wood Waste (10^3 GPU/yr.)	(3) Wood Waste Required for Displacement of of fossil fuel (10^3 GPU/yr.)	(4) Additional Wood Waste Required for Electricity (All power boilers at 1250 psi) (10^3 GPU/yr.)	(5) Total Wood Waste Demand (Total of columns 2, 3, and 4.) (10^3 GPU/yr.)
Southern Coast Zone					
Estimated wood waste production in 1980: 3,805 10^3 GPU/yr.					
	Crofton	113	415	167	695
	Elk Falls	227	341	176	744
	Harmac	208	291	168	667
	Port Alberni	354	111	127	592
	Port Alice	47	234	60	341
	Port Mellon	101	142	79	322
	Powell River	238	197	121	556
	Tahsis	81	96	74	251
	Woodfibre	108	210	87	405
	Totals	1,477	2,037	1,059	4,573
Estimated deficit of wood waste in 1980: 768 10^3 GPU/yr.					
Northern Coast and Skeena Zone					
Estimated wood waste production in 1980: 490 10^3 GPU/yr.					
	Kitimat	0	286	110	396
	Prince Rupert	103	384	160	647
	Totals	103	670	270	1,043

Estimated deficit of wood waste in 1980: 553 10^3 GPU/yr.				
Kamloops, South Cariboo, Shuswap Zones				
Estimated wood waste production in 1980: 1,097 10^3 GPU/yr.				
Kamloops	272	157	148	577
Estimated surplus of wood waste in 1980: 511 10^3 GPU/yr.				
West Kootenay, Arrow Lakes Zone				
Estimated wood waste production in 1980: 534 10^3 GPU/yr.				
Castlegar	117	62	65	304
Estimated surplus of wood waste in 1980: 230 10^3 GPU/yr.				
East Kootenay, Kinbasket Zones				
Estimated wood waste production in 1980: 489 10^3 GPU/yr.				
Skookumchuk	0	119	49	168
Estimated surplus of wood waste in 1980: 321 10^3 GPU/yr.				
Central and North Cariboo Zones				
Estimated wood waste production in 1980: 982 10^3 GPU/yr.				
Quesnel	172	72	94	338
Estimated surplus of wood waste in 1980: 644 10^3 GPU/yr.				
Prince George, East and West Zones				
Estimated wood waste production in 1980: 1,740 10^3 GPU/yr.				
Northwood	28	201	84	313
Prince George	156	358	178	692
Totals	184	559	262	1,005
Estimated surplus of wood waste in 1980: 735 10^3 GPU/yr.				

TABLE 9–2. Transportation distances covered by fossil fuel replacement value of hog fuel

Zone	(1)	(2)	(3)	(4)	(5)	(6)
	With Credit for Fossil Fuel Burner			Without Credit for Fossil Fuel Burner		
	By Slow Truck (Miles)	By Fast Truck (Miles)	By Rail (Barge) (Miles)	By Slow Truck (Miles)	By Fast Truck (Miles)	By Rail (Barge) (Miles)
Southern Coast Zones	377	566	(465)	294	440	(349)
Northern Coast and Skeena Zone	234	351	(258)	161	243	(150)
Kamloops, South Cariboo, Shuswap Zones	170	255	162	56	84	46
West Kootenay, Arrow Lakes Zones	117	175	83	0	0	0
East Kootenay, Kinbasket Zones	266	399	173	183	275	122
Central and North Cariboo Zones	173	259	116	50	75	42
Prince George, East and West Zones	173	259	116	70	105	54

Table 9–2 lists these distances for wood waste used to displace natural gas or oil. It is divided into two parts, using values of wood waste burned in a new steam plant, the cost of which is (1) partly offset by an equivalent fossil fuel burner or, (2) not offset by an equivalent fossil fuel burner.

Using the lower imputed value, mills in the Southern Coast Region could still afford to barge wood wastes for considerable distances within the region or from other regions, with some residual value left over for hauling hog fuel over land to the coast. The trucking distance for this region indicates that almost any mill in the region could have access to any source of wood waste in the region.

In the Northern Coast Region the transportation range for fossil fuel replacement is reduced by about 50 percent by the low price of natural gas, varying with the mode of transport considered. In addition, the lack of an accounting credit for a new natural gas burner results in an additional drop of 25 to 35 percent in each transportation radius. The value of hog fuel used to replace fossil fuel is high enough to barely cover transportation costs from the Babine Region. It is estimated, in Reid, Collins, and Associates

TABLE 9-3. Transportation distances covered by electricity generation value of hog fuel

Zone	*(1)*	*(2)*	*(3)*	*(4)*	*(5)*	*(6)*
	Adding to Current Generating Capacity			*Assuming No Current Generating Capacity*		
	By Slow Truck (Miles)	*By Fast Truck (Miles)*	*By Rail (Barge) (Miles)*	*By Slow Truck (Miles)*	*By Fast Truck (Miles)*	*By Rail (Barge) (Miles)*
Southern Coast Zones						
Crofton	280	419	(328)	290	436	(344)
Elk Falls	289	433	(342)	292	438	(345)
Harmac	0	0	0	148	221	(128)
Port Alberni	0	0	0	278	417	(325)
Port Alice	0	0	0	80	120	(26)
Port Mellon	44	66	0	33	50	0
Powell River	0	0	0	275	413	(321)
Tahsis	162	243	(150)	166	249	(156)
Woodfibre	94	141	(47)	118	178	(84)
Wtd. Avg.	209	313	(265)	210	316	(252)
Northern Coast and Skeena Zone						
Kitimat	252	379	286	269	403	312
Prince Rupert	0	0	0	182	273	122
Wtd. Avg.				217	325	234
Kamloops, South Cariboo, Shuswap Zones						
Kamloops	0	0	0	198	298	132
West Kootenay, Arrow Lakes Zones						
Castlegar	150	226	103	150	226	103
East Kootenay, Kinbasket Zones						
Skookumchuk	150	226	103	150	226	103
Central and North Cariboo Zones						
Quesnel	0	0	0	134	200	93
Prince George, East and West Zones						
Northwood	0	0	0	171	260	116
Prince George	210	314	138	210	314	138
Wtd. Avg.				197	296	131

(1978) that the Babine Region will produce 590,000 Units of wood waste per year in 1980, enough to completely offset the deficit in wood wastes in the Northern Coast and Skeena Regions. All other regions of the province are likely to have some surplus wood waste production.

The effects of electricity pricing are more interesting and more complex. Electricity, as it is priced in 1978, results in the value of wood waste used to produce electricity being considerably lower than its value to displace fossil fuel. A cost of acquiring hog fuel much greater than zero results in no electricity being generated.

At the other end of the range of possibilities is the pricing of electricity at B.C. Hydro's cost of electricity from new projects. Such a price would result in a greater private value for hog fuel used in electricity generation than in fossil fuel displacement.

Under B.C. Hydro's announced price structure for 1980, electricity may be profitably cogenerated in regions that have large amounts of wood waste available. However, mills in regions in which there is currently an apparent deficit cannot undertake more extended searches for wood waste. Were electricity prices high enough to increase the value of wood waste, in this use, to a level equal to or above the value of wood waste used to generate heat alone, the profit maximizing mill would collect all the wood waste that it could, at the latter price, to both replace fossil fuel consumption and to generate electricity.

The effect of electricity prices on the demand for wood wastes is explicitly demonstrated in Table 9-3, which lists transportation distances in both an idealized "greenfield" case (i.e., with no current stock of power boilers or generators) and in the case of mills adding to their current electric generation stock. For the oil-consuming mills in the Southern Coast Region, the value of wood waste used to displace relatively expensive oil exceeds its value for the production of electricity under B.C. Hydro's current rate structure. The extent to which fossil fuel displacement dominates electricity production depends on the current structure of the power plant at the mill.

Thus, Tables 9-1, 9-2, and 9-3 indicate that, in the Southern Coast Region, the estimated supply of hog fuel is large enough to displace oil used in the power boilers, with the value of that wood waste being large enough to justify transporting it betwen any two points within the region. However, several mills in this region, already mentioned, are not likely to add to their electrical generating capacity.

In the Northern Coast and Skeena Regions, Table 9-1 indicates that the two mills there will experience a shortage of hog fuel in their regions if they attempt more than a 70-percent conversion to wood waste utilization for natural gas displacement, but have some possibility (from Table 9-2) of transporting hog fuel from the Babine Region. Table 9-3 indicates that the mill at Kitimat would also be able to purchase some wood waste from the Babine region for the production of electricity.

In the other regions of the province, supplies are adequate to permit full use of hog fuel without any hog fuel being shipped between regions. While supplies of wood waste appear to be adequate in the interior, the low cost of natural gas results in low transportation distances for that fuel's substitution. The electricity price structure, particularly for electricity sold to B.C. Hydro, reduces the transportation distance to zero for four interior mills, though others appear to have a large economic incentive to transport hog fuel for the production of electricity.

9.6 CONCLUSIONS

We have discussed some aspects of energy production from an industrial by-product in one industry. We have examined several considerations that affect the profitability of such projects to the firm: (1) previous investment decisions, (2) energy prices, (3) special tax provisions and federal initiatives, and (4) wood waste supply. The most important is the cost of energy. Fuel and electricity prices that reflect the future costs of supply provide ample return to investment in hog fuel projects. This return is large enough to overcome the second major obstacle to such investments; that of the existing stock of fossil-fueled burners and lower pressure boilers. This obstacle will eventually be removed as old boilers have to be replaced, leaving the value of wood waste to rise to a value limited by its relative burning efficiency, relative capital costs, operating and maintenance costs, and the price of conventional energy sources.

The impact of tax and expenditure incentives is insubstantial in fossil fuel replacement projects. These financial tools play a far smaller role than do required energy prices. The impact of these federal initiatives is far more noticeable in electricity cogeneration projects. However, we are again forced to conclude, from a comparison of the social returns and the private returns to the electricity projects, that a pricing schedule more closely in line with B.C. Hydro's replacement cost of electricity would encourage a more appropriate pattern of investment in electricity cogeneration projects.

We finished by looking at the regional balances of hog fuel demand and supply. While shortages appear to exist in some areas of the province, indicating the need for some shipment between regions, it is important to point out that the supplies estimated to date have been based on a low (or zero) price for hog fuel. As the value of wood waste as an energy source comes to be better recognized, and potential users become willing to pay more for this material, more of it will become available.

REFERENCES

Department of Energy, Mines and Resources. 1976. *An energy strategy for Canada,* Ottawa.

Case, L. S., and Lave L. B. 1970. Cost functions for inland waterways transport in the U.S. *Journal of Transport Economics and Policy* 4:181–191.

Cox, A. J. 1978. An economic evaluation of the use of wood wastes to generate heat and electricity at pulp and paper mills in British Columbia. Resources Paper No. 20, Programme in Natural Resource Economics, University of British Columbia.

Cox, A. J., and Helliwell, J. F. 1978. Economic modeling of energy supply from burning wood waste at B.C. pulp and paper mills. Resources Paper No. 21, Programme in Natural Resource Economics, University of British Columbia.

Helliwell, J. F., and Cox, A. J. 1979a. Wood waste as an energy source for the British Columbia pulp and paper industry: Economic implications and institutional barriers. In *Energy policy: The global challenge,* ed. P. N. Nemetz. Montreal: Institute for Research in Public Policy.

Helliwell, J. F., and Cox, A. J. 1979b. Electricity pricing and electricity supply: The influence of utility pricing on electricity production by pulp and paper mills. *Resources and Energy* 1: No. 3.

Helliwell, J. F., and Cox, A. J. 1978. Simulation analysis of energy production in the British Columbia pulp and paper industry. Proceedings of *Simulation, modeling and decision in energy systems,* sponsored by the International Association of Science and Technology for Development, Acta Press, Calgary.

Osler, S. L. 1977. An application of marginal cost pricing principles to B.C. Hydro. Resources Paper No. 12, Programme in Natural Resource Economics, University of British Columbia.

Reid, Collins, and Associates. 1974. *The availability of hog fuel for generation of thermal power in British Columbia,* Vancouver: B.C. Hydro and Power Authority.

Reid, Collins, and Associates. 1978. *Hog fuel availability in British Columbia for the co-generation of steam and power.* Vancouver: British Columbia Energy Commission.

H. A. Simons (Int.) Ltd. 1974. *British Columbia pulp and paper industrial electrical energy report.* Report for B.C. Hydro and Power Authority, Vancouver.

10 SIMULATION OF TAR SANDS MINING OPERATIONS*†

F. Paul Wyman

The energy crisis is upon us and new sources of energy must be tapped. One such pool is the vast reserves of the Athabasca Tar Sands in Alberta, Canada. Of the estimated 600 billion barrels of oil locked in the sands, 300 billion barrels are deemed recoverable. The problem has been to extract the oil by a method both feasible and economic.

Syncrude Canada Limited is to mine this raw material plus overburden at a rate of approximately 150 million tons annually in order to extract 125,000 bbl/day of bitumen. The tarsand must ultimately be moved several miles to an extraction plant. The mining scheme decision involved a capital cost in excess of half a billion dollars.

The productivity of five mining schemes, four using bucket wheel excavators and one using draglines, was investigated in 1973 using dynamic simulation. The simulation models, written in GPSS V and Fortran, consisted of five

*This paper documents work which was the result of the efforts of employees of the Bechtel Group as well as Syncrude Canada, Ltd. Special acknowledgement is given to Harold J. Helfand, who led the simulation task described herein. Other members of the simulation team included Pat Brennan, Daniel Dunne, Harvey Elwin, Neil O'Henley, and the author. The paper was also reviewed and corrected by Syncrude Canada, Ltd.

†This paper is reprinted from *Interfaces* vol. 8, no. 1, Part 2 (November 1977): 6–20 with the permission of the author and publisher.

essentially independent modules: mining, transportation, storage, extraction, and weather. Approximately ten runs were made for each scheme. Factors investigated included mining procedures, equipment availability, and equipment sizes.

The simulation runs were a major factor in the final selection of the mining scheme. For the plan selected, numerous sensitivity runs were performed to improve details of the mining design. The model continues to be a valuable tool in debottlenecking and the on-going refinement of the mining scheme.

10.1 INTRODUCTION

For decades it has been known that vast quantities of crude oil are locked in the Athabasca Tar Sands of Canada. Estimates run up to 600 billion barrels with the recoverable volume estimated at 300 billion barrels. The latter is roughly one-fourth of Saudi Arabia's presently known oil reserves. With the energy crisis growing in significance each year it has been crucial to initiate development of this resource.

This paper reports a case study of successful application of the Management Science technique of dynamic simulation to the process of selecting, checking, and refining the design of the mining equipment to be used by Syncrude Canada Limited. Syncrude is a consortium of several government and oil companies, authorized by the Alberta Government to design and implement petroleum recovery, upgrading, and pipeline facilities for the Mildred Lake Project, near Fort McMurray in Alberta. Canadian Bechtel Limited was retained to manage detailed engineering and construction work. Initially Bechtel evaluated the base case mining concept. This scheme was found to require modification in order to meet the production goals under the unique conditions of tar sand mining. The Management Science contribution performed by Bechtel was to estimate the system availabilities and production levels of several mining conditions. Extensive details were built into each model to reflect the blockages and maintenance activities that would occur in actual operations. Moreover, the facility to handle variations in the ore grade and reject materials was built into the model. The simulation activity achieved credibility by incorporating mining details, meeting tight schedules, and producing realistic and consistent results in response to numerous sensitivity tests requested by mining engineers. The Syncrude Project startup date depended upon the timing of the order of mining equipment, due to a three- to four-year lead time. Simulation helped to resolve doubts and to establish a consensus on the equipment selection decision. The risk of delaying the entire two billion dollar project due to mining equipment selection was thereby greatly reduced.

The results of all the design and simulation effort culminated in a comparison of five schemes, which were carefully considered during a crucial meeting to choose the final plan to be presented to Syncrude. The equipment was selected based on the simulation indications of productivity and on capital and operating costs. This equipment selection contributed to Bechtel's role in both the engineering design and construction management of this project.

10.2 HISTORICAL BACKGROUND

10.2.1 History of the Tarsands

Since the days of early explorers, there has been interest in the outcrops of oil sand along the Athabasca River in the north part of Province of Alberta in Canada. This mixture of sand and heavy oil, the Athabasca Tar Sands, lies under an area of some 12,000 square miles near the town of Fort McMurray. In some places the Athabasa Tar Sands are shallow enough to allow recovery by surface mining. Smaller tar sand deposits are in the vicinity of Cold Lake and Peace River, but the tarsand is buried 2000 feet below the ground, and requires other recovery methods. According to the Alberta government more than 26 billion barrels of synthetic crude oil are presently recoverable by surface mining. Advanced mining techniques might recover 60 billion barrels more. By using the "in situ" techniques of forced hot water injection and/or burning, up to 200 billion barrels may be recovered by conventional drilling operations. Out of the known 600 billion barrel of reserves, 300 billion are thought to be recoverable.

For several decades the tar sands were not developed due to the high cost per barrel relative to ordinary crude. Moreover, early attempts at oil recovery from the tar sands were not economically feasible primarily because of their limited scale. But in the 1960s, Great Canadian Oil Sands (GCOS) initiated development of surface mining, extraction, and crude upgrading facilities. This project came into production in 1967, long before the pressures of the Arab oil embargo. The GCOS plant was designed to produce 45,000 barrels of crude oil per day, but it took several years of experience and development to reach this level of production. Now it has achieved 70,000 barrels on peak days.

10.2.2 Syncrude Canada Limited

Since the 1950s Cities-Service Athabasca (now Syncrude Canada Limited) has invested a great deal of time and effort in considering mining plans for the Lake Mildred site. The charge of Syncrude was to develop and execute the engineering plan for mining the tarsand, extracting the bitumen, and upgrading bitumen to synthetic crude oil. Several tradeoffs had to be considered, such as excavation capacity, maintenance, ore movement, economies of scale, ease of operations, and so forth. The equipment considered had included shovels and trucks, bucketwheels like those in the GCOS scheme, scrapers, and draglines. After extensive proceedings, the Alberta Government, in 1971, gave Syncrude authorization to develop a plant to produce up to 125,000 barrels per day of synthetic crude oil.

10.2.3 Canadian Bechtel Limited

At this point Canadian Bechtel Limited was selected as contract manager for the detailed engineering and construction management. Bechtel was chosen for its refinery and mining expertise as well as its experience as the engineering, procurement and construction manager of the GCOS facility. Bechtel's initial task was to carefully examine the Syncrude mining scheme and to suggest modifications, if necessary, prior to ordering the mining equipment. This activity began in early 1972.

10.3 TECHNICAL BACKGROUND

10.3.1 Scope and Significance of the Syncrude Project

Because of the lengthy proceedings required to obtain government approval of a large-scale plant, the basic design criterion was whether production could be met. Capacity had to be sufficient to produce the authorized 125,000 barrels per day while minimizing the equipment and operating costs.

One can readily appreciate the importance of continuous flow of ore material by considering the scale factor. Roughly two tons of acceptable grade tarsand are required to produce one barrel of crude. The volume equivalent of one day's production would cover a football field nearly forty yards deep. Excluding the overburden and reject (low grade) materials, there must be an average flow of 1.65 cubic yards of tarsand per second over the twenty-five-year life of the mine. The capital required is large too. The present estimated cost of the total project is on the order of two billion dollars. The mining and extraction plant represent more than half a billion dollars.

10.3.2 Syncrude's Base Case Mining Scheme

The large volume of material to be handled requires large scale mining equipment and a transportation system capable of commensurate volume and high reliability. Figures 10–1 and 10–2 illustrate dragline and bucketwheel equipment which are two of the main alternatives for large-scale surface mining. Draglines function by dragging a huge bucket into the side of an embankment of ore material. Then the draglines lift and swing the bucket filled with ore to a pile and drop it there. Draglines in the scale foreseen weigh several thousand tons to balance the long boom and bucket. A bucketwheel excavator (BWE) uses a large wheel with bucket attached to the edge. When the wheel revolves, the buckets scoop the material, lift it up and dump it out on a conveyor moving away from the wheel.

Draglines are attractive due to their ability to drop overburden and reject directly into the area previously mined while bucketwheels require transportation of this material over long distances. However, bucketwheel excavation (in use by GCOS) was the only proven mining scheme for tarsand. Syncrude had specified two large draglines plus a dedicated train in its base case mining scheme in late 1971.

During 1972 close examination of the dragline/train scheme by Syncrude and Bechtel revealed potential problems. In the severe winter conditions, the tarsand hardens, making the material more difficult to dig. Productivity declines because the cold weather affects both workers and equipment. Moreover, it was questionable whether large draglines were sufficiently selective to discriminate layers of reject or ore materials as thin as five feet.[1] The draglines dig out the ore and pile it behind them in a "windrow." Large bucketwheels were to reclaim and move the ore from the windrow to a waiting train. The interface between the continuous mining and the batch train process could result in excessive blockages. For example, the dragline could be blocked if the pile behind it were so small as to interfere with the reclaimer. In addition, productivity of the specified draglines was in doubt.

1. This concern was a significant part of the motivation underlying the requirement that mine ore data inputs allow layers of varying thickness.

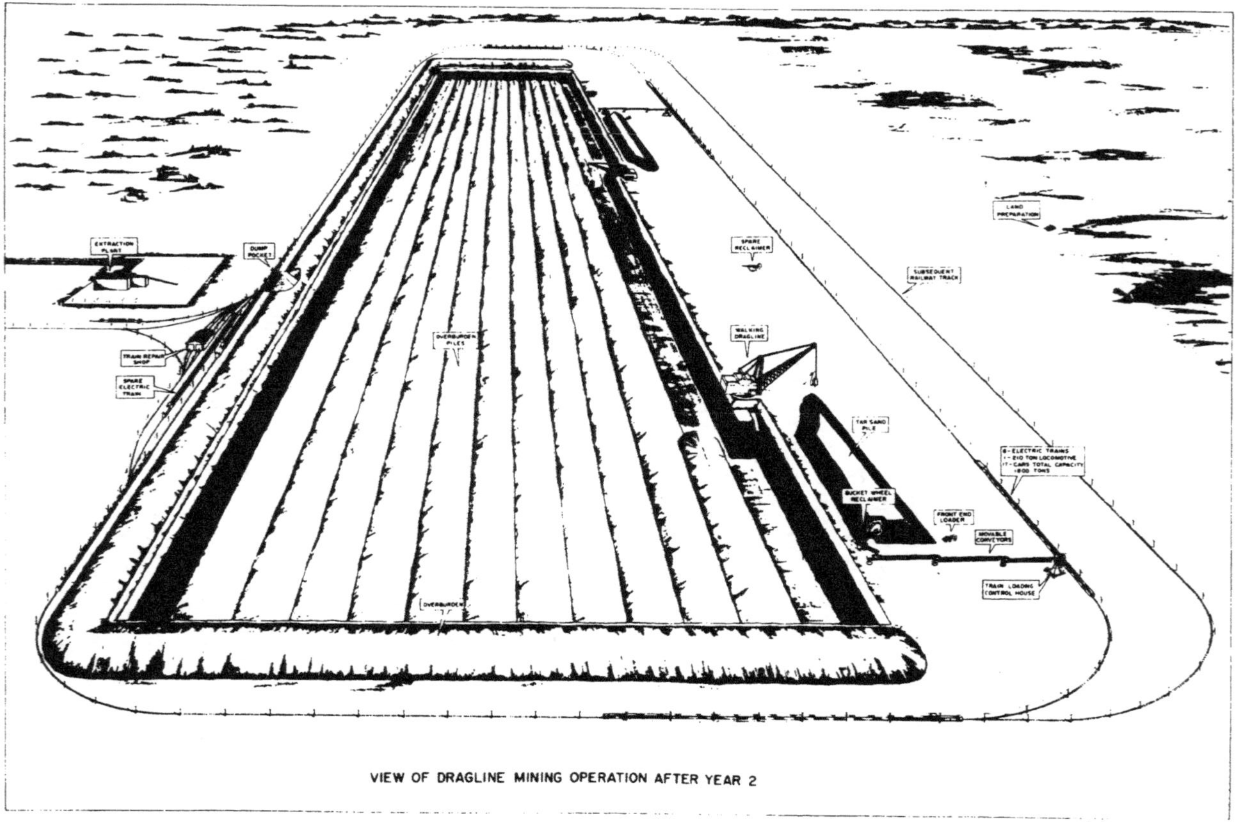

FIGURE 10–1. Dragline excavation illustration

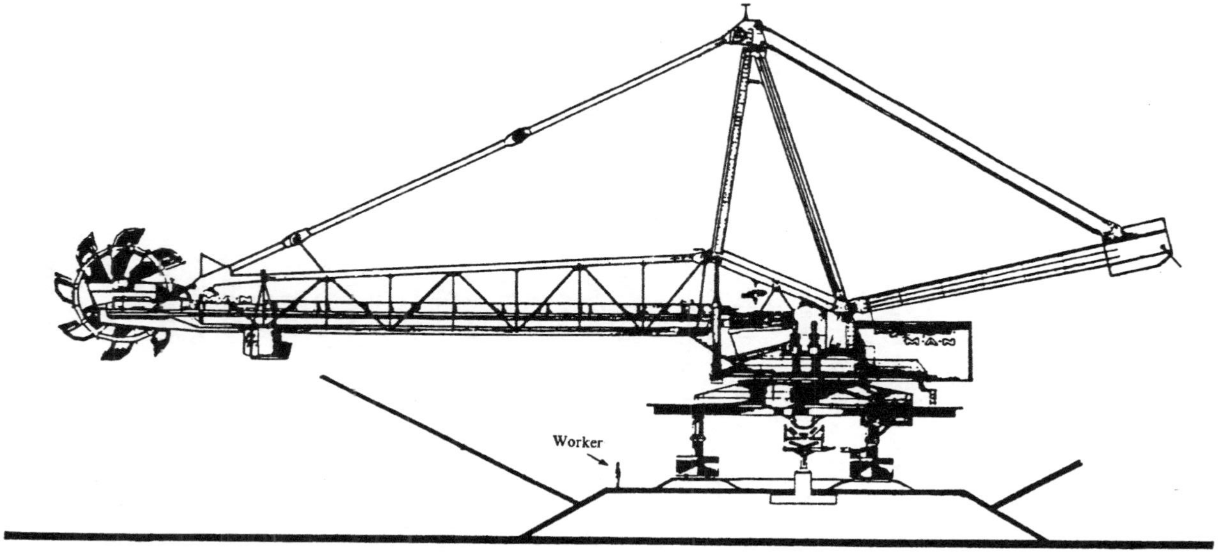

FIGURE 10–2. Bucketwheel excavator illustration

Test results of a seventeen-cubic yard dragline in actual operation in winter conditions in 1972–1973 substantiated some of the anticipated productivity problems. To remedy these problems several changes were contemplated including more but smaller draglines, conveyor transportation, different pit designs, etc. However, time was growing short.

10.3.3 Use of Simulation

Syncrude had been using a simulation program for some time to model the dragline/train operations. Bechtel came on the job in 1972 and evaluated the base scheme. This led to a consideration of a bucketwheel scheme as a contingency while the original scheme was being revised, since a delay in the final definition of the mining scheme could delay the entire project schedule. Three to four years are required to procure and erect large draglines.

The alternative scheme was a combination of bucketwheel excavators and a conveyor transportation system. This scheme provided a continuous flow process, but it was still possible that system availability might be too low because of the serial connection of several miles of conveyors. To improve availability, creative schemes of maintenance were suggested, and a surge pile was planned between the conveyor system and the extraction plant.

Betchel proposed the use of dynamic simulation to investigate the total system availability and production level of the several versions of the bucketwheel scheme being considered. It also became increasingly apparent that the mining equipment selection was on the critical path of the entire project. In mid-1973 pressure was also growing because Syncrude was to tell the Alberta government by August 31 whether the project would proceed. Considering all the complexities involved, Syncrude determined that simulation was a desirable way to rapidly study blockages and bottlenecks, and to size the bucketwheel equipment appropriately. However, the existing simulation model was not sufficiently flexible to incorporate bucketwheel excavators and conveyors, or to accommodate significant alterations to the dragline scheme. At this point the equipment ordering deadline was only a few months away. In order to make the recommendation, Syncrude needed solid evidence of at least on a workable scheme. Therefore Bechtel was given approval by Syncrude to develop a new dynamic simulation model in a seven-week period for the 105,000 barrel per day bucketwheel excavator scheme.

10.4 SIMULATION EFFORT

10.4.1 Magnitude of the Simulation Task

In order to appreciate the implications of a seven-week development schedule, the reader must understand the scope of detail required. Conventional availability models had been considered but found incapable of reflecting geological variation of the mine. The schemes were complex systems of several bucketwheels or draglines plus a conveyor network ultimately several miles in length. In bucketwheel schemes, the reject and tarsand must be moved by conveyor, and therefore different routing for ore and reject must be provided. This requires consideration of complex sequences of events that result in varying rates of flow through the mining and extraction system. For example, when a conveyor belt fails, the adjacent equipment may also have to stop operating. If scheduled maintenance is nearly due on the idled equipment, it may be performed ahead of schedule, resulting in somewhat higher total system availability. How much higher is difficult to determine except by simulation. Over each year simulated, the model traced each event that changed the rate of material flow through each piece of equipment. The final code was 2200 lines of GPSS V plus 2100 lines of FORTAN IV, and the schedule included systems analysis, design, coding, debugging, and testing. Technical details of the model are discussed in Appendix A (section 10.6).

10.4.2 Task Organization, Consensus and Credibility

In order to meet the seven-week deadline it was critical to establish efficient teamwork procedures. Activities were scheduled by days with manhours and computer costs budgeted for each activity.

The simulation model was organized into five modules: Mining; Transportation; Storage; Extraction; and Weather. Nontechnical flowcharts were developed for each module. A sample page is shown in Figure 10-3. These flowcharts were presented in step-by-step detail to the Syncrude and Bechtel engineers in Edmonton. When in error, flowcharts were corrected on the spot. This process required two full days of a large joint meeting. In this way, each engineer had an opportunity to voice his concerns and determine whether more detail should be added to the model. This activity provided a foundation of consensus which was to be critical during the simulation task.

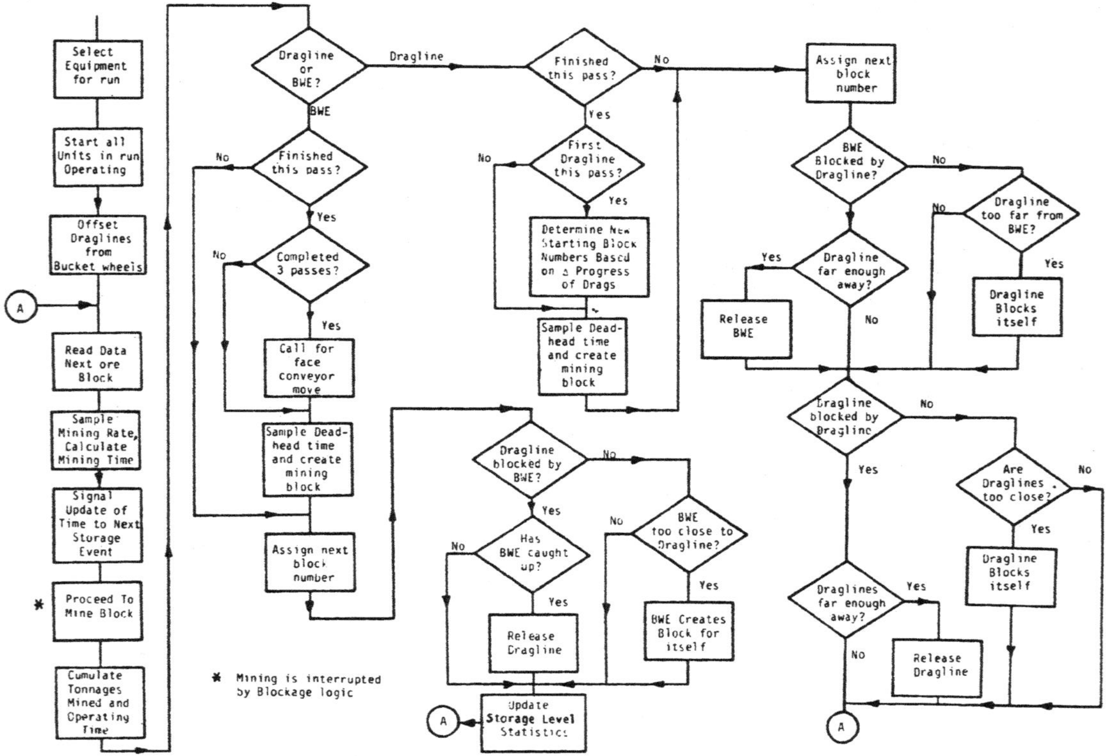

FIGURE 10–3. Nontechnical flowchart example (mining model)

Weekly one-page progress reports were issued to key Bechtel management and Syncrude client representatives showing percent completion and resources expended. This practice (in addition to the engineering involvement) helped to reassure our management and clients and to build credibility during a near-crisis period.

Modular program development is frequently claimed but not as frequently achieved. In this case it was successfully achieved because of the careful design of communications between modules plus the sheer enforcement of programming rules to avoid conflicts between modules. Communications were absolutely minimized, even at the expense of program inefficiencies to reduce possibility of logic errors when the modules were assembled. The pivotal device of enforcement involved the use of a Project Control Book, which was a record of variable names, arrays, labels, and transactions. The first programmer to register his resource requirements or communication conventions in the Control Book was given priority in case of conflict.

It was clear that Bechtel, Syncrude, and the consortium members took the simulation effort seriously. First, Bechtel's tarsand mining engineer most experienced in simulation was flown in to systematically scrutinize the model development. Next, Syncrude and Atlantic Richfield (ARCO) sent engineers to monitor Bechtel's simulation work. At each point of determining policy for the program logic these engineers were on call to suggest the proper details for correctly modeling the mining operations. Once the modules were coded, the team of five analyst/programmers went on split-shift to keep program development in progress twenty-four hours a day. Work weeks of sixty to seventy hours were typical during the compilation and debugging stage. The most serious program logic bug required one week to correct. It involved two simultaneous GPSS events, occurring in an illogical sequence. Because of the extremely small probability of such an occurrence, the problem did not appear until the model had simulated a full year of operations and consumed twenty-five minutes of computer time. Despite this difficulty the model for the alternative mining scheme was completed in seven weeks.

10.4.3 Model Change Requests

Because of the need to rapidly evaluate changes in the dragline case, Syncrude requested Bechtel to modify the simulation program to evaluate the revised mining scheme, which included four smaller draglines, bucketwheel reclaimers (BWR) and conveyor transportation. The simulation group responded in three weeks time and was then requested to perform three additional modifications to the bucketwheel excavator mining scheme.

10.4.4 Model Descriptions

The five models are briefly summarized in Appendix B (section 10.7). Each was run to test the sensitivity of several factors:

- failure time variability;
- winter startup times;
- fifteen-foot layers instead of five-foot;
- conveyor availability of 93 percent versus 97 percent;
- changes of bench height;
- seventh and thirteenth year of ore data;
- reclaimer rate;
- extraction rate;
- random number seeds;
- number of serial connections of collecting conveyors;
- overlapped maintenance; and
- bench priorities for the radial stacker.

Approximately ten combinations of factors were run for each model. Because of extensive participation of mining engineers from Bechtel, Syncrude and ARCO during the programming stage, as well as during the initial flowcharting of concepts, the simulation results were generally accepted as definitive once any anomalies due to errors in input were corrected.

10.5 SELECTION OF MINING EQUIPMENT

10.5.1 The Bechtel/Syncrude Meeting

Prior to reporting the recommendation to Syncrude's Mining Subcommittee, project personnel from both Bechtel and Syncrude agreed to meet to consider the entire set of data and to decide jointly upon the scheme to be recommended to Syncrude's participants. The staff engineers advocating each scheme carefully presented and summarized the positive and negative aspects, qualitative as well as quantitative, for each plan. The simulation had shown that a feasible scheme existed for meeting production using draglines and a scheme using bucketwheels. It also showed that the amount of equipment required in the BWE scheme resulted in higher capital and operating costs. This difference had not been anticipated prior to the simulation work. Nevertheless, the fact remained that the GCOS bucketwheel concept was still the only scheme proven by actual experience for tarsand mining. After considerable deliberation the consensus of the meeting was to recommend the dragline scheme to the Syncrude Management and participants. The significance of this recommendation was shown by the fact that shortly afterward, the mining equipment was ordered.

10.5.2 Impact of the Decision

Needless to say, the impact on the equipment suppliers was considerable, for both successful and unsuccessful companies. The impact on the state of the art of actual mining practice was to establish a new scheme for mining tar sand. The impact upon Bechtel, as construction manager, was to help relieve the most constraining activity on the project's critical path, thereby avoiding delay of project startup because of the mining equipment lead time. The impact upon Syncrude was most significant because selection of mining equipment of this order of magnitude is practically an irreversible decision once it is made. Syncrude was fully aware of this fact and had spent ten years in extensive deliberation upon the question. The simulation was useful in helping to estimate production capability under detailed engineering considerations while also showing the most economical balance of equipment sizes to achieve that production.

10.5.3 Subsequent and Future Use of the Model

Once the mining scheme had been selected, the dragline base case model was used for thirty-two sensitivity test runs to further refine the mining plan. The analysis showed the system production to be rather insensitive to single factors but sensitive to combinations of factors such as the surge pile size, conveyor flexibility, equipment capacities, and equipment availabilities. The need for the planned conveyor capacity was substantiated. It was possible to see how effects of individual changes are damped by the effect of interactions with other parts of the system. For example, increased conveyor availablility may increase BWR hours available but not necessarily production since the extraction plant capacity may become limiting. This was highly dependent on inputs used.

The model was recently modified to estimate hourly power consumption of the mining and extraction equipment. It continues to be used for planning the details of balancing the operations. It is to be used as a de-bottle-necking and long-range planning tool as the actual equipment capacities and availabilities become known.

10.6 APPENDIX A

10.6.1 Details of the Model Design

The basic modeling philosophy of the simulation was briefly perplexing due to the fact that the underlying process involved continuous flows of ore and reject materials interrupted by both scheduled and random changes of flow rate. The combined discrete event/continuous flow nature of the problem was modeled in GPSS V by defining the transactions entities in SIMSCRIPT or GASP) to be changes in flow rate such as plant break-downs, changes in mining geology, weather interruptions, scheduled main-tenance, conveyor moves, and full or empty storage-pile events. Using this concept, GPSS V was found to be a highly effective simulation modeling language. The rate-changes were generated, delayed until their time of occurrence, and then allowed to disrupt the rate of material flow through draglines, bucketwheels, conveyors, or extraction plant as appropriate.

Figure 10–4 shows the module relationships. The information communi-cated between modules was crucial to the model design concept. The Mining

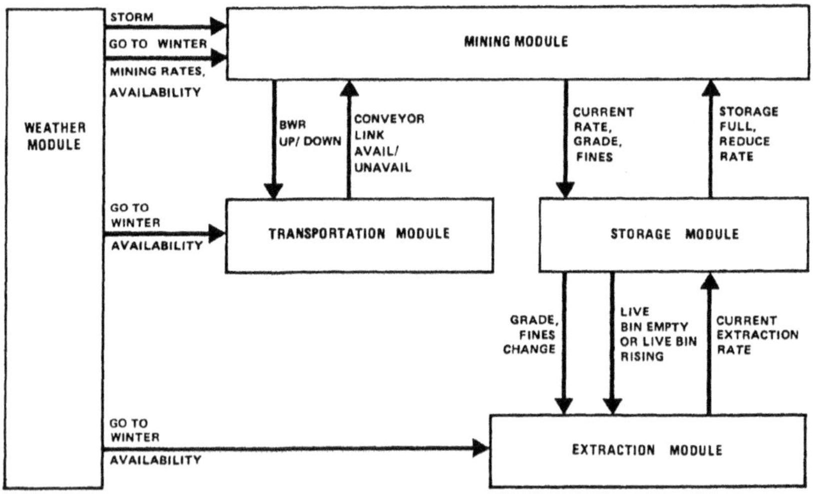

FIGURE 10–4. Module relationships

Module receives information about weather changes, conveyor shutdowns, and storage changes, and processes the changes in mining rates. It also signals Transportation when reclaimers stop or start, and signals the Storage Module when the ore changes in grade, fines, or flow rate. The Storage Module signals Extraction when grade or fines change to reflect change in froth production, when the extraction plant is to stop or start based on feed to the live bin. Extraction signals Storage when the extraction rate changes due to equipment failing or coming back into operation. The Weather Module signals changes in equipment availability and mining rates due to severely cold temperatures. Also, storms occur periodically which make mining impossible, thus shutting down all equipment.

In the Mining Module, mine ore input data is read for ore blocks of 200 feet × 80 × depth of the ore body. Up to six different layers are allowed in each block, though normally three were sufficient. Each layer has data of tons, grade, percent fines, and mining rate. Figure 10–5 illustrates the mine ore geology conceptualization. If a layer of subgrade material is more than five feet in thickness it is cast into the pit as reject, otherwise it is included as feed to the extraction plant. The onset of each winter reduces the basic mining rate. Detailed events include time for keycuts, deadheading, moving the conveyors, and logic to maintain appropriate distances between pieces of excavating equipment. Six types of maintenance and repair categories are

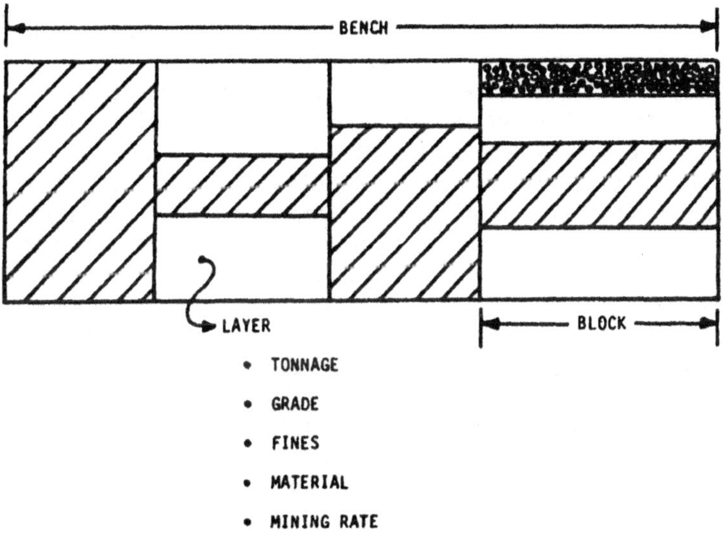

FIGURE 10–5. Mine ore data

provided, each with unique time distributions specified by mining engineers. The blockage logic receives information from the Transportation Module as to conveyor availability, surge pile status, weather, and mining unit interferences. The blockages states are recorded and progress is delayed until the blockages are removed. The mine layout as modeled is shown in Figure 10–6. Two faces advance outward from the center of the mine. The two large draglines on each face work in opposite directions and deadhead back to the centerline of the faces after each cut. If one dragline is eight blocks ahead of the other, it will deadhead two blocks beyond the centerline to allow the slower dragline to catch up. Draglines and BWRs must stay within 400′ to 2200′ of each other to avoid interfering with each other. The logic is designed to maintain this distance when operating rates are changed.

The Transportation Module handles a network of up to thirty-four conveyors which include loading, shiftable (mine face), collecting, and radial stackers. The tarsand moves progressively through these four sets of conveyors from the mine to the live storage pile. Shiftable conveyors must be moved once every two passes of the bucketwheel reclaimer as the mine face moves away from the centerline. Conveyor failure, conveyor moves, reclaimer failure and recovery are the events that drive this module. Upon conveyor failure the logic routes tarsand to other operating conveyors whenever possible.

In the Storage Module, the tarsand is stored in one of four surge piles and a live storage pile. The surge piles are sized to one eight-hour shift of average production. The storage module strives to insure a continuous supply of tarsand to the extraction plant by keeping the live bin as full as possible. To this end the storage module issues requests to change the mining or extraction rates. The storage state logic examines rates of flow to and from storage to determine whether the full or empty condition imminent. The module strives to prevent these conditions from occurring because a full surge pile blocks mining while empty surge pile blocks extraction. Figure 10–7 shows the physical arrangement that exists near the surge pile.

The extraction plant is illustrated in Figure 10–8. It consists of four extraction lines, a froth tank, pumps, two trains of primary and secondary centrifuge units and a bitummen storage tank. The froth tank limits flow when it is full or empty analogous to the storage bin. Each centrifuge unit is in one of four states: operating, idle (blocked), repair or maintenance, or multiple failure. Live bin events can modify the grade or fines being fed to extraction. This in turn affects the volume being extracted, the volume of froth, the centrifuge flow rate and the resulting rate of increase or decrease in the bitumen storage tank. The live bin being empty or full also impacts the flow rate and equipment status. Multiple failures occur for power outages and annual maintenance. Three other identifiable categories of random failure and repair were included. The strategy built into the Extraction Module was to prevent the froth tank going empty or full in order to avoid the resulting blockages. This was achieved by randomly idling centrifuge units when the froth tank was nearing depletion and by mobilizing extraction trains when possible. When the froth tank was nearly full, the model mobilized centrifuge and/or idled the operating extraction trains randomly.

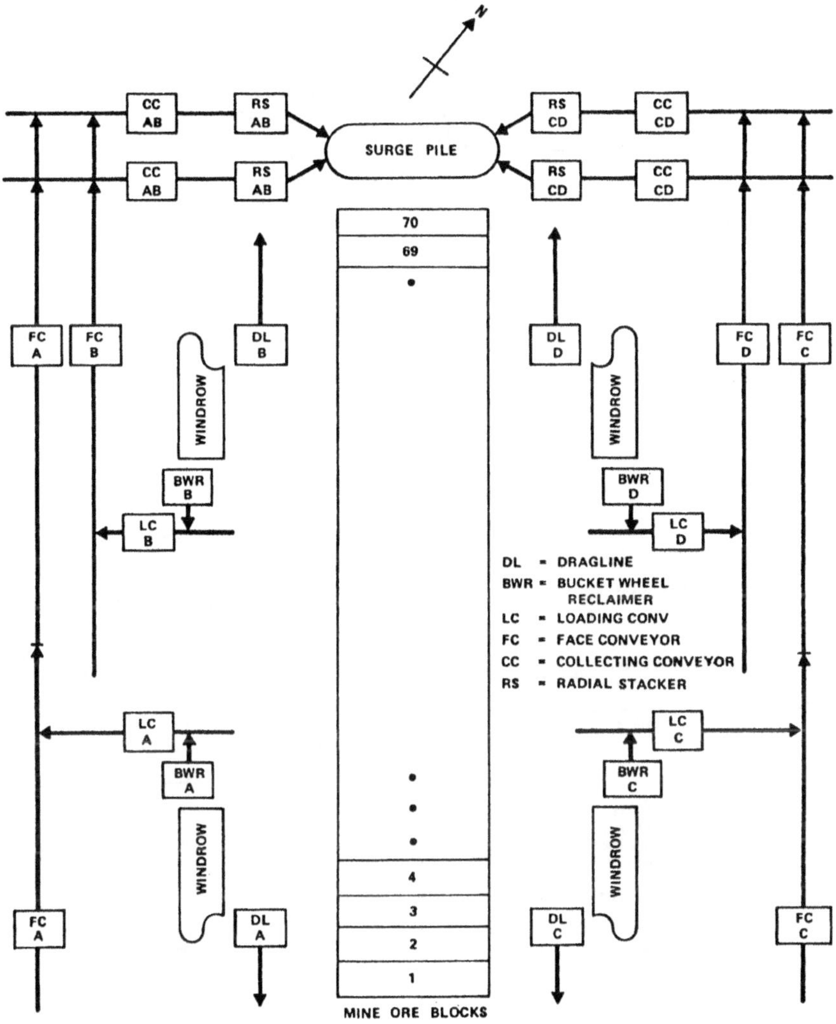

FIGURE 10-6. Mine layout

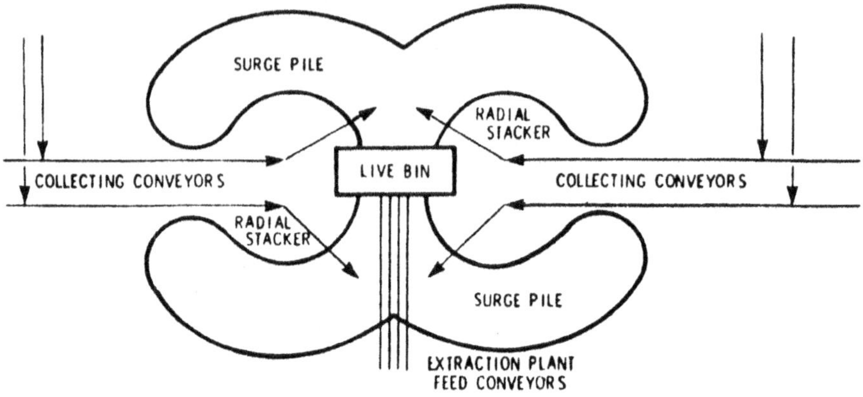

FIGURE 10–7. Surge pile diagram

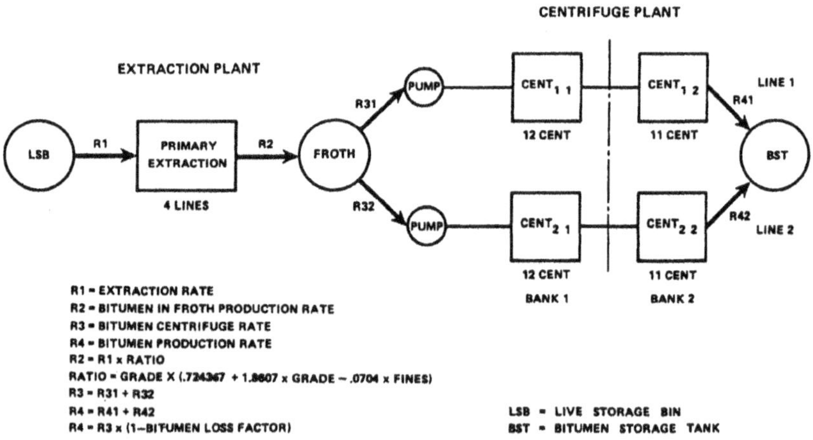

FIGURE 10–8. Extraction plant layout

10.7 APPENDIX B

10.7.1 Five Model Descriptions

6 BWE: 105,000 bbl/day. This model represented six bucketwheels positioned on three benches of a single 15,000-foot mine face. The mine face was divided by a central berm with a pit on either side. Two BWEs were on each bench on either half of the mine. Tarsand was moved from the BWEs via a loading conveyor to a movable face conveyor which carried the material to a tarsand collecting conveyor. The upper bench consists mostly of overburden which was moved to reject collecting conveyors at the extreme sides of the mine. The face conveyors reversed direction to switch between ore and reject material. The tarsand collecting conveyors fed to a radial stacker which could either direct ore to the surge pile or to the live bin.

6 BWE: 125,000 bbl/day. This case had six larger BWEs, and a single large pit with a 20,0000-foot mine face with all collecting conveyors to one side of the mine. Each BWE could feed either of two tarsand collecting conveyors. The mining rate was proportional to the ore layer thickness, because the mining rate is much lower for ten-foot layers as compared to seventy-foot layers. Higher capacity conveyors and extraction units were used to accommodate the larger volume of tarsand.

4 BWE: 125,000 bbl/day. Four larger BWEs were used in this model on two benches, with a central berm similar to the first model. Each BWE was able to feed any collecting conveyor by means of slewing belt wagons at each transfer point. This allowed the use of lower capacity conveyors. Exraction plant maintenance operations were improved.

4 BWE: 125,000 bbl/day Case 2. In this model four larger BWEs were used. However, a central berm was not used, making additional ore available. Two collecting conveyors were at each extreme side of the mine, one per BWE. A different conveyor network was used to allow spreading reject in two areas. Each BWE had access to either of two collecting conveyors.

Dragline: 125,000 bbl/day. The dragline model consisted of four draglines on two benches, with overburden stripped away in advance. The nominal mining rate per dragline was about two-thirds the comparable rate for the BWEs of the four-BWE cases. Four small draglines move ahead of the large draglines depositing tarsand on the windrows. Material was placed in a working pile and reclaimed by a bucketwheel reclaimer (BWR) to a loading conveyor and then to the collecting conveyors. Downtimes of the BWRs tended not to block excavating, and downtime of excavating tended not to impede reclaiming. The BWRs could operate more continuously because they did not have to handle reject.

10.8 ADDENDUM (OCTOBER 30, 1978)

The computer models described in this paper were conveyed to Syncrude Canada in late 1973. They were occasionally enhanced by Bechtel staff, although Syncrude had taken charge of exercising the programs. Several studies have been conducted by Syncrude over the years to reflect new ore data, changes in pit plan, and reject material handling. As Syncrude draglines now go into operation, the model is being used by Syncrude to evaluate new mining schemes at another site. In fact the project leader of the simulation task is presently an independent computer consultant, and periodically provides assistance to Syncrude in a continuing series of enhancements to the model.

11 A MODEL OF ENERGY SUPPLY FROM WESTERN CANADA*

John Rowse

This paper discusses a static multiregional linear programming model of energy supply from western Canada. This model has been constructed as part of an effort to measure production labor requirements, regional wealth accrual, and economic resource rents associated with different energy resource development scenarios. Demands and prices are exogenous to the model and supplies determined to maximize the increment to gross domestic product generated by energy resource production. The optimal solution yields a pattern of production and economic rent distribution which would be obtained if actual prices were specified exogenously and energy markets functioned in a perfectly competitive manner to meet demands. Thus the most economic supply alternatives are utilized most intensively, low-cost producers rewarded most heavily, and highest rents awarded to production capacities and reserves in particularly short supply. Two major advantages of approach are (1) the most economic patterns of production and transport of energy products can be determined

*Without implicating him, I would like to express my deep appreciation to Dr. Lawrence W. Copithorne of the Economic Council of Canada for many helpful suggestions relating to conceptual and practical problems of the modeling approach described here and for helpful comments on a preliminary draft of this paper. This paper is a highly condensed version of my "Energy Supply from Western Canada: Preliminary Work on a Comprehensive Programming Energy Model for Canada." I am grateful to Bill Ziemba for very helpful editorial assistance.

independently of the externally imposed restrictions characterizing Canadian energy product markets, allowing inefficiencies to be pinpointed and quantified, and (2) it allows the price of each energy product to have a direct impact on the shadow prices of constraints on energy production and consumption, in turn allowing empirical estimation of changes in natural resource rents as energy product prices change. The model can be used to address such supply-oriented questions as: (1) the short term consequences to provincial wealth accrual and economic rents of energy price adjustments in international markets, (2) the impact of increased or reduced restrictions on energy product supply or transportation, (3) the implications of technical developments in product supply or co-product yields, and (4) the outcome of government attempts to promote economic development of specific provincial energy industries.

11.1 INTRODUCTION

This paper describes work carried out in 1977 on the construction of an energy model for Canada. See Rowse (1977) for details. An inquiry into the role of natural resources in regional economic disparities, production labor employment potential, and regional economic growth has provided the impetus for this work. Two other studies forming a part of this inquiry are Copithorne (1976) and Copithorne and Quiroga (1977). The modeling approach of this paper is very similar to the approach of these two studies.

The central objective of the modeling effort has been to construct a vehicle capable of examining, within a single consistent framework, the interrelated issues of: (1) regional economic activity associated with the production of crude oil, natural gas, coal, and electrical energy; (2) regional economic disparities flowing from differential natural resource rents attaching to conventional energy forms in relatively short supply, namely crude oil, natural gas, and hydroelectric potential; (3) the influence upon these natural resource rents of transport costs and technological change in energy production; and (4) the consequences for economic activity in the energy production industries and natural resource rents regionally of government imposed restrictions on the way in which energy can be produced. Resource rents and wealth accrual from resource production have been singled out for particular attention because of their role in regional economic disparities, their potential for widening or narrowing such disparities, and their size relative to federal equalization payments. Furthermore, given the present federal-provincial jurisdictional dispute concerning the capture of resource rents, it has become imperative to quantify these resource rents and analyze the impact upon their magnitude of restrictions on production and transportation to understand better how resolution of the jurisdictional issue will affect the economic position of government and energy product suppliers.

To examine these issues a general model is essential. In the case of Alberta thermal coal, for instance, restrictions on strip mining and shipment of coal outside the province may have numerous and far-ranging effects, including increased cost of coal to Ontario Hydro customers, a possible shift toward nuclear power in Ontario, hastened exploitation of lignite coal deposits in southern Saskatchewan to supply Ontario markets, and possibly slowed development of an Alberta industry devoted to coal gasification, with corresponding implications for the regional distribution of income and jobs. A comprehensive model must have the detail and generality to trace these consequences. Furthermore, potential rents accruing to conventional oil and gas require measurement in a framework which allows for adjustments to production and transport costs, price variations in domestic and export markets, differential exploitation of these resources according to different growth rates in demands through time, the consequences for such rents of additions to reserves through exploration, and shifts toward alternative energy supply sources. Similarly, hydro rents depend crucially upon the costs of alternative sources of electrical energy, and must fluctuate with the cost of capital, the cost of thermal fuels, social discount rate, and the price charged for electrical energy. All these elements require a place in the framework.

Linear programming has been adopted for modeling the necessary breadth of diverse elements and the detail of specific elements. The research effort has so far yielded a static energy model embracing the individual western provinces of Canada. The multiple time-period framework essential for examining questions of intertemporal adjustment and measuring economic rents is not yet present. The model structure is described in section 11.2, with brief attention to differences between the approach adopted and other modeling efforts. Illustrative comparative static results from the model are presented in section 11.3.

11.2 STRUCTURE OF THE MODEL

11.2.1 Preliminaries

The static linear programming model describes energy production and transportation in western Canada and does not yet constitute a national model. Since western Canada possesses more than 95 percent of indigenous known reserves of natural gas, crude oil, and coal, and all of Canada's heavy oil and oil sands, the model captures the most important elements of the Canadian supply system for these energy resources. Hydro resources, however, are more widely dispersed across the country. Activity in the energy industries is represented in the model for the year 1974, the most recent year for which data have been available.

Model construction has been much simplified by largely avoiding the processing of crude energy into refined products. Energy products included are: (1) light/medium crude oil, consisting of conventional light and medium crudes, field condensate, the generic category of pentanes plus, and synthetic crude from the oil sands of Alberta; (2) heavy crude oil; (3) natural gas; (4) bituminous, subbituminous, and lignite coals; and (5) electric power. Hydro resources are included only as existing supplies of hydroelectric energy. The model has a high degree of aggregation; model production sources, consumption centers, and transportation networks are stylized representations of western Canadian production-transport-consumption systems. For instance, each supply activity represents production from numerous spatially dispersed sources, such as oil wells, gas wells, coal mines, or electric power-generating facilities.

For the light/medium crude oil network of the model, each province of western Canada has one representative producing center save for Alberta, which with oil sands production capacity at Fort MacMurray has two. Vancouver, Edmonton, Regina, Winnipeg, and Sarnia-Toronto are representative consumption centers, and Cherry Point (Washington), Billings (Montana), and Chicago are representative consumption centers for the U.S. Petroleum Administration for Defense (PAD) Districts V, IV, and II, respectively.

Other resource networks exhibit similar detail. For heavy crude oil, production sources are confined to Alberta Saskatchewan, and foreign export is confined exclusively to PAD District II in the United States. The natural gas network is very similar to that for light/medium crude (henceforth simply light crude), two major differences being that there is no transmission link from Alberta production sources to British Columbia consumption centers and that Manitoba produces no natural gas. The coal network embraces both metallurgical coal and thermal coals, markets for the former consisting almost exclusively of Japan and southern Ontario, while markets for the latter consist primarily of power utilities in the prairie provinces. Finally, the electric power network of western Canada has been constructed around the three publicly-owned provincial electric utilities of B.C. Hydro, Saskatchewan Power and Manitoba Hydro, and an aggregate of the four principal Alberta power utilities.

11.2.2 Activities and Constraints

Model activities for coal, crude oil, and natural gas are confined to: extraction variables, representing quantities of resources extracted on a provincial basis and brought to a central location for distribution; transport variables, representing the movement of these products from one domestic location to another within Canada or to representative locations in the United States; marketing variables, representing resource products consumed in any particular location; and variables measuring production labor requirements associated with resource extraction. For electric power, an additional set of variables measuring the conversion of coal or natural gas into electrical energy is included.

The model structure is displayed schematically in Table 11–1. For each province there are constraints (where applicable) on reserves of oil, natural gas, and coal, which require that aggregate intertemporal extraction of these fossil fuels cannot exceed exogenously specified reserves. Such reserves constraints are redundant in a static model since reserves cannot be exhausted in a single time period. Next, there are constraints on provincial productive capacity of oil and gas wells or coal mines, which limit the quantity of oil, gas, and coal which can be extracted in any particular year. Constraints on market demand specify upper limits on the quantity of energy products which can be absorbed by consumption centers at exogenously specified prices. Constraints for oil, gas, and coal comprise either mass balance constraints, which require that product supply equal demand, or accounting constraints, which record production labor requirements, transportation costs, or volumes of co-products associated with crude oil or natural gas production. Only the mass balance constraints require elaboration. For example, the balance constraint for natural gas in Alberta equates supplies of natural gas, namely marketable gas produced from natural gas wells and associated gas derived as a co-product from crude oil production, to demands for natural gas, which consist of shipments of natural gas south to the United States and east to Saskatchewan, domestic non-electric demands for natural gas within Alberta, and demands in Alberta for natural gas for electric power generation. For different products and regions the form of the balance constaint is similar but not identical. There is, for instance, no direct conversion of crude oil into electrical energy in the model for any province.

Similar constraints apply for electric power provision: constraints on power capacity and energy generation limit supply from each provincial source, marketing constraints establish maximum quantities of power to be absorbed in each domestic or American consumption center, while conversion constraints transform quantities of electric power generated into requirements for natural gas, coal, and fuel oil. Mass balance constraints require that power consumed exactly equal power supplied, and accounting constraints aggregate quantities of operating labor required for electric power generation. Power demands have required special attention because

TABLE 11-1. Schematic diagram of linear programming model constraints*

Constraint Name \ Activity Type		OIL, GAS & COAL: Pro-duction	Trans-port	Mark-eting	Co-Products	Labour Use	ELECTRIC POWER: Gener-ation	Trans-mission	Con-version	Mark-eting	Labour Use	Constraint Type	Constraint Right Hand Side
Objective Function		■	■	■	■	■	■			■	■		
Oil Gas & Coal	Demands			■								≤	Specified Demands
	Prod^{n} Capacity	■										≤	Capacity Estimates
	Reserves	■										≤	Reserve Estimates
	Mass Balances	■	■	■					■			=	0
	Labour Req'ts	■				■						=	0
	Transport Costs	■	■									=	0
	Co-Products	■			■							=	0
Electric Power	Demands									■		≤	Specified Demands
	Power & Energy Generation						■					≤	Generating Capabilities
	Mass Balances						■	■		■		=	0
	Conversion						■		■			=	0
	Labour Req'ts						■				■	=	0

* Shaded entries denote nonzero activity and objective function coefficients.

of their variability over time, both daily and seasonally. In this model, a highly simplified representation has been adopted: a peak load demand extending for 1 percent of the year, and a base load demand extending for the full year.

To illustrate actual matrix entries, Table 11-2 lists input requirements and co-product yield ratios associated with light/medium crude oil production in each province. Production activities for coal and natural gas have similar entries, but with certain differences. Coal, for instance, has not associated co-products, whereas natural gas has co-products of condensate, propane, butane, and sulphur, with co-product ratios varying considerably between provinces. Likewise, electric power generation has a similar structure but with constraints on both power and energy generation and a mass balance constraint for each of the base and peak demands.

11.2.3 The Objective Function

The increment to gross domestic product (GDP) in all energy industries is to be maximized. For each industry and province, this aggregate consists of the value of the energy product sold less: (1) payments to other industries for fuel, materials, and supplies (save for electric power, where fuel choice is made explicitly by the model); and (2) wage payments for production labor, which are incurred as a result of energy product supply, with appropriate credit for any co-products produced. This aggregate consists of value added net of payments to production labor, and will be abbreviated to "net value added" Attainment of this objective in fact rewards the low-cost producers and awards highest rents to their production capacities and reserves in particularly short supply, yielding a pattern of production and rent distribution which would be obtained if prices were truly specified exogenously and energy markets functioned in a perfectly competitive manner to meet the ceilings on demands. Two major advantages of the approach selected are: (1) the most economic patterns of production and transport of energy products can be determined independently of the externally imposed restrictions characterizing Canadian energy product markets, allowing inefficiencies to be pinpointed and quantified; and (2) it allows the price of each energy product to have a direct impact on the shadow prices of constraints on energy production and consumption, in turn allowing empirical estimation of changes in natural resource rents as energy product prices change.

Interaction of the electric power industry and the other industries may well play a role in shaping model demands and supplies. For instance, the increment to GDP in the coal industry and electric power industry together

TABLE 11–2. Energy model per unit data for light/medium crude oil production

					Production Activity		
Type	*Constraint Name*	*Units*	*Light Crude in B.C.*	*Light Crude in Alberta*	*Synthetic Crude in Alberta*	*Light Crude in Sask.*	*Light Crude in Manitoba*
$\leq$	Productive Capacity	10^3 BBL	1.0	1.0	1.0	1.0	1.0
$\leq$	Crude Oil Reserves	10^3 BBL	1.0	1.0	1.0	1.0	1.0
=	Mass Balance	10^3 BBL	1.0	1.0	1.0	1.0	1.0
=	Labor Requirements	Man-Years	0.005481	0.005458	0.244727	0.005245	0.005896
=	Gathering Costs	10^6 $	0.000800	0.000300	0.000250	0.000250	0.000100
=	Fuel and Materials	10^6 $	0.000116	0.000136	0.004500	0.000286	0.000139
=	Co-Product: Gas	10^6 MCF	0.000769	0.000707	0.0	0.000475	0.0
=	Co-Product: Sulphur	10^3 L.T.	0.0	0.0	0.007000	0.0	0.0

Sources: Coefficients in this table have been calculated using data from Statistics Canada, the National Energy Board, the Alberta Energy Resources Conservation Board, provincial ministries of energy and mineral resources, and discussions with various individuals. See Appendices A & B of Rowse (1977) for further information.

will have an important influence upon which types of existing generating capabilities are selected for use. If net value added in coal production is high but that of coal-fired generation for electric power is not — relative to some other type of generation — the model may still select the coal-fired generation since the combined increment to GDP is higher.

Although the model displays some similarities to other supply models, it also displays some notable differences. For instance, it embraces minimal processing of energy resources (excluding oil refining entirely) and maximizes net value added in energy industries subject to ceilings on demands instead of minimizing costs of energy provision subject to floors on demands, as does the LORENDAS model (Rapoport et al., 1977), which also exhibits far greater detail in the modeling of energy supply capabilities. Another element that differs somewhat from other models is the attention paid to the dual variables emerging from the optimal solution, a focus that formed a central part of Nordhaus's (1973) study on optimal world energy resource depletion. The economic rent or windfall gain attaching to a resource in scarce supply depends upon many factors, including the price of the final product or products for which the resource is used, the timing of resource production and sale, costs of cooperating factors and the technology used in production, the quantity and value of co-products in resource extraction, and the costs of transport of the product to consumption centers. The linear programming approach allows for all these separate factors and, at the optimum, the dual variables provide estimates of their combined quantitative importance. See Appendix F in Rowse (1977) for an algebraic statement of how, in a highly simplified energy model, the shadow price of reserves is related to these factors. Finally, one minor difference between the present model and other models is its emphasis upon employment of production labor. This emphasis could also be supplemented with allowance for job creation potential for professional labor if desired, and stems from an interest in the employment growth potential of energy resource development.

11.3 ILLUSTRATIVE MODEL SOLUTIONS AND COMPARATIVE STATICS

Because a dynamic version of the model is not yet available, the results it is capable of providing must be regarded as illustrative. Furthermore, since the solution detail which it generates is considerable, only salient results will be discussed.

Tables 11-3 and 11-4 provide selected model statistics and shadow prices respectively for the Base Case and Low Price Scenario. The solution results

TABLE 11–3. Selected model energy statistics—the base case and low price scenario (entries for the low price scenario are listed in parentheses if they differ from the base case)

Production, Labor, or Value Statistic	*British Columbia*		*Alberta*		*Saskatchewan*		*Manitoba*	
Net Value Added*—Oil & Gas (10^6\$)	216.2	(94.2)	4006.3	(2140.4)	407.5	(212.7)	27.9	(16.6)
Labor—Oil & Gas (Man-Years)	271.		3805.	(3795.)	424.	28.		
Production of Oil** (10^3 bbl)	10,713.		582,551.		77,409.	4749.		
Production of Gas (10^6 mcf)	407.2		2117.	(2093.6)	56.4		—	
Production of Propane (10^3 bbl)	613.		34,058.	(33,682.)	702.		—	
Production of Butane (10^3 bbl)	683.		22,619.	(22,369.)	299.		—	
Production of Sulphur (10^3 l. tons)	65.		7038.	(6960.)	3.		—	
Net Value Added*†—Coal (10^6 \$)	105.	(38.)	47.	(16.8)			—	
Labor†—Coal (Man-Years)	1937.	(1822.)	1307.	(1371.)			—	
Production of Bituminous (10^3 s. tons)	8076.	(7792.)	3652.		—		—	
Production of Subbituminous (10^3 s. tons)	—		3722.	(4657.)	—		—	
Production of Lignite (10^3 s. tons)	—		—		3414.		—	
Generation of Electrical Energy (10^6 kwh)	25,696.5		13,513.3		7126.7	14,271.1		
Labor—Electrical Energy (Man-Years)	2130.		1882.		965.	1341.		
Prime Motive Source: Gas (10^6 mcf)	29.7		82.9	(60.7)	15.9	0.43		
Prime Motive Source: Subbit. Coal (10^3 s. tons)	—		3491.7	(4426.5)	—		—	
Prime Motive Source: Lignite Coal (10^3 s. tons)	—		—		2810.9		—	
Prime Motive Source: Fuel Oil (10^3 bbl)	—		—		—		—	
Net Energy Transmission (10^6 kwh):								
To Ontario	—		—		—	1814.4		
To Manitoba	—		—		273.		—	
To Saskatchewan	—		—		—		—	
To Alberta	—		—		—		—	
To British Columbia	—		—		—		—	
To United States	1348.7		—		—	1495.3		

Definitions:

* = Net value added consists of value added less production labor wage payments.

** = Oil production includes light, medium and heavy oil, condensate, and pentanes plus, for Alberta, also synthetic crude.

† = Alberta and Saskatchewan net values added for coal production have been aggregated to derive a single figure for comparison with actual

TABLE 11–4. Selected model shadow prices—the base case and low price scenario (entries for the low price scenario are listed in parentheses if they differ from the base case)

Consumption Centre \ Shadow Price		Demand for Light Crude Oil ($/bbl)	Demand for Heavy Crude Oil ($/bbl)	Demand for Natural Gas (¢/mcf)	Demand for Bituminous Coal ($/s. ton)	Demand for Thermal Coal* ($/s. ton)	Hydro Energy (Mills/kwh)
British Columbia		5.37 (2.99)	—	30.58 (5.83)	8.16 (0.00)	—	4.03 (4.20)
Alberta		5.37 (2.99)	4.50 (2.12)	44.30 (20.77)	8.16 (0.00)	0.10	1.71
Saskatchewan		5.37 (2.99)	4.50 (2.12)	44.30 (20.77)	—	0.28	2.03
Manitoba		5.37 (2.99)	4.50 (2.12)	44.30 (20.77)	8.16 (0.00)	—	3.18 (4.83)
Ontario		5.37 (2.99)	4.50 (2.12)	44.30 (20.77)	8.16 (0.00)	—	—
Exports to U.S.	South from B.C.	5.37 (2.99)	—	30.58 (5.83)	—	—	—
	South from Alta.	5.37 (2.99)	—	44.30 (20.77)	—	—	—
	South from Man.	5.37 (2.99)	4.50 (2.12)	44.30 (20.77)	—	—	—
Exports to Japan		—	—	—	8.16 (0.00)	—	—

*Thermal code denotes subbituminous coal in Alberta and lignite in Saskatchewan.

for the Low Price Scenario (if they differ from the Base Case) are recorded in parentheses. The Base Case solution indicates how the energy model would supply 1974 demands for crude oil, natural gas, coal, and electric power using prices and productive capacity constraints for that year. Details of the actual Base Case and Low Price Scenario results are in chapter 3 of Rowse (1977). The Base Case solution basically replicated the actual western Canadian energy supply pattern. There are, however, some notable exceptions, stemming from such causes as government-imposed restrictions on the functioning of product markets, simplifications such as linearity inherent in the model, and problems arising from quality variations in energy products existing in the real world but assumed away in the model. Particular supply features characteristic of western Canada were duplicated, such as the dominance of Alberta in oil and gas supply, followed by British Columbia as a natural gas producer, and Saskatchewan as an oil producer. Model net values added for oil and gas were relatively close to those actually observed for all provinces except British Columbia, the difference for the latter province owing in large part to noncompetitive gas pricing for gas producers. Net values added for the coal industry were not relatively close to what was actually experienced, however; in part because the model sought to use as much natural gas for electric power generation and as little thermal coal as possible since the combined increment to net value added from gas production and gas-fired power generation exceeded the combined increment with coal. This result would not arise in a dynamic model which recognized an explicit opportunity cost for natural gas in the form of future production and sale, and could have been eliminated had such an opportunity cost been specified in the static model. Hydroelectric power generation has been excluded from the table. Regarding Table 11-4, only those shadow prices attaching to maximum demands for crude oil, natural gas, and coal, and to available hydroelectric energy have been included. Shadow prices of light and heavy crude and bituminous coal are identical for all model demands because wherever incremental demands occur in the respective networks, the marginal supply source is the same. For crude oil this source is Alberta, while for bituminous coal this source is British Columbia. Thus, for example, wherever a barrel increase in demand for crude oil is registered in the oil networks, Alberta production will increase by one barrel. Shadow prices for natural gas and thermal coals do differ according to demand location, however. For gas, there is no transmission link between Alberta and British Columbia and hence there are two marginal sources in the gas network. For each of lignite and subbituminous coal there is only a single demand center and a single supply source. Hydro energy shadow prices differ for several reasons, a principal one being that electrical energy prices differ considerably across provinces.

To examine how energy industries might have performed in the absence of the sharp upward adjustment in oil, gas, and coal prices that occurred during 1974, and to measure the consequences for net values added provincially, the Low Price Scenario was analyzed. Oil, gas, propane, butane, sulphur, and bituminous coal prices were adjusted downward to their 1973 averages while thermal coals and electrical energy were taken unchanged in price. In this case, therefore, the same production technology actually used during 1974 was implicitly assumed available for use when lower prices were taken to prevail. In the new solution, all figures for net value added shrink. For example, oil and gas in British Columbia experienced a decline of almost 56 percent, and in Alberta a decline of 47 percent, the latter representing a reduction of $1866 million. Results for the coal industry are similar despite the fact that more subbituminous and lignite coal is produced under this scenario. But there is minimal change in the quantities of production labor employed. Demands remaining unchanged, and there being little provincial shift in production patterns, labor employment registers virtually no change. The only substantial adjustment is that lignite and subbituminous generating sources substitute for natural gas because gas production and transformation into electrical energy is less attractive than that for coal under lower gas prices. Shadow prices are seen to adjust downward sharply for all non-electrical demands, even to zero for bituminous coal, exhibiting the direct influence of product sale price on constraint shadow prices. Hydro energy shadow prices for British Columbia and Manitoba rise slightly because an extra kwh of hydro energy would displace one kwh of natural gas generation, now no longer as attractive as before. An extra kwh of hydro in Alberta and Saskatchewan would displace one kwh of thermal coal generation as before, and since thermal coal is unchanged in price, the shadow price of hydro energy remains unchanged for these two provinces.

The most notable result of the Low Price Scenario is that, mirroring reality, the model has generated consequences for disparities in provincial wealth accrual stemming from fossil-fuel price increases from 1973 to 1974 that are enormous, indeed almost staggering. Such disparities are, of course, caused primarily by the huge windfall gains to oil production in Alberta and natural gas production in British Columbia that are wrought by these price increases.

11.4 CONCLUDING REMARKS

This paper has discussed the construction of a static economic model of energy supply from western Canada. This model is intended to lie at the core of a dynamic national energy model to trace and analyze regional and temporal adjustments to wealth accrual, natural resource rents, production labor requirements, and economic growth potential associated with different energy resource development scenarios. Model construction has been tempered by the goals motivating study of the Canadian energy system. Hence, for example, the representation of energy resource processing has been minimized and emphasis placed upon measuring production labor requirements associated with resource production and quantifying economic rents through dual shadow prices. Although the objective has been to model competitive market behavior for energy supply, the model can readily be used as a planning tool for assessing different strategies shaping energy resource development, both at the national and regional levels.

Model solutions previously displayed exhibit a part of the detail generated by model use, notably the provincial aggregates of net values added, resource production, labor requirements, and certain of the dual shadow prices. In its present form, the model can only be used to address such supply-oriented questions as the short term consequences to provincial wealth accrual and economic rents of price adjustments in international markets, the impact of increased or reduced restrictions on energy product supply or transportation, the implications of technical developments in product supply or co-product yields, or the outcome of government attempts to promote economic development of specific provincial energy industries. Several questions of this sort have been examined in Rowse (1977).

REFERENCES

Copithorne, L. W. 1976. The role of gold and base metals in regional economic activity. Economic Council of Canada, Ottawa, unpublished.

Copithorne, L. W., and Quiroga, J. 1977. The role of forest products in regional economic activity: A study in spatial and temporal optimization. Paper presented at the Canadian Economics Association Meetings in Frederickton, New Brunswick.

Nordhaus, W. 1973. The allocation of energy resources. *Brookings Papers on Economic Activity* 3:529–576.

Rapoport, L., et al. 1977. LORENDAS model documentation, volume 1: Mathematical concepts and formulation. LORENDAS Project, Virginia Polytechnic Institute and State University, Blacksburg, unpublished.

Rowse, J. 1977. Energy supply from western Canada: Preliminary work on a comprehensive linear programming energy model for Canada. Department of Economics, Queen's University, Kingston, unpublished.

12 THE INCORPORATION OF NEW TECHNOLOGIES IN ENERGY SUPPLY ESTIMATION*

J. Daniel Khazzoom

This study integrates engineering and economic approaches to estimating energy supply in the short, intermediate, and long run—using a linear programming framework. It is motivated by the need to derive credible supply estimates under different price conditions, which incorporate explicitly new supply technologies in the estimation process. New technologies can be incorporated in this system as long as the technologist can specify the input requirements for investment in and operation of the new technology. Whether a technology will contribute to supply depends on its competitiveness with existing technologies, under the assumed conditions. The system developed is consistent with the 1967 input-output table for the U.S. economy. It is specified as a disequilibrium model to allow for the fact that under certain price conditions, excess demand (or excess supply) may exist. The energy sector includes 85 vectors of energy technologies and 850 vectors of investment requirements,

*Research of this project is supported by the Electric Power Research Institute, Contract No. RP1011-1 and the Federal Energy Regulatory Commission, Contract No. FPC 77-C-0018. This research is a continuation of that reported in Khazzoom(1975, 1977a) and Bechtel Corporation (1975). The author wishes to acknowledge the contribution of Win Lin Chou and Ilan Idler. Paul Rech, David Avis, Mark Chesters, and Alan Deikman helped in various ways. Special thanks are due to E. A. Parson and W. T. Ziemba for extensive editing of the paper for this volume.

allowing for an investment lead time of up to ten years. The timing and extent of investment in each energy technology is determined endogenously. There are sixty-two energy and energy-related products. The supply results focus on oil (including synthetic), gas (including synthetic), coal, and electricity. Preliminary ex post test results are reported.

12.1 INTRODUCTION

Economists generally represent the behavior of a profit-maximizing producer by a function giving a relationship between output and commodity prices. Such supply curves are convenient for storing much information compactly, however, a price is paid for this simplicity and convenience. The technological and institutional details behind the supply curve may be tedious to work with. However their absence deprives us of the flexibility of inquiring how supply is affected by changing technology or by modification of other underlying constraints. This limitation is particularly serious when we are dealing with a long time horizon or an industry in which major new technological developments are expected to occur. This is a major problem in modeling the energy sector.

Agencies with long-term planning responsibilities need long-range energy supply estimates. Yet estimated supply curves derived from econometric estimates generally do not model technological change satisfactorily, and so will be invalidated almost as soon as they are estimated.

This study integrates the engineering and economic approach to derive the supply curves of energy in a short, intermediate, and longer time horizone from an economic system which incorporates energy technology explicitly. The analysis departs from economic theory only in that the estimated supply curves must be interpreted in the context of an explicitly stated breakdown of final demand for nonenergy product.

12.2 SCOPE OF THE APPROACH

We focus on four major energy resources: oil (including synthetic), gas, coal, and electricity under assumed price conditions. Consider a standard economy wide input-output model with a technology matrix giving the dollar value of each input required for a dollar of output, for all outputs. Suppose there are s columns representing energy sources. To this model make the following modifications:

1. Replace the s columns of energy used by m ($m>s$) vectors of energy technologies, where the input requirement for each vector is based on engineering data for each technology.
2. Corresponding to the m vectors of operating requirements of energy technologies, use $10m$ vectors of investment in the energy sector (based on engineering data) to allow for a lead time of up to ten years.
3. Replace the matrix of dollar input per dollar of non-energy sale in the standard I-0 format by a matrix which expresses the Btu input per dollar of non-energy sale.
4. Expand the labor matrices L_N and L_E to include twenty-five categories (instead of one row) of labor input.

These changes are incorporated in the model formulated in section 12.3. The energy industry is represented by 85 vectors of energy technologies with 850 vectors of investment technologies allowing for lead time of up to ten years. The non-energy sector has 92 vectors. The work in Khazzoom (1977a) allows for a labor input of twenty-five categories for the non-energy and energy industries. The matrix of energy input into non-energy technologies (T_{EN}) has four rows and the matrix of energy input into energy (T_{EE}) has thirty-six rows. The model has a profit maximizing objective, conditional on the prices of energy sources and various constraints. The model outputs a schedule of energy availability as a function of energy prices, and a schedule of associated investment requirements in energy technologies over the same time horizon. A by-product is a list of the energy facilities that were completed during the time horizon of the model; an account of the existing capacity; and a list of the stock of investment in progress initiated during the time horizon covered by the model.

12.3 THE MODEL

There are thirty-six energy and energy related products generated by the model and used as input in various energy technologies. Additionally, there are twenty-six energy related products that appear as output of the model, but that are not used as input, e.g., hot water, chilled water, etc). All energy and energy related products appear in the model in physical units. Changes in energy price affect not only the profit in the objective function, but also the cost of each of the eighty-five energy technologies. Recall the energy input for (investment in and operation of) each technology is expressed in

Btu. When the price of crude oil increases in the future, the profitability of oil exploration and production increases (revenue per barrel increases by more than the cost of energy input per barrel), but the profitability of electricity generated from oil-fired plants decreases, and other things being equal, leads to a shift to a greater reliance on coal or uranium for electricity generation.

Define the following variables:

K_E^t = vector of the capacity of energy production in billion Btus, except for uranium which is measured in short tons throughout,
PQ^t = vector of proved reserves of crude oil and natural gas in year t, in billion Btus,
Q^t = vector of ultimately recoverable resources for gas, oil, coal, uranium, and shale oil in year t, in billion Btus (except for uranium),
X_N^t = vector of non-energy sales (in 1967 dollars) in year t,
X_E^t = vector of energy supply in year t, in billion Btus (except for uranium),
X_R^t = vector of oil and gas exploration in year t for different depths, in billion Btus,[1]
X_{IE}^t = vector of investment in energy production capacity in year t, in billion Btus (except for uranium),
X_{IR}^t = vector of investment in oil and gas exploration capacity in year t for different depths, measured in billion Btus.[1]

The objective is to maximize total discounted profits of the energy sector over the horizon using only profitable technologies:

$$\text{Max} \sum_{t=1}^{T} \rho^t \left(P_E^t X_E^t - P_R^t X_R^t - \sum_{s=1}^{t} P_{IE}^{t,s} X_{IE}^s - \sum_{s=1}^{t} P_{IR}^{t,s} X_{IE}^s\right) \quad (12.1)$$

where

P_E^t = vector of calculated operating profits of each energy technology in year t,
P_R^t = vector of calculated operating cost of exploration technologies in year t,
$P_{IR}^{t,s}$ = vector of calculated cost in year t for exploration initiated in year s,
ρ = discount factor.

1. While data for technologies to explore at different depths have been compiled, they have not been implemented yet, since the resource stimates do not break down the resources by depths.

The first set of constraints guarantee satisfaction of the non-energy final demand:

$$(I - T^t_{\mathrm{NN}})X^t_{\mathrm{N}} - T^t_{\mathrm{NE}}X^t_{\mathrm{E}} - T^t_{\mathrm{NR}} - \sum_{s=1}^{t} T^{t,s}_{\mathrm{NIE}}X^s_{\mathrm{IE}}$$

$$- \sum_{s=1}^{t} T^{t,s}_{\mathrm{NIR}}X^s_{\mathrm{IR}} = b^t_{\mathrm{N}}, \qquad (12.2)$$

where

T^t_{NN} = input-output matrix of the non-energy sector in year t,
T^t_{NE} = matrix of the required input to non-energy into the production of energy in year t,
T^t_{NR} = matrix of the required input of non-energy into the exploration of energy in year t,
$T^{t,s}_{\mathrm{NIE}}$ = matrix of the required input of non-energy in the *t-th* year of energy investment initiated in year s,
$T^{t,s}_{\mathrm{NIR}}$ = matrix of required input of non-energy in the *t-th* year of exploration investment initiated in vear s,
b^t_{N} = vector of stipulated final demand of non-energy products in year t (including non-energy investment, personal consumptions expenditures, government purchases, and net export).

The following constraints guarantee that the domestic supply plus the imports of energy will be sufficient (assuming a feasible solution exists) to support the final demand for non-energy products over the horizon. Constraints (12.4) are aggregates of (12.3), necessitated by differences in data availability:

$$- T^t_{\mathrm{EN}}X^t_{\mathrm{N}} + D^t_1(D^t_0 - T^t_{\mathrm{EE}})X^t_{\mathrm{E}} - D^t_1T^t_{\mathrm{ER}}X^t_{\mathrm{R}} - \sum_{s=1}^{t} T^{t,s}_{\mathrm{EIE}}X^s_{\mathrm{IE}}$$

$$- \sum_{s=1}^{t} T^{t,s}_{\mathrm{EIR}}X^s_{\mathrm{IR}} \geq 0, \qquad (12.3)$$

$$(D_0 - T^t_{\mathrm{EE}})X^t_{\mathrm{E}} - T^t_{\mathrm{ER}}X^t_{\mathrm{R}} \geq 0, \qquad (12.4)$$

where

T^t_{EN} = matrix (4 × 84) of required input of energy into the production of non-energy. The rows of this matrix correspond to an aggregate of the energy products to four classes (crude oil and gas, refined products, coal, and electricity),
T^t_{EE} = input-output matrix (36 × 77) of the energy sector,

T^t_{ER} = matrix (36 × 8) of the required input of energy into the exploration of energy,
$T^{t,s}_{\mathrm{EIE}}$ = matrix (4 × 77) of the required input of energy in the *t-th* year of energy investments initiated in year *s*,
$T^{t,s}_{\mathrm{EIR}}$ = matrix (4 × 8) of the required input of energy in the *t-th* year of exploration investment initiated in year *s*,
D^t_0 = summation matrix (36 × 77) aggregating the output of all technologies that produce the same energy or energy-related products to thirty-six energy types used as input in the energy sector.[2] D_0 brings aggregation to the level of three decimal expanded BEA categories defined in Khazzoom (1977a, pp. 24–26).
D^t_1 = a 4 × 36 summation matrix (4 × 36) aggregating the energy products to the level of T^t_{EN} which brings the aggregation down to the level of crude oil and gas, refined products, coal, and electricity.

The following constraints restrict the use of labor (by classification) to the existing labor force in each year *t*. As in constraints (12.3) and (12.4) aggregation of labor may be necessary if sufficiently detailed data are not available:

$$L^t_{\mathrm{N}}X^t_{\mathrm{N}} + L^t_{\mathrm{E}}X^t_{\mathrm{E}} + L^t_{\mathrm{R}}X^t_{\mathrm{R}} + \sum_{s=1}^{t} L^{t,s}_{\mathrm{IE}}X^s_{\mathrm{IE}} + \sum_{s=1}^{t} L^{t,s}_{\mathrm{IR}}X^s_{\mathrm{IR}} \leq b^t_{\mathrm{L}}, \quad (12.5)$$

where

L^t_{N} = matrix of required labor (by classification) for the production of non-energy in year *t*,
L^t_{E} = matrix of required labor for the production of energy in year *t*,
L^t_{R} = matrix of required labor for the exploration of energy in *t*,
$L^{t,s}_{\mathrm{IE}}$ = matrix of required labor for the *t-th* year of energy investments initiated in year *s*,
$L^{t,s}_{\mathrm{IR}}$ = matrix of required labor for the *t-th* year of exploration investments initiated in year *s*,
b^t_{L} = vector of available labor in year *t*.

The following two sets of constraints define the capacity of energy technologies in each year:

$$K^1_{\mathrm{E}} = b^1_{\mathrm{K}}, \text{ and} \quad (12.6)$$

$$K^t_{\mathrm{E}} - K^{t-1}_{\mathrm{E}} - \sum_{s=1}^{t} M^{t,s}_{\mathrm{IE}}X^s_{\mathrm{IE}} = b^t_{\mathrm{K}}, \quad (12.7)$$

2. There are sixty-two energy or energy-related products in the model. However, only thirty-six of these are used as input in energy technology. The rest appears as output but not as an input. The system now prints only the thirty-six products but not the rest.

where

$M_{IE}^{t,s}$ = diagonal matrix representing the availability in year t of energy technologies due to investments initiated in year s (e.g., $(M_{IE}^{t,s})_{\ell\ell}$ is 1 whenever the investment in the ℓ-th technology initiated in year s takes $t - s$ years to be ready for production, and -1 when the investment in the ℓ-th technology initiated in year s takes $t - s$ years until the end of productive life),

$$b_K^t = \begin{cases} \text{for } t = 1: & \text{vector of initial capacities of energy technologies,} \\ \text{for } t > 1: & \text{vector of change in the capacity of energy technologies in year } t \text{ (due to the existence of investment in progress at the year of initiation of the model).} \end{cases}$$

The constraints that define exploration capacity are:

$$K_R^1 = b_R^1, \tag{12.8}$$

$$K_R^t - \sum_{s=1}^{t} M_{IR}^{t,s} X_{IR}^s = b_R^t, \tag{12.9}$$

where

$M_{IR}^{t,s}$ = (diagonal) matrix (analogous to $M_{IE}^{t,s}$) representing availability in year t of exploration technologies due to investment initiated in year s,

b_R^t = capacity vector of exploration technologies in year t, defined in a manner similar to b_K^t.

The energy production and exploration in year t is restricted to the capacity in that year by the constraints:

$$X_E^t - K_E^t \leq 0, \text{ and} \tag{12.10}$$

$$X_R^t - K_R^t \leq 0. \tag{12.11}$$

The following constraints define the resource base in year t:

$$Q^1 = b_Q^1, \text{ and} \tag{12.12}$$

$$Q^t - Q^{t-1} + \begin{bmatrix} D_3 \\ \hline 0 \end{bmatrix} X_E^{t-1} + \begin{bmatrix} 0 \\ \hline D_2 \end{bmatrix} X_R^{t-1} = 0, \tag{12.13}$$

where

$\begin{bmatrix} D_3 \\ \hline 0 \end{bmatrix}$ = a summation matrix aggregating the resources of coal, uranium, and shale oil used as inputs into the production of energy in year t,

$\begin{bmatrix} 0 \\ \hline D_2 \end{bmatrix}$ = a summation matrix aggregating the discoveries of all gas and oil,

b_Q^t = ultimately recoverable resources of coal, uranium, shale oil, oil, and gas.

The following constraints are similar to (12.12) and (12.13), except that they correspond to proved reserves of crude oil and natural gas:

$$\text{PQ}^1 = b_{\text{PQ}}^1, \text{ and} \quad (12.14)$$

$$\text{PQ}^t - \text{PQ}^{t-1} + U^{t-1}X_E^{t-1} - D_2X_R^{t-1} = 0, \quad (12.15)$$

where

U^t = matrix of proved reserves of oil and gas used as input in energy production facilities in year t.

Constraint set (12.13) below limits the production of coal, uranium, and shale oil to a fraction of their resource bases. It also limits the exploration and discovery of oil and gas to a fraction of the oil and gas resource base. The constraint (12.17) restricts production of crude oil and natural gas to a fraction of their proven reserves. (The model does not have a separate exploration sector for coal, uranium, and shale oil. For these energy sources, production is made directly from the resource base without a transition through an exploration stage. For oil and gas, however, exploration is modeled separately. This accounts for the appearance of X_R^t separately in (12.16).) These constraints are:

$$\begin{bmatrix} D_3 \\ \hline 0 \end{bmatrix} X_E^t + \begin{bmatrix} 0 \\ \hline D_2 \end{bmatrix} X_R^t - \underset{\sim}{\lambda} \begin{bmatrix} I & 0 \\ I & 0 \end{bmatrix} Q^t \leq 0, \text{ and} \quad (12.16)$$

$$U^tX_E^t - \underset{\sim}{\delta}\, PQ^t \leq 0, \quad (12.17)$$

where

$\underset{\sim}{\lambda}$ = vector of extraction limits on coal, uranium, shale oil, oil, and natural gas,

$\underset{\sim}{\delta}$ = vector of fractions of existing proved reserves in year t.

The non-negativity constraints are:

$$X_N, X_E, X_R, X_{IE}, X_{IR}, K_E, \text{PQ}, Q \geq 0. \quad (12.18)$$

12.4 OBSERVATIONS ON THE MODEL

1. The model is a disequilibrium model. Difficulties of the equilibrium approach are discussed in Khazzoom (1976). There is no requirement

in this model that the demand for every type (or any one type) of energy must be met, for existing prices may not be high enough to yield a return deemed adequate by the producer.

2. The timing and extent of the investment in each type of energy technology is determined endogenously, the specification of the expected future input requirements (for investment and operation) of each new technology. This is accomplished by the explicit incorporation of lead time requirements for each technology in the model.
3. The use of optimization methods in a descriptive (rather than prescriptive or normative) sense for deriving the supply curves of energy is a new innovation. It makes it possible to capture many effects that we have not been able to estimate satisfactorily by other methods, such as the threshold effect of the supply response to prices, and the dependence of supply on future as well as past and present prices. The use of optimization methods does raise difficult issues: the treatment of the energy industry as one sector,[3] the implications of estimating the behavior of the energy industry in the context of the economy as a whole, the choice of the time horizon, and the implication for model validation for a historical period. We will not deal with these issues here; see Khazzoom (1977b).
4. "Inefficiencies" built into our energy use are reflected in the model structure. For example, because of internal inconsistencies in the relationship between the prices of oil and natural gas, it is conceivable that producers may choose to inject one-and-a-half Btu of natural gas to recover one Btu of oil. From the point of energy use, this is clearly an inefficient process, but it is the result of internal inconsistencies in the price structure of energy sources. These inconsistencies are built into the model formulation.
5. Other questions that may be addressed to this model are: How will changes in resource availability affect the supply forecast? How does the R&D implicit in the model's result compare, under a given set of price conditions, with the existing program? If under a given energy price structure, a certain technology is not profitable; what is the effect of change in the price structure on the use of this technology, and on other competing technologies? The model can also be used to simulate the impact of policy measures designed to stimulate energy supply.

3. This may not be a serious problem if certain inputs are used only in one industry, but not others within the energy sector; for example, nuclear engineers are used in the electric not the oil or coal industry; hence, no confusion or substitution of nuclear engineers with, say, civil engineers will result.

6. The LP's size can be reduced by eliminating the set of nonenergy constraints. The resulting solution is feasible for (12.1) through (12.18) and hence is optimal. Assume that $(I\text{-}T_{NN})^{-1}>0$ and T_{NE}, T_{NR}, T_{NIE}, T_{NIR}, b_N, X_E, X_R, X_{IE}, $X_{IR} \geq 0$. Premultiply (12.1) by $(I\text{-}T_{NN})^{-1}$. Denote the resulting expression for X_{N_t} by (12.1 ′). Premultiply (12.1 ′) by T_{EN}, add to (12:2) yielding (12.2 ′). Premultiply (12.1) by $-L_N$, add to (12.5) and denote by (12.5 ′). The optimal solution of the equivalent system with (12.1 ′) deleted and (12.2 ′) and (12.5 ′) replacing (12.2) and (12.5), when substituted in (12.1 ′) yields $X_N \geq 0$.
7. Table 12-1 shows the preliminary results available. They were obtained using the simples code GUMPS at the Lawrence Berkeley Laboratory.

TABLE 12-1. Three-year run: Ex-post forecast of domestic energy supply in 10^{16} Btu

		1967	*1968*	*1969*
Natural Gas	Model Forecast	1.88	2.00	2.07
	Actual	1.94	2.07	2.22
Crude Oil	Model Forecast	1.87	1.94	1.85
	Actual	1.87	1.83	1.86
Electricity	Model Forecast	.40	.69	.80
	Actual	.41	.45	.49
Coal	Model forecast	1.59	1.59	1.79
	Actual	1.42	1.40	1.42

Sources: Energy supply data were derived from American Gas Association (1976), American Petroleum Institute (1975), and U.S. Department of the Interior (1976).

REFERENCES

American Gas Association. 1976. *Gas facts 1975.* Arlington, Va.: American Gas Association.

American Petroleum Institute. 1975. Annual statistical review: Petroleum industry statistics 1965–74. Washington, D.C.: American Petroleum Institute.

Bechtel Corporation. 1975. *The energy supply planning model, vols. I and II.* Final report to the NSF Office of Energy R&D Policy, August.

Khazzoom, J. D. 1975. A proposed framework for net energy analysis. *Proceedings of NSF Conference of August 25–28, 1975, at Stanford University on Net Energy Analysis,* pp. 151–173.

Khazzoom, J. D. 1977a. *Final report to EPRI: Critical assessment and modification of the energy planning model of Bechtel Corporation,* March 31.

Khazzoom, J. D. 1977b. *Third quarterly report to the Electric Power Research Institute: Incorporation of new technologies in supply estimates* (Contract No. RP 1011-1), October 31.

Khazzoom, J. D. 1976. *Proceedings of the workshop on modeling the interrelationships between the energy sector and the general economy.* Special Report No. 45, Electric Power Research Institute, Palo Alto, California.

U. S. Department of Commerce, Bureau of Economic Analysis 1974. The input-output structure of the U.S. economy: 1967 *Survey of Current Business* 54

U. S. Department of the Interior 1976. *Energy perspectives 2.* Washington, D.C.: Government Printing Office

III COAL AND TRANSPORTATION MODELING

Ernest Koenigsberg

The economic and strategic importance of the large coal reserves in North America has become a matter of public discussion since the 1973 oil embargo. It is generally recognized that expanded coal use, while presenting some serious environmental and ecological problems, can allow Canada and the United States time to plan to develop alternate energy sources before world oil reserves reach a critical level.

An important study of coal supply and demand in the United States is described in Griffith's paper. The study was undertaken by a special group working under the auspices of the Energy Modeling Forum at Stanford University. The study was a comparative analysis of the ways in which various energy models treat the major forces which can affect the supply and demand for coal in the United States. The analysis was carried out by subjecting the several models to a number of plausible coal supply and demand scenarios. The secnarios consider the alternate end uses of coal (electricity generation, metallurgical processes, synthetic fuels, and industrial uses), alternate limitations on emissions and on mine reclamations, alternate prices of competing fuels, and alternate plans regarding regional production.

The results indicate that the several models with different structures and assumptions lead to similar conclusions on the future demand for coal. There are differences in the ratio of western coal produced to eastern coal depending on emission limitations and transportation costs, but the resulting price of electric power is not strongly dependent on the regional mix. Coal production will increase significantly over the next twenty years; the absolute magnitude of the increase will not be limited by supply constraints. The demand will depend on the price of oil and government policy on oil imports. The outcome, in terms of coal production and consumption, is relatively independent of national policy on sulfur emissions, land reclamation and eminent domain, and state policy on severance taxes.

Because of technological problems relating to process design and process efficiency, most experts, including the Coal in Transition study group, see only a small production of gas and liquid fuels from coal before the turn of the century (Bowden, 1976; Cochran, 1976; Fumich, 1975; Perry, 1974). This implies that large tonnages of coal will move by rail, barge, ship (Great Lakes), and, perhaps, slurry pipelines (University of Illinois, 1977; Input-Output Computer Services, 1976a, 1976b; Resources for the Future, 1976). The next three papers deal with the movement of coal in North America and point out the important problems and issues associated with energy transportation.

The problems of and potential for rail hauling of coal by the Canadian National Railroad are discussed in Armstrong's paper. While he examines the situation faced by one company, his comments apply to railroads in general and to mountain railroads in particular. The reader should note Armstrong's comments on the technology of rail transportation when heavy loads are carried: grade and curvature not only limit speed (and hence equipment utilization) but also have a very strong influence on rail and wheel wear (and hence maintenance cost). He reports that the Canadian railroads, with improvements using existing technology, can haul 120 million tons of coal and other products per year from coal areas in British Columbia and Alberta to western markets (including exports from Vancouver and Prince Rupert). The capacity to eastern markets is much larger than that figure. We note here that other studies indicate that with suitable improvements in critical regions, the U.S. railroad and waterway system will be able to move the tonnages envisaged in 1985 (Desai and Anderson, 1976; Manalytics, 1976, 1979; Reebie and Associates, 1976; Resources for the Future, 1976; University of Pittsburgh, 1975).

Ott and Boon report on two different studies of coal slurry pipelines as alternatives to railroads for the movement of coal. Ott's study, carried out for the Office of Technology Assessment, is concerned with regulatory, environmental, and water issues as well as the economic evaluation of coal transportation systems in the United States. The OTA report covers several potential pipeline movements of both Eastern and Western Coal.

Boon's paper deals with a very specific movement — that of coal from western Canada (Saskatchewan) to coal markets in Ontario. Thus Boon compares rail-ship movements with pipeline-ship movements — all ship movements out of Thunder Bay, Ontario. Both studies indicate that rail is generally cheaper than pipeline in the circumstances studied, but under favorable conditions for pipelines (and poor conditions for railroads) pipelines may be advantageous. In both cases, the cost of dewatering slurry is not discussed in any detail. It would appear that slurry pipelines would be preferred to a new railroad, but given the existing rail network with excess capacity, rail remains the more economical mode, at least in the short term. Similar results have been reported elsewhere (The Hudson Institute, 1976; University of Illinois, 1977).

Slurry pipelines are an attractive alternate under the following conditions:

1. Large coal volumes from a single or closely spaced mines;
2. Large coal consumption at a single or closely spaced plants;
3. High inflation rates;
4. Availability of water at low cost;
5. Absence of a parallel navigable waterway; and
6. Unfavorable railroad conditions or inefficient rail operations.

World exports of coal exceed 100 million tons, and this quantity may well double or even triple by the year 2000. The paper by Lauga deals with the design of coal export terminals. It emphasizes the problems created by the nonhomogeneity of coal, the uncertainty in supply availability, and the randomness of ship arrivals. The port studied here, Richards Bay, Union of South Africa, has an annual capacity of 20 million tons per year and an ultimate capacity of 30 million tons per year. The simulation model considers not only the loading rate of ships and the unloading rate of trains, but also the dynamic allocations of coal types to storage areas and the dynamic assignment of loader-stacker cranes.

Coal terminal design models are being used for marine coal terminals for domestic movements in the United States (Lake Superior, Lake Erie, Mississippi River) and Canada (Lake Superior). Domestic movements via large terminals in North America may exceed 150 million tons per year before the turn of the century. Large marine terminals for the export of North American coal are now in operation in Vancouver, Norfolk, and Baltimore (Input-Output Computer Services, 1976b; Manalytics, 1976, 1979; Matson Research Corp., 1970; Resources for the Future, 1976).

These papers deal with coal and represent the results of analysis by models. The models are of many forms; simulation, mathematical programming, macroeconomic, microeconomic, regional, national, cost analysis, process analysis, and facilities planning models. Most of the studies of coal — supply, transportation, and process analysis — are recent, dating from the oil embargo of late 1973. Until then, coal had received little attention by model builders and policy makers, except for models of particular operations (e.g., the Roberts Bank coal terminal). The papers here represent a sample of the work done in the past five years. Other key references are Ferrell (1977); Ford Foundation (1974); ICF (1976); MIT (1975); and Zimmerman (1975).

The paper by Devanney and Kennedy deals with the production, transportation, and processing of petroleum on a world scale. Their mathematical programming model allows crudes, intermediate products, and final products to retain their identity. The model is very large; however, computation is eased by the block structure which allows special decomposition procedures to be used.

The paper is a progress report rather than a completed study. In its present form the most important users of the model would be crude oil producers, refiners, and perhaps tanker operators. The model assumes: (1) fixed capital investment (tanker fleets, refiners, etc.); (2) perfect competition; (3) inelastic supply and demand; and (4) refineries do not blend crudes. Within these somewhat restrictive assumptions the model shows promise as an aid in planning crude allocation and tanker assignments, and as an aid to national planning.

Coal, which was the major energy source in North America in the first quarter of the century, may be a major source again by the end of the century. The growth of the use of coal for generating electric power and process steam can reduce our dependence on imported oil, and serve as a bridge to the era of solar and nuclear power. The models presented here deal with the availability, transportation, and use of coal over the next twenty years. There are many other problems or concerns not covered here or only briefly mentioned, but which are of major concern in energy planning. Several have been studied using modeling techniques.

Griffith discusses coal used for the production of synthetic gas and liquid fuels. It is estimated that only a small portion of coal will be used to produce synthetic fuels by the end of the century. While coal has been used to produce town gas since 1850 and liquid fuels since the 1930s, the processes are generally inefficient and uneconomic at this time. See Bowden (1976); Cochran (1976); and Fumich (1975).

Modeling has been helpful in other areas of concern. The Ford Foundation Policy (1974) project reported on models of open cast mining with emphasis on reclamation and environments.

Several policy modeling studies have been carried out to examine the effects of increased coal production and transportation on the environment (National Academy of Sciences, 1978; University of Pittsburgh, 1975). In other reports (May, 1976; Three R Corporation, 1979) the concern is the effect of increased railroad traffic on small communities along the right of way. The problems are noise, coal dust, interference with normal traffic flows, as well as environmental damage in the coal producing region.

We have found no references on the use of energy policy modeling in the area of mine safety and health. Such models could begin with an analysis of the differences, in terms of dust, accident proneness, and safety performance using the various methods of underground mining (e.g., longwall cutting, shortwall with continuous mining machines, conventional room and pillar mining, and hydraulic mining).

There have been a number of modeling studies of energy transportation which can provide policy makers with a framework for decisions (University of Illinois, 1977; MIT, 1975; National Academy of Sciences, 1978). There are some technical uncertainties, to be sure, but these are not the major cause of delays by government policy makers. Thus we have no policy on bulk terminals for crude oil or LNG, on pipeline conversion, on slurry pipelines, or railroad limitations. In the absence of decisions, we have no investment. It would appear, from the results presented by Griffith and others (The Hudson Institute, 1976; University of Illinois, 1977; Manalytics, 1979; University of Pittsburgh, 1975) that the end results in terms of energy use and flow depend very little on the standards set by government policy. Investments will be made by producers, transporters, and users, once the ground rules are firmly established.

REFERENCES

Bowden, J. R. 1976. Prospects for coal as a direct fuel and its potential through application of liquefaction and gasification. *Energy Sources* 3:1–11.

Cochran, N. P. 1976. Oil and gas from coal. *Scientific American* 234:24–29.

Desai, S. A., and Anderson, J. 1976. Rail transportation requirements for coal movement in 1980. U.S. Department of Transportation, Office of Transportation and Transportation Systems Center. Springfield, Va.: NTIS.

Ferrell, G. C. 1977. Energy strategies and options: An analysis of coal in the United States. Third IIASA Conference on Energy Resources, Moscow, November 28–December 4.

Ford Foundation Energy Policy Project. 1974. Rehabilitation potential of western coal lands. Cambridge, Mass.: Ballinger Press.

Fumich, G., Jr. 1975. Clean energy from coal: A research program. *Mechanical Engineering* 97:14–21.

The Hudson Institute. 1976. Research analysis of factors affecting transportation of coal by rail and slurry pipeline. Prepared under a grant from Burlington, Northern Inc., Croton-on-Hudson, New York, 1976.

ICF Inc. 1976. The national coal model description and documentation. Prepared for Federal Energy Administration. Springfield, Va.: NTIS.

University of Illinois, Urbana. 1977. Comparative coal transportation costs: An economic and engineering analysis of truck, belt, rail, barge and coal slurry and pneumatic pipelines. Prepared for U.S. Bureau of Mines and Federal Energy Administration. Springfield, Va.: NTIS.

Input-Output Computer Services, Inc. 1976a. Rail transportation requirements for coal movement in 1980. Prepared for U.S. Department of Transportation, Office of Transportation, Energy Policy and Transportation Systems Center. Springfield, Va.: NTIS.

Input-Output Computer Services, Inc. 1976b. Water transportation requirements for coal movements in the 1980s. Prepared for U.S. Department of Transportation, Office of Transportation, Energy Policy and Transportation Systems Center, Washington, D.C.

Manalytics, Inc. 1976. Coal transportation capability of the existing rail and barge network. Prepared for Electric Power Research Institute. Springfield, Va.: NTIS.

Manalytics, Inc. 1979. Cost models for coal transportation by common carrier. Prepared for Electric Power Research Institute. Palo Alto, California.

Massachusetts Institute of Technology. 1975. *Multiregional economic impacts of energy and transportation policies.* Springfield, Va.: NTIS.

Matson Research Corp. 1970. Transocean tug barge systems: A conceptual study. Prepared for U.S. Maritime Administration. Springfield, Va.: NTIS.

May, O. N. 1976. Criteria and limits for wayside noise from trains. *Journal of Sound and Vibration* 46:537–550.

National Academy of Sciences. 1978. *Energy modeling for an uncertain future.* Washington, D.C.

Perry, H. 1974. Gasification of coal. *Scientific American* 230:19–25.

Reebie and Associates, Inc. 1976. National intermodal network feasibility study. Prepared for U.S. Department of Transportation, Federal Railroad Administration, Office of Policy and Program Development. Springfield, Va.: NTIS.

Resources for the Future, Inc. 1976. Inland waterway transportation: Studies in public and private management and investment decisions. Baltimore, Md.: Johns Hopkins Press.

Three R Corporation. 1979. An analysis of the interactions between coal development and transportation alternatives in Colorado. Prepared for Colorado Energy Research Institute. Denver, Colorado.

U.S. Transportation Systems Center. 1977. *The railroad performance model.* Cambridge, Mass.

University of Pittsburgh, School of Engineering. 1975. Feasibility of considerably expanded use of western coal by midwestern and eastern utilities in the period 1978 and beyond. Springfield, Va.: NTIS.

Zimmerman, M. B. 1975. *Long run mineral supply: The case for coal in the United States.* Cambridge, Mass.: MIT PhD. dissertation.

13 MODELING U.S. COAL SUPPLY AND DEMAND

Edward D. Griffith

Recent studies have indicated that world oil production is likely to peak during the next twenty-five years, and nations may turn to coal as a major alternative fuel. In assessing the outlook for coal, we must carefully analyze the economics of mining, transporting, and burning coal; as well as political, social, and environmental implications. One effort to better understand the interplay of these forces is the Energy Modeling Forum study entitled, "Coal in Transition: 1980 to 2000." In this project, a group of energy modelers conducted a comparative analysis of how various mathematical models treat the major forces affecting the outlook for coal supply and demand in the United States. It was designed to highlight the policy implications of alternative coal supply/demand scenarios. It produced important insights on regional coal production patterns, transport flows, and the requirements for coal infrastructure development in response to differing economic and policy assumptions. This paper summarizes the major findings of this study.

13.1 INTRODUCTION

A number of recent studies of the long run energy outlook for the free world (such as the Workshop on Alternative Energy Strategies) anticipate tightness in the supply of oil and gas later in this century. As a result, many people now believe that the world must begin a transition away from its heavy reliance on oil and gas to alternative forms of energy. One of the most likely transitions is toward the use of more coal in the major energy-consuming nations. The potential magnitude of this transition is discussed in the International Energy Agency's report, "Steam Coal, Prospects to 2000."

The United States, in particular, is likely to increase coal use as domestic production of oil and gas decline, and policy makers perceive the need to reduce dependence on imported oil through exploitation of vast and relatively inexpensive reserves of coal. While the logic for turning to coal is obvious, there are many specific economic issues that require detailed analysis and policy concerns that must be addressed. Some of these issues include the likely environmental impacts of expanded coal use, the economics of coal development, the need for transportation and coal handling facility expansion, and the strain on other resources such as water requirements and land use that may result from greatly expanded coal production.

The renewed interest in coal that has come about in recent years has generated a number of efforts to better understand the outlook for coal and coal-related policy issues. One such effort was the "Coal in Transition: 1980–2000" project of the Energy Modeling Forum. The EMF is administered through the Stanford University Institute for Energy Studies. Its purpose is to promote communication between model users and developers through the comparative application of current energy models to the analysis of priority U.S. energy issues. The Coal in Transition project brought together a group of energy model developers and energy modeling users from the academic, business, and government sectors to study the outlook for coal supply and demand in the United States and to compare the results of various models against a set of common scenarios. The main conclusions of the study are: (1) coal production in the United States will increase substantially through the end of this century given the assumptions about increasing world oil prices and nuclear power capacity in the United States; (2) there is sufficient coal to meet reasonable or even large demand levels; (3) western coal production is likely to increase dramatically — eastern coal production will also increase, but at a modest rate; (4) regional coal production patterns vary among the various scenarios and appear to be sensitive to differences in production costs between regions and to varying standards for controlling air pollution from coal burning; (5) the establishment of stricter environmental standards will increase the cost of coal use. However, the choice of how to administer stricter environmental standards between lowering new source emissions standards to one-half prior levels or alternatively requiring best available control technology yields equivalent results in terms of cost. The choice does not appear to impact total coal production levels, although it will have a minor impact on the regional pattern of coal production; (6) the ability to substitute other fuels for coal in end-use markets and competition in the supply of coal will moderate coal price increases. In only one scenario are significant real increases in the supply price of coal anticipated; and (7) the price of electricity is expected to trend upward as new plants replace older plants. However, the potential for substitution in the fuels used to supply electricity and to substitute other fuels for electricity in end-use markets is expected to moderate electricity cost increases for the ultimate user.

The various conclusions of the workshop are generally supported by all of the models; although there are also important differences in detailed results contained in the models. In the following sections I discuss the findings and scenario results obtained. See Energy Modeling Forum (1978) and Griffith and Clarke (1979) for further results and discussion.

13.2 COAL IN TRANSITION PROJECT

The study utilized ten different models grouped into three different types. There were five energy sector models with significant coal detail: the Gulf SRI Model, the Brookhaven Tesom Model, the Department of Energy PIES Model, the Dartmouth Fossil 1 Model, and the DRI Zimmerman Model. (See the paper by Fuller and Ziemba in Volume II for brief descriptions of the first three of these models; Greenberg's two papers in Volume II also discuss the PIES model.) There were four regional models of coal supply, transportation, and demand: the Argonne National Coal Model, the ICF Inc. Coal Model, the Bechtel Response Model and the Pepco/CRA Coal Model. There was one facilities planning model: the Bechtel Energy Supply Planning Model. In addition to the builders of the listed models and the staff of EMF, there were representatives of model users and policy makers from the Department of Energy, the Edison Electric Institute, the Institute of Gas Technology, the Electric Power Research Institute, Pennsylvania State University, Atlantic Richfield Company, Gulf Oil Corporation, the United States Congress, and the Environmental Protection Agency. Dr. David Sternlight of Atlantic Richfield was the chairman of the "Coal in Transition" working group.

13.3 COAL DEVELOPMENT SCENARIOS

To analyze how different models treat coal supply and demand issues, it was necessary to develop alternative scenarios that could be used to test various policy issues. A reference scenario was established assuming aggregated annual energy growth in the United States of 2.5 percent during 1980–2000. It was assumed that the electricity growth rate would be 5.6 percent from now to 1985 and 4 percent from 1986 to 2000. Industrial steam coal was postulated to grow at 8 percent, and three quads of coal equivalent would be required for synthetic fuels by the year 2000. To fully test the range of possible coal demand, high and low coal demand scenarios were developed. The precise assumptions are given in Table 13-1. Other scenario assumptions, which would remain the same in all cases, were as follows: (1) imported oil would cost $13.00 per barrel escalated at 2.75 percent annually from 1975 in constant 1975 dollars; (2) domestic oil would follow current price regulations until it was decontrolled in 1980; (3) natural gas was assumed to be priced at the Btu equivalent of crude oil plus 50 cents per million Btu as an environmental and convenience premium; and (4) nuclear electric capacity was assumed to be 125 gigawatts in 1985, 200 in 1990, and 300 in 2000, slightly below recent Department of Energy estimates.

A number of additional alternative scenarios were necessary to test critical coal issues. To test alternative regional economics, deemphasize East and deemphasize West cases were developed. The deemphasize East case assumed a real increase of 2 percent per year in mine input factor costs in Eastern mines beyond the costs assumed in the Reference Scenario. In the scenarios deemphasizing Western coal, it was assumed that Western states would impose a severance tax of 40 percent on the cost of production of Western coal and strict surface mine regulations would effectively remove

TABLE 13-1. Coal in transition scenarios, alternative demand levels

	Demand Level Scenarios		
	Reference	*High*	*Low*
Aggregate energy growth rate (percent per annum)	2.5	3.5	1.5
Electricity growth rate (percent per annum)			
1975–1985	5.6	7.0	4.0
1986–2000	4.0	6.0	2.0
Industrial steam coal growth rate (percent per annum)	8	10	6
Coal required for synthetic fuels (quads)	3	5	1

50 percent of Western coal reserves from the available resource base. Other assumptions in those two scenarios would be the same as the reference scenario.

Two scenarios were designed to test the effect of alternative environmental standards. In the Reference Case emmision controls were assumed to be equivalent to July, 1977, New Source Performance Standards. One alternative environmental scenario assumed that the emission limits would be reduced to one-half of the July, 1977, New Source Performance Standards. In the other stringent environmental case, best available control technology was established as the requisite criteria for controlling emissions from new facilities. This was defined as requiring the removal of 90 percent of the original sulfur content of all coal burned.

One final case, the "Crunch" scenario, was devised in which everything goes wrong for the production, supply, and use of coal. In this case, coal demand equivalent to the High Demand Scenario was assumed. Eastern mining costs were assumed to escalate at 2 percent per year, the Western severance taxes were set at 40 percent, and the 90 percent emmission standards was applied.

13.4 MODEL RESULTS

For each of the scenarios, the models calculated that coal production will increase between now and the year 2000. Figure 13-1 shows the estimated medium projections of coal production in 1985 and 2000 for each scenario as derived by the various models. In the Reference Case, coal production increases from fifteen to twenty-five quads by 1985, and to over fifty quads by the year 2000. This is equivalent to about 2.5 billion tons per year. In the low demand case, coal demand reaches twenty-three quads or about 1 billion tons per year in 1985 and thirty-four quads in the year 2000. This is equivalent to just over 1½ billion tons. In the high demand scenario, coal production reaches twenty-eight quads in 1985, equivalent to 1¼ billion tons, and seventy-five quads or about 3.8 billion tons in the year 2000. While there is a great difference in ultimate coal production between the low and high cases, the expectation is that coal production will rise on an overall basis. The Reference Case represents a better than three-fold increase in U.S. coal production by the end of the century.

In no case were supply constraints triggered and there is no significant depletion of resources. The conclusion of no supply problems is also supported by a comparison of medium projections of coal production calculated by energy models compared to the assumptions about coal production

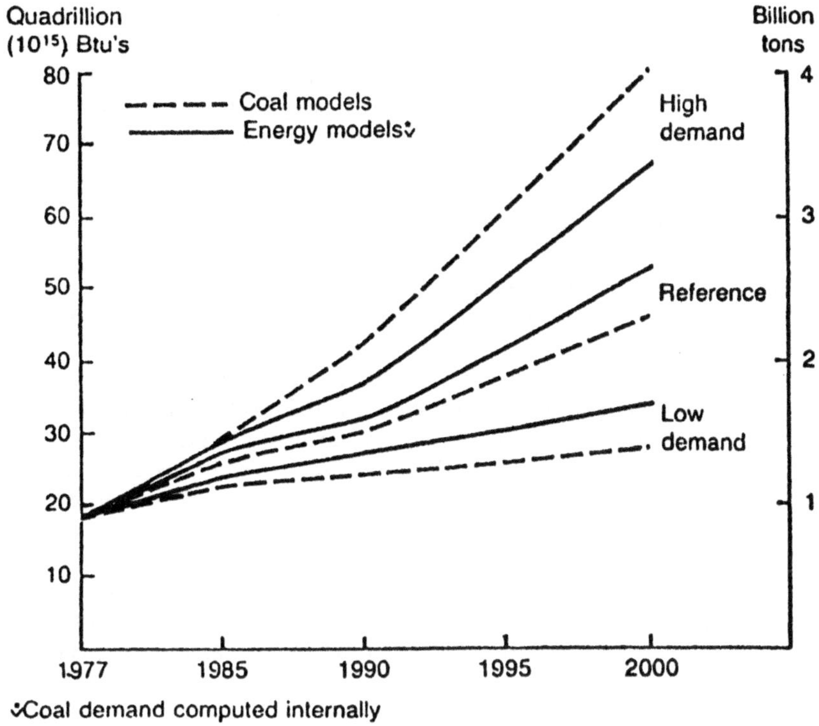

FIGURE 13-1. Domestic coal production, median projections

used to drive coal models. The important distinction is that the energy models were given assumptions about overall energy and electricity demand growth and internally calculated the likely mix of major fuels, including coal, required to meet those demands. The coal models had the level of coal demand specified in advance. In most scenarios the energy models gave internally calculated coal production that was reasonably consistent with the prior assumptions about coal demand used to drive the coal models. In comparing the scenario results for the year 2000, we find differences in the range of 16 to 20 percent between the two types of models. Significantly, however, in the Low Demand and Reference scenario the energy models calculated coal production levels higher than assumed externally for the coal models. However in the High Demand scenario the energy models calculated lower levels of coal production than assumed for the coal models. The energy models were unable to generate sufficient demand to require the high levels of coal production assumed for the coal models in the highest case. This was primarily a result of the inability of the energy models to replicate the high levels of electricity demand, and thus coal demand for electric generation, that would be necessary to meet the high levels of coal production specified for the coal models (see Table 13-2). In the Low Demand and Reference Scenarios, the energy models internally calculated slightly higher but consistent electricity demand compared to the external assumptions about electricity generation assumptions used in the coal models. This difference is further confirmed by reviewing the composition of coal consumption in the year 2000. The median projection of the coal models indicates 69 percent of coal consumption would go to the electric utility sector, compared to the 60 percent median projection produced by the energy models.

An important concern to policy makers is the potential regional split between Eastern coal production and Western coal production. The scenarios used in this project produced a significant range of estimates for total U.S. coal production. The range of variation in Western coal production is even greater as shown in Table 13-3. In all scenarios, Western coal production increases dramatically by 1985. In the Low Demand scenario, for example, 1985 production is projected to be about 3½ times 1975 production. By the year 2000, it is over 6 times as great. In the High Demand scenario, Western coal production increases roughly five fold by 1985, and 25 times to nearly 2.6 billion tons by the year 2000. Even the Deemphasize West scenario,

TABLE 13-2. Coal production and electricity generation—year 2000

	Coal (10^{15} Btus)	*Electricity (Tkwh)*
Low Demand		
Energy models*	35.6	4.30
Coal models	29.9	3.67
Reference		
Energy models*	55.0	5.96
Coal models	47.5	5.74
High-Demand		
Energy models*	68.6	7.20
Coal models	80.8	8.76
1977	18	2.12

*Internally calculated in these models.

TABLE 13-3. Western coal production* (million tons)

Scenario	*1975*	*1985*	*2000*
Reference	112	491	1,610
High demand	112	560	2,588
Low demand	112	408	758
Crunch	112	349	1,607
Deemphasize East	112	549	1,955
Deemphasize West	112	370	1,055
1/2 NSPS	112	456	1,461
BACT (90% Sulfur)	112	488	1,376

*Median projections across models.

which was designed to test stringent disincentives for Western coal, shows median projections of Western coal production of 370 million tons by 1985 compared to 112 million tons in 1975 and over a billion tons of Western coal production by the year 2000. The directional consistency of these results clearly indicates the likelihood for massive increases in overall levels of coal production in the Western United States.

The working group was also interested in the impact on Western coal production of the policy choice between one-half new source performance standards or 90 percent sulfur removal as alternative approaches to enforcing more stringent air pollution standards. The median projections produced by the various models showed a relatively small difference in western coal production between the two scenarios. This surprised the working group members as it had been anticipated that these different approaches would lead to different proportions of low sulfur coal production and thus different levels of Western coal production. (Most of the coals in western United States have low sulfur contents.) But a review of projections of low sulfur coal production in relation to total production also shows very little differences between these two scenarios (see Table 13-4).

In both cases involving more stringent environmental standards, low sulfur coal as a percentage of total coal only increases by about 10 percentage points from 1975 to 2000. It is believed that this similarity results from the economies of scale of flue gas desulfurization. Even in the one-half new source performance standards scenario, most utilities would be required to install scrubbers either to meet state implementation standards or to ensure continuous compliance. Srubbing equipment is extremely captital intensive and once installed there is no longer an incentive for most utilities to incur

TABLE 13-4. Low sulfur coal production, percent of total coal

Scenario	*1975*	*1985*	*2000*
Reference	29.4%	43.7%	52.1%
High demand	29.4%	45.8%	53.5%
Low demand	29.4%	47.3%	54.5%
Crunch	29.4%	36.0%	32.2%
Deemphasize East	29.4%	42.9%	55.8%
Deemphasize West	29.4%	39.5%	41.2%
1/2 NSPS	29.4%	38.9%	39.0%
BACT (90% Sulfur)	29.4%	37.7%	39.4%

additonal cost to acquire low sulfur coal. Both of the more stringent environmental standards scenarios do, however, result in significantly less low sulfur coal as a portion of total coal than the reference scenario. In the Reference Scenario, July 1977 emission standards are assumed, and there is a significant quantity of low sulfur western coal than can meet these earlier emissions standards without scrubbing.

Emission standards promulgated under the August 1977 amendments to the Clean Air Act require up to 90 percent sulfur removal from all coal burned as the EPA's interpretation of the "Best Available Control Technology" mandated by those amendments. (Final regulations issued subsequent to this analysis would allow between 70 percent and 90 percent sulfur removal from certain low and intermediate sulfur coals.) An important policy issue is the potential impact on the cost of electricity generation. The results of the project concerning coal in transition indicate that 90 percent sulfur removal would increase the average cost of electricity generation by only about 3 percent, compared to the Reference Case by 1985, and about 4 percent compared to the Reference Case by 2000 (see Figure 13-2). The one-half new source performance standard scenario gave very similar results to the 90 percent sulfur removal case. While these increases appear to be relatively small on a national basis it should be noted that the performance standards apply to new plants constructed during the interim period and that those specific utilities (and their customers) which are adding significant new capacity will bear a proportionally greater share of those costs.

The models used in the project also calculated the effect on the supply price of coal of the various scenarios. In all but one scenario the median projections for the average supply price of coal show rather modest and gradual increases in real terms compared to the 1975 cost in dollars per million Btus, (see Figure 13-3). The scenario that provides an exception is the

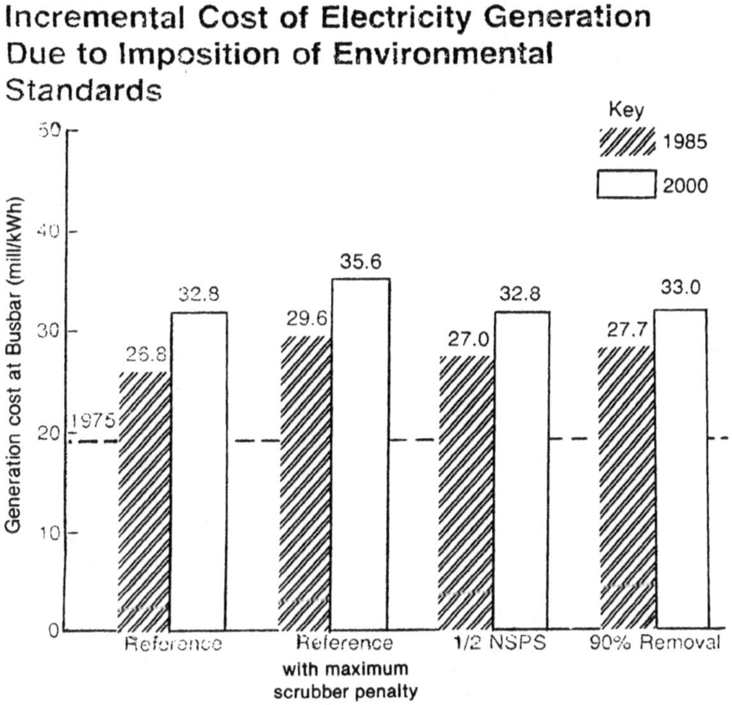

FIGURE 13-2. Incremental cost of electricity generation due to imposition of environmental standards

"Crunch" scenario which was designed to test the resiliency of the coal supply system under circumstances which provided maximum credible penalties to coal use and supply. In this case, the average supply price of coal is expected to increase by about 19 percent by 1985, compared to the 1975 price and another 66 percent by the year 2000 over 1985. This represents a 2.8 percent annual rate of increase in the supply price of coal over the entire twenty-five-year period rising to 3.4 percent during 1985–2000. Similarly, the average supply of electricity at the busbar is expected to rise at a moderate rate over the period. (The "busbar" is the connecting link between electric generating plants and the electricity delivery system.) Only in the "Crunch" case is the likely projection significantly different than the Reference Case with the anticipated supply price (in 1975 dollars) rising from about 19 mills per kilowatt hour in 1975 to 30 mills, and in 1985 to about 38 mills by 2000 (see Figure 13-4).

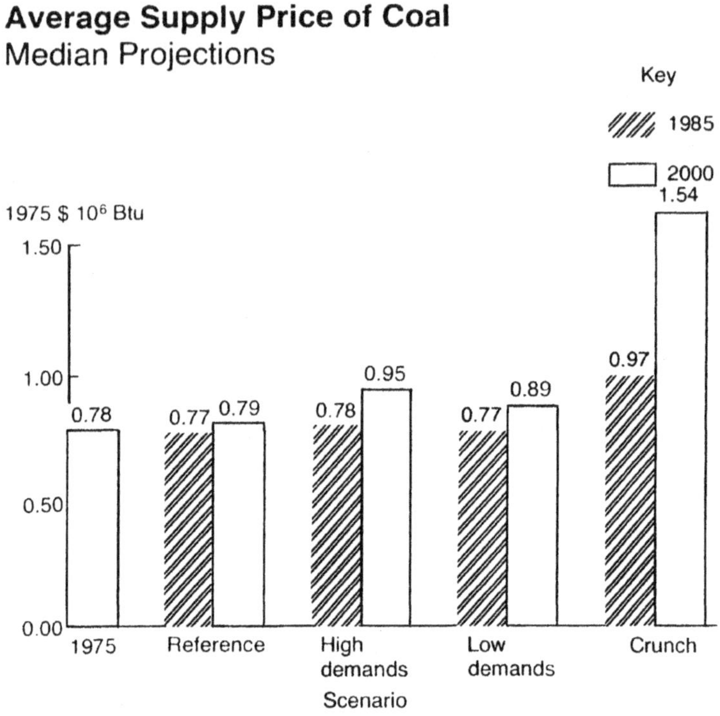

FIGURE 13-3. Average supply price of coal, median projections

13.5 ASSESSMENT OF ENERGY INFRASTRUCTURE REQUIREMENTS

The final area addressed by the study was the impact of anticipated large increases in coal production and use on transportation systems and secondary industries. The Bechtel Energy Supply Planning Model was used to calculate the resource requirements in terms of mine capacity, mining equipment, labor, transportation system capacity, transportation equipment, construction materials and labor, and overall capital requirements for the Reference Low Demand and High Demand Scenarios. Having made these calculations, the project team then asked a number of knowledgeable individuals about the resources and industries involved to comment on the feasibility of the U.S. economy meeting these requirements.

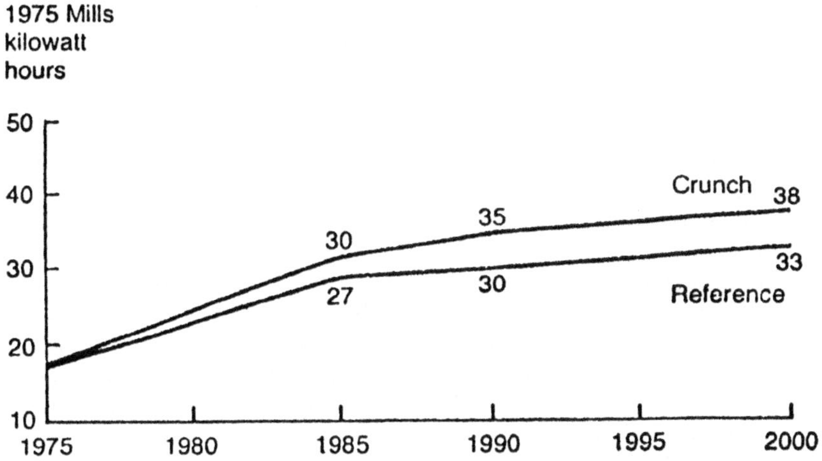

FIGURE 13–4. Average supply price of electricity at the Busbar, median projections

These assessments indentified no significant constraints in either the Low Demand or Reference Scenarios for meeting the needs calculated for those scenarios. In the High Demand Case, however, some difficulties were identified which could potentially lead to short term constraints on production expansion and/or potential increases in the cost of providing the resources or equipment in question. Specifically, the High Demand Case would require significant additional capacity in the United States for producing drag lines for surface mining use. While it was felt that such capacity additions were feasible, sufficient lead time would be required for the capacity to be developed.

A similar situation was identified in the castings and forgings industry with the anticipation that the High Demand Case would strain capacity and would probably lead to price increases. However, in this case foreign suppliers might be capable of meeting part of the demand. In the steel plate case the High Demand Scenario would probably create some restrictions on supply. This would be particularly true if synthetic fuel implementation were to exceed the levels assumed by the EMF.

Water requirements are a subject of particular interest, especially as much of the increased coal production may be in semi-arid portions of the western states. In the Reference Case, for example, overall water requirements were projected to grow by 4.4 percent per annum. However, the Bechtel results indicate that over 90 percent of the water consumption in the year 2000 in the energy industry would be for cooling water in the electric utility sector. The water needed specifically for coal processing at the mine and for the levels of slurry pipelines assumed were judged to be within the capabilities of water resources available in the western states. (Nine percent of total coal production would be moved by slurry pipelines.) While this refers to the physical availability of water, it does not answer the very real question of whether political decisions can be made to make that water legally available to the energy sector.

Manpower requirements were judged to be manageable for both construction labor and mining labor in the Reference Case. The High Demand Case may create some labor shortages, particularly for electricians and pipefitters in the construction trades. There is also some concern about potential labor shortages in the High Demand Case for underground mining in eastern United States. The experts felt that any shortages in mining personnel would tend to be transitory and local. Coal mining is a very small portion of the total labor force and manpower needs can probably be met over the long term. A key issue is whether relative wage rates will be high enough to attract the necessary new entrants. Presumably, sufficient coal demands would facilitate coal price increases to justify appropriate wage rate increases to attract these workers.

Capital requirements to meet expanded coal production infrastructure needs were also reviewed. In the Reference Case, it was calculated that energy-related capital requirements would be consistent with historic shares of total capital devoted to energy related industries. The High Demand Case would require that the energy sector increase its share of total capital from the historic level of about 20 to 23 percent in 1985, and to 28 percent by the year 2000. Those consulted indicated a view that these increases would be manageable. The issue would not be total capital availability, but the ability of energy projects themselves to attract sufficient capital. The ability to attract capital is, of course, dependent on expectations of economic returns from energy projects, which are expected to be high enough to raise the needed capital.

An important caveat on all these assessments is the question of lead times. In all cases, relatively constant growth rates over time are assumed which allow for the gradual build-up of supply capabilities. In the cases where possible constraints were identified, they are expected to be in the early part of the time period as sufficient lead time for new capacity development is not available. In the longer run, all of the relevant industries could adjust, although adjustment may imply higher prices.

REFERENCES

Energy Modeling Forum. 1978 Coal in transition: 1980–2000, vol. 1, Stanford Calif.: Stanford University.

Griffith, E. D., and Clarke, A. W. 1979. World coal production. *Scientific American* 240:38–47.

International Energy Agency. 1978. Steam coal—Prospects to 2000. Paris.

Report of the National Coal Policy Project, Center for Strategic and International Studies, Georgetown University. 1978. *Where we agree.* Boulder, Colo.: Westview Press.

Wilson, C. L. (Project Director). 1977. *Energy: Global prospects 1985–2000.* Report of the Workshop on Alternative Energy Strategies. New York: McGraw-Hill Book Company.

14 THE TRANSPORT OF ENERGY BY RAIL

C. F. Armstrong

An examination of physical and operating problems of the mountain railroads of Canada indicates that rail capacity can be adequate to meet the potential demands for Canadian coal over the next fifteen years. Significant investment will be required for track improvements, siding and signaling on the existing main lines of Canadian National (CN) and Canadian Pacific (CP), to Vancouver and particularly for the CN Line to Prince Rupert (the former Grand Trunk Pacific).

14.1 INTRODUCTION

To competently model Canada's energy future we must not only project domestic and international markets, but we must also assess our transportation capabilities and whether these will be a constraining factor. The transport of energy by rail in today's context is mainly concerned with the movement of coal. However, there are situations where rail handling of liquid and liquefied fuels makes sense. The major task, however, will be that of coping with the very significant — in fact almost staggering — increases in thermal and metallurgical coal traffic now under consideration.

The ultimate tonnages will be determined by many factors: the economic health of traditional and prospective markets, governmental attitudes toward resource extraction, the performance of alternative suppliers, and our own productivity. Projections are difficult to make and lack authority. There is a measure of consensus that total western Canadian coal marketings (thermal and metallurgical) could top 40 million tons by 1990. CN is presently handling about 4 mty (million tons a year) of western coal, and CP Rail about 10 mty. With the addition of 4 mty of thermal coal to Ontario, the total will rise to 18 mty. The prospect over the long term is something more than a doubling of present volumes. For CN itself, the figures may be more demanding. If our projections prove correct, then CN handlings could perhaps rise four-fold to 16 mty.

14.2 GROWTH OF RAIL CAPACITY

Can we produce the physical rail capacity to handle this much coal and, if so, can we achieve that capacity at prices which help to ensure the continued economic viability of the Canadian coal sources? If not, we must develop new technology which will do the job or accept that transportation will in fact place limits on our energy future.

The first issue is physical capacity. Coal is the volume leader and the rate of growth in coal traffic will certainly out-strip that of other principal movements. Nevertheless, our rail planning must acknowledge that there are other commodities and that each has a legitimate claim on the capacity of the plant. The movements of sulphur will increase as Alberta sends this once unwanted by-product to growing offshore markets and new continental markets previously served with sulphur produced by the frasch process, itself a victim in part of increasing energy costs. Grain handlings will continue to rise as production increases and emphasis shifts to markets served through the West Coast. Potash traffic will increase as the Saskatchewan mines respond to the demands of a hungry world largely dependent on higher agricultural production. The movement of forest products will also rise as cutting areas in northern British Columbia and Alberta share in the markets created by increased construction activity at home and in the United States. Thus CN must plan for an increase of about 20 mty in rail usage, of which about 12 mty will be for coal shipments. This represents more than a doubling of present handlings. Can we cope with a growth in traffic of this order? Some observers see railway capacity to be without limit. However there are limitations imposed by geography, the present technology of railroading, and the cost of plant additions in some of the most difficult terrain in the world.

Railway capacity is a complex subject. Setting aside the obvious questions of motive power and cars, it starts with a measure of how many trains of what length can be handled in a day over a particular section of rail. This is a function of siding spacing, siding length, effective speed of movement, etc. This capability is then converted into tons of product on the basis of other factors, including the carrying capacity of the car equipment, the uniformity of the flow, and the balance by direction. The rail in western Canada is largely a one-way system. The major traffic elements — coal, grain, sulphur, and potash — are westbound for overseas movement and the cars return to the loading point empty. The other major commodity, forest products, is also one-way since, while it is generally eastward traffic, it cannot be handled in the car equipment used for other resource products and suitable equipment must move empty in the westward direction. There are exceptions, but the challenge is to meet the needs of directional tonnage and some of the usual yardsticks for railway capability do not apply.

Any discussion of railway capacity must start with what can be termed a basic system — a single main line, sidings at extended intervals, and "train order control." This system would have a capacity under mountain conditions of perhaps twelve trains a day. Using the shorter trains and smaller cars typical of an earlier generation, it would do well to handle about 10 mty of one-way product. Our capacity planning uses a series of models designed to evaluate train performance, terminal capability, car utilization, motive power performance, etc. We have no overall model that provides any such ready measure of tonnage capability; therefore, the figures given are somewhat speculative. With additional sidings to reduce train "stand-offs" and signal control, we can handle about twenty trains a day. With longer trains and increased carrying capacity we should be able to handle 20 mty of one-way product. This is where the CN was on the mountain route a few years ago. Adding sections of double track in bottleneck areas and extra signals reduces train headway. More trackage is installed at intermediate terminals to allow "train fleeting," that is, the operation of several trains in one direction and then a reversal of flow to operate a series of trains in the opposite direction. Add to the mixture matching improvements to speed up the handling of trains and cars in terminal areas — a combination of better facilities and the rapid loading/unloading which is part of the unit train concept. We are doing this in CN and our planning is directed toward a further doubling of our capacity — to a system capable of handling perhaps 40 mty by the same rules.

Is there anything to be done after this goal has been achieved? The usual answer, of course, would be the progressive extension of double track with frequent high speed connections and a signal system designed for two-direction running on each track. One finds this between Montreal and Toronto, between Winnipeg and Portage la Prairie and in the higher density traffic areas of the United States.

The realities of mountain railroading limit what we can do. CN enjoys the advantages of the best gradients on the North American Continent — a legacy of exacting British engineering three-quarters of a century ago. Nevertheless, much of the length of the line is located in narrow canyons where every foot in width means hundreds and thousands of cubic yards to be removed to establish a stable back slope. Given environmental concerns, an individual siding a mile in length represents a major engineering challenge at a cost of several million dollars. Extended double track requires major tunnels of up to forty miles in length in formations where faults, brecciated rock, and subterranean water are not uncommon. Such tunnels may well be part of our future and the advantages of an environmentally safe "inside" railway are intriguing. The costs and operating problems will be a real threshold in our efforts to increase capacity.

There remains then little more than the gains to be made through changes in train length and the on-going replacement of smaller, last generation equipment with cars capable of handling 100 tons. With what we know today of train dynamics and the resulting forces on the rail, trains much beyond the present ninety-eight-car standard for coal handling will come only with a new technology. Nor is there a case for increasing gross vehicle weights beyond the current 263,000-pound limit. The benefits of longer trains and higher car capacity have already been realized in large measure and future gains will be a fine-tuning process. Our modeling is in terms of a highly sophisticated single track plant with present car capacities and train lengths as general parameters. This indicates that the potential capacity to the lower mainland is a little more than 40 mty for CN.

CP rail on the parallel route handles, because of the more mature coal mining operations in southeastern British Columbia, greater tonnage than CN. CP has the advantage of more double track already in place and the disadvantage of more severe gradients. Plans have been made public, however, for major grade reduction programs which, according to the material available, will increase plant capabilities by perhaps four trains a day. In one-direction movement this represents another 5–7 mty. It is probably likely that CP, notwithstanding what gradient problems may remain after the major expenditures now contemplated, has an ultimate tonnage threshold similar to that for CN.

The story is not complete since route alternatives must be considered. The CN of today is an amalgam of literally hundreds of rail properties including the Grand Trunk Pacific Railway which completed the line into

Prince Rupert in 1912. History has not treated Prince Rupert kindly in terms of original expectations that it would become, because of the shorter sailing distance to the orient, the focal point of our western export trade. This honor went to the lower mainland which was the western terminus of both CP and CN. However, some two-thirds of a century later we are very aware of the northern route to Prince Rupert and its implications for the future of western Canada. The Rupert line, finished by exacting engineers, provides literally a water level right-of-way with maximum grades of 0.4 percent — an outstanding engineering achievement. Present traffic on the Prince Rupert line is approximately 6 mgtm (million gross ton miles) per mile on that segment of the plant west of Prince George and rises to about 10 mgtm per mile east of Prince George. There forest products traffic from CN stations and British Columbia Railway joins together in its movement toward markets in eastern Canada and the United States. We are handling on this British Columbia north line approximately one-quarter of the traffic associated with the principal route to the south.

The northern route poses special problems in terms of grade stabilization along parallel water courses and through the Bulkley Canyon immediately west of Smithers. These problems are being resolved, however, and we can consider again building up the basic rail plant to the higher levels of sophistication on the Vancouver route. The ultimate rail capacity through the western mountains is perhaps 120 mty. This capability will not serve all traffic sources or a port of choice, and ultimately resource extraction programs will have to be designed along with transportation capacity. With this constraint, the rail system has the capability of handling volumes perhaps threefold current demands which should carry us to any reasonable planning horizon. Beyond this, who can say whether we can continue to assess our needs in terms of present transportation patterns or whether these patterns will be drastically altered by new technologies such as the solids pipeline or changes in the form in which our products reach their ultimate market? From my perspective, an ability to see forward ten to fifteen years is perhaps all the insight we should claim.

Achievement of this capacity will require a step-by-step build-up of our plant in extremely difficult operating terrain. It will also have to be done "under traffic," adding new dimensions to cost and operating problems. There must also be a parallel expansion of our port capabilities.

Common to all of this is the issue of adequate financing. I will not discuss freight rate levels, the cost of the social roles which have historically been shouldered by the railway, or the specifics of the statutory grain rates. However, if technical and engineering solutions are available, as I believe they are, then the expansion of rail capacity hinges entirely on a cash flow adequate to finance the necessary work. CN is investing about 70–80 million a year in current dollars in the mountain plant. This will increase with the more difficult construction problems, and our cash flow must match these expenditures.

This brings us to the issue of whether, with the high capital costs involved, we can achieve the additional capacity at a price that shippers and receivers can afford. The answer will be determined by several factors: the productivity of our economy and the wage and price structure which evolves, CN's productivity as a corporate entity, and our ability to solve some problems that plague us. One of these problems is rail wear — the speed with which we consume rail. Between Jasper and Vancouver, about 550 miles in length, we have 120 miles which is in curvature. By present standards, heavy steel (132 lbs. to the yard) will survive 700 mgtm of wear on tangent track. The figure drops, however, to only about 90 mgtm on curvature of at least four degrees. Thus, at present traffic levels, some 120 miles of rail will be completely exhausted in about thirty months. Hence, about 50 miles per year of rail must be replaced to maintain the present system. Add the cost of rail and the disruption to traffic services while replacement is made and rail wear becomes our biggest problem.

14.3 PRESENT ACTIVITIES AT CN

However, progress is being made:

1. We have supplemented our rail lubrication programs.
2. We have adopted a new wheel profile on captive unit train equipment that enlarges the area of contact.
3. We are installing concrete ties on all curvature over two degrees to maintain better gauge and to eliminate the waste of wooden ties through spike killing.
4. We are moving to a heavier rail section, up from 132 to 136 pounds to the yard with the extra metal in the head.
5. We are experimenting with additional grinding capacity to measure the benefits in removing rail corrugation as soon as it appears.
6. We are at the test stage with a new freight car wheel assembly, developed by a manufacturer with assistance from CN, which will allow the axles of an ordinary freight truck to articulate up to six degrees. If the field results measure up to lab experiments, we will shortly make this modification to all car equipment assigned to heavy traffic movements. These programs add together to give us considerable leverage on rail life and the results are beginning to show.

We are also making other productivity gains through better coordination of maintenance of way activities, better traction through our own improved diesel slip-control devices, and the addition of more intermediate signals to reduce train headway. Soon we will achieve a downward adjustment in the size of our train crews in main line service through long-standing programs for radio communication, improved cabooses, and hot box detector systems.

One of the exciting areas of development has been the computer system. CN has one of the finest on-line operating control systems available to any railroad in the world. It is built around some 400 mini-computers in the field linked to major central computers which we have duplicated in a distant location for back-up. This provides, in printed form or cathode ray tube display, current information on fleet status, individual cars and locomotives, and failures previously undetected.

For CN productivity has been a matter of survival. The simple economies of longer trains and elimination of steam locomotive firemen are behind us. Other changes are taking place, however, and while the productivity gains of the future may be less spectacular, they should continue.

There is no special insulation against further rate increases. Such a formula does not exist and rates will have to take into account real costs and, in some instances, to improve our position on certain movements where the rate of return is not adequate. We can no longer live on the heritage of surplus capacity left us by the frantic railroad building activity in the early two decades of our century. The present rail plant is operating close to optimum level in many areas and additional capacity must be bought and paid for.

14.4 CONCLUDING REMARKS

Considering Canada's energy future from the perspective of a railroader, I see that: (1) as a fuel efficient carrier, the railways will have an increasingly important role to play in meeting the country's transportation needs; (2) since fuel is a significant element in our total direct costs, increases in energy price will mean a significant increase in our cost base; (3) the transport of coal will be the major component in a potential doubling of demands for rail transportation in the next ten to fifteen years; (4) segments of the present rail plant are now handling optimum traffic levels or do not meet the exacting standards required for heavy traffic. The capacity to handle this increased traffic will have to be created by continuing substantial investments in additional line plant, new rail, and better terminal facilities. This demands an adequate cash flow from rates which recognize present construction costs and the escalating costs of doing business. Speaking for CN Rail, we see as well that a major block of this additional capacity will be oriented to the alternative port of Prince Rupert and that this will have to be reflected in planning future resource exploitation; and (5) the railways have the capability to meet the total rail transportation needs, including coal, for the foreseeable future.

15 COAL SLURRY PIPELINES: A TECHNOLOGY ASSESSMENT

Marvin C. Ott

At the request of the Congress, the Office of Technology Assessment (OTA) carried out an analysis of the potential economic, environmental, social, and legal-regulatory implications of coal slurry pipeline development. Major findings include: (1) under certain conditions slurry pipelines are the least costly mode for transporting coal; (2) the current regulatory framework does not insure an optimal choice between rail and pipeline from a societal perspective; (3) the introduction of slurry pipelines is not likely to affect materially the rate of coal resource development and use on a national scale; and (4) sufficient unused quantities of suitable water are physically present although not necessarily legally available for the operation of several slurry pipelines from Western coal-producing regions.

15.1 TECHNOLOGY ASSESSMENT AND THE ROLE OF THE OTA

In recent years the concept of "technology assessment" has gained considerable currency in the academic, governmental, and industrial communities. Behind this development lies a growing appreciation of the powerful influence of technology upon the modern world as well as the extraordinary complexity of technology-society interactions. The impact of technology is not only potent and complex, it is highly dynamic as well due to the rapid and accelerating pace of technological innovation. The pace of technological change has tended to strain, if not outrun, the capacity of social and political institutions to adapt. The lag is manifested in myriad ways; e.g., the failure to develop an agreed code of ethics in dealing wtih advances in medical technologies relating to life support systems, abortion, test tube conception, and recombinant DNA; the absence of a comprehensive means of coping with the land use impacts of the automobile; and the inability of diplomats to negotiate an international legal regime for the oceans in response to the development of deep sea mining technology. In the past such dislocations have been broadly regarded as a necessary and bearable cost of "progress." However, as the pace, scope, and impact of technological change continue to grow, so do the actual or potential costs. In recent years an increasing willingness to question the acceptability of such costs has been evident. Examples range from anti-technology overtones of the "back to the land" movement embraced by many people to public opinion surveys which indicate a growing willingness to accept a slowing of the pace of conventional technological and economic progress in return for a lessening of the environmental and other costs accompanying such change. While these attitudes are not yet dominant, there is a clear risk that technological innovation will be the casualty if means cannot be found for containing the external costs associated with the process. The discipline of technology assessment has emerged in response to the latter concern. The basic objective is to devise methods and institutions for anticipating and averting, to the maximum extent possible, adverse impacts of technological innovation and change.

The Congress has not been immune to these concerns. Legislators are confronted with an increasing array of policy issues containing a substantial technological dimension and with major implications for the future of the United States and the world. These range from defense matters (e.g., whether to build the neutron bomb), to energy (e.g., how to handle the problem of nuclear waste disposal), to communications (e.g., how to protect civil rights while permitting the introduction of centralized electronic data gathering systems). In order to deal effectively with such questions, the Congress needs expert assistance to understand the complex technical questions involved and to anticipate the range of possible consequences, intended or otherwise, of technological applications and of public policy concerning them. To be useful such analysis must be unbiased and carried out independently of the Executive branch agencies. With these considerations in mind, the Office of Technology Assessment was created in 1972 as an advisory arm of the Congress. Its official task is "to help legislative policymakers anticipate and plan for the consequences of technological changes and to examine the many ways, expected and unexpected, in which technology affects people's lives. The assessment of technology calls for exploration of the physical, biological, economic, social and political impacts which can result from applications of scientific knowledge."

OTA has a staff of 130 and a budget of about $11 million. The professional staff is drawn largely from the physical and natural sciences and engineering, but there is also a significant number from the social sciences and a few from the humanities. Much of the Office's research is conducted through contractors, closely supervised by OTA staff. Contractor research can be an important source of information and analysis, but it is only an input. The final study is written by the OTA staff relying to a greater or lesser extent on contractor contributions. The policy analysis and conclusions are produced entirely by the staff. Most assessments originate as a request from the Chairman of one or more committees of the House or Senate. Before any study can be undertaken or published, it must be approved by a twelve-member Congressional board evenly divided between House and Senate and Democrats and Republicans. The chairmanship rotates with each Congress and is presently occupied by Senator Edward Kennedy. The intent has been to create an agency that is responsive to Congressional needs but that is insulated from partisan political manipulation.

It is probably too early to judge whether OTA will be able to perform effectively the role assigned it. Examples of energy-related studies include nuclear proliferation and safeguards, enhanced oil recovery, onsite solar energy systems, the proposed national energy plan, coal slurry pipelines, direct combustion of coal, and residential energy conservation. Other assessments underway examine energy from biological processes, global energy trends, solar satellites, liquid natural gas, nuclear waste disposal, and alternative U.S. energy futures. Studies completed to date have been the basis for Congressional committee briefings and hearings and, as a consequence, have directly influenced legislation. In addition, they have in several cases been used within the Executive branch to modify policy and shape legislative proposals.

The OTA analysis of coal slurry pipelines is a representative example of technology assessment (OTA, 1978). It examines the proposed large scale application of a relatively new technology with a possible wide range of attendant impacts — economic, environmental, social, and political. OTA's task in this study is to assess the nature and extent of those impacts and the policy options available to the Congress to mitigate the adverse ones.

15.2 THE SLURRY PIPELINE STUDY: AN OVERVIEW

President Kennedy suggested in early 1962 that coal slurry pipelines might be a way of transporting coal more economically, thereby improving the depressed condition of the coal mining industry. Since that time, a substantial measure of public debate has centered on the desirability of applying this technology as an alternative to transportation by rail. A slurry pipeline involves pumping finely ground coal suspended in water or other liquid medium through a pipe over a long distance. At the terminus the coal and liquid are separated and the coal is prepared for combustion or other use. The unit train is a complete train of dedicated cars operating on a regularly scheduled movement between a single origin and a single destination. It contrasts with ordinary carload movements in which many commodities are combined and recombined in one train as they are transported from many origins to many destinations. Two such pipelines have been built and put into operation in the United States. One was closed after the introduction of competing unit trains and the approval by the Interstate Commerce Commission (ICC) of a separate rate structure for this more efficient form of rail service. Another has been carrying coal for six years and has demonstrated that a coal slurry pipeline of the size required to serve a large electric generating station is economically feasible. Most of the current public controversy has surrounded legislative proposals at both the federal and state levels to grant the power of eminent domain for right-of-way acquisition to coal slurry pipeline enterprises and to impose certain restrictions and requirements upon their activities. Railroad, pipeline, coal, and utility interests have a major stake in the outcome and have lobbied heavily as a consequence.

Assessing the potential economic and environmental consequences of coal slurry pipeline development necessitates forecasting the coal transportation market in which coal pipelines would compete. Although large industrial facilities, gasification plants, and foreign countries represent possible future customers for slurry coal, the OTA report concentrates on coal for steam production by domestic electric utilities, since they represent the predominant present users that could receive coal in quantities that would take advantage of pipeline economies. A model of utility industry behavior at the powerplant level provides estimates of how much coal would be purchased from what sources to meet both hypothetical demand growth and environmental requirements at the lowest cost. These results are aggregated to arrive at total projected coal flows from nine producing regions to forty-eight consuming states at five-year intervals through the year 2000.

With this measure of demand for transportation as a starting point, the economic analysis seeks to establish relative cost relationships for railroads and pipelines and to hypothesize a plausible share of the traffic that pipelines might capture if their development were not constrained by institutional or legal factors. Potential savings to customers served by pipelines can then be estimated, as well as the impacts of diverting the traffic in question from the railroad industry. The impacts of pipeline development are evaluated in terms of their effect upon the cost and quality of rail service, availability of water for other uses, demands on related industries and markets, levels of employment, and regional economic development. Simplifying assumptions were necessary to carry out the market, cost, and impact analyses. These include an approximately 2.9 percent annual rate of growth in both rail revenue traffic and GNP, as well as continuation of present trends in some elements of rail costs.

Complementing the economic analysis, a parallel study examines the environmental impacts of constructing and operating coal pipelines, as contrasted with the corresponding effects of moving the same volumes of coal by railroad. With regard to pipelines, particular attention is focused on water use and disposal and on construction impacts. Principal impacts specific to railroads include traffic accidents and interruption at grade crossings, train-caused fires, diesel emissions, and land-use interference. Energy and materials, use, occupational health and safety, and social impacts and perceptions are explored for both modes.

In the legal and regulatory study, the existing legal systems, including relevant statutes, regulatory policies, and judicial precedents, are discussed with particular attention to contrasting the framework for coal slurry pipelines with the regulatory environment for other similar or competing transportation modes. Issues examined include the implications of common carrier status, rate setting, and contractual arrangements between carriers and shippers. In addition, provisions of water law were explored to determine what access a pipeline operator would have to water sources under a variety of conditions and how much control could be exercised over the use of water for slurry pipeline purposes by state agencies as opposed to the federal government. Provisions of environmental law related to pipeline and rail construction and operation are also investigated, as are precedents for and implications of granting the power of eminent domain for acquisition of transportation right-of-way at the federal and state level.

The coal-flow forecasting model embodied preliminary assumptions about the cost of transportation. Additional analysis was therefore necessary to determine what effect findings from the economic analysis of rail and pipeline costs might have on the coal transportation demand projections. This later work also incorporates some improvements in the model and includes data from the President's National Energy Plan, which became available after the first set of coal flows were derived.

15.3 MODELING TECHNIQUES USED*

The assessment utilized formal quantitative models for three analytical tasks. The first was designed to forecast the coal transportation market in which slurry pipelines would compete by determining what patterns of coal use utilities are likely to follow under various conditions of electrical demand growth, generating plant configuration, and environmental regulation. The second provided estimates of rail and pipelines costs and of plausible traffic scenarios if pipelines were not constrained by institutional or legal factors. The third permitted an estimate of the possible impact of coal slurry pipeline competition on the financial health of the railroad industry.

The market model focused on coal for steam production by electric utilities, since they are the principal domestic users of coal in sufficient quantities to take advantage of pipeline economics. The model, originally developed under the sponsorship of the Environmental Protection Agency to predict local air quality impacts of alternative policies, provided estimates of how much coal would be purchased from what sources to meet both hypothetical demand growth and environmental requirements at the lowest cost. Key features of the model include the following:

1. Coal is assigned to each generating unit on the basis of least cost to the utility, taking into account applicable sulfur-emission standards, coal Btu and sulfur content, and mining and transportation costs.
2. Coal prices per Btu are comprised of an f.o.b. mine raw coal price, a transportation cost from the region of origin to the state of consumption, and additional components representing local severance taxes or market premiums and the cost of FGD (flue gas desulfurization) as a function of sulfur content.
3. No constraints are postulated on the transport of coal. Transport costs were calculated by multiplying the straight-line distance from the center of the relevant supply region to the center of the consuming state by generalized transportation tariffs (0.8 cents per ton-mile for coal orginating in the West, 1.2 cents for coal originating in the

*I would like to thank Bradford Hollomon for reviewing this section.

Midwest and East). This calculation was revised for later runs to reflect likely routes and tariffs by barge and rail.

4. Starting with actual electricity sales in 1973, a national average growth in peak and average power demand is specified exogenously to the model. This average rate is made to vary by region to normalized variations in population growth rates.

Two sets of variables were incorporated in the model. The first specified government energy policy and the utilities' response to that policy by expressing the following factors quantitatively:

1. Energy policy
   a. Influence of government management of supply and demand,
   b. Availability and price of fuels,
   c. Regulations for powerplant fuel conversions,
   d. Effect of natural gas curtailment.

2. Utility Response
   a. Schedule for additions to capacity by fuel type and state,
   b. Schedule for conversions of gas and oil-fired plants to coal.

The second involved government environmental policy and the utilities' response. Assumed policy instruments include:

1. Current state implementation plans,
2. Current New Source Performance Standards,
3. Siting prohibitions in Class I and nonattainment areas.
4. A Best Available Control Technology (BACT) requirement regarding SO_2 emissions from new sources (online after 1981). This was interpreted to mean mandatory Flue Gas Desulfurization with 90-percent removal efficiency (Clean Air Act Revisions of 1977 as then understood).

The results were aggregated into scenarios giving total coal flows from nine producing regions to forty-eight consuming states at five-year intervals through the year 2000. Eight such scenarios were executed to provide insights into the sensitivity of the model to changes in variables. One was selected as the basis for market assumptions in the subsequent economic analysis.

The projections generated by the model under the selected scenario approximate an average annual compound growth rate for utility steam coal consumption of 4.2 percent. The total volume is projected to be 942 million tons in the year 2000 compared with actual deliveries to electric utilities of 429 million tons in 1975 (see Figure 15–1). A comparison of the results obtained for all eight scenarios reveals that the magnitudes of the flows are quite dependent on assumed demand growth rates, and that the spatial distribution of the coal movements are highly sensitive to environmental regulation and transportation cost assumptions. Penetration of western coal into eastern markets, for example, is highly dependent on transportation costs and BACT requirements.

Having modeled the utility coal market, the economic and environmental consequences of introducing coal slurry pipelines can be ascertained by positing specific routes and comparing the features of a rail or slurry system serving those routes. The critical characteristics to be specified for each system are cost and traffic volume and distances. A national scenario without pipelines would be one in which railroads, along with other existing modes, would meet the demand for utility coal transportation. The alternative involves a hybrid rail and pipeline system with traffic allocated to the cheaper mode from the shipper's standpoint. The second scenario is, of necessity, highly conjectural depending not only on the projections of the coal transportation market, but also on crude cost estimates and uncertain predictions of the behaviour of transportation firms, their customers, and government regulatory bodies.

Four hypothetical transportation routes were selected and arbitrarily assigned specific states of origin as follows:

1. Central Western coal from Wyoming to Texas,
2. Northwestern coal from Montana to Minnesota and Wisconsin,
3. Central Western coal from Utah to California,
4. Southern Appalachian coal from Tennessee to Florida.

These four origin and destination pairs exhibit differences in (1) region of the country, (2) condition and circuity of the rail system, (3) type of terrain, (4) access to water, (5) type and concentration of mining activity, and (6) volumes of coal to be transported.

These costs considered here are incremental ones from the viewpoint of a railroad or pipeline enterprise, and they therefore represent the rates that a firm providing the transportation would have to charge its shippers in order not to lose money on the traffic in question. They do not necessarily represent the rates that would be charged in the current regulatory environment, and they include neither profit beyond a minimum cost of capital for direct investment nor any contribution to the fixed costs of a larger railroad or pipeline system. The estimates presented also provide for no change in technology or productivity with time for either mode.

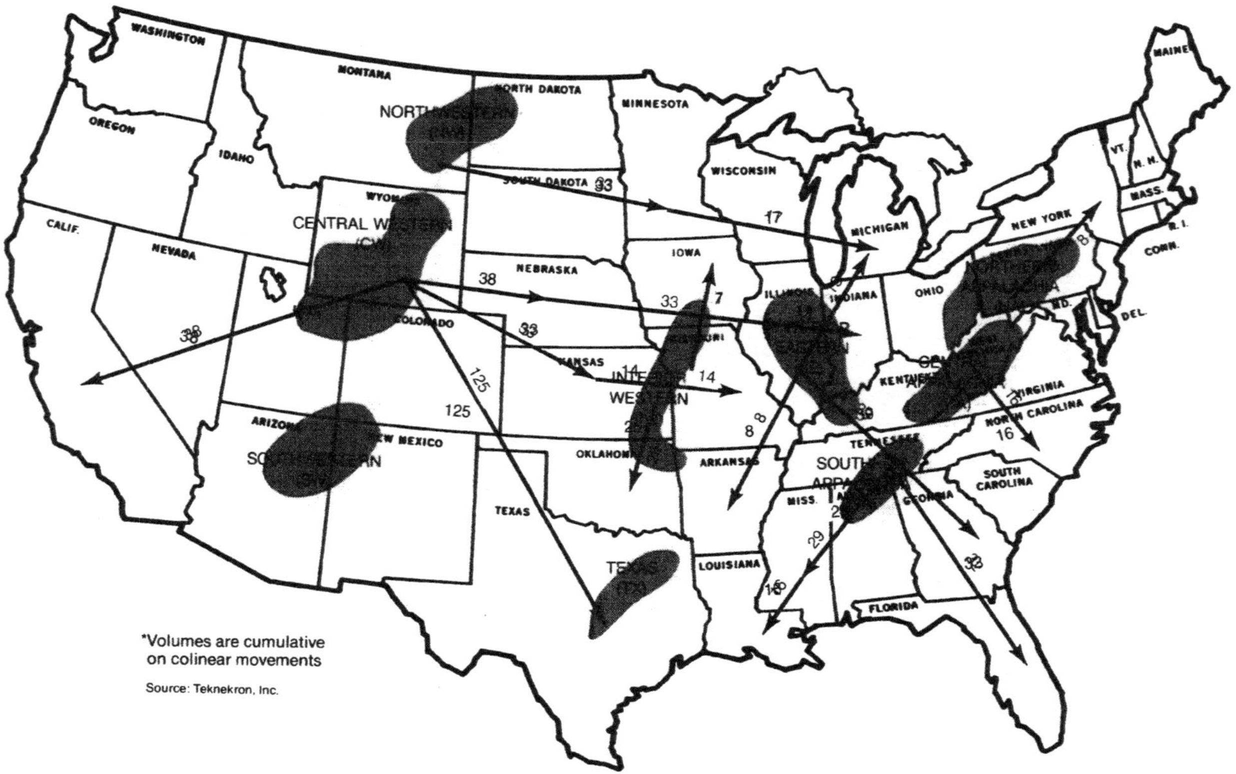

FIGURE 15-1. Year 2000 potential utility coal movements of more than 5 million tons per year over distances greater than 200 miles (millions of tons per year)*

The analysis of the four routes indicated that the principal factors influencing the relative costs of unit trains and slurry pipelines for coal transportation are the following:

1. Annual volume of coal,
2. Distance to be traversed,
3. Terrain along the route,
4. Expected rate of inflation,
5. Real interest rate,
6. Size and spacing of mines,
7. Presence of large volume customers for the coal,
8. Water availability and cost,
9. Relative costs of diesel fuel and electricity,
10. Railroad track characteristics,
11. Length and speed of trains.

Creating a plausible scenario for the purpose of evaluating the overall economic effects, as opposed to the localized costs, of the development of a coal slurry pipeline industry required a determination, by some general criteria, of which coal flows might be carried by pipeline. To accomplish this, assumed distances and coal volumes were varied artifically and calculations repeated to determine those combinations of values for which rail and pipeline costs are equal under the conditions governing each of the four cases. The resulting "indifference curves" appear in Figure 15-2. For each set of conditions, traffic volumes and distances above and to the right of the curve would be carried more economically by pipeline, while rail would be more advantageous otherwise.

The flows of coal from producing regions to consuming states in the transportation demand scenario could be compared to the indifference curves and assigned to pipelines whenever the combinations of distance and sustained volume fell in the region favorable to pipelines. A highly speculative but plausible traffic scenario derived in this necessarily somewhat arbitrary manner is illustrated in Table 15-1. All other coal is assumed to travel by another mode, probably rail or barge. These postulated volumes are in no way intended as a projection of pipeline market penetration. They only provide a starting point for an analysis of what might happen if the equivalent of approximately eight pipelines averaging 25 million tons per year were to be built between now and the year 2000.

The remaining task of the economic modeling was to estimate the effect that development of coal slurry pipelines would have upon the railroad

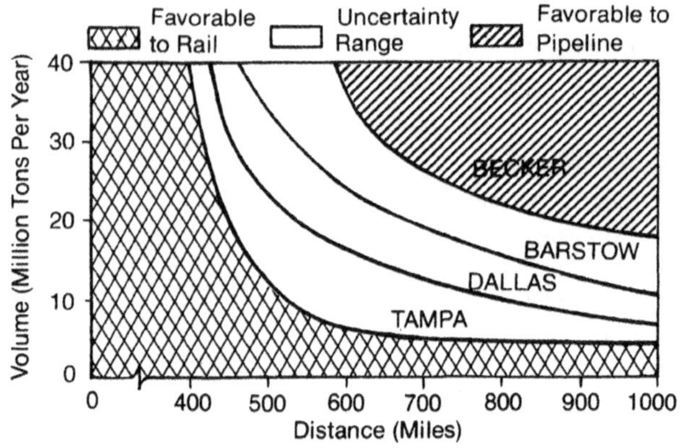

Source: General Research Corp.

FIGURE 15-2. Rail versus pipeline cost indifference curves based upon site-specific case study conditions

TABLE 15-1. Pipeline traffic scenario (millions of tons per year)

Origin / *Destination*	*Year* 1985	1990	1995	2000
Central Western				
Indiana	17	17	17	17
Kansas	—	—	19	19
Missouri	14	14	14	14
Texas	35	72	93	125
Southern Appalachian				
Florida	16	16	16	32
Total	82	119	159	207

Note: This scenario has been developed for illustrative purposes and does not represent a prediction that the coal volumes will be transported by pipeline or any other mode between the listed origins and destinations.

industry, its employees, suppliers, and customers. This required a four-step analysis:

1. A baseline projection of total rail traffic (distance and volume) by region for all commodities,
2. A projection of railroad costs by region as a function of traffic levels identified in step one,
3. An estimation of the reduction in regional railroad revenues and costs due to the postulated diversion of traffic to pipelines (see Table 15-1),
4. A calculation of the impact on rates of return of the reduction in net railroad revenues under ICC tariff regulations.

The first step was accomplished by using GNP growth assumptions, an input-output model of the overall economy developed by the International Research and Technology Corporation under Department of Energy auspices which translated the input-output structure into freight flows by transport mode over time. Railroad revenue shares and operating costs by region were established primarily by regression analysis on both sectoral and time series data. It was then possible to calculate what impact the projected capture of coal traffic by pipelines (as shown in Table 15-1) could have on the net earnings of railroads by region. The impact on return on capital for the railroad industry could be estimated under different assumptions about ICC tariff regulation policies affecting revenues from commodities other than coal. The result can also be expressed as the percentage by which tariffs on all other commodities would have to increase to offset the lost coal traffic and provide a given minimum necessary return on investment.

15.4 THE RESULTS

Major findings of the assessment based upon simplifying assumptions and considerable speculation about the future are:

1. Based on the analysis performed in this assessment, coal slurry pipelines do represent under some specific circumstances the least costly available means for transporting coal. Whether this is true of any particular pipeline can only be determined by detailed evaluation of the conditions specific to the route. The following conditions tend to favor pipelines on any particular route: high annual volumes of coal shipped, long distances to be traversed, high anticipated rates of in-

flation, low real interest rates, large closely spaced mines, a secure market of several large customers located in such a way as to permit them to receive coal from a single pipeline, terrain characteristics favorable to pipeline excavation and construction, availability of sufficient water at low delivered cost, low cost of electric power for pipeline pumping relative to that of diesel fuel for railroad locomotives, circuitous rail routes, poor track (or other conditions unfavorable to railroads), inefficient rail operations (including short or slow trains), and absence of a parallel navigable waterway.

The choice of pipeline transportation over rail represents in part a decision to incur capital costs, which can be amortized at a predictable rate, rather than operating costs, which are subject to inflation. This decision rule involves weighing the real interest rate one must pay on invested capital against the uncertain inflation component of future operating expenses. Comparisons of rail and pipeline economics in OTA's analyses are based on total life cycle costs, and they take the greater exposure of rail expenses to inflation into account. However, managers of electric utilities, the potential customers for slurry pipelines, may prefer the greater stability and predictability of pipeline costs even where an analysis of life cycle costs favors railroads.

The necessity to predict future construction costs, labor productivity, and inflation rates adds a major element of uncertainty to the relative costs of the two modes. In fact, the range of uncertainty associated with predictions of rail and pipeline costs in a given case is often as great as the difference between them.

2. The current regulatory framework does not guarantee that market-based choices between slurry pipelines and rail will necessarily minimize the cost to society of transporting coal. This is true because common carrier status and Interstate Commerce Commission rate regulation place railroads at a disadvantage relative to less stringently regulated pipelines. Thus, with the power of eminent domain, coal pipelines would enjoy significant regulatory advantages over railroads in four major areas.

First, rail rates contain an element of fixed system costs and losses which result from the requirement to maintain certain unprofitable services. This creates a distortion in relative rates, permitting selection of pipeline transportation in some cases where rail represents a lesser cost to society. Second, permitted rates of return on rail investment have historically been considerably less than those allowed in the present pipeline industry. Railroads therefore will find it more difficult to effect capital improvements that would reduce total costs than will pipelines. "Real" rail costs as estimated in this study are not as low as those that railroads could achieve with an improved ability to attract needed investment. Third, prohibitions against long term contracts with shippers impede railroads from undertaking otherwise economical investments that would only pay for themselves over a period of time. Pipelines, on the other hand, enjoy cost escalation clauses within long term delivery contracts.

3. The development of a substantial slurry pipeline industry is likely to diminish the growth in future revenues of competing railroads, primarily in the West, unless rates paid by remaining shippers are adjusted to compensate.

Assuming that pipelines carry a share of coal traffic increasing to approximately 200 million tons per year by the end of the century, western railroads will experience slower increases in coal revenues than they would otherwise have expected. Although any reduction in revenue could represent a threat to the financial health of a particular railroad, the potential impact of coal slurry pipelines on the railroad industry as a whole appears to be substantially less than that of either a possible adverse federal regulatory policy or a decline in the present rate of improvement in productivity.

Average rail tariffs, adjusted for inflation, are declining and are likely to continue to do so for the next twenty years based on the market and cost assumptions of the analysis. Even if railroads were to respond to pipeline competition by modifying their rate structure to preserve the net income they would otherwise have realized without pipelines, the rate of decline in tariffs would be lessened but not reversed.

4. The introduction of coal slurry pipelines is not likely to affect materially the rate of coal resource development and use on a national scale. It may, however affect the regional pattern of coal mining and distribution in such a way as to expand the use of western coal to greater distances from its area of origin.

The choice between transportation modes will not be determined by their respective capacity limitations. Sufficient investment in either can keep transportation capabilities abreast of forseeable needs. The pattern of distribution of coal from producing areas to points of use, however, is sensitive to transportation costs. Thus, relative reduction in coal freight rates in the West due to the introduction of coal slurry pipelines will encourage the use of western coal at greater distances from where it is mined.

5. Pipelines employ less labor than does rail over their respective useful lives, but if a substantial pipeline industry were to develop, enough people would probably be employed in construction and supplying industries to offset cumulative employment impacts in the rail industry for the rest of the century.

Even without the competition of pipelines for new coal traffic, railroad employment is expected to remain at a constant level, or even decline, until 1990. If slurry pipelines capture a significant portion of the coal transport market during this period, especially if they do so after railroads have expanded their operations to carry new coal traffic, the decline in railroad employment may outstrip attrition and result in actual layoffs. This effect, however, is not likely to be great on a national scale.

6. In the three western coal-producing areas studied, sufficient water is physically, although not necessarily legally, available to service both existing uses at present levels and a substantial number of coal slurry pipelines as well. However, pipelines do compete directly with other possible future uses. These include alternative forms of energy development involving *inter alia* facilities for coal mining, electric power generation, and shale oil. Consequently, a decision to construct a coal slurry pipeline will require consideration now of alternative uses for water in the future.

The allocation of water for any use can potentially have a significant impact upon: (1) the physical environment by diminishing surface stream flows or depleting ground water supplies; and (2) the economic and social well-being of the populace in the water source areas as choices are made between competing water uses. The water-related impacts of coal slurry pipelines can be mitigated if sources of water can be found which are usable for slurry but not for most other purposes. There are three promising possibilities: irrigation return flows, primary or secondary sewage effluent, and most important, saline ground water. In each instance the water may need some purification for use as a slurry medium but this appears to be manageable. Sewage effluent will not be available in sufficient quantities in many areas to serve as more than a supplementary water source, and the size and location of saline ground water sources are generally not well known. An additional means of mitigating the pressure on limited water resources is to recycle the recovered slurry water by return pipeline. The limiting factors are the high, but not necessarily prohibitive, cost of such a self-contained system and the fact that not all of the water can be readily separated from the coal.

7. The environmental choice between coal pipelines as opposed to unit trains primarily involves weighing the water use impacts of slurry pipelines against the community disruption resulting from increased train traffic.

Community disruption can take a variety of forms: increased exposure to train noise, dislocation of land use patterns, interruption of commuting and other automobile traffic, additional accidents at grade crossings, and interference with cattle movements as rangeland. Some of the adverse impacts that result from increased unit train activity can be mitigated. Grade separations permit the safe movement of vehicle and pedestrian traffic across tracks, though these are expensive and the costs are borne in part by the public. Cattle passes may facilitate the movement of herds from one range to another, though their impact is uncertain. New highway and rail construction can be planned so as not to intersect if at all possible. New tracks can be laid to avoid residential areas, and land alongside existing track can be zoned nonresidential.

Other environmental and social impacts associated with either coal slurry pipelines or unit trains (e.g., air pollution, construction impacts, revegetation, and occupational health and safety) are not particularly serious or are roughly equivalent for the two modes.

8. The development of a coal slurry pipeline industry would be possible, but very difficult, without eminent domain authority at the federal level.

All other pipeline systems except natural gas were built largely with state eminent domain authority. However, not all states have statutes granting the power of eminent domain to slurry pipelines. Those that do, require that the pipelines serve shippers or consumers within the state. More recent statutes limit use of state water for slurry pipelines and subject them to state regulation as common carriers. Federal legislation in this area would facilitate coal slurry pipeline development by removing the need to direct routes, possibly at prohibitive cost, around states without eminent domain provisions, and by eliminating the requirement that the pipelines serve a public purpose within each state along the route.

A judgment concerning the desirability of slurry pipelines as a form of coal transportation will depend on the subjective weights that one assigns to the factors discussed above. The overall issue, however, extends beyond the question of whether coal slurry pipeline development by itself would have a favorable impact on society. The judgment will therefore also depend on one's views concerning broader problems, of which the coal slurry pipeline controversy is only one aspect. These include: (1) the current railroad regulatory structure, (2) the present systems for allocating water resources in the West, and (3) the availability of mechanisms by which conflicting regional differences over energy development can be reconciled.

REFERENCES

Office of Technology Assessment, U.S. Congress 1978. *A technology assessment of coal slurry pipelines.* Washington, D.C.: Government Printing Office.

16 COSTING THE MOVEMENT OF WESTERN CANADIAN COAL TO THUNDER BAY: AN INCREMENTAL APPROACH*

Christopher J. Boon

The problem of selecting the appropriate mode or combination of modes for the movement of western Canadian coal to Ontario through the year 2000 is studied. The analysis includes the development of coal demand and supply forecasts, and an assessment of rail traffic and line capacity in western Canada. Marginal capital and operating costs for four alternative systems — rail/lakeboat, slurry pipeline/lakeboat, high-voltage direct-current transmission, and coal gasification — are developed, and tariff schedules for each system through 2000 calculated using a discounted cash flow computer model. A sensitivity analysis on the model parameters and cost estimates is performed.

16.1 INTRODUCTION

The cost data employed in this analysis are based on publicly available information. Although the level of accuracy is appropriate for a prefeasibility

*This paper describes the results of a research project carried out under the supervision of Dr. R. W. Lake of the Canadian Institute of Guided Ground Transport, as part of the author's MBA program at Queen's University. Support was provided by a Transport Canada Research and Development Center Research Fellowship and by CIGGT.

study, these data should not be regarded as definitive. This paper will focus on the methodological framework of the study, and on some of the implications of the results obtained.

16.1.1 Coal Demand

Ontario is the largest Canadian market for both thermal and metallurgical coal, having consumed over 16 million tons in 1976. Nearly all of this coal comes from U.S. sources, reflecting the price advantage enjoyed by nearby American producers (Cooke, 1973; Darling and Shaw, 1975). However, recent developments indicate that Ontario's principal coal consumers plan to seek future supplies within Canada, while retaining their current sources whenever possible (*Globe and Mail,* 9 March 1977). Beginning in the fall of 1978, Ontario Hydro will receive shipments of bituminous thermal coal from two western Canadian sources. Announced contractual agreements call for these supplies to reach 3.5 million tons by 1980 (Banks and Associates, 1973). Hydro has also contracted for the delivery of one million tons annually of lignite from Saskatchewan, beginning in 1980 (*Canadian Mining Journal,* 1977; Drolet, 1976).

The steel industry's interest in Canadian sources of coking coal is also increasing. Both STELCO (Steel Company of Canada) and DOFASCO (Dominion Foundry and Steel Co.) have acquired equity positions in metallurgical coal properties in western Canada, and small shipments of coking coal have already been made to DOFASCO in Hamilton from the west coast ports via the Panama Canal (*Globe and Mail,* 15 April, 1976).

The ultimate size of the Ontario market is not certain, but projections based on the assumption that no new U.S. sources will be available before the mid-1980s suggest that the demand for Canadian bituminous thermal coal could grow to as much as 22.7 million tons by 2000 (Energy, Mines and Resources Canada, 1976a, 1973a, 1976b; Erdmann and Gorbet, 1977; NEB, 1969; Ontario Hydro, 1976, 1975), while the demand for metallurgical coal could increase from 1.7 million tons in 1980 to around 7 million tons over the same period (Shelpac Research and Development, 1975).

The question of availability of U.S. coal is of great significance to any attempt at forecasting domestic demand. While no one is seriously suggesting that existing coal supplies will be cut off, a growing desire on the part of the Americans to retain or increase the availability of Canadian natural gas and crude oil might prompt the restriction of coal exports as a means of forcing the establishment of an energy *quid pro quo* (*Time Magazine,* 4 April 1977). Such restrictions were actually suggested during the oil price crisis that followed the 1973 supply embargo, and might well be faced again in the future (*Canadian Petroleum,* 1971). In any event, the continuing labor unrest and declining productivity of mines in eastern United States has rendered short term supply interdiction a reality, to the extent that, "Ontario has committed itself to retaining its current [U.S.] supplies, but where possible to add incremental tonnages from Canadian sources . . . " (Martin and Eng, 1977).

A further uncertainty with a potentially great impact on the demand for thermal coal in Ontario will be the ability of Ontario Hydro to finance and complete on time its very ambitious program for the expansion of nuclear generating capacity. Current plans call for 66 percent of the base-load generating capacity to be nuclear by 1995, as opposed to just 13 percent in 1975 (Neter and Wasserman, 1974). With cost overruns and delays on existing nuclear projects and growing public opposition to the nuclear alternative raising the possibility of lengthy litigation, the ability of this program to meet the demand for base-load capacity must be questioned *(Engineering Journal,* 1975). Were coal-fired generators to replace even 5 percent of the planned nuclear base-load, an additional 4.7 million tons of coal would be needed by the turn of the century. Even the prospect of considerable delays in nuclear power-plant construction *could* necessitate such a switch in base-load capacity planning. Should such a shift occur, the demand for thermal coal in Ontario could grow dramatically.

16.1.2 Coal Supply

The question of coal supply really encompasses two elements which must be treated as separate entities: physical availability and deliverability. Although estimates of the physical reserves of coal vary considerably, depending, to a large extent, on the definition adopted for the term "reserves," even the most conservative estimates indicate that adequate resources exist to meet projected levels of demand well beyond the turn of the century (Energy, Mines and Resources Canada, 1973b, 1974, 1976d; Geological Survey of Canada 1957, 1967). In addition to these "measured" and "indicated" reserves of metallurgical bituminous and subbituminous thermal coal in Alberta and British Columbia, there are sizeable reserves of lignite (5.5 billion tons) in Saskatchewan (Boyd, 1973; Lake et al., 1975).

The question of deliverability — the ability of the industry to produce and deliver coal at an attractive price — is considerably more complex. Although both Ontario Hydro and the steel industry have stated that price will not be the principal determinant in supply diversification decisions in the immediate future, the longer term demand for western Canadian coal will remain price-sensitive to a degree (Mineral Industry Research Laboratory, 1973).

The major sources of uncertainty with regard to deliverability are, on one hand, the escalating recovery costs associated with the switch from open-pit to underground mining operations, and on the other, the possible escalation of transportation tariffs to unacceptable levels. A third element — the cost penalties imposed by stringent environmental and reclamation requirements, and by restrictions on new development in some areas — has been the target for extensive criticism by the coal industry, but these costs are *relatively* insignificant in the context of the Ontario market. The ultimate impact of these factors on coal availability is unclear, but prices will unquestionably rise to some extent. Since both Ontario Hydro and the steel companies are committed to supply diversification despite the availability of U.S. coal at lower prices, short run demand is unlikely to be affected. Over a larger period, higher prices could be expected to limit the growth of demand *if adequate supplies are available from the United States.* If such supplies are not available, the impact of rising prices may be negligible.

16.2 SYSTEMS ANALYSIS

16.2.1 Some General Comments

Such comparative costing analyses as were available in the literature reviewed for this study exhibited, almost without exception, a strong bias toward one mode and against all alternatives (Campbell, 1975; Canadian Artic Gas Study Limited, 1973; McLaughlin, 1974, 1972; Ontario Hydro, 1976; Shelpac Research and Development, Limited, 1975). The range of costs attributed to a given mode was quite spectacular, even allowing for inflation and cost escalation. Further, these was a tendency on the part of some authors to cost portions of the relevant system, rather than all components, then compare these partial costs to the full costs of other modes (Transportation Research Forum, 1974, 1976; Vanderlund, 1974).

In analyzing the four systems initially selected for study — unit train/lakeboat, slurry pipeline/lakeboat, high-voltage direct-current (HVDC) transmission, and coal gasification — an attempt was made to follow a middle course amongst high and low estimates. This did not always prove possible. For example, two sources of cost data were available for the HVDC system, and both apparently overstate the costs. The figures developed by Canadian Arctic Gas Study Limited (CAGSL) were derived to justify the position that there was no preferable alternative to a Mackenzie Valley gas pipeline. On the other hand, the costs developed by Ontario Hydro lack this intentional bias, but given the environment prevailing in such conservative organizations, there is a strong incentive not to underestimate costs, especially in the preliminary stages of project costing. It is much more acceptable to "save" money during the detailed design and construction phases than to risk a cost overrun.

Although it had been anticipated that the HVDC and coal gasification alternatives would not be cost-competitive, the magnitude of the difference, as shown in Figure 16-1, was surprisingly large — about three times that expected.

16.2.1.1 The model. Since the selection of a transportation mode by a shipper — or in the case of coal by the consumers — is typically a long term decision, the use of a *single* tariff rate generated using the discounted cash flow (DCF) methodology is an inadequate means of assessing the available alternatives. This analysis utilizes the DCF resource transportation tariff computer model MRAIL, which offers a significant improvement over the conventional DCF approach (Lake, 1975; Lake et al., 1977a). What MRAIL does to overcome this problem is to assume that the transportation tariffs are not fixed over the long term, but rather vary so that the carrier will cover the costs of operating the system, and receive a fair rate of return on equity investment.

The program requires, as input, schedules of estimated operating costs and capital expenditures, estimates of the proceeds from the disposal of assets, and the projected annual traffic volume. As well, values must be specified for a number of model parameters, as summarized in Table 16–1. The values given therein are for the "base case" used for comparison of the tariff schedules generated by the program. Given these parameter values, and the input data, the MRAIL program solves a discounted cash flow equation, with the present value set equal to zero and the discount rate at

TABLE 16–1. Base case values for MRAIL parameters

Return on Equity:	11½%
Bond Interest Rate:	11%
Delay in Development:	0 years
Escalation Rate:	5%
Debt: Equity Proportion in Capital Structure:	75:25
Term of Debt:	30 years
Life of Capital Goods:	30 years

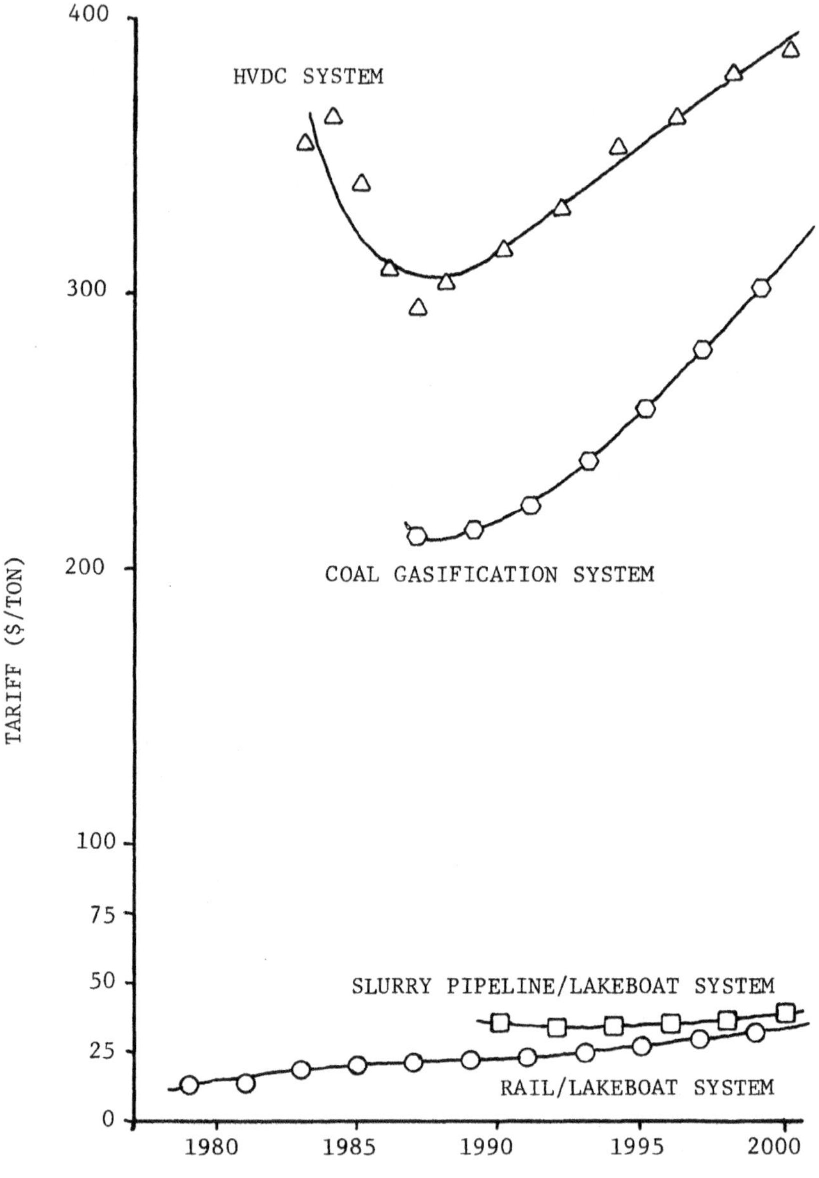

FIGURE 16-1. Annual systems tariffs, per ton of coal or the equivalent in coal-derived energy, delivered to Ontario for use

the designated parameter value. This yields a tariff schedule which will generate adequate annual revenues over the relevant time period.

16.2.1.2 The costing methodology. In order that the resulting tariff schedules be truly comparable, it was necessary to employ a consistent costing methodology for all modes. The approach selected, after some consideration, was to identify the *minimum* incremental capital and operating costs associated with the movement of the projected coal traffic on each system, and to use these cost estimates as the input data for MRAIL. The impact of this approach on the slurry pipeline costs is relatively small, since the bulk of this investment is purely incremental. However, the unit train alternative represents incremental traffic on what is essentially an existing infrastructure, with all the problems of joint costs and benefits that this entails. By restricting the costs to those which could not, under any reasonable set of assumptions, be assigned to other traffic, it has been possible to obtain consistent minimum incremental capital and operating costs for both alternatives. Since the lakeboat and Thunder Bay transshipment components are common to both systems, these have also been eliminated from further study, allowing the analysis to focus on the unit train versus slurry pipeline decision.

The following cost-allocation rationale was developed to handle the problem of allocating the costs of upgrading the relevant portions of the existing rail system between the projected coal traffic and other traffic moving over the same lines: (1) projections for other traffic were prepared (Canadian Transport Commission, 1968–1972, 1973, 1974, 1977; Canadian Wheat Board, 1975–1976; Corneil et al., 1976; Government of Canada, 1977; Hedlin, Menzies and Associates, 1969; Kates, 1972; Statistics Canada, 1976, 1974–1975; Transport Canada, 1975; Weinberg and McLaughlin, 1971); (2) an estimate of capacity for the relevant rail links was obtained (Macdonald et al., 1976; Railway Advisory Committee, 1976); (3) coal traffic (in trains per day in each direction) required to move the projected annual demand was allocated to each rail system; (4) links with capacity restrictions, inadequate siding lengths, and other limitations were identified (Canadian National Railways, 1976a through 1976h; Corneil et al., 1976; CP Rail, 1976a, 1976b; Transport Canada Research and Development Center); (5) the CP rail-weight standards (Princeton University, 1974) for upgrading based on annual gross tonnages were adopted as a guide to the weight of rail each link should contain, based on current (1976) traffic levels; and (6) links which would require upgrading only with the addition of coal traffic were thus identified, and these costs charged against this traffic.

The results of this analysis indicate that one cannot say that the cost of upgrading all existing mainline trackage to 132-lb continuous welded rail (CWR) standards *should* be assigned to the incremental coal traffic. However, the costs of upgrading the three critical links identified could quite reasonably be so allocated, and have been for the purposes of this study. In addition, the costs of upgrading, lengthening, and in some instances constructing, sidings, and signal systems as required to handle unit train consists, plus the costs of upgrading the Foothills Subdivision branch line into the Coal Valley region of Alberta, should be assigned to the movement of coal (Ahlf, 1975; American Railway Engineering Association, 1975; Canadian National Railways, 1977; Danzig et al., 1976; Lake et al., 1977b; Maughan et al., 1975; Transportation Research Forum, 1973). Finally, the incremental cost of upgrading the relevant Canadian National (CN) links with 136-lb RE CWR, which offers a superior section and hence improved performance with lower maintenance costs under unit-train traffic, should be charged against the coal traffic, together with allowances for work on other track structures and on curves and gradient sections.

Capital costs for rolling stock and motive power were based on the acquisition of 100 percent new equipment, plus spares, as required for a 145-hour cycle for CN and a 130-hour cycle for Canadian Pacific (CP) Rail services (Energy, Mines and Resources Canada, 1976d; *Time Magazine,* 4 April 1977). It has been assumed that no improvement in trainset productivity will occur over the period of the study. Operating costs were developed on a purely incremental basis; incremental demand was taken to occur at the start of each year, and the additional trainsets required were assumed to be in operation for the full year (*Modern Railroads; Progressive Railroading;* Rail Systems Research and L. E. Peabody, 1976; *Railway Age; Railway Gazette International; Railway Management Review; Railway Track Structures;* Roney, 1975; Sillcox, 1977).

16.2.2 Unit Train Costs

Table 16–2 summarizes the capital expenditures for roadbed and track structures, and motive power and rolling stock, for each railway, and presents the schedule of capital outlays used as input for the MRAIL program.

The operating costs for the unit train movement of coal to Thunder Bay include track maintenance costs over and above the level required by non-coal traffic, plus the actual costs of train operation, plus interference costs which were assessed at 15 percent of total operating costs. These costs are summarized in Table 16–3.

TABLE 16–2. Capital outlays for the unit train movement of coal to Thunder Bay ($1977 10^6)

	Canadian National	*CP Rail*	*Total*
Track & Structures	40.26	41.70	81.96
Rolling Stock & Motive Power	186.22	200.88	387.10
Total	226.48	242.58	469.06

Schedule of Expenditures

Year	1978	1979	1980	1981	1982	1983	1984	1985	1986	1987	1988	1989
Outlay	78.44	30.37	36.86	8.2	15.37	31.77	9.37	2.20	22.65	22.54	14.45	15.37
Year	1990	1991	1992	1993	1994	1995	1996	1997	1998	1999	2000	
Outlay	7.17	7.20	22.54	7.17	14.34	23.60	7.17	15.37	22.57	22.54	31.76	

TABLE 16–3. Rail system operating "expenditures" including interference ($1977 10^6)

	Canadian National	*CP Rail*	*Total*
Maintenance	86.43	52.59	139.02
Operating Costs	1,115.47	1,012.96	2,128.43
Interference	180.29	159.83	340.12
	1,382.19	1,225.38	2,607.57

Total Operating Cost Schedule

Year	*Total Cost*	*Year*	*Total Cost*	*Year*	*Total Cost*
1978	29.11	1986	82.95	1994	147.50
1979	38.04	1987	95.69	1995	164.74
1980	47.51	1988	104.14	1996	169.43
1981	47.94	1989	113.05	1997	178.43
1982	52.24	1990	117.51	1998	191.49
1983	65.35	1991	122.06	1999	203.29
1984	69.67	1992	134.75	2000	222.31
1985	70.09	1993	139.20		

16.2.3 Slurry Pipeline Costs

The slurry pipeline alternative costed here is largely based on the system studied by Shelpac Research and Development Ltd. (1975), with the addition of a gathering component to collect the coal at a central slurry preparation site near Drumheller, Alberta. To maintain comparability, it has been assumed that the pipeline will be designed to handle both thermal and metallurgical coal movements to Thunder Bay through the end of the century (Wallace, 1977). The design would be able to accommodate a maximum annual throughput of some 30 million tons. This would require an approximately forty-four inch diameter pipeline (Transportation Research Forum, 1974).

Although such a pipeline could be *constructed* in as little as three years, this assumes that all needed preparatory work has been completed, the right-of-way acquired, and the design finalized (McLaughlin, 1974). Shelpac's study is much less optimistic on this matter. The development plan proposed by that group would require eleven years from design inception through start-up. This would make the earliest start-up date sometime in 1988.

Four components must be costed: the gathering network, the central slurry preparation facility, the pipeline itself, and the dewatering and water purification facility at Thunder Bay.

The capital costs associated with the gathering component include the upgrading of 402 miles of track to mainline standards, as discussed in section 16.2. This will include extensive siding construction as well as improvements to the track and roadbed. It has been assumed that existing trainsets will be switched over as required, since these will be consumer-owned rather than railway-owned. Under this assumption, no new trainsets would be required before 2000. The capital cost of a slurry preparation facility is uncertain, but historical data for similar facilities suggest costs of the order of $0.70 to $1.25 per annual ton of throughput. However, recent discussions have indicated that capital costs in the neighborhood of $4.50 per annual ton would now be more realistic (Pemel, 1977). No costing or design study was available for an 1100-mile forty-four inch slurry pipeline. However, the available data indicate that a capital cost of the order of one billion dollars would be appropriate. Considering that the 1048-mile, thirty-six inch line proposed for the United States was estimated to cost $750 million in 1975, this is probably not unreasonable.

The provision of adequate facilities to separate the coal from the water, dry it to an acceptable level of surface moisture, and decontaminate the water used in transporting the coal, is crucial to the viability of a slurry pipeline system. Estimates from within the industry indicate that the cost of the dewatering facilities will be on the order of \$3.50 per annual ton, with up to an additional \$5.50 per annual ton required to provide treatment facilities for the very acidic, highly contaminated water. Table 16-4 summarizes the proposed schedule of capital expenditures, while Table 16-5 summarizes the operating costs for the slurry pipeline alternative.

16.3 TARIFF SCHEDULES AND ANALYSIS

The cost schedules reported in section 16.2 were used as the primary input data for MRAIL, together with the "base case" financial parameters summarized in Table 16-1. Further, thirty-year-old equipment was assumed to be salvageable at 5 percent of initial cost, with the salvage value prorated over the life span of the equipment. Capital cost allowance was assumed to flow through the other corporate operations, and it was assumed that debt would be issued for all capital expenditures up to the specified proportion. Each system was assumed to operate for thirty years, with annual operating costs held constant after 2000 (in terms of current dollars). Each system was then evaluated on the basis of the tariff schedule through 2000. The derived "tariff" schedules are shown in Table 16-6.

Although the unit train alternative is preferable through 2000, the advantage it enjoys is steadily decreasing. Further, the development of the systems "tariff" has been based on the *minimum incremental* capital and operating costs, and this approach does not consider allocated costs that would, or *could*, be charged against the service. Since the bulk of the pipeline expenditures are purely incremental, the impact of these allocations on the competitiveness of the unit train alternative is the central issue.

In this context, the answer is relatively clear. The incremental analysis developed a basic "tariff" rate which provides for the recovery of all direct capital and operating costs, plus a reasonable rate of return on the marginal investment. However, in *pricing* the service to the shipper, the railways would set rates at the highest level that would capture the traffic and satisfy all regulatory considerations, with the additional revenue providing a contribution to system fixed costs (overhead) and possibly a margin of real economic profit. The regulatory agencies governing rail freight rates have repeatedly encouraged this type of pricing policy, and could likely be expected to continue to do so in the foreseeable future.

In order to ascertain the sensitivity of the results to the various study assumptions, further analyses were undertaken with different parameter values and cost estimates. The range over which each input was varied is

TABLE 16-4. Annual capital expenditures slurry pipeline alternative (\$1977 10^6)

Project Year	1978	1979	1980	1981	1982	1983	1984	1985	1986	1987	1988
Annual Expenditure	11.00	16.21	24.91	41.28	55.02	76.36	69.98	98.26	279.22	508.25	302.73
Cumulative Expenditure	11.00	27.21	52.12	93.40	148.42	224.78	294.76	393.02	672.24	1180.49	1483.22

TABLE 16-5. Total annual slurry pipeline operating costs (\$1977 10^6)

Year	*Gathering*	*Slurry Prepar-ation*	*Pipeline*	*De-watering*	*Total*	*Total Tonnage (in tons 10^6)*	*Average Cost/Ton*
1989	28.38	13.34	30.00	21.63	93.36	14.32	\$6.519
1990	28.38	15.51	30.00	23.26	97.15	15.50	\$6.268
1991	31.00	16.55	30.00	24.73	102.27	16.59	\$6.165
1992	31.00	17.44	30.00	25.98	104.42	17.54	\$5.953
1993	33.56	18.71	30.00	27.94	110.21	18.92	\$5.825
1994	36.18	19.83	30.00	29.26	115.27	20.12	\$5.729
1995	38.60	21.00	30.00	30.86	120.45	21.38	\$5.634
1996	41.22	22.38	30.00	32.74	126.33	22.88	\$5.521
1997	43.78	23.91	30.00	34.81	132.50	24.56	\$5.395
1998	46.40	25.52	30.00	36.98	138.90	26.32	\$5.277
1999	46.40	27.37	30.00	39.52	146.10	28.32	\$5.159
2000	49.02	28.78	30.00	41.48	149.28	29.78	\$5.013
Total					1,436.24		

TABLE 16-6. Tariff schedules for movement of coal to Thunder Bay (\$/ton)

Year	*Unit Train*	*Slurry Pipeline*	*Difference*
1978	9.162	—	—
1980	11.700	—	—
1982	12.964	—	—
1984	13.914	—	—
1986	14.743	—	—
1988	16.172	—	—
1989	16.837	31.368	14.531
1990	17.531	30.389	12.858
1992	18.994	29.464	10.470
1994	20.797	29.140	8.343
1996	22.851	29.554	6.703
1998	24.969	30.510	5.541
2000	27.514	32.101	4.587

summarized in Table 16–7. The transportation decision proved to be insensitive to variations in the base case financial parameters over the range of values indicated above. However, the results are sensitive to the relative overestimation and underestimation of costs.

Since it is entirely conceivable that both capital and operating costs were overstated or understated (Neter and Wasserman, 1974), the sensitivity of the decision to total cost was examined. The results in Figure 16–2 demonstrate that were the total costs for rail to increase by 25 percent, while the total costs for the slurry system decreased by 25 percent, then the decision would be reversed. This is not the only combination of changes that could result in a decision reversal, but the examination of decision sensitivity to a 25 percent range in total cost is believed to be reasonable and satisfactory for a preliminary study.

16.4 POLICY IMPLICATIONS

These tariff rates provide for the recovery of all direct capital and operating costs, plus a reasonable rate of return on the marginal equity investment. However, a railway company cannot be expected to base its price on marginal costs. The actual rate faced by the shipper would be at the maximum level which would capture the traffic and satisfy regulatory considerations, with the additional revenue providing a contribution towards system fixed costs, and possibly a margin of real economic profit.

TABLE 16–7. Summary of base case and sensitivity parameter values

Parameter	*Base Case Value*	*Sensitivity Value(s)*
Debt/Equity Ratio	3.0	1.5, 0.0
Bond Interest Rate	11%	8%, 9%, 10%, 12%, 13%
Return on Equity	11½%	7½%, 8½%, 9½%, 10½%, 12½%, 13½%, 14½%, 20%
Delay in Construction	0	4 yrs
CCA Flowthrough	yes	no
Salvage Included	yes	no
Cost Escalation	5%	10%
Capital Costs	100%	125%, 75%
Operating Costs	100%	125%, 75%
Total Costs	100%	125%, 75%

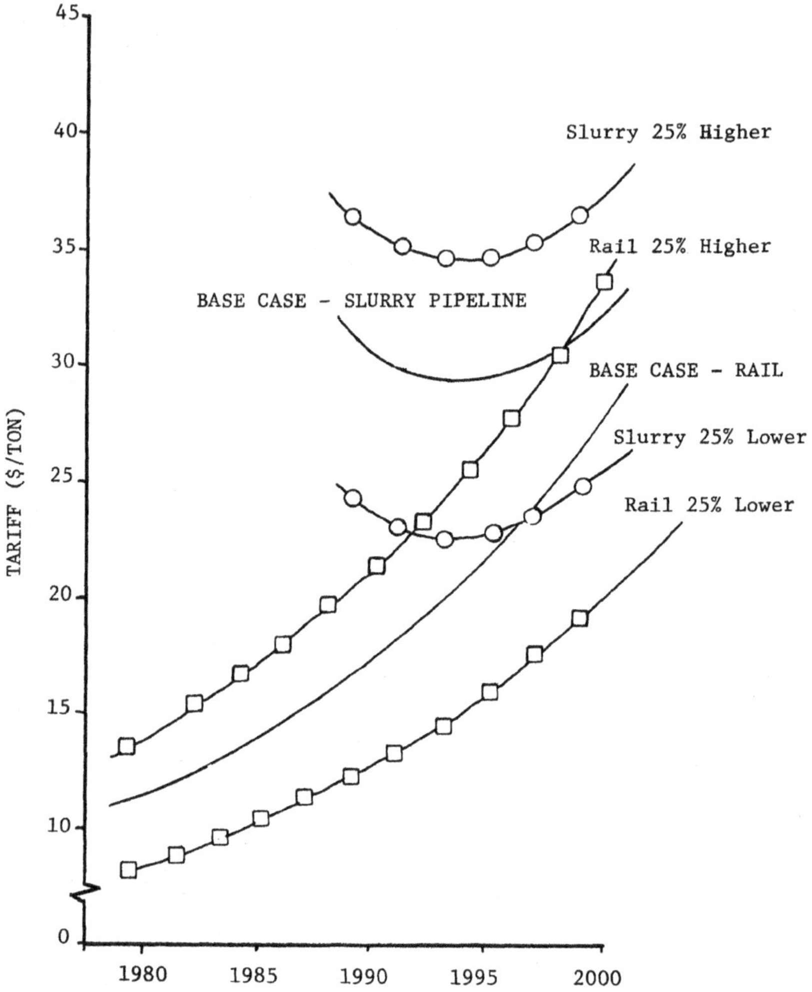

FIGURE 16–2. Tariff sensitivity to changes in total systems costs

This possibility raises a number of interesting policy issues. The National Transportation Act (NTA) of 1967 stated, as its objective, the development of "an economic, efficient, and adequate transportation system . . . at the lowest total cost." In other words, the NTA was intended to achieve the maximization of net economic benefits to the nation, *without particular concern for the distribution of these benefits.*

At the present time, the Canadian National/Canadian Pacific consortium enjoys an effective monopoly on the long-haul movement of western Canadian coal, so that the price levels which may be faced by shippers and/or consumers, and the degree to which those groups might be forced to cross-subsidize noncompensatory railway movements, is the real concern. (The legal obligation of CN and CP to move grain at the rates prevailing in 1899 — the so called Crow's Nest rates — results in sizeable losses to the railways (Schriever, 1972).) While recognizing that the railway costs developed in this study do not correspond *exactly* to the railway costs employed for regulatory purposes, the calculated "tariff" schedule should be a reasonable approximation for long run variable cost. Under the provisions of the NTA dealing with *captive shippers*, the railways could set rates at up to 250 percent of this amount, which would imply rates well in excess of the calculated "tariffs" for the slurry pipeline alternative over the period 1989–2000. If the outcome of the Gimli, Manitoba, case is considered a precedent, the shippers and/or consumers would be required to actually construct a slurry pipeline system before the regulatory process would force the railways to provide service at *competitive* rates. Since the removal of this coal traffic from the two railways could have potentially far-reaching effects on the level of general transportation service which CN and CP could provide, approval for the construction of such a system would constitute an implicit alteration in transportation policy.

The proposed amendments to the NTA do not remove the policy implications of this modal selection process, but rather result in a shift in emphasis. One of the revisions contained in Bill C-33 would provide that "where no effective competition exists, transportation rates should be so regulated as to give transportation users the same protection as they would have if effective competition existed." Since no long-distance, high-volume slurry systems have been built in Canada — and none *of this length* anywhere in the world — the establishment of what constitutes a "competitive" rate would require extensive engineering and economic analysis on the part of the regulatory agency, and would draw government even deeper into the swamp of economic regulation, with all the potential for distention and inefficiency this implies. Under these circumstances, a failure to provide accurate and comparable systems costs could have disastrous implications, both for the specific coal movements considered here, and for Canadian transportation in general.

REFERENCES

Ahlf, R. E. 1975. Heavy four-axle cars and their maintenance of way costs. *American Railway Engineering Association Bulletin* 653.

American Railway Engineering Association. 1975. *Manual for Railway Engineering*.

Banks, R. L., and Associates. 1973. Preliminary estimates of the cost of moving coal by unit train from Alberta mines to Ontario destinations or to ports for further movement by water. Executive summary to unpublished report prepared for Ontario Hydro.

Boyd, B. 1973. Coal resources of the Yukon Territory — A review. Department of Indian and Northern Affairs, Ottawa.

Campbell, T. C. 1975. Transporting western Canadian coal: Unit train or slurry pipeline? *The Logistics and Transportation Review* 11.

Canadian Arctic Gas Study Limited. 1973. Alternative modes study, volume VI — H.V.D.C. transmission.

Canadian Mining Journal. 1977. Vol. 98.

Canadian National Railways. 1977. *Keeping Track*. June.

Canadian National Railways. 1976a. Timetable no. 1. Mountain Region, 25 April.

Canadian National Railways. 1976b. Timetable no. 30. Prairie Region, 25 April.

Canadian National Railways. 1976c. Timetable no. 31. Prairie Region, 25 April.

Canadian National Railways. 1976d. Timetable no. 71. Prairie Region, 17 October.

Canadian National Railways. 1976e. Timetable no. 68. Prairie Region, 31 October.

Canadian National Railways. 1976f. Timetable no. 78. Prairie Region, 31 October.

Canadian National Railways. 1976g. Traffic density report — Pacific region.

Canadian National Railways. 1976h. Traffic density report — Mountain region.

Canadian Petroleum. 1971. Vol. 12.

Canadian Transport Commission. Commodity flow analysis, Canadian carload all-rail traffic. Traffic and Tariffs Branch, Reference Papers 1.0 (1968–72), 1.1 (1973), and 1.2 (1974).

Canadian Transport Commission. 1977. Transport review, trends and selected issues.

Canadian Wheat Board. Annual report, 1975–76.

Cooke, J. L. 1973. Coal transportation on the Great Lakes. Ontario Hydro.

Cooper, H. E. H., Jr. 1975. Environmental and energy aspects of coal energy transshipment through railroad electrification. University of Texas.

Corneil, E. R., et al. 1976. Canadian railway electrification study, phase I, vols. I and II. Canadian Institute of Guided Ground Transport, CIGGT Report No. 76–2.

CP News Summary. 1977. Vol. 33, Nos. 4, 9, 15, 17, 19, 20, 21, 22, 23, 24, 27 and 28; 1976. Vol. 32, Nos. 11, 35, 37 and 39; 1975. Vol. 31, Nos. 29, 31, 38, 44, 45, 46.

CP Rail. 1976a. Timetable no. 87. Pacific Region, 25 April.

CP Rail. 1976b. Timetable no. 97. Pacific Region, 25 April.

Danzig, J. D.; Rugg, J. A.; Williams, J. H.; and Hay, W. W. 1976. Procedures for analyzing the economic costs of railroad roadway for pricing purposes, volume 1: Procedures.

Darling, H. J., and Shaw, G. C. 1975. The Canadian lake shipping industry today. Research Report No. 29, York University/University of Toronto Joint Program in Transportation.

Drolet, J. P. 1976. The demand and limitations governing the mineral production of western Canada to 1990.

Energy, Mines and Resources Canada. 1976a. Electric power in Canada, 1975. Energy Policy Sector, Ottawa.

Energy, Mines and Resources Canada. 1973a (two volumes). An energy policy for Canada, Phase I. Ottawa.

Energy, Mines and Resources Canada. 1976b. An energy strategy for Canada — Policies for self-reliance. Ottawa.

Energy, Mines and Resources Canada. 1975a. Mineral area planning study. Mineral Development Sector, Ottawa.

Energy, Mines and Resources Canada. 1976c. Mineral industry trends and economic opportunities. Mineral Policy Series Paper MR-158, Ottawa.

Energy, Mines and Resources Canada. 1973b. Proceedings, 25th Canadian conference on coal.

Energy, Mines and Resources Canada. 1974. Proceedings, 26th Canadian conference on coal.

Energy, Mines and Resources Canada. 1975b. Proceedings, 27th Canadian conference on coal.

Energy, Mines and Resources Canada. 1976d. Proceedings, 28th Canadian conference on coal.

Engineering Journal. May/June 1975.

Erdmann, R. W., and Gorbet, F. W. 1977. Energy demand projections for Canada: An integrated approach. Energy, Mines and Resources Canada.

Geological Survey of Canada. 1957. Geology and economic minerals of Canada. Ottawa.

Geological Survey of Canada. 1967. Geology and economic minerals of Canada, part B. Ottawa.

Globe and Mail, 25 May 1976, 9 March 1977, 15 April 1976, 21 July 1977, 29 January 1976, 18 July 1975, 27 July 1976.

Government of Canada. 1977. Grain and rail in western Canada, vol. 1. Report of the Grain Handling and Transportation Commission (Hall Commission).

Hedlin, Menzies and Associates. 1969. The Canadian northwest transportation study, vol. I — The mineral potential, vol. III — A consideration of transportation factors.

Kates, Peat, Marwick & Co. 1972. Grain transportation in eastern Canada, volumes I and II.

Lake, R. W. 1975. An economic decision model for mineral development in Canada. Unpublished Ph.D. thesis, Department of Mining Engineering, Queen's University at Kingston.

Lake, R. W., et al. 1975. Forecast of demand for transportation systems in a Mackenzie Valley corridor. Unpublished report, prepared for the Canadian Artic Resources Commission.

Lake, R. W., et al. 1977a. A model to evaluate modal alternatives on the basis of complete transportation tariff schedules. Canadian Transport Research Forum, St. Andrews, N.B.

Lake, R. W., et al. 1977b. Progress report: Preliminary exploration and project definition stage, railway costing order review.

Macdonald, J. A., et al. 1976. A conceptual basis for estimating rail line productivity and capacity. Unpublished CIGGT Report No. 76-4.

Martin, P. S., and Eng P., Dames and Moore Ltd., Toronto. 1977. Reported in the *Toronto Globe and Mail*, 9 March.

Maughan, R. G.; Smith, J. S.; Lake, R. W.; et al. 1975. Arctic oil and gas by rail: Volume one, introduction and summary; Volume three, railway operations and maintenance; Volume four, petroleum products processing and handling; Volume five, relevant considerations; Volume six, cost data and analysis.

McLaughlin, G. M. 1974. Economic comparison of rail and slurry pipeline for the domestic movement of western Canadian coal to central Canadian markets. Bulk Freight Division, Canadian Transport Commission, Report No. 123.

McLaughlin, G. M. 1972. Applications, technology and economics of slurry pipelines. *Logistics and Transportation Review 8.*

Mineral Industry Research Laboratory. 1973. Transportation economics of coal resources of northern slope coal fields, Alaska. University of Alaska.

Modern Railroads. Vol. 32, nos. 2 and 6.

National Energy Board. 1969. Energy supply and demand in Canada, 1966–*1990. Ottawa.*

National Transportation Act, 1966–67. C.69s.2, Section 3, "National Transportation Policy," p. 5474, Hansard.

Neter, J., and Wasserman, W. 1974. *Applied linear statistical models.* Homewood, Ill.: Richard D. Irwin, Inc.

Ontario Hydro. 1976. Memorandum to the royal commission on electric power planning with respect to public information hearings: Fuels supply, load forecasting, generation-technical, generation-environmental, transmission-technical, transmission-environmental, and system interconnections.

Ontario Hydro. 1975. Sulphur content in relation to fuels supply program, 1970–1990. Fuel Resources Planning, Fuels Division, Ontario Hydro.

Pemel, F. W. 1977. Personal communication.

Princeton University. 1974. Design and analysis of railroad track. Rail Transportation Series, Office of Professional Educaton, School of Engineering and Applied Science Transportation Program.

Progressive Railroading. 1977. Vol. 20, nos. 3, 4, 5, 6 and 7; 1976. Vol. 19, nos. 4 and 6; 1975. Vol. 18, no. 9; 1974. Vol. 17, no. 1.

Rail Systems Research Associates/L. E. Peabody and Associates, Inc. 1976. Analysis of track and roadbed maintenance cost variability.

Railway Advisory Committee, Transport Canada Research and Development Center. 1976. Railway capacity tradeoff study.

Railway Age. 1976. Vol. 177, nos. 10 and 12; 1975. Vol. 176, nos. 9 and 22.

Railway Gazette International. 1971. Vol. 127, no. 2.

Railway Management Review. 1973. Vol. 73, no. 3.

Railway Track Structures. 1977. Vol. 73, nos. 2, 3 and 6.

Roney, M. D. 1975. Multivariate functional relationships in railway right of way costing. Unpublished M.Sc. thesis, Department of Civil Engineering, Queen's University at Kingston, Ontario.

Schriever, J. 1972. *Transportation: The evolution of Canada's networks.* Toronto: McGraw-Hill/Ryerson/MacLean-Hunter.

Shelpac Research and Development, Limited. 1975. A coal pipeline system, western Canada to Ontario.

Sillcox, L. K. 1977. Car-time cost — The dilemma of railway dead-time, idle investment and unequal treatment by Congress. Presented to Department of Civil Engineering, University of Illinois, Urbana, Illinois, April 22.

Statistics Canada. 1976. Railway freight traffic. 52–002, Quarters 1–4.

Statistics Canada. 1974–1975. Railway transport, part V — Freight carried by principal commodity classes. 52–211.

Time Magazine, April 4, 1977.

Transport Canada. 1975. An interim report on freight transportation in Canada. Ottawa.

Transport Canada Research and Development Center. *Transportation development news.* 1977: January/February, March/April, May/June; 1976: January/February, March/April, May/June, July/August, September/October, November/December; 1975: September/October; 1974: June; 1973: January, April.

Transportation Research Forum. 1973. Proceedings, 14th annual meeting. Oxford, Indiana: R. B. Cross and Co.

Transportation Research Forum. 1974. Proceedings, 15th annual meeting. Oxford, Indiana: R. B. Cross and Co.

Transportation Research Forum. 1975. Proceedings, 16th annual meeting. Oxford, Indiana: R. B. Cross and Co.

Transportation Research Forum. 1976. Proceedings, 17th annual meeting. Oxford, Indiana: R. B. Cross and Co.

Vanderlund, W. A. 1974. Solids pipelining. Speech to Canadian Railway Club, Montreal, Quebec.

Wallace, I. 1977. The transportation Impact of the Canadian mining industry. Center for Resource Studies, Queen's University, Kingston, Ontario.

Weinberg, E., and McLaughlin, G. M. 1971. Slurry pipeline research information circular no. 1. Canadian Transport Commission, Report 13.

17 SIMULATION MODELING OF COAL TERMINALS

T. J. Lauga

Coal terminals justify the effort and expense of simulation modeling because they are critical connectors between coal transport modes and have a strong influence on the end cost of coal. Three major factors to be considered by the modelers are: coal terminals have special characteristics in terms of queuing theory; they require modeling of commodity storage; and they have complex materials handling facilities. As a case study, Richards Bay Coal Terminals in South Africa illustrates a complex operational and corporate problem which presented a challenge to the simulation method of modeling.

17.1 JUSTIFICATION FOR SIMULATION MODELING

The need for simulation models of coal terminals arises from the high proportion of transportation cost in the end cost of coal energy. As links in transportation systems, terminals can have a strong influence on costs by limiting the capacity and efficiency of a transportation system.

An underdesigned terminal begins a chain reaction of excess costs. These cost effects can start with idleness costs to ships or trains at the terminal then work through the transport system to disrupt mine production at the source or interrupt delivery at the destination. For example, it can cost \$15,000 a day to delay a large bulk ship or \$500,000 to shut down a metallurgical coal mine for a day.

In spite of these strong system influences, the terminal's direct contribution to total transport cost is usually small. For example, order of magnitude costs to ship western Canadian coal to Japan are \$35 a ton to mine the coal, \$12.50 a ton to bring it to the coast by rail, and about \$5.00 a ton for a ship to take it across the Pacific to Japan. Terminal costs are modest by comparison at \$1.25 a ton. Because a terminal has strong cost influences while having relatively small direct costs, efforts to save money by providing minimum facilities may provide only illusory economies.

17.2 MODELING CONSIDERATIONS AT COAL TERMINALS

Coal terminals are a distinct type of port facility. Three major factors to be considered by the modeler are: coal terminals have special characteristics in terms of queuing theory, they require modeling of commodity storage, and they have complex materials handling facilities. The resulting simulation model includes most of the elements of a general port simulation model with the addition of additional elements that are peculiar to coal terminals.

17.2.1 Queuing Theory

Coal terminals are characterized by approximately exponential distributions of interarrival times and Erlangian service time distributions (see Table 17-1). They are an M/E_K S type of queuing problem. This means that they have random ship arrivals and ship times at berth which range fairly close to average values. Unfortunately when the terminal can serve more than one ship at a time one must solve some complicated equations.

Further, the most common reason to use queuing theory is to estimate average ship waiting time. However, at coal terminals, historical records of ship waiting time indicate departures from theoretical expectations due to two factors: intelligent human intervention to avoid congestion, and delays due to lack of cargo. Complex decisions to minimize delays and accounting for cargo are difficult to model with queuing theory.

Although ship arrivals, when aggregated, have roughly exponentially distributed interarrival times, the arrival pattern according to individual grades of coal does not conform to the expectations of queuing theory. Since individual grades of coal must be modeled in order to account properly for

TABLE 17-1. Queuing theory characteristics of coal terminals

Terminal	*Interarrival Distribution*	*Service Time Distribution*
Hay Point, Australia	Exponential	Erlang, $n = 4$
Roberts Bank, Canada	Exponential	Erlang, $n = 6$
Richards Bay, South Africa	Exponential	Erlang, $n = 6$

stock inventory at the terminal, grade-by-grade ship arrival patterns have to be created in the model. These arrival patterns are governed by the type of shipping arrangements for the terminal under study. For example, if coal shipments are generally made in ships hired on a single voyage basis, then ship arrivals will be scheduled to conform with the arrival of coal at the terminal with due allowance for unforeseen delays such as weather. Similarly, the arrival of trains at the terminal is governed by seasonalities of mining production and other factors which may vary between different grades of coal carried to the terminal.

When queuing theory is applied in most port simulations, the number of servers is assumed to be equal to the number of berths. This assumption may not be valid at all coal terminals. The competition among ships at a coal terminal for the use of the materials handling system may be more relevant than the number of berths. Using a two-berth coal terminal as an example, the operations may be described as a one- or a two-server system. Loading is carried out according to a single server model when the two ships at berth are loaded sequentially by allocating the materials handling system as a single entity. When the materials handling capacity is split between two ships, the operations are similar to two server systems.

The management of the terminal makes the operational decision about the most efficient allocation of materials handling equipment to ships at berth. This decision depends on changing variables such as the availability of equipment, grade distribution of stored coal, and grades required by the ships at the berth. For the queuing modeler, the question of defining the terminal as a one or two server system remains unresolved, since the terminal may be both at various times.

17.2.2 Commodity Storage

The aspects of greatest interest, and importance, to the terminal designer are the second and third factors previously mentioned, the physical distribution of stock at the terminal and the arrangement of the materials handling equipment.

Modeling of the physical distribution of stock is important to the terminal simulation because the lack of stock and the arrangement of stock affects, respectively, the ship waiting time and the ship service time. The stock problem will also affect the trains arriving at the terminal. An excess of stock which has filled all of the available storage space will cause disruptions to train schedules and may delay the unloading of trains when secondary materials handling equipment. The stock accounting problem places rigorous demands on the model. The model must be of sufficient detail to be able to report statistics such as twenty-three trains a year of grade #3 were delayed due to overstocking, or $100,000 a year will be spent for secondary materials handling of grade #2. Lack of stock will cause delays to ships. However, the physical arrangement and distribution of the different grades of coal on the site also has a significant bearing on the service time of ships. Grades whose annual throughputs are not large do not justify large storage facilities accessible to all of the materials handling equipment. Whereas, grades that form a large proportion of the total throughput need to be located in as many points accessible to the materials handling equipment as possible and require generous storage capacities. The materials handling system will work more efficiently and load ships faster when storage facilities are large and numerous. However, the allocation of the limited land area and reach of fixed materials handling equipment is governed by cost and engineering feasibility. The simulation must be detailed enough to measure the performance of the terminal in engineering and financial terms when various schemes for the arrangement of stock are tested.

17.2.3 Materials Handling Facilities

In designing a coal terminal, the arrival pattern and characteristics of ships and trains, harbor conditions, and train handling methods, must be modeled but there is very little room for variation in design with respect to these variables. The model, therefore, must have flexibility and provision for the testing of numerous schemes in the area of the on-shore materials handling system. In the view of the terminal designer, it is here that the simulation must prove its worth. Modeling the materials handling equipment requires that the simulation model includes such things as individual stockpiles for different grades of coal; specialized materials handling machinery such as stacker reclaimers, conveyor systems, train car dumpers, surge bin silos, shiploaders; and secondary equipment such as bulldozers.

When evaluating different materials handling schemes, sensitivity tests of engineering data are often required. For example, the rate at which material should be removed from stock by stacker reclaimers may be estimated at 3250 tons an hour. However, in recognition of the variance of engineering data, the actual rate may range from 3000 tons an hour to 3500 tons an hour. A sensitivity test would be a simulation run comparing the 3500 tons an hour rate with the 3000 tons an hour. The terminal designer would be interested in the number of hours that the materials handling machines worked, the amount of time lost due to breakdowns, the amount of time available for maintenance, and that spent on maintenance, etc. The 3000 tons an hour rate for the stacker reclaimer to remove coal from stock and transfer it for placement into a ship will require that the machine work for more hours to move the same amount of coal. The consequence would be a reduced time remaining for preventive maintenance to be carried out. This may indicate that long run operations at this slower rate would result in steadily deteriorating terminal performance due to insufficient maintenance. For this machine, the stacker reclaimer, the simulation must be able to model time utilization in great detail. It is necessary to know the amount of hours placing coal into stock, removing coal from stock, hours in maintenance, hours moving from one stock position to another, and hours broken down.

As a consequence of detailed modeling of stock arrangement and materials handling systems, routing problems develop. Material arriving to the terminal in trains must select a route into the materials handling system for storage or possibly directly to ships at the berth. In either case, the routing question requires consideration of the state of repair of materials handling equipment, the current occupancy of the machines, the current stock position on a grade-by-grade basis, current loading condition of the ship, and the problem of maximizing materials handling rates over as many routings as possible. These routing problems lead to decision rules which simulate day-to-day decisions by the terminal operators. Examples are: Which of several designated storage locations should be used to store a particular grade of coal now being dumped at the terminal? Should the grade of coal in a train recently arrived at the terminal be put into stock, the surge storage, directly onto a ship, or into a waiting line of trains? Should shiploading be interrupted so that incoming coal can be placed into storage? How should the materials handling capacity be allocated among the ships at berth?

17.3 CASE STUDY: RICHARDS BAY, SOUTH AFRICA

The task at hand was the master planning of a multiproduct export terminal handling thirteen separate grades of coal. These grades arrived from a number of inland origins in two types of unit train systems which annually deliver a total of 20 million tons to the terminal. Approximately 5500 trains and 300 ships were expected to be handled by the terminal in one year. The terminal was located in a protected harbour and was served by a one-way approach channel which brought ships from anchorage to the terminal for berthing. Ships moored alongside a 700-meter quay wall and were to be loaded by two shiploaders of a peak capacity of 7200 tons an hour.

In order to handle the expected 20 mty (million tons a year), the existing facilities designed for 12 mty required expansion. The existing plant consisted of two rail car dumpers, two dual purpose stacking and reclaiming machines with associated conveyors and sampling facilities, and two ship loaders.

The ownership of the development was split between eight separate national and international companies. Each owner had an economic point of view which required consideration. Owner interest varied according to proportion of throughput, time of entry into the terminal operations, and degree of ownership of the transportation system served by the terminal. Ships and trains were expected to carry both single grade and multigrade shipments.

In developing the master plan for the terminal, the fundamental economic justification for the facility had already been established by other studies. The main objective for master planning was the selection of the most appropriate design for the terminal to handle 20 mty and the development of a scheme for smooth transition from existing operations at 12 mty to 20 mty. Over a total study period of two years, five separate simulation studies were conducted to progressively refine the final design. These studies were required consideration of the following factors: (1) four basic materials handling schemes with numerous subvariations required comparative evaluation; (2) adequacy of storage with each materials handling arrangement and the possible requirements for supplementary materials handling was reviewed at each stage; (3) during the transition period from a 12 mty terminal to a 20 mty terminal a dynamic situation where throughputs, materials handling capacity, and the number of participants in the development was progressively changing, had to be handled by the analysis; (4) arrangement of stock for the various materials handling schemes was of major importance. Considerations were that contamination of different grades of coal was not to be permitted and multiple locations for different grades of coal increased the shiploading rate potential. However, multiple locations for different grades decreased the overall storage capacity because of end effects of the stockpiles; and (5) the analysis required a level of precision which allowed one to distinguish the effects of detailed changes to operations, procedures, stockpile layouts, materials handling arrangements such as surge capacities and varying patterns of machinery breakdowns. Table 17-2 shows a sample of some of the output for this study.

TABLE 17-2. Detailed ship waiting and service times

Detailed Times in Hours Per Ship	*4 Stacker-Reclaimers only*	*4 Stacker-Reclaimers + Silo Scheme*	*4 Stacker-Reclaimers +* High *Capacity Stacker*	*4 Stacker-Reclaimers +* Low *Capacity Stacker*
Wait for Berth	6.16	5.24	5.94	5.55
Wait for Cargo	0.03	0.06	0.69	0.35
Wait for Bunker Ships	0.30	0.19	0.43	0.35
Congestion Incoming	0.33	0.33	0.33	0.33
Total Wait Time	6.82	5.82	7.39	6.58
Approach & Mooring	1.33	1.33	1.33	1.33
Documentation & Gear Delay	2.00	2.00	2.00	2.00
Bad Weather Delay	1.18	1.03	0.99	0.95
Wait for S/R to move	0.65	0.59	0.45	0.51
Wait for Available S/R	4.92	4.43	4.85	4.89
Load with 1 S/R	13.57	13.11	13.02	12.98
Load with 2 S/R's	3.79	4.03	3.64	3.59
Load with 3 S/R's	0.61	0.59	0.83	0.86

(continued)

TABLE 17-2. *Continued*

Detailed Times in Hours Per Ship	*4 Stacker-Reclaimers only*	*4 Stacker-Reclaimers + Silo Scheme*	*4 Stacker-Reclaimers +* High *Capacity Stacker*	*4 Stacker-Reclaimers +* Low *Capacity Stacker*
1st Draft Survey	1.00	1.00	1.00	1.00
2nd Draft Survey	0.19	0.19	0.19	0.19
Deballast Time	0.03	0.02	0.05	0.03
Congestion Outgoing	0.33	0.33	0.33	0.33
Departure Time	1.00	1.00	1.00	1.00
Total Berth Time	30.60	29.65	29.68	29.66
Total Port Time	37.42	35.47	37.07	36.24

17.4 CONCLUSION

First, terminals are critical connectors in transport systems. They have high costs when things go wrong and relatively low costs when designed properly. Second, models of coal terminals are distinct from other port models: (1) the queuing theory is different, (2) storage accounting is important, and (3) the physical layout and material handling system must be modeled in considerable detail yet with flexibility for changes.

18 A SHORT RUN MODEL OF THE WORLD PETROLEUM NETWORK BASED ON DECOMPOSITION

J. W. DeVanney III and M. B. Kennedy

Progress to date on a large model of the world petroleum network is outlined. This model is unusual among its peers in its assumption of completely blocked operation of each refinery. This allows each intermediate feedstock to retain its crude identity all the way to final blending and downstream process coefficients to be tailored to the properties of each crude. This added realism is bought at a high cost in model size. The resulting linear program contains some 20,000 rows and 65,000 columns. Fortunately, the assumption of blocked operation allows the model to be decomposed in an extremely natural manner. By taking advantage of this structure, computational costs per run have been achieved which are approximately equal to those obtained with considerably less descriptive models. Prospects for further improvements in computational efficiency are discussed.

18.1 INTRODUCTION

The emergence of OPEC as an effective petroleum producers' cartel and the subsequent dislocations in the world energy system have generated considerable interest in models of the world petroleum network. Such models have a variety of uses ranging from assessing the impact on both flows and prices caused by changes in supply offered by source, by changes in demand by market and product, by changes in terminal and canal draft limitations, and by changes in refinery capacity by location and process. A reasonably complete description of this network generates a very large model mainly because each major crude is a unique combination of hydrocarbons with its own refining characteristics. To model differences in crude quality and their effects, one must keep track of the flow of each crude on each route in each size tanker while at the same time modeling each refinery sector down to the major process unit level. One result is that almost all existing large-scale world petroleum network models employ linear programming, assume inelastic demand and supply, and search for competitive (minimum cost) equilibria. If one attempts to solve such linear programs by the simplex method (Dantzig, 1965) one is limited to roughly 5000 rows and 20,000 columns and computation costs can be quite extravagant, ten thousand dollars per run or more. In order to obtain even these very large computer bills, these models commonly assume that all crudes charged to a particular refinery are blended immediately. This implies, for example, that there is only one, light straight-run naptha in each refinery. Intermediate feedstocks lose their crude identity as soon as they leave the distillation column. This implies in turn that downstream process yields and intermediate feedstock characteristics cannot depend on the properties of the crude being refined. In essence, in such models, crude quality is a function only of the distillation curve and, to a very limited extent, the characteristics of the straight-run feedstocks. For a number of applications — crude pricing, embargo contingency planning, and strategic reserve purchases — the resulting inaccuracies can be extremely important.

We have turned to a larger model and decomposition. Any world petroleum network model is an obvious candidate for decomposition. Assuming no intermediate feedstock shipments between refinery sectors, each such refinery sector is not linked directly to any other refinery. The coefficient matrix exhibits the angular structure for which Dantzig-Wolfe decomposition and its variants were designed (Dantzig, 1965). The reported experience with decomposition in the energy area has been mixed at best. While our own efforts are far from complete, the results to date indicate that by taking rather specialized advantage not only of decomposition by refinery sector but also by crude-refinery combination, an order of magnitude improvement in computational efficiency can be obtained.

18.2 OVERALL DESCRIPTION OF MARTINET

Our model MARTINET is based on the following four fundamental assumptions:

1. Strictly short run. All capital investment including the tanker fleet by vessel size category and refinery capacity by process unit is fixed as far as the model is concerned.
2. Perfect competition throughout the world petroleum network.
3. Completely inelastic (exogenously fixed) fob crude supply and cif product demands.[1]
4. Each refinery sector processes only one crude at a time. Crudes in any one refinery are processed sequentially, not simultaneously.

The first three assumptions are near-standard in large scale, short run models of the world petroleum network. Usually, the fourth assumption is replaced by the assumption that feedstocks from all crudes are blended as soon as they leave the distillation column. In reality, one of the goals of refinery scheduling is to schedule crudes sequentially, in order to take full advantage of the differences in each crude. This is known as block operation. A refinery's job is to split crudes apart, not to mix them together. Sometimes such block scheduling is logistically impossible and to the extent that it is not, this assumption may be slightly optimistic with respect to overall results. But Assumption 4 seems more realistic than the other extreme of assuming that straight-run feedstocks from all crudes are (1) always blended, and (2) the resulting blended feedstocks always have 'average' characteristics as far as downstream process yields and costs are concerned.

MARTINET divides the world petroleum network modeling problem into two separate but interrelated steps. One step models in considerable detail the internal operations of each of the world's major refinery sectors in processing each of the world's major crudes. The result is a set of product yields for each such combination of crude and refinery. The second step uses these yields in solving for the competitive equilibrium set of crude and product flows for the postulated crude production and product consumption patterns. These two steps are repeated until the internal refinery operations are in equilibrium with the overall crude and product flows.

Figure 18–1 describes this iterative procedure. The process begins with an initial estimate of the equilibrium ex-refinery product values for each of seven product types in each of fifteen major refining regions. These prices, together with a fairly detailed description of each of fifty-four major crudes and a description of the capabilities of each of the fifteen refining regions, are fed to a program known as REFOPS. This program constitutes a full-scale, refinery operations model. REFOPS contains 61 rows and 200

1. MARTINET "floats" Arabian Light at the marker crude price. That is, f.o.b. supply is inelastic except for the marker crude whose supply is assumed to be totally elastic at the user-specified limit. Also, there is an involuntary conservation option which represents a relaxation of the completely inelastic assumption on the demand side.

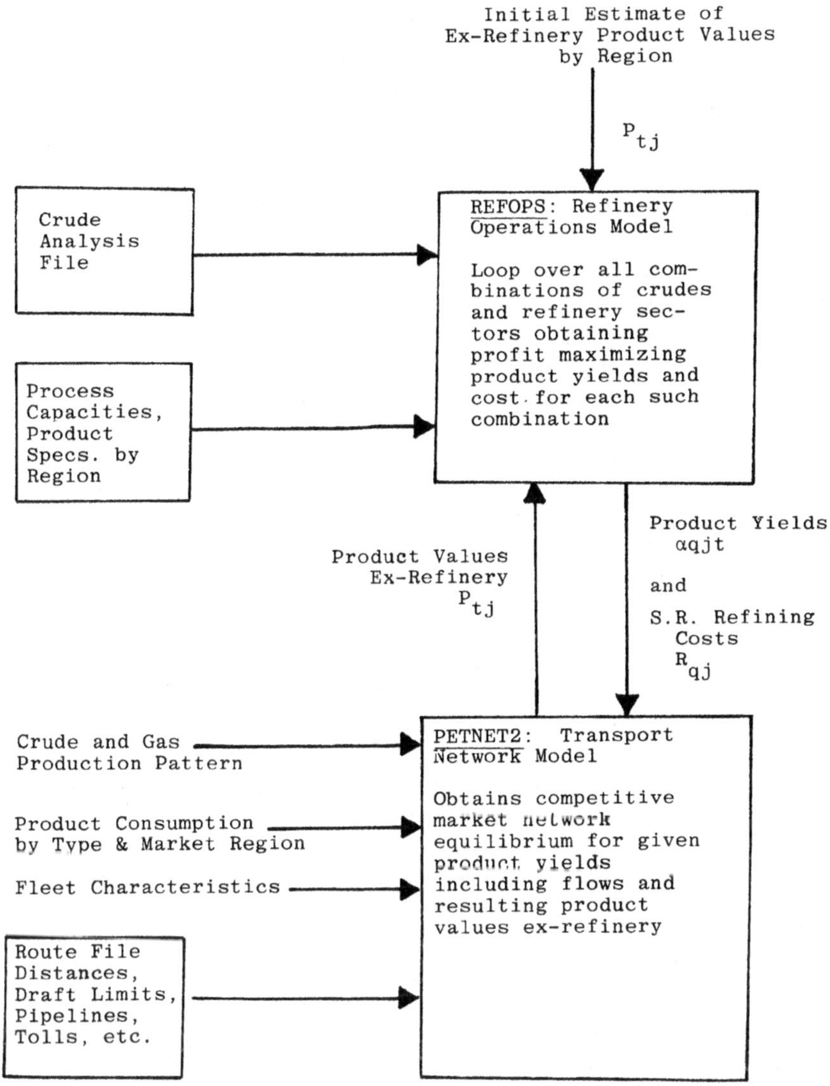

FIGURE 18-1. Martinet decomposition

columns. It keeps track of thirty-seven different intermediate product streams. Each refining sector is described by thirteen process capacities: atmospheric distillation, vacuum distillation, catcracking, hydrocracking, desulferization, hydrotreating, alkylation, isomerization, coking, visbreaking, thermal cracking, catreforming, and polymerization. Three of these units, catcracking, catreforming, and hydrocracking, can be operated at varying degrees of severity. Final products are aggregated into seven major product types:

1. Pipeline gas
2. LPG — naptha
3. Motor gasoline
4. Jet fuel — kerosine
5. Diesel oil — No. 2 fuel
6. Low sulfur heavy fuels
7. High sulfur heavy fuels

A self-documenting, easily modified data base which contains process unit capacities, product specifications, and economic data for each of fifteen major refinery sectors has been developed. REFOPS refers to this data base as required. REFOPS also takes as input a fairly detailed description of the refining characteristics of each of the world's major crudes. These crude analyses are also stored in a computerized file which contains the crude's distillation curve, sulfur content by fraction, specific gravity by fraction, the clear octane number and lead susceptibility of the gasoline fractions, and the crude density, overall sulfur, and nickel and vanadium content.

The most important feature of REFOPS is that downstream process yields, and intermediate feedstock properties may and do depend on the characteristics of each individual crude being charged. Fully 90 percent of the downstream process coefficients in REFOPS change as the characteristics of the crude being run to the refinery change. To put it another way, there is a completely different REFOPS model for each combination of crude and refinery.[2] Each intermediate feedstock maintains its crude identity until final product blending. In an undecomposed approach, straight-run feedstocks from different crudes are generally blended immediately, crude identity is lost, and 'average' values for the downstream coefficients must be used. This can lead to important errors. For an obvious example, the catreformer yield of a naptha high in aromatics will be quite different

2. Programming (some 500 statements) has been developed to automatically generate each of these coefficient matrices from the crude and refinery characteristics.

from that for a highly paraffinic crude. REFOPS models this difference. A model in which straight-run feedstocks from different crudes are blended cannot.

Returning to the basic process, Figure 18-1, REFOPS combines the description of each refining sector and each crude analysis with the assumed product prices to obtain, for each combination of crude and refining sector, the short run profit maximizing set of product yields. It computes a separate set of seven product yields for each of fifty-four crudes in each of fifteen different world refining sectors.[3] These yields then form part of the input to the network model, PETNET2. PETNET2 computes the equilibrium set of flows by route and tanker size category for the postulated crude production pattern, product consumption pattern, the specified fleet afloat, and the given yields, generating, among other things, the marginal value of each product ex-refinery in each of the refining sectors. That is, the duals of each product production constraint at each refinery. This set of product prices produced by the network program is compared with the set of product values last used by REFOPS. If the two sets of prices are significantly different, the old prices are adjusted toward the new prices. REFOPS is then rerun over all combinations of crude and refinery sectors with these adjusted prices.[4] This generates a new set of product yields which are then passed to the network model. This process is continued until convergence on the ex-refinery product prices is obtained.

The network model, PETNET2, is capable of handling up to ninety-nine crudes and twenty natural gases; ninety-nine crude loading, ninety-nine product loading, ninety-nine crude discharge, and ninety-nine product discharge ports; fifteen refining sectors; seven final product types; fifteen products regions; ten oil tanker size categories; and LNG and LPG carriers. The programming will accept any self-consistent input data describing the network. An unlimited number of arcs can be handled. Defaults are supplied for almost all variables. The user need enter only changes. Users can insert or remove large subsets of routes by issuing a single command, e.g., open or close Suez Canal. Lower and upper bounds on individual arcs are accepted. This allows one to represent long-term lifting contracts and political limitations on particular flows, e.g., Canada's limiting exports to the

3. Actually, some crude-refinery combinations are not analyzed on the grounds that they will almost certainly be of no interest, e.g., Algerian crude in Japanese refineries. At present, the number of crude-refinery combinations for which product yields are computed is about 350.

4. In practice, at each iteration, the REFOPS prices are usually changed for only a few refining regions and REFOPS rerun only over the crude-refinery combinations corresponding to these regions. This generates a more economical, more stable convergence process.

USA. PETNET2 properly accounts for the fact that a higher proportion of time is spent in port on short routes than long routes, deadweight lost to bunkers, and emergence enroute and its effect on effective terminal draft restrictions. If the stipulated demands cannot be met with the given tanker fleet, PETNET2 employs special logic to simulate the resulting tanker market boom and indicates which tanker size categories will participate in the boom.

PETNET2 contains an integrated natural gas sector. The sulfur content and richness of up to twenty natural gases are explicitly modeled. Natural gas products are allowed to compete with refined products in the pipeline gas markets, LPG-naptha markets, and NGL in gasoline. At user option, natural gas may also compete in regional fuel oil markets. This latter feature could be a valuable tool in modeling moderately short run gas for oil substitution during a prolonged embargo.

Despite all these features, PETNET2 costs only about $125 per run. This is about two orders of magnitude less than other network models in which simplified refinery sectors are included within the network proper. In our approach, the refinery operating decisions for each crude and each refinery are handled separately by REFOPS. In any given run of PETNET2, the product yields associated with a given crude and a given refinery are fixed. Although refinery operating decisions are modeled in considerable detail in REFOPS, they are not modelled explicitly within PETNET2. This allows us to represent each refinery sector by only eight rows in the network model — one for each final product type and one refinery capacity constraint.

The disadvantage of this approach in its present form is that it is a trial-and-error method. In order to compute the profit maximizing yield for each crude and each refinery sector, REFOPS, prior to running the network model, requires a set of product values for each refinery region. However, the market clearing prices ex-refinery associated with any given crude production pattern, product consumption pattern and set of product yields are determined endogenously by the network model and are not known until after the network computations. This implies that we must:

1. First estimate what these ex-refinery product values will be and run REFOPS over all possible combinations of crude and refinery to obtain the resulting product yields.
2. Use these yields to run the PETNET2 network model obtaining, among other things, the competitive market values of each product ex-refinery.

3. Compare these product values with the values used in the last run of REFOPS and, where necessary, rerun the crude-refinery combinations with new values, obtaining new product yields. Return to Step 2.

Step 3 at present is not mechanical and in fact considerable judgment must be exercised by the analyst in determining what combination of the olds and new product values should be used in the next set of REFOPS runs.

The overall process has been developed and tested on a network consisting of fifty-four crudes, ten oil tanker size categories, a 1500-arc world petroleum network, fifteen refining sectors, seven final products, and five market regions. Undecomposed, this network generates an extremely large linear program — approximately 20,000 rows and 65,000 columns. Since models with one-fourth as many rows and columns cost over ten thousand dollars per run, a brute force approach to this network is not economically feasible.

Using the iterative procedure, we have been able to obtain convergence within 10 cents per barrel on f.o.b. crude prices with a total computer bill of less than $10,000. Convergence has proven to be rather touchy, requiring a great deal of care and judgment on the part of the analyst. The basic problem is that, since product consumption is taken to be fixed, the process involves the intersection of vertical cif product demand curves with usually rather inelastic cif product supply curves. However, with sufficient patience it can be done.

Hindsight runs based on actual 1975 and 1976 data generated cif product prices that were always within 50 cents per barrel of actual spot values and usually within 20 cents per barrel. The one exception was gasoline which tended to be $1.00 to $2.00 per barrel too low. The model generated ex-refinery values for gasoline of about $125 per ton when actual spot prices were $135 to $140 per ton. We suspect that the gasoline problem is caused by REFOPS ignorance of vapor pressure specs and/or the aggregation of all gasolines into an 'average' gasoline. Overall we believe the results to date are encouraging for those who feel that the world petroleum system can be modeled by competitive market approaches; but the gasoline anomaly could be the result of market imperfections. Further work on the gasoline sector in REFOPS is required before this possibility need be accepted. Tanker spot rates were always within 10 percent of actual prices by route in the hindsight runs at convergence. There is no doubt about the competitiveness of this market. From an f.o.b. crude pricing point of view, it is worth noting that a $1.00 error in cif product valuation usually translated into a much smaller error (perhaps 20 to 25 cents) error in fob crude valuation. From an embargo contingency planning point of view, it is worth noting that the objective function (total short run cost of transport and refining) stabilized much faster than the duals. The model generates near optimal solutions in two or three iterations.

18.3 COMPUTATIONAL IMPROVEMENTS

We have not really begun to take advantage of the computational potential of the decomposed structure of MARTINET. The great bulk of the work to date has been in the individual development of REFOPS and PETNET2, and demonstrating that the REFOPS-PETNET2 iterative process can be made to converge manually. In this section, we suggest some obvious computational improvements which should cut computer costs per iteration by an order of magnitude. We then discuss complete mechanization of the algorithm by implementation of full-scale Dantzig-Wolfe decomposition and its potential for further reduction in computational cost.

Almost all the computational effort expended in the overall iterative process is spent in the multiple runs of REFOPS. As Figure 18–2 indicates, the 350 crude-refinery combinations make up the great bulk of MARTINET. A single run of a particular crude-refinery combination costs about \$4.00. Hence, to run all 350 of them costs about \$1400. Potentially, all these computations must be repeated at each iteration in the overall process. Actually, we only rerun a subset of all combination at each iteration. Still the multiple REFOPS runs currently constitute better than 90 percent of the total computational effort.

REFOPS in its present form is capable of improvements which could cut per-run computer bills by as much as an order of magnitude. Currently, REFOPS uses a rather crude, revised simplex written entirely in Fortran. Hand optimization of a portion of this code, especially the pivoting and inversion routines, could be expected to generate substantial improvements.[5] Experienced CDC personnel who have examined our REFOPS code as compiled by the CDC FTN compiler have offered the opinion that hand optimization should decrease solution times by a factor of from two to four.

Still larger improvements should be achieved by Last Basis Saving (LBS). The only change from one REFOPS run for a particular crude-refinery combination to the next is in the objective function where the new ex-refinery prices replace the old. The optimal solution from the last run is not only

5. Hand optimization is the process of rewriting the most time consuming portions of the code in assembler language. The primary goal is more efficient use of the computer's register stack.

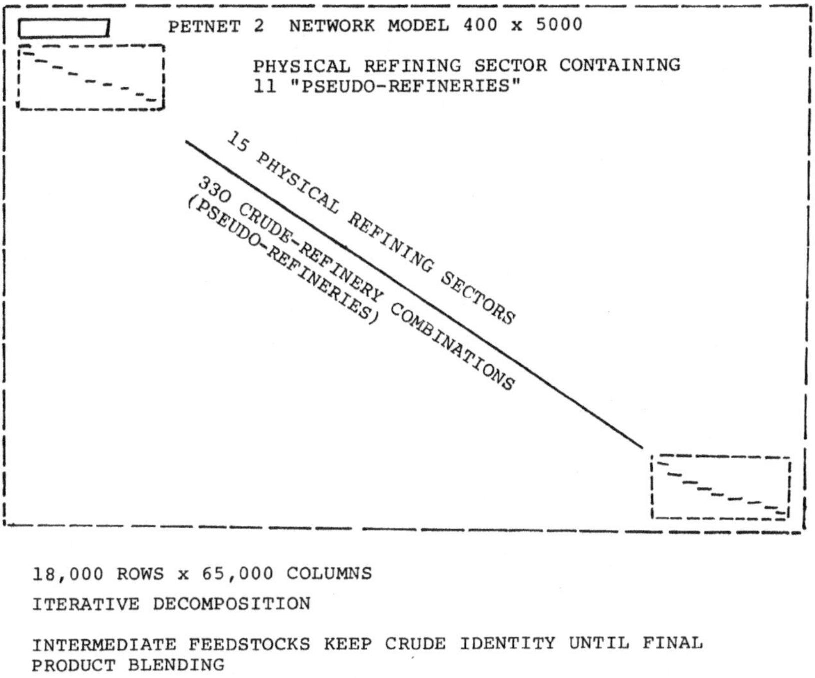

FIGURE 18–2. Basic structure of the Martinet matrix

basic feasible for the new problem but also likely to be very close to the new optimum especially in the latter iteration where product prices are not changing drastically. REFOPS tends to use the same feedstocks and the same blending columns over a wide range of product prices. REFOPS spends about half its time in Phase 1 which would be entirely eliminated by LBS. Overall an order of magnitude improvement in REFOPS computer bills is not out of the question by the simple expedient of using the last basis as the initial solution in each iteration.

Now consider PETNET2. Implementation of full Dantzig-Wolfe decomposition (discussed later) will, everything else being equal, substantially increase PETNET2 per-run computation cost — perhaps by as much as a factor of three. Since less than 10 percent of the current total cost is in the PETNET2 computations, we probably could afford to pay this price, if we had to, to obtain the benefit of Dantzig-Wolfe. Fortunately, we do not have to. Under Dantzig-Wolfe decomposition, the optimal solution from the last iteration will be basic feasible for the next and often very close to the new optimum. Hence, by implementing LBS for the expanded PETNET2, we will obtain the same kind of computational savings as in the REFOPS case and more. PETNET2 is a very short and wide linear program. It has over ten times as many columns as rows — typically 5000 versus 500. This is a characteristic of world petroleum network models that break the tanker fleet down into multiple vessel size categories. We have another world petroleum network model with a similar shape: 2000 columns and 100 rows. This program, known as PETNET1, is basically PETNET2 without the refinery rows and without differentiation of crudes. When we implemented LBS for PETNET1 we obtained a factor of fifteen decrease in per iteration computer costs. Similar improvements with PETNET2 are to be expected.

A more fundamental problem with the current algorithm is that it is not mechanical. User intervention is required at the point where the new ex-refinery values are determined for the next set of REFOPS runs. Convergence is quite sensitive to the choice of these new values. In the present algorithm, simply replacing the old values with the new PETNET2-generated values will result in unstable behavior and an exploding cobweb. If we are to have an easily used, operational tool, this step must be mechanized. Further, the mechanism suggested below will completely avoid the troublesome overshoot phenomenon observed in our manual runs. This in turn should markedly decrease the number of iterations required to obtain satisfactory convergence. The obvious attack on this issue is to exploit and extend the similarities between the current algorithm and Dantzig-Wolfe decomposition without destroying the special structure of MARTINET.

MARTINET in its present form has some relationships to standard decomposition. The network model PETNET2 plays the role of the master problem. Each individual REFOPS run is a subproblem. As in decomposition, the master communicates to the subproblems by transferring its duals to the subproblem objective functions. The major difference is in the transfer of information from the subproblems to the master, i.e., the column generation step. After all 350 refinery operations runs are computed at each iteration, 350 new sets of product yields are transferred to the Master and the old yields discarded. That is, the old yields are forced out of the basis. If the Master chooses to use a particular crude-refinery combination, it must do so at the new yields.

The proposed change is conceptually simple but with far reaching implications. At the second iteration of the process, the new yields are added to the master and the old ones retained. The master (PETNET2) will be free to use the old yields, or the new yields, or any convex combination. At the third iteration, the new set of yields would be added to the other two, and the master allowed any convex combination of all three sets, etc. A set of yields would not be dropped from the master until the master freely chooses to drop it from the basis.

Physically, this change corresponds to allowing the refinery sectors to operate in more than one mode in processing a particular crude. Each refinery sector will be free to spend a portion of the time it is charging a particular crude in one operating mode and then switch to other modes for the remaining portion. Figure 18–3 sketches this process for the case of a two-product world (gasoline and fuel oil). The set of yields labeled A represents an all-out gasoline mode, i.e., a set of yields generated by a very high relative gasoline price. Suppose this set of yields was generated on the first REFOPS iteration. The set of yields labeled B represents an all-out fuel oil mode, i.e., a set of yields generated by a relatively low gasoline price. Suppose this set of yields was generated on the second REFOPS iteration. At present, PETNET2 is forced to operate at Point A in the first iteration if it uses this particular crude refinery combination, and at Point B in the second iteration. Point B may well represent an overshoot reaction to the overly high gasoline price used in the first iteration generating a glut in gasoline and a relatively low gasoline dual going into the second iteration. Under the proposed change, PETNET2 at the second iteration will be free to operate anywhere along the line joining the two points, say, at Point C which represents 50 percent all-out gasoline mode and 50 percent all-out fuel oil mode. Hence, the overshoot and the failure to automatically converge will be avoided. The third iteration of REFOPS might then generate a point such as D which represents a balanced gasoline-fuel oil mode for this crude refinery combination and hence generates both more gasoline and more fuel oil than the alternative of running half the time all-out gasoline and half the time all-out fuel oil with the inefficiencies and poor process utilization associated with running 100 percent of the time way off the plant's design point. In the third PETNET2 iteration, PETNET2 would be free to use any combination of all three modes, which is to say any point in the shaded area in Figure 18-3. If we are near convergence at this point and the product prices generated by the third iteration of PETNET2 are close to those used in the third iteration of REFOPS, then we can be sure that PETNET2 will choose to operate the refinery at a point close to Point D in Figure 18–3.

This change will entail a considerable increase in the potential number of columns in PETNET2 — as much as a factor of three. However, as discussed earlier, the combination of LBS for PETNET2, the basic feasibility of the last solution, and the fact that currently PETNET2 represents less than 10 percent of the total computation effort imply that the overall

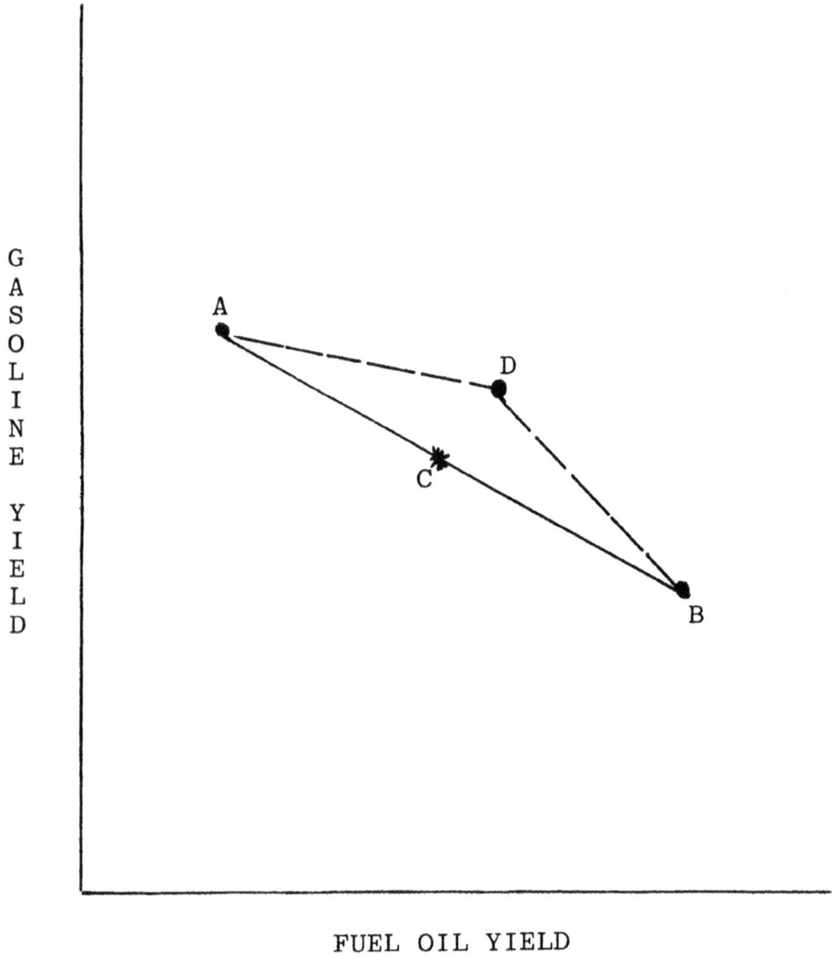

FIGURE 18-3. Diagramatic sketch of change in product yields

increase in computational cost due to this increase in the number of variables should be scarcely noticeable. In exchange, we receive the following benefits.

1. The algorithm becomes completely mechanical with assured convergence in a finite number of iterations.[6]
2. The troublesome overshoot phenomenon in the present process will be avoided for the master need not go all the way to the new yields in order to use a particular crude in a particular refinery, but can use any combination midway between the old and the new yields. This should significantly reduce the number of iterations required to reach satisfactory convergence.
3. We also obtain the Dantzig-Wolfe lower bound on the optimal value of the objective function which can be used in cutting the algorithm off before strict optimality is obtained if desired. This will be particularly useful in embargo contingency planning where we are not really seeking a competitive equilibrium but rather a "good" response to a very unusual situation.

At the same time, we retain and build on most of the nice features of the present algorithm. We feel that a key reason for the at least partial success of the present process is that each subproblem is linked to the master by only eight coefficients. The assumption that each refinery processes only one crude at a time makes the decomposition a very strong, natural one. It is this particular structure, together with our computational results to date, which encourages us to believe that we may be able to achieve the long-sought breakthrough in applying decomposition to energy networks.

REFERENCE

Dantzig, G. B. 1965. *Linear programming and extensions,* 2nd ed. Princeton, N.J.: Princeton University Press.

6. The refinery capacity constraints in the current PETNET2 model play the role of the convexity rows (Dantzig, 1965). Hence there is no need to augment the Master with 350 convexity rows. It is interesting that the number of convexity rows is equal to the number of physical refinery sectors (currently 15) rather than the number of Subproblems (the 350 crude-refinery combinations). Note also that despite the number of Subproblems, the number of dual variables which must be converged is equal to only the number of final products times the number of physical refineries reflecting the economic fact that there can be only one price for each product fob each refinery.

IV THE PROBLEMS AND INTERACTIONS OF ENERGY, ENVIRONMENT, AND CONSERVATION*

S. L. Schwartz and W. T. Ziemba

This section contains four papers concerned with the interactions of energy, environment, and conservation. By conservation we mean the management of energy resources to maintain long-term supplies while minimizing negative impacts on the environment and the depletion of critical resources. The first three papers discuss the development and use of simulation models to analyze, the contribution solar energy might make to our energy future, economic and environmental impacts of various electric utility futures, and the assessment of electricity conservation initiatives. The final paper studies end-use conservation policies in homes and appliances.

Bennington assesses the relative impacts and interactions of various solar technologies in terms of development, uncertainty, cost, and socio-economic barriers likely to be encountered. He discusses a number of solar technologies currently under study and development, including wind power, water temperature differentials use, energy from plant biomass, and thermodynamic and photovoltaic processes. The SPURR model (System for Projecting the Utilization of Renewable Resources) is used to

*Special thanks are due to Joan Rush for research assistance concerning this introduction.

simulate the market decisions to purchase solar versus conventional technologies in the different market sectors and regions of the United States. One difficult area of development in the SPURR model has been to determine the market potential for several new technologies simultaneously attempting to compete with a number of conventional systems. This is approached by employing a methodology which assigns a Figure of Merit (FOM) based on performance and cost for each conventional system and new technology. Market shares are then based on the FOM and the number of years since the solar system is announced to be commercially available. From the analysis of solar designs and market projections, Bennington concludes the solar energy may eventually displace significant quantities of fossil and nuclear fuels. He stresses the benefit of a federal program of policies and incentives to promote strongly accelerated acceptance and use of solar technologies. A major cost-sharing program for solar heat, for example, could increase the year 2000 fuel displacement from 2.0 to 3.5 quads, at a federal cost of $1.2 million. The paper briefly addresses other long-term benefits of solar energy including cost averaging and ecological benefits.

The MITRE study presents an optimistic supply scenario for solar power. Whether or not such estimates will be realized depends largely on whether or not the high capital intensive costs of solar technologies can be brought down to a level that is competitive with alternative sources of energy. Although solar is not yet a major contributor to U.S. energy supplies (see Abelson and Hammond (1978) for a recent assessment), it has emerged as an explosive growth area of research in recent years which might suggest substantial contributions in the future. One of the difficulties is that solar research funding in North America has not been given a high priority. There are signs that this may be changing and certainly sharply increased prices and limited availability of alternative fuels will put pressure on the development of reasonably priced solar energy power. In Canada, although still of modest proportions, solar research and development programs have received sharply increased funding — approximately $6 million for the 1978–1979 fiscal year (McCutcheon, 1978). There is wide scope in the size of technology. A forceful argument for the use and development of small collectors and individual efforts appears in Lovins (1977). For more recent data, see Lovins (1978). Large solar collectors have already have been successfully used in Israel. The most grandeoise scheme is the solar power satellite. The satellite is a highly debatable and emotional issue (see Grey (1979) for a "plea for rationality"). It would transmit electric power to land-based receivers from photovoltaic arrays or solar thermal power plants in space. The costs (in the billions) and potential benefits are enormous; the American

Institute of Aeronautics and Astronautics suggests (Grey, 1979) a level of research support of about $30 million per year for five years. For more detail, see Glaser (1977) and Machol (1978).

The paper by Van Horn, Large, and Smith describes the application of the Utility Simulation Model (USM) in the assessment of the impact of government policies, economic conditions, and technological conditions on the future investment and operating decisions made by utilities and the resulting impacts on local and regional air quality. The model evaluates the environmental implications of alternative policies which might be adopted to meet the goals of the U.S. Clean Air Act.

The USM simulates decisions for system planning and operation, utility financing, and the operation of individual technical processes such as pollution control devices. The model estimates factor demands, financial statistics, and average electricity prices for various geographical regions under different scenarios. It is also used to: (1) quantify the impacts of revised New Source Performance Standards (NSPS) requiring Best Available Control Technology; (2) identify local air quality problem areas; and (3) determine the extent of the need for regional, rather than national, environmental policies. The authors have found that revising the NSPS will substantially reduce SO_2 emissions, although the financial cost of revised NSPS is not likely to be met by that portion of electricity price increases representative of pollution control.

The authors consider the air quality impacts of clustering power plants. Their assessment concludes that not only should clustering be avoided, but that existing plants in specific subregional areas will need to be controlled in order to permit any future growth. They also argue the need for regional, rather than national, emission control policies on the basis that entire regions are affected by meteorological phenomena. For example a significant portion of Pennsylvania's nonattainment of SIP (State Implementation Plans) pollution standards can be attributed to SO_2 sources in the upwind states of Ohio and West Virginia.

There are several models in use that estimate the environmental impact of electric power generation. One such model is the Electricity Impact Model (EIM) developed by Buehring and Foell (1976) at the University of Wisconsin-Madison and IIASA (the International Institute for Applied Systems Analysis in Laxenburg, Austria). This model also considers the impacts associated with an energy system that may occur outside the region where the electricity is generated, which gives the EIM a somewhat more holistic approach than the USM.

One of the difficulties faced in environmental (and many other energy related) studies is concerned with the tradeoffs that must be made between the many and conflicting objectives. A framework based on the general theory (see, for example, Keeney and Raiffa (1977)) for the analysis of multicriteria environmental problems along with some sample results using the EIM is presented in Buehring, Foell, and Keeney (1976).

Smith, Johnston, and Meyer have used the Rate Simulation Model (RSM) to examine the impacts of implementing time-of-day and flat rate structures on utilities in the United States. The model simulates future developments in the electric utility industry in response to selected pricing, energy, economic, and environmental alternatives. The forecasted responses to alternative rate structures are for the customer classes: (1) residential; (2) commercial; (3) industrial; and (4) other (railroads, government bodies, and miscellaneous). The responses are based on technological alternatives for each end use, and their costs of acquisition and operation. The analysis shows that time-of-day rates are effective in suppressing growth in peak demand periods. However, the authors also point out some of the unintended consequences which are likely to arise when innovations in rate setting are adopted without consideration of the system-wide effects. One consequence of implementing time-of-day rates is that rate increases to residential customers are about three times the rate of cost increases, giving other customers a cost decrease. Also, if major peak period users find other forms of energy during peak hours (or entirely), such as greater use of cogeneration technology by industry, then the cost to other customers for energy becomes greater. One consideration that seems to be overlooked, however, is the fact that a reduction in peak period demand will reduce future capacity requirements. This might result in a reduction of average long-term cost to all customers. Also to be considered are the ecological and efficiency benefits of such conservation practices as cogeneration.

The analysis uses a highly optimistic supply scenario. In particular they assume low coal prices, low construction costs for new capacity, and the absence of regulatory constraints on new capacity additions. These assumptions may not be entirely valid in the future.

Although not currently used in the United States or Canada, peak load pricing is a common energy policy in Europe. In their study, Acton, Mitchell, and Manning (1978) conclude that ". . . if U.S. firms were to exhibit the degree of load shifting demonstrated by their European counterpart industries, the savings in the long run to U.S. energy and capital costs would be significant. . . . It appears that time-of-day pricing of electricity will offer important opportunities to assist in the goals of more prudent use of energy by more accurately reflecting the costs of supply." A second study is concerned with residential response to peak load pricing; see Acton, Manning, and Mitchell (1978) for a preliminary report. A study by Utterback, Rich and Sirbu (1977) concludes that: ". . . if the higher costs of added production and the social costs of energy use were reflected in prices, consumers would have strong incentives to employ a multitude of conservation measures.'' An earlier study by Acton and Mowill (1975) describes how the curtailment ordinance regarding electricity (largely produced by oil-fired generators) in Los Angeles in response to the 1973 oil embargo resulted in a rapid and substantial drop in consumption once the situation was thoroughly recognized by all classes of customers. The reaction to that ordinance might have significant importance for nationwide application.

The third energy modeling forum study (Cherry, 1979) presents an extremely thorough analysis concerning forecasts of peak load and electricity consumption. As with the previous two EMF studies (see the discussion in Volume II and Griffith's paper in this volume), the object is to bring together a number of modelers and policy makers to provide a vehicle for communication between these groups in the analysis of an important energy-economic area. Ten models based on econometric and engineering approaches participated in the study of the complexities and uncertainties of electric utility demand forecasting. Some of the findings are: (1) future electricity consumption is likely to grow more slowly than it has in the past; (2) implementation of time-of-use pricing and load management will require accurate forecasting of load shapes; (3) comparing and evaluating various models is extremely difficult; (4) improved data and model and data consistency is needed; and (5) improved models would result by combining or using in combination econometric models (that utilize statistical methods to analyze historical data to estimate the effects of changes in prices, incomes, demographic, and other macro data) and engineering models (which are concerned with end use details of residential, commercial, and industrial energy use). More discussion of this ''marriage'' of the engineering and economic approaches appears in Volume II.

Rosenfeld, Goldstein, Lichtenberg, and Craig describe and investigate various simple and inexpensive means by which homes and appliances (especially refrigerators) can be made to consume much less energy and to perform much more efficiently. They advocate mandatory standards for manufacturers of ranges, refrigerators, and other applicances, to achieve maximum conservation of energy. Their research reveals that gas ranges and dryers are much more fuel efficient than are electric ranges and dryers and that consumers prefer the gas appliances. Despite this fact, most pre-built homes are automatically equipped with electric appliances.

By examining the energy savings available from weatherproofing homes in Oakland, California, it is apparent that ''. . . under conditions of increasing energy prices, there are attractive weatherproofing measures that go substantially beyond the present ERCDC (California Energy Resources Conservation and Development Commission) standard for new homes.'' The authors make the point that ''under these circumstances, policies are justified that ensure conservation to a point where, from a societal point of view, no investments are made to expand energy supply when there are better investments to be had in conservation.'' The policies they advocate are sufficiently long range to allow manufacturers time to innovate, design, and retool their plants.

A study by Hirst (1979) is consistent with the Rosenfeld et al. results and estimates the potential reduction in annual energy use by refrigerators with present-day technologies at 50 percent. The same reduction is possible in the ''thermal performance'' of homes by adding sufficient insulation, weatherstripping, etc. The ORNL (Oak Ridge National Laboratory) engineering-economic model (Hirst and Carney, 1978) shows that a minimum energy growth future of 0.4 percent per year is technically and economically feasible; see also Hirst (1979). Passage of the National Energy Act in 1978 confirmed the conservation of energy in buildings as a U.S. policy objective. A National Program Plan for Building Thermal Envelope Systems and Insulating Materials was issued by the U.S. Department of Energy in January 1979. Federal Support for the program (1978–1980) is $9.5 million. See Bales et al. (1979) for a summary of the plan. As part of the national effort to reduce energy consumption in the United States, the appliance industry is investing heavily in research of efficient refrigeration systems (see, for example, Berenbaum, Allen, and Mastroianni (1976)). An interesting area of research (Grot and Galowin, (1976)) is the feasibility of integrated appliances into one unit, in which waste heat from refrigerators, freezers or air conditioners is recovered to preheat water.

Additional discussions related to the interaction of energy, environment and conservation may be found in Abelson and Hammond (1978), Ashley, Rudman, and Whipple (1976), Biswas (1974), Energy, Mines and Resources (1977), Hayes (1976), Hirst (1976), Hollander and Simmons (1976), Knelman (1975), Lovins (1977, 1978) and Tinkleman (1977).

REFERENCES

Abelson, P., and Hammond, A. L., eds. 1978. *Energy II: Use, conservation and supply*. Washington, D.C.: American Association for the Advancement of Science.

Acton, J. P.; Manning, W. G., Jr.; and Mitchell, B. M. 1978. Lessons to be learned from the Los Angeles rate experiment in electricity. Santa Monica, Calif.: Rand Corporation, R-2113-DWP.

Acton, J. P.; Mitchell, B. M.; and Manning, W. G. Jr. 1978. Projected nationwide energy and capacity savings from peak-load pricing of electricity in the industrial sector. Santa Monica, Calif.: Rand Corporation, R-2179-DOE.

Acton, J. P., and Mowill, R. S. 1975. Conserving electricity by ordinance: A statistical analysis. Santa Monica, Calif.: Rand Corporation, R-1650-FEA.

Ashley, H.; Rudman, R. L.; and Whipple, C. 1976. *Energy and the environment.* New York: Pergamon Press.

Bales, E. L.; Freeman, E. C.; Lundy, T. S.; McElroy, D. J.; Carroll, W. L.; and Powell, F. J. 1979. The national program plan for building thermal envelope systems and insulating materials: A summary by the authors of the plan. *ASHRAE Journal* 21:39–43.

Bell, C. R. 1977. Solar energy task progress report for 1975/76: Evaluation of solar energy options. IIASA, Laxenburg, Austria, RM 77-20.

Berenbaum, M. B.; Allen, R. A.; and Mastroianni, M. J. 1976. Energy conservation through more efficient refrigerants. Mimeo, Allied Chemical Corporation.

Biswas, A. K. 1974. *Energy and the environment.* Environment Canada, Ottawa.

Buehring, W. A., and Foell, W. K. 1976. Environmental impacts of electrical generation: A system-wide approach. IIASA, Laxenburg, Austria, RR-76-13.

Buehring, W. A.; Foell, W. K.; and Keeney, R. L. 1976. Energy-environment management: Application of decision analysis. IIASA, Laxenburg, Austria, RR-76-14.

Cherry, B. H., et al. 1979. Electric load forecasting: Probing the issues with models: Volumes 1 and 2. Energy Modeling Forum Report 3, Stanford University.

Energy, Mines and Resources. 1977. *Energy conservation in Canada: Programs and perspectives.* Report EP 77-7.

Glaser, P. E. 1977. The potential of satellite solar power. *Proceedings IEEE* 65:1162–1176.

Grey, J. 1979. Solar power satellite: A plea for rationality. *Science* 203.

Grot, R. A., and Galowin, L. S. 1976. Integrated household appliances and utility services for energy conservation in dwellings. Proceedings of the Technical Opportunities for Energy Conservation in Appliances, Boston.

Hayes, D. 1976. Energy: The case for conservation. *Worldwatch Paper* 4.

Hirst, E. 1976. Transportation energy conservation policies. *Science* 192.

Hirst, E. 1979. Reducing residential energy growth. *ASHRAE Journal* 21:44–46.

Hirst, E., and Carney, J. 1978. The ORNL engineering-economic model of residential energy use. ORNL/CON-24, Oak Ridge National Laboratory, Tennessee.

Hollander, J. M., and Simmons, M. K., eds. 1976. *Annual review of energy,* vol. 1. Palo Alto, Calif.: Annual Reviews Inc.

Keeney, R. L., and Raiffa, H. 1977. *Decision analysis with multiple conflicting objectives: Preferences and value tradeoffs.* New York: Wiley.

Knelman, F. H. 1975. *Energy conservation.* Science Council of Canada Background Study No. 33, Ottawa.

Lovins, A. B. 1978. Soft energy technologies. *Annual Review of Energy, 1978.* Annual Reviews Inc., pp. 477–517.

Lovins, A. B. 1977. *Soft energy paths.* New York: Harper Colophon Books.

Machol, R. E. 1978. Satellite solar power systems. In *Energy policy,* eds. J. S. Aronofsky; A. G. Rao; and M. F. Shakun. *Studies in the Management Sciences* 10:227–244.

McCutcheon, S. 1978. A technology in ferment: Solar heating. In *Science Dimension* (NRC) 10. *Solar heating,* ed. L. Racine.

Tinkleman, M. 1977. Energy analysis and environment: Philosophy of approach and research accomplishments at the Electric Power Research Institute. Mimeo, EPRI, Washington, D.C.

Utterback, J. M.; Rich, D.; and Sirbu, M. A. 1977. Strategic alternatives for energy conservation. CPA-77-1, Center for Policy Alternatives, MIT, Cambridge, Massachusetts.

19 PROJECTIONS OF SOLAR ENERGY UTILIZATION: A GUIDE TO FEDERAL PLANNING*

Gerald E. Bennington

The Metrek Division of The MITRE Corporation was funded by the United States Energy Research and Development Administration (now the Department of Energy) to perform a comparative analysis of the likely utilizations of solar energy and to use this analysis to develop recommendations for planning the research, development, and commercialization of solar energy. To this end, Metrek has developed an energy data base, a set of scenarios of likely trends in demand and energy prices, and a computer simulation model. The energy data base contains engineering cost data on conventional and solar technologies based on the development of comparable generic system designs derived from a synthesis of the latest available information. The National Energy Plan, as proposed in April 1977, was used as the baseline scenario for the analysis. Projections of solar energy utilization were made by computer simulations of regional market decisions to use solar or conventional technologies in each market sector on a year-by-year basis.

*This article is based on MITRE Corporation reports, particularly *Solar Energy: A Comparative Analysis to the Year 2020* and *A System for Projecting the Utilization of Renewable Resources,* that were coauthored by Paul Curto, Grant Miller, Kathy K. Rebibo, Peter Spewak, Rick Vitray, and Gerald E. Bennington. The original work was funded by ERDA Contract No. E-(4918)-2322. The ongoing work is sponsored by Contract No. EM-78-01-5147 with DOE. Thanks also go to S. L. Schwartz for her help in preparing the paper for this volume.

19.1 INTRODUCTION

The oil embargo of 1973 was a major shock to the United States. It was soon followed by long lines at gas stations, shortages of home-heating oil, curtailments of natural gas, and a quintuple increase in fossil-fuel prices. The federal government initially responded with Project Independence, a plan to resolve the nation's energy crisis by 1985. Since then, the energy crisis has come to be viewed as a complex political and socioeconomic problem requiring planning into the twenty-first century and a long-term commitment to its solution. Solar energy is seen by many as a solution to the problem. Old concepts have been refurbished and new concepts proposed to exploit this important renewable resource.

Solar energy — sunlight — is readily available and virtually inexhaustible. It interacts with the environment in many ways that can be exploited to produce usable power. Winds, caused by sunlight heating the air of various regions differently, create air currents whose energy can be used by wind machines to produce mechanical power. This power can be used directly (to pump water for irrigation, for example) or converted to electricity by a generator. Sunlight heating the upper layers of the oceans while deep ocean waters remain significantly colder can create a temperature differential of 40 degrees Fahrenheit between upper and deep ocean waters. This differential can be used to drive heat engines producing usable power. Plants use sunlight directly to produce biomass. Trees or crop residues may be burned to produce heat or power or used to produce energy-intensive products such as synthetic fuels, ammonia, or methanol. Sunlight is collected or concentrated through the use of solar collectors. Some collectors are designed to use the sun's energy to heat hot water, heat space in buildings, provide heat for industrial processes, cool through the use of absorption coolers, or produce electricity by several thermodynamic processes. Other collectors directly convert sunlight into electricity (photovoltaics). Figure 19-1 graphically depicts some of the solar technologies under consideration, while Table 19-1 lists the technologies included in Metrek's comparative analysis.

Advocates of each solar program present strong arguments on why their program is essential to the solution of the energy problem. Other constituencies pursue coal and nuclear energy with a similar fervor and dedication. Part of this healthy competition for staff, resources, and program funding focuses on the likely impacts of the various solar technologies. A widely divergent set of claims of potential energy savings has emerged. In a sense, projected impacts have become a "scorecard" for determining the winners and losers.

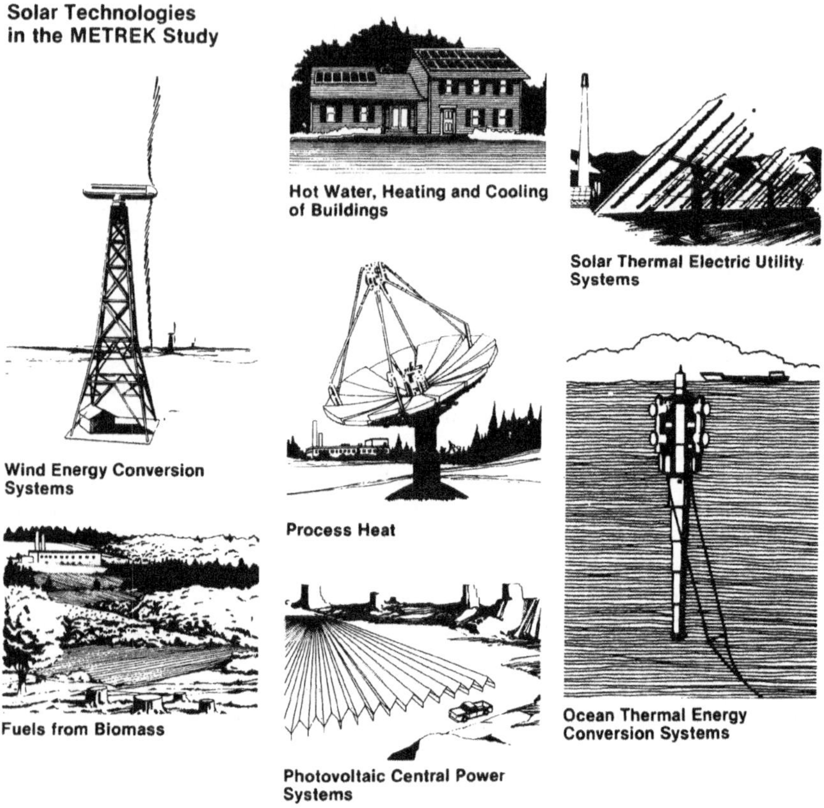

FIGURE 19–1. Solar technologies in the Metrek study

Although policy options, technological development, and national and international political situations are in a state of rapid flux, the tools and analysis described here provide a useful bench mark for continued solar energy planning. Models can provide guidance in the broader decision-making process. The goal of the work at the MITRE Corporation is to provide a means for assessing the relative impacts and interactions among the solar options in the broader context of the nation's energy supply/use patterns. We have sought to do this in a manner that incorporates the state of development, relative uncertainty about eventual performance and cost of each type of solar system, and the socioeconomic barriers likely to be encountered in the many diverse applications of solar energy.

TABLE 19-1. Solar technologies included in Metrek's comparative analysis

Market Sector	*Solar Technologies*
Heating and Cooling for Buildings	Hot water Hot water and heating (air collector) Hot water and heating (liquid collector) Hot water, heating, and absorption cooling Hot water, heating, and cooling with heat pump auxiliary
Process Heat	Convecting solar ponds Flat plate collectors Evacuated tubular collectors Compound parabolic concentrations Segmented mirror concentrators Parabolic trough collectors Parabolic dish concentrators
Electric Utilities	Wind Energy Conversion System (WECS) (100-ft rotor diameter) Wind Energy Conversion System (advanced design with 300-ft rotor diameter) WECS with combustion turbine auxiliary WECS-I water saver Solar thermal central receiver Solar thermal central receiver with thermal storage Solar thermal central receiver with combined cycle auxiliary Ocean Thermal Energy Conversion System Photovoltaics (silicon) with battery storage Photovoltaics (thin film) Photovoltaics (thin film) with battery storage Photovoltaics concentrator with battery storage Combustion of wood biomass
Synthetic Fuels	Pyrolysis of wood to produce synthetic natural gas Pyrolysis of wood to produce methanol Pyrolysis of wood to produce ammonia Pyrolysis of wood to produce synthetic crude oil

The original focus of this work was to provide input to energy planners who make decisions about specific solar research and development programs. The scope was quickly broadened to incorporate the assessment of a wide range of incentive options intended to accelerate the commercialization of solar technologies. To address the wide range of technical and economic issues, the level of detail of the modeling and analysis is designed to distinguish between different hardware configurations and possible technological advances through the remainder of this century. The analysis must also be robust enough to incorporate changing assumptions on end-use demand in a wide variety of applications.

19.2 CAPTURING THE DYNAMICS OF THE SOLAR TRANSITION: THE SPURR MODEL

Metrek's energy data base contains data on solar and conventional technologies and the economic data describing potential economic/energy futures. The SPURR computer model (System for Projecting the Utilization of Renewable Resources) simulates market decisions to purchase solar or conventional technologies in each market sector and region of the United States to satisfy a given energy demand on a year-by-year basis. The SPURR methodology is depicted in Figure 19–2.

Market decisions are based primarily on economic factors, although risk, market inertia, and resistance to technological change are also incorporated (e.g., by way of S-shaped logit curves of market penetration). Experience curves were estimated based on engineering and cost analysis (Solar Energy Project Team, 1977). These are used to model cost reductions of new equipment as a function of projected cumulative experience. See Figure 19–3. Projections of the utilization of solar components (such as solar flat plate collectors and photovoltaic cells) result in price reductions on these components in subsequent years as manufacturers gain experience. Utilization of a system in regions with favorable climatic conditions can therefore cause price reductions that make the system competitive in other regions in later years.

To obtain results on a national and regional basis within the limits of time and effort available, it was necessary to deal with representative or average data for buildings, utilities, and industries. Regional analyses allow the model to account for regional variations in sunlight and wind; for differences in the cost of fossil fuels, construction, and operation and maintenance; and for the regional demands for energy. The regional variations in the cost of fossil fuels, particularly coal, which varies by as much as a factor or two, result in markedly different regional solar market penetrations.

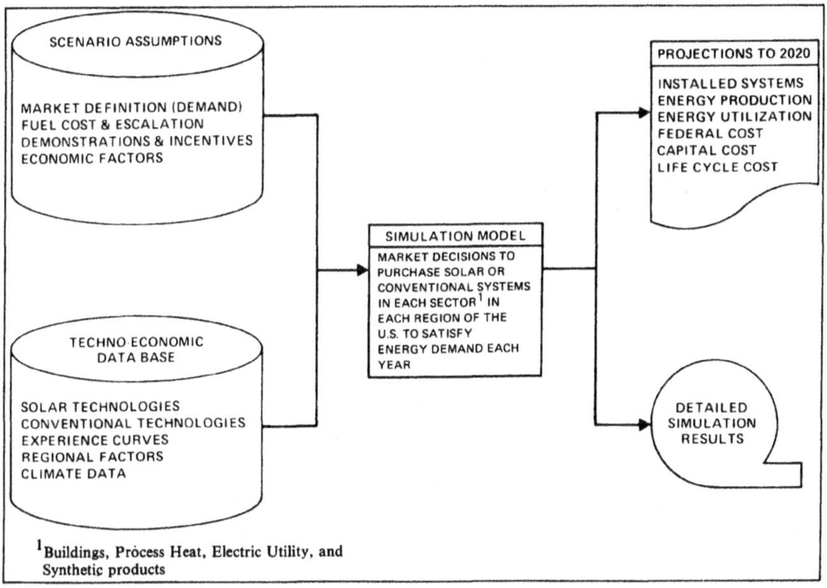

FIGURE 19-2. Spurr methodology

Certain solar electric options — solar thermal central receivers, photovoltaic central power stations, and ocean thermal energy conversion systems — are limited to specific regions. The conversion efficiencies of solar collectors competing in the buildings and process heat sectors also show considerable regional variations.

The market definition or demand for energy is input to the model for the scenario to be analyzed. The demand for process heat is segmented into six system types: coal, oil, gas, synthetic natural gas, electric resistance, and electric heat pump. Solar energy systems then compete against each of these fuel types separately. In the buildings sector, solar competes against electric resistance system and against heat pumps. This segmentation of the market varies by region and over time.

Limitations on the availability of fossil and nuclear fuels are handled by adjustment to the fuel escalation rates. Regional supply curves are used for biomass feedstocks with costs adjusted during the simulation as a function of the available supply remaining in the region.

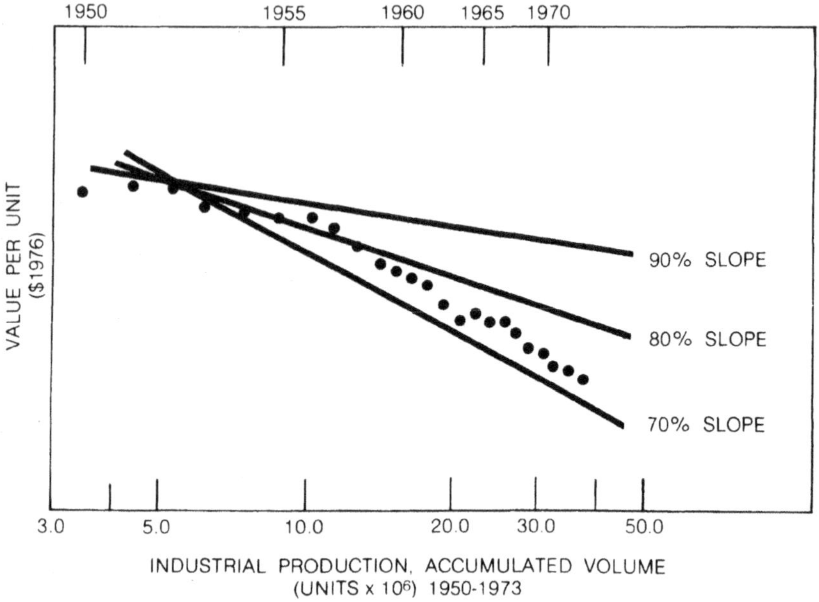

FIGURE 19-3. Experience curve: Forced warm air furnaces, non-electric, 1947–1973

Model output reports show the projected installed systems, energy production, fuel utilization, and private and federal costs for selected years of simulation. Additional reports are written for each market sector. More detailed reports and graphs can be produced by a CALCOMP plotter by processing a transaction tape generated during simulation.

One of the most challenging areas in the development of the SPURR model has been how to allocate the demand among the competing technologies. There is a substantial body of literature on the penetration of a single new technology into an existing market. For example, see Blackman (1972) and Fisher and Pry (1971). More data are required to understand utility markets where several new technologies compete with several conventional systems, and the buildings and process heat markets where solar energy systems must compete against conventional systems using different fuels of varying costs (all of which seem to get a share of the market regardless of the economic implications). A brief description of the buildings component illustrates the market segmentation, technology-costing methodology, and market allocation algorithms.

19.3 THE BUILDINGS COMPONENTS: AN EXAMPLE

The buildings component market is segmented into nine building types, new and retrofit systems; sixteen regions; and three or more conventional systems to supply hot water, heating, and/or cooling. Figure 19–4 provides an overview of the market penetration methodology. The optimal solar system with storage and auxiliary backup is determined for each market segment using design charts to compute a collector area that minimizes costs. Design charts for hot water and heating applications were developed through exten-

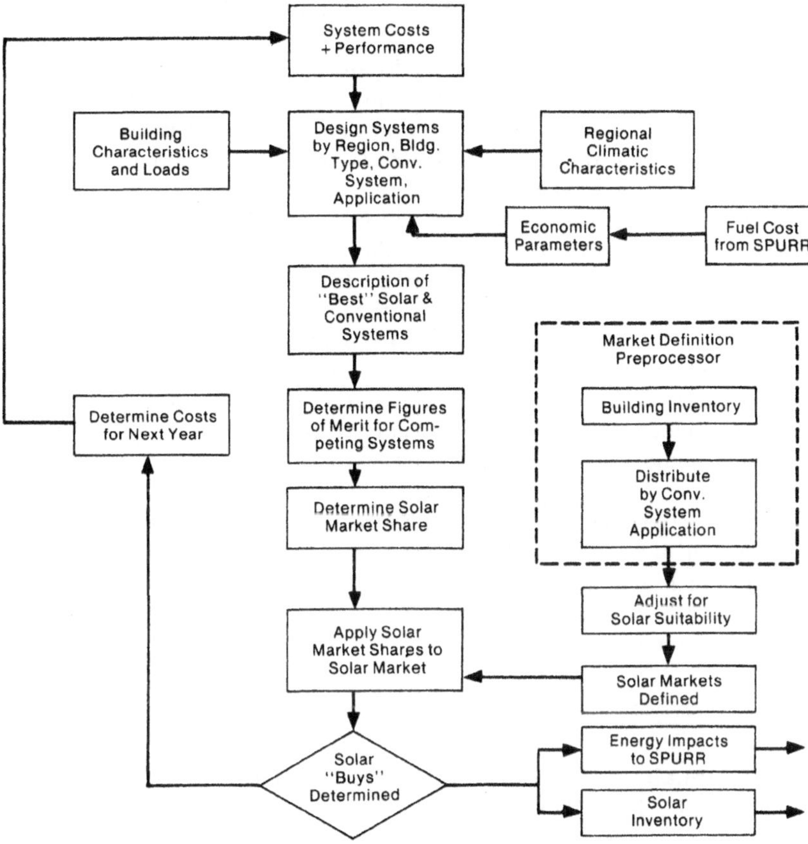

FIGURE 19–4. Market penetration flow chart

sive simulations (Hughes, 1977; Rebibo et al., 1977); and incorporate regional climatic data, collector performance, and building energy demands. Additional design charts were developed by Metrek to approximate the performance of solar cooling (Connolly et al., 1976; Energy Research and Development Administration, 1977). To represent the relative competitiveness of the new technology, a figure of merit (FOM) for each conventional system and best solar combination is calculated. A solar water system with an FOM of 2, is then twice as good as the conventional system. For one- and two-family living units, the FOM is a function of initial cost and annual savings. For other building types, the ratio type of life-cycle conventional costs to solar costs is used as the FOM. The calibration of the FOM and market share function was based on historic examples (Connolly et al., 1976; Fisher and Pry, 1971) and preliminary solar survey data (Scott, 1976).

Market shares are based on the FOM and the number of years since the solar system was assumed to be commercially available. Figure 19–5 illustrates how the market share function changes as potential users become more familiar with the system and perceive solar as a mature technology. When the systems are valued as equal (FOM = 1), the new system will get only 14 percent of the market after ten years and 36 percent after twenty years. If the new system is of greater value than the competitor (FOM > 1), it will gradually capture the entire market. If it is of lesser value (FOM < 1), it will initially get a small percentage of the market, but this will decline and the system will eventually disappear from the marketplace. The rate at which a particular class of users will shift to new products is a second parameter which defines the shape of the market share function. The market shares in Figure 19–5 illustrate a twenty-five-year time constant; with a FOM of 1, almost one-half of the market would be captured in twenty-five years.

The time constant is chosen based on the nature of the market, available nonfinancial incentives, and associated regulations. At present, the time constant is selected based on past experience; a causal model is needed for this critical area to extend the early work (Blackman, 1972; Fisher and Pry, 1971) for the more general case.

19.4 SUMMARY OF PROJECTIONS OF SOLAR ENERGY UTILIZATION

The end-use demand assumptions used in the baseline scenario are given in Table 19–2. Although the estimates incorporate the likely effects of the cur-

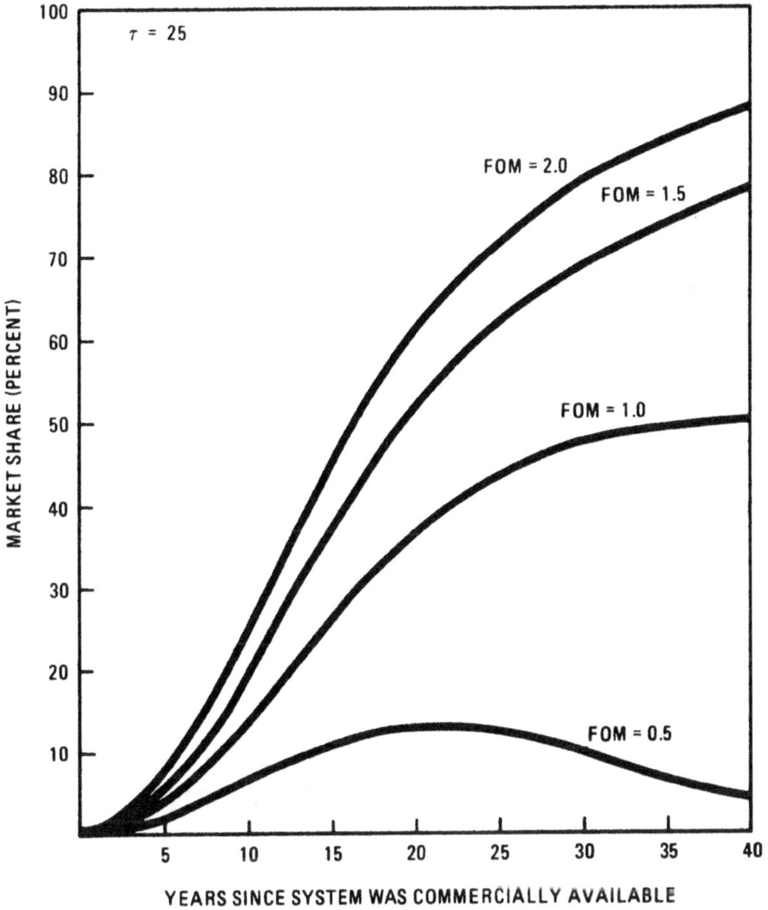

FIGURE 19–5. Metrek market share function

rent energy conservation programs, the end-use demand in houses, stores, and industrial processes is projected to more than double by the year 2020.

Our analysis of solar designs and market projections yielded the following conclusions for the potential use of solar technologies versus other energy technologies: (1) Solar energy may eventually displace significant quantities of both fossil and nuclear fuels. See Table 19–3 for a comparison with the other energy sources. (2) Although solar applications are regionally dependent, solar makes significant contributions in all regions. (3) Near-term solar applications are primarily in distributed markets for heating and

TABLE 19-2. Projected U.S. end-use demand (quadrillion Btus)

	1985	*2000*	*2020*
Buildings			
Electric	5.6	10	13
Total	14.4	17	22
Industry			
Process heat	8.0	13	27
Total	19.0	31	63
Transportation	18.5	21	25
Total end-use demand	52.0	69	110

TABLE 19-3. Energy consumption under the national energy plan (fossil fuel equivalent quadrillion Btus per year)

	1985	*2000*	*2020*
Oil	33	31	32
Gas	16	13	11
Coal	27	45	83
Nuclear	7	17	27
Hydro	3	3	3
Solar	—	6	33
Total	86	115	189

hot water for buildings and process heat for industry and agriculture (Table 19-4). Additional incentives and R&D funds for process heat applications are expected to have the maximum impact on accelerating solar energy commercialization. (4) Without additional incentives, large-scale production of electricity and synthetic fuels and products will probably require a longer development cycle than previously anticipated, but will still provide a large contribution once commercialized. A federal program of policies and incentives to promote solar electric technologies could strongly accelerate their acceptance and use.

The big payoffs from solar are projected to begin in about forty years: a total of 33 quads[1] of energy per year by 2020 — nearly 18 percent of the

1. Quad-quadrillion Btu. One quad of energy is equivalent to enough energy to heat 500,000 homes for 20 years or enough crude oil to fill a fleet of 75 supertankers (325,000-ton supertankers, each with a capacity of 2.3 million barrels).

TABLE 19-4. Projected energy savings from solar technologies under the National Energy Plan[1,2] (fossil fuel equivalent in quadrillion Btu per year)

Solar Technology	*1985*	*2000*	*2020*
Hot water and space heating of buildings (direct thermal)	0.15	1.6	3–5[3]
Process heat (direct thermal)	0.02	2.0	13
Wind Energy Conversion Systems			
Electric utility	—	1.7	6.6
Distributed	*	*	*
Solar thermal			
Electric utility	—	0.3	2.9
Total energy systems	*	*	*
Photovoltaics			
Electric utility	—	—	0.2
Distributed	*	*	*
Ocean Thermal Energy Conversion Systems	—	—	2.4
Biomass—Electricity			
Wood	—	—	0.6
Other biomass	*	*	*
Biomass—Fuels			
Wood	0.3	0.4	4.4
Other biomass	*	*	*

1. Although these estimates may be reduced due to delay in implementing the National Energy Plan or increased as a result of federal policy and program alternatives now under consideration, they represent a consistent base upon which to evaluate changes.

2. Electricity is converted to equivalent quads of primary energy based on 10,000 Btu/kwh.

3. An estimate based on an extrapolation of the simulations up to the year 2000, adjusted with the likely addition of penetration of the gas and oil market.

—Less than 0.01 quads.

*Included in ongoing Metrek analyses.

nation's total energy needs (Figure 19-6). While solar's major contribution to the nation's energy needs may not be important until after the turn of the century, this study projects that with the incentives in the National Energy Plan, solar could contribute 0.2 quads of energy by 1985, and 6 quads of energy by 2000. These are significant contributions. Some twenty years ago, the first commercial nuclear reactor was still on paper. Today, with investments totaling billions of dollars, nuclear energy still displaces less than half of the 6 quads it is projected solar will displace after a like period of

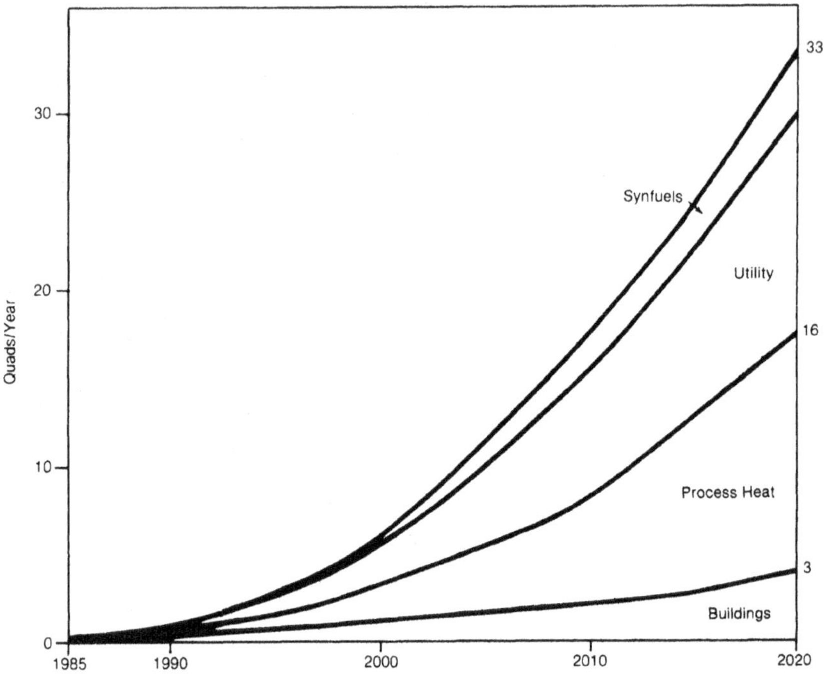

FIGURE 19-6. Fuel saved under the national energy plan scenario

development. Solar hot water systems are commercially available now, and space heating and cooling systems are in an advanced stage of development. Near-term (by 1985) contributions from solar can therefore be expected primarily from these systems. By 2000, solar energy applications for agriculture and industry should have cleared most of the hurdles of market resistance to new technologies and be cost-competitive. Solar agricultural and industrial process heat systems are projected to be competitive in cost with conventional systems before the year 2020, resulting in a major energy contribution — 13 quads per year, or 35 percent of their potential market.

Wind energy conversion systems producing electricity for utilities will be especially attractive as a fuel-saver (solar systems without storage or backup used primarily to save fuel from fossil-fuel burning plants). By 2020, a wind system is expected to displace sufficient fuel over its lifetime to save three to four times its initial cost, resulting in a projected energy displacement of more than 6 quads.

Synthetic products and fuels produced from wood are projected to supply more than 4 quads by 2020. Costs of fuel from mill residues and silvicultural energy frams are so inexpensive relative to alternative fuels such as coal that all readily available supplies are projected to be used by 2020.

19.4.1 Alternative Incentives Programs

In addition to the assessment of the likely impact of the National Energy Plan, a series of alternative incentives were investigated to see if there is potential for further acceleration of the use of solar energy. The analysis of these alternative incentives indicated that: (1) The provision of the tax credits in the National Energy Plan was as effective as other cases examined and substantially better than the case with no incentives; (2) A major cost-sharing program for solar process heat emphasizing a 65 percent federal share in 1978 declining to 20 percent in 1985, coupled with an accelerated R&D program, would increase the year 2000 fuel displacement from 2.0 quads to 3.5, at a federal cost of $1.2 billion; (3) An incentive program for solar utility applications, featuring a 10 percent additional investment tax credit, the use of oil and gas/solar hybrids, and an accelerated utility planning program, might increase the year 2000 fuel displacement from 2 quads to 4 quads at an additional federal cost of $10.3 billion; and (4) A 20 percent investment tax credit for synthetic fuels and products from biomass would increase the biomass utilization in the year 2000 from .4 to .8 quads at an additional federal cost of $600 million.

19.4.2 Other Long-Term Benefits of Solar Energy

This analysis does not represent the maximum potential for solar energy. Reasonable changes in the pace of R&D, market response (a large demand for dispersed solar electric systems, for example), and other assumptions could result in a substantially higher growth of solar energy. Moreover, if shortages in fuels result in frequent plant shut-downs, the cost resulting from a loss of business might be more important than the average energy cost.

The societal or ecological benefits of using solar energy instead of coal and nuclear fuels have also not been taken into account. Only the direct cost of likely pollution abatement equipment has been included. Recognition of these other long-term benefits of using solar energy would add additional momentum to the transition to this important renewable resource.

REFERENCES

Bennington, G. E., et al. 1977. *Solar energy: A comparative analysis to the year 2020.* MTR-7579. McLean, Va.: The Mitre Corporation.

Blackman, A. 1972. A mathematical model for trend forecasts. *Technical Forecasting and Social Change* 3:441–452.

Connolly, M., et al. 1976. *Solar heating and cooling computer analysis: A simplified sizing design method for non-thermal specialists.* ERDA Contract No. E(11-1)-2876. Denver: Martin Marietta Corporation.

Energy Research and Development Administration. 1977. *SOLOCOST: A new simplified design method for residential and light commercial solar heating and cooling.* Washington, D.C.: Division of Solar Energy, Technology Transfer.

Fisher, J. C., and Pry, R. H. 1971. A simple substitution model of technological change. *Technological Forecasting and Social Change* 3:75–88.

Hughes, P. J. 1977. *FCHART version 2.0 variable description.* University of Wisconsin-Madison College of Engineering.

Klein, S. A.; Bechman, W. A.; and Duffie, J. A. 1975. A design for solar heating systems. *Solar Energy.* 18:113–127.

Rebibo, K., et al. 1977. *A system for projecting the utilization of renewable resources.* MTR-7570. McLean, Va.: The Mitre Corporation.

Scott, J. E. 1976. *Consumer demand analysis solar heating and cooling of buildings.* Final Report, COO-2598-1. Newark: University of Delaware.

Solar Energy Project Team. 1977. *Systems descriptions and engineering costs for solar-related technologies,* vols. I–IX. MTR-7485. McLean, Va.: The Mitre Corporation.

20 MODELING THE ECONOMIC AND ENVIRONMENTAL IMPACTS OF ALTERNATIVE ELECTRIC UTILITY FUTURES

Andrew J. Van Horn, David B. Large, and Lowell F. Smith

Teknekron's Utility Simulation Model was developed to examine the effects that alternative energy and environmental policies and economic conditions will have on U.S. electric utility behavior through the year 2000 and the impacts of this behavior, in turn, on utility emissions of pollutants to air, water, and land. The model includes data on each existing and announced generating unit through 1987; for the years after 1987 it simulates units sited at the county level. We describe the model and discuss its recent application and results in an ongoing study (for EPA) of the environmental and economic impacts of alternative revisions to the New Source Performance Standards for SO_2, NO_x, and particulates. We also describe two recent air quality studies in which the model's county-by-county emission forecasts and exogeneous meterological and air quality data were analyzed in an integrated manner as a necessary prelude to dispersion modeling in order to determine: (1) the local impacts of emissions in the Lower Ohio River Basin; and (2) the regional air quality problems that arise when meterological conditions and the spatial distribution of power plants promote the long-range transport of pollutant emissions and concentrations across state boundaries.

20.1 INTRODUCTION

As a significant energy supplier, consumer of primary fuels, and producer of wastes and emissions to air, water, and land, the electric utility industry through its investment and operating decisions influences the nation's economy and the environment. The utilities' decisions, in turn, are influenced by various factors: government energy and environmental policies, economic conditions, and technological considerations. Teknekron has developed a framework for assessing in an *integrated* manner the impact of these factors on the future investment and operating decisions made by utility firms. Some of the elements in our framework are illustrated in Figure 20-1. The figure shows that the growth and development of the U.S. electric utility industry will be influenced by regulatory constraints, electricity demand, the costs and availability of technologies for electricity generation and pollution control, and conditions in the nation's economy. Utility investment and operating decisions, in turn, will be reflected in revenue requirements, which determine electricity prices, and in fuel consumption, which leads to releases of air and water pollutants and to the generation of solid wastes. These decisions and their impacts in terms of electricity prices and pollutant releases are forecast by the Utility Simulation

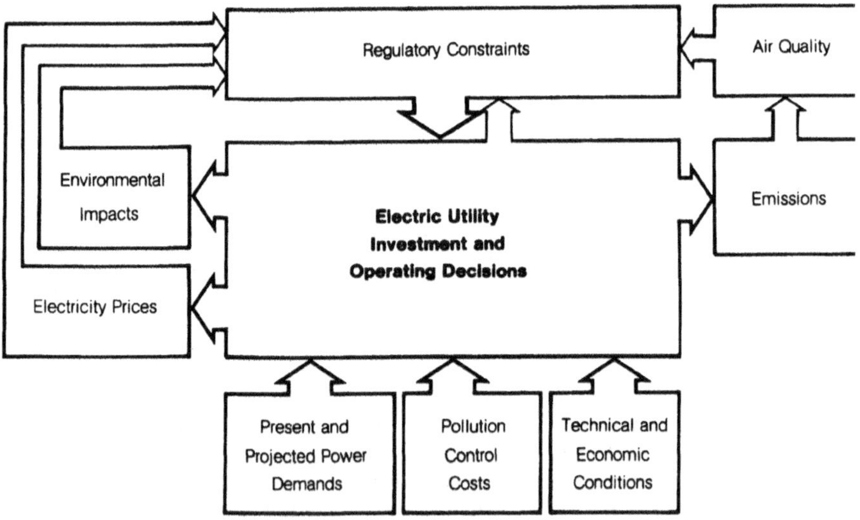

FIGURE 20-1. The integrated assessment process

Model (USM), developed under the sponsorship of the U.S. Environmental Protection Agency.

One major focus of our assessment has been to analyze the local and regional air quality impacts of the decisions utilities are likely to make in response to alternative energy and environmental policies and economic and technical conditions. For each set of alternatives, we have determined the probable air quality impacts first by using the USM to forecast the spatial distribution of power-plant emissions (by county), and then by applying statistical analyses of historical meteorological data and air transport models. Thus the outputs of the USM serve as inputs to the meteorological models. Several of the results obtained so far have profound implications for the EPA in terms of the Agency's meeting the requirements of the Clean Air Act as amended in 1977.

The U.S. Clean Air Act has several goals. As indicated in Table 20–1, three of the most important are the attainment of acceptable air quality, the maintenance of acceptable air quality, and the prevention of significant deterioration of air quality. The USM has been designed to evaluate the economic and environmental implications of several alternative policies the EPA or utilities might adopt to achieve these goals. Table 20–1 lists some of the policy tools available to the Agency.

20.2 THE UTILITY SIMULATION MODEL

The USM consists of several interconnecting computer modules and data bases that simulate decisions for system planning and operation, utility finance, and the operation of individual technical processes such as pollu-

TABLE 20–1. Air pollution control goals and policy tools

Goals	*Tools*
1. Attainment of air quality	1. State Implementation Plans
2. Maintenance of air quality	2. Revised State Implementation Plans Emission offsets Siting restrictions New Source Performance Standards Best Available Control Technology
3. Prevention of significant deterioration	3. Siting restrictions Emission offsets Best Available Control Technology

tion control devices. The model is driven by exogenous scenario elements that include electricity demand levels, financial market conditions, fuel prices and availabilities, advanced technology deployment, and environmental regulations. For each scenario, the model calculates the following by geographical region, for each county or state, for future years up to 2010:

1. Factor demands, including:
   a. fuel use, by type and for coal by region of origin
   b. electricity generated, by type of unit and for individual units
   c. capital requirements, by source (e.g., debt, common equity, preferred equity)
   d. plant and equipment requirements
   e. releases of air and water pollutants and generation of solid wastes, by county
2. Financial statistics for utility firms
3. Average electricity prices

In order to produce these calculations at the required level of detail, the model considers generating-unit sites located in each county in the forty-eight contiguous states where electricity is produced, fuel and water are consumed, and pollutants are released. Since utilities operate as integrated systems, the model presently simulates the joint operation (i.e., dispatching) of all generating units owned by utilities based in a state. Finally, the responses of utility firms to the external environment in which they function may be changed by the model user by modifying present data bases or by specifying alternate choices for future system planning and operation. Some results of that analysis will be presented in the following section.

Figure 20-2 is a simplified diagram of the USM. The model includes the following major components:

1. Demand projection by year, including:
   a. retail and wholesale sales and purchases
   b. energy generation (i.e., average load growth)
   c. peak load growth
2. System Planning projection by year, including:
   a. choice of generating-unit type
   b. choice of fuel type, quality, and coal region of origin
   c. choice of pollution control technology
   d. expansion of transmission and distribution networks
   e. siting of generating units by county

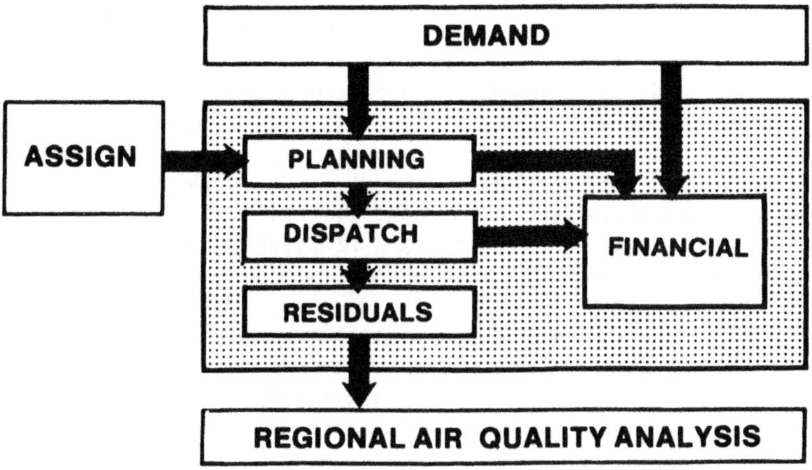

FIGURE 20-2. Teknekron's utility simulation model

3. Dispatch seasonally for typical days, including:
   a. unit capacity factors for each typical day of operation, by class of unit
   b. total fuel, operation, and maintenance expenses for electricity generation
   c. fuel consumption, by type and for coal by region of origin
   d. pollution control costs and operating characteristics for the various types of pollution control devices
4. Financial considerations by year, including:
   a. projected production expenses integrated with construction expenditures
   b. the firm's balance sheet, income statement, sources and uses of funds, and other financial statistics
   c. revenue requirements and electrcity prices
5. Residuals released and resources consumed, including:
   a. release rates at the generating-unit site for numerous air and water pollutants and for solid wastes
   b. consumption of water and other resources
6. Inputs to air quality models, including:
   a. forecasts of the counties that will have high emissions from utility and industrial boilers

For air quality modeling, historical meteorological data are analyzed to determine the preferred paths for the downwind transport of emissions from the source locations; and emissions,. air quality, and meteorological data are analyzed to develop source-receptor relationships for sulfur dioxide emissions and sulfate concentrations. The air quality models are then applied to determine ambient concentrations of sulfur dioxide, oxides of nitrogen, particulates, and sulfates. A number of detailed data bases — including data on each installed and announced generating unit in the United States, financial and operating statistics submitted by utilities to the former Federal Power Commission, fuels data, and so forth — provide inputs to the model.

The USM is not a linear program that seeks to minimize the national cost of producing electricity. Rather, for each state it projects year-by-year investments, operating costs, fuel usage, and pollutant releases. For these projections it makes maximum use of data sets that reflect the current condition and composition of utility systems, utilizes ten- and twenty-year forecasts made by individual utility firms, and takes into account the factors (including economic costs) that influence utility decision makers in their current and future choices.

In response to an exogenously specified forecast of demand, the System Planning module builds new capacity consistent with the announced plans of utility firms modified to reflect specified reserve requirements and national energy policies. For each year through 1987, for each state, the model adds new generating units from a data base of announced utility plants and sites. For each year after 1987 it simulates units as capacity is added to ensure that reserves are sufficient to exceed projected annual peaks and to meet seasonal electrical energy requirements given the system composition and availability of units projected for that year. Future unit siting is based on weight derived from engineering criteria and the type of generator, as well as air quality exclusionary criteria for each county. The selection of fuel and pollution controls to meet specified regulations is performed by utilizing the Coal Assignment model. This model reviews delivered prices and pollution control costs for over thirty different coal types and selects that combination of coal supply source and pollution control equipment that results in compliance with state and federal air pollution control regulations at least cost. The Planning module also effects announced plans for fuel conversion and plant retirement and calculates capital investment requirements for each year of the simulation. Investment needs serve as one input to the Financial module.

The Dispatch module reviews the operating costs among seventeen classes of generating units for the available generating capacity and apportions the electrical loads so that the total system cost of producing electricity is minimized for the system of existing plants and new plants built by the Planning module. Thus, the Dispatch module makes it possible to calculate both fuel consumption by category of plant and total system operating costs. Operating costs are input to the Financial module, while fuel consumption results are passed on to the Residuals module.

The Residuals module calculates releases of air and land pollutants and the generation of solid wastes for individual generating units located by county. This level of geographical detail is necessary for assessing environmental impacts and allows us to forecast the spatial and temporal distribution of emissions projected by the Planning and Dispatch modules. The disaggregated emission forecast is essential for proper evaluation of the regional and subregional impacts of alternative pollution control policies. By "impacts" we mean, for example, the distribution of price increases and pollutant reductions arising from pollution control regulations, shifts in the market for coals from different supply regions, and the existence of high-emission areas that can lead to deterioration of regional air quality.

The Financial module performs annual updates of the base-year income statement and balance sheet for the utility firms merged at the state level. Needs for external financing to accommodate the investment requirements forecast by the Planning module, as well as the cost of this financing, are calculated by source of capital. Average prices for each succeeding year are calculated considering all costs of operation including a return on the rate base. Separate treatment is provided for investor-owned and non-investor-owned utilities in each state because of their different financial status.

20.3 APPLICATIONS OF THE MODELING AND ITS RESULTS

We now discuss three important applications of the Utility Simulation Model and of the model's results. These applications were carried out for the EPA to: (1) quantify the impacts of revised New Source Performance Standards requiring Best Available Control Technology; (2) identify local air quality problem areas; and (3) determine the extent of the need for regional, rather than national, environmental policies.

20.3.1 The Impacts of Revised New Source Performance Standards

In response to a petition by the Sierra Club and to Section III of the Clean Air Act as amended in 1977, EPA's Office of Air Quality Planning and

Standards (OAQPS) is investigating alternatives for revising the New Source Performance Standards for emissions of SO_2 and particulate matter from coal-fired utility boilers. Teknekron's Utility Simulation Model is a key analytical tool being used by the EPA to investigate the regional energy, economic, and environmental impacts of possible regulatory revisions.

The impacts of alternative policies are most effectively revealed through comparison with *baseline* projections of the impacts of continuing with current policies. The baseline projections developed in our NSPS evaluation take into account many elements of current national and subnational environmental policies. These elements include, for example, the curtailment and phasing out of natural gas as an electric utility boiler fuel, the coal conversion program under the Energy Supply and Environmental Coordination Act, siting restrictions in Class I or nonattainment areas, retrofitting of cooling towers and other required pollution control measures, and compliance with current State Implementation Plans (SIPs) and New Source Performance Standards (NSPS) for the control of SO_2, NO_x, and particulates.

For one set of our analyses of alternative NSPS revisions 3 and 4, the following emissions standards were assumed:

1. For generating units on line prior to 1977: SIP limits
2. For generating units on line between 1977 and 1982: current NSPS
3. For generating units on line after 1982: revised NSPS

The SIP limits vary by state and county. Current NSPS for emissions from coal-fired boilers are: 516 nanograms per joule (ng/J), or 1.2 lb/10^6 Btu, for SO_2; 43.0 ng/J (0.10 lb/10^6 Btu) for particulates; and 301 ng/J (0.7 lb/10^6 Btu) for NO_x. As for the revised NSPS, we considered a range of possible SO_2 and particulate standards that might ultimately be adopted by the EPA. Because of space limitations, we present the results for just two here. The first is a revised SO_2 standard stipulating Best Available Control Technology (BACT), which implies the use of flue gas desulfurization, and 90 percent mandatory postcombustion SO_2 removal with an upper limit on emissions of 1.2 lbs/10^6 Btu. (Note that the baseline case, the current NSPS for SO_2, involves no mandatory percentage postcombustion removal.) The second is a revised particulate standard of 12.9 ng/J (0.03 lb/10^6 Btu).

The results given here for the NSPS revision analysis include those obtained under the following projections of growth in electricity demand: "high growth" is taken to be 5.8 percent per year nationally until 1985 and 5.5 percent per year thereafter (more recent Teknekron analyses have used lower projections), while "moderate growth" is 5.8 percent per year nationally until 1985 and 3.4 percent per year thereafter.

TABLE 20-2. U.S. electric utility system capacity mix, 1976 and 1995

		1995 Capacity (GW)	
Capacity Type	*1976 Capacity (GW)*	*Moderate Growth*	*High Growth*
Nuclear	40.5	314.4	328.5
Coal	196.9	411.5	568.8
Oil	87.3	119.0	119.7
Gas	60.3	5.5	5.5
Combined cycle	1.2	17.6	23.3
Hydro	67.6	100.3	109.4
Turbines	45.7	115.4	124.7
Geothermal	0.3	3.6	4.6
Total (GW)*	500	1087	1285

*Totals rounded.

Table 20-2 shows the capacity mix for the U.S. electric utility system in 1976 and in 1995 under the two nominal projections of growth in electricity demand. The USM projects capacity additions for the investor-owned and publicly-owned sectors by year and by state, at the county level. For each year the model also simulates a least-cost dispatch of the available units in each state to meet the projected load curves for typical weekdays and weekend days in each of the summer and winter seasons. The shapes of the load curves can be varied to examine the effects of different rates of growth in peak and average electricity demand. However, for the NSPS review, peak and average loads were assumed to grow at the same rate, leaving the shape of the load curves unchanged.

20.3.1.1 Emission reductions. One benefit of revising the NSPS will come from substantially reduced SO_2 emissions. The reduction in SO_2 emissions (assuming high growth of electricity demand) is illustrated in Figure 20-3 by the difference between the top curve (current NSPS) and the middle curve (revised NSPS with 90 percent SO_2 removal). The revised SO_2 standards will have the greatest relative impact in those regions that do not presently have a large base of coal-fired generation: compared with current standards, the revised NSPS will reduce emission by 56 percent in the West South Central region, by 53 percent in the North Mountain region, by 47 percent in the South Mountain region, by 42 percent in the Pacific region, and by 23 percent in the New England region. The spatial distribution of these percentage emission reductions is indicated by the darkest areas in

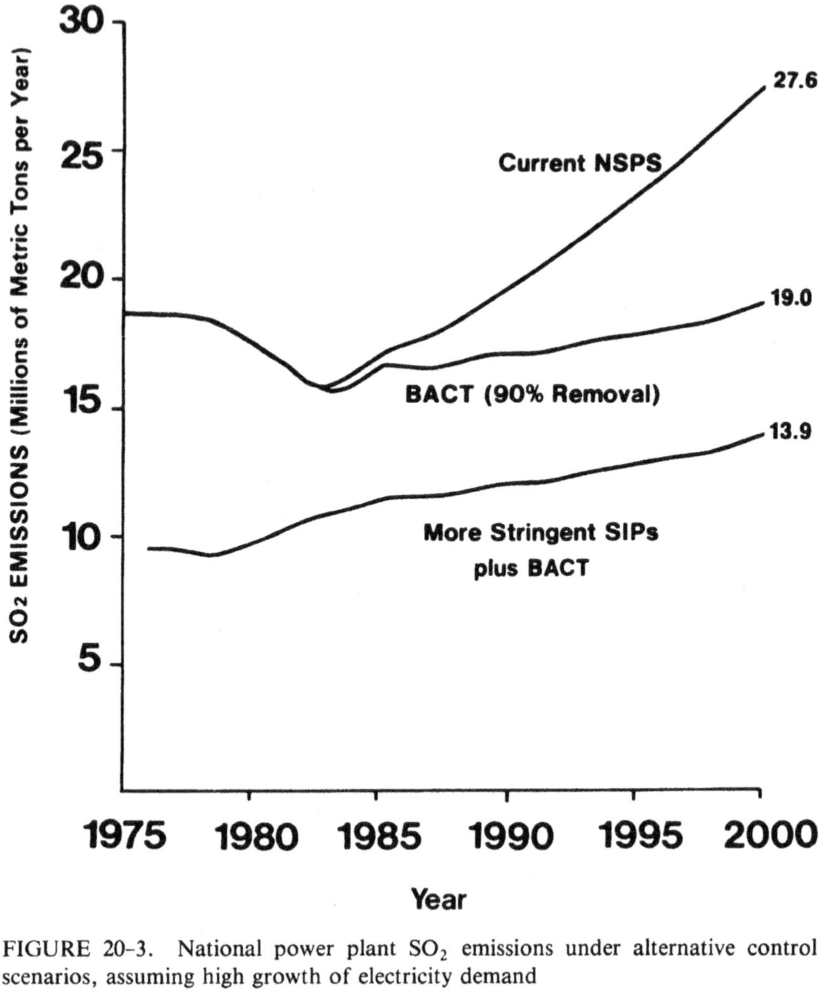

FIGURE 20-3. National power plant SO_2 emissions under alternative control scenarios, assuming high growth of electricity demand

Figure 20-4. In terms of reduced SO_2 emission tonnages, the West South Central, East North Central, and South Atlantic regions will have the largest reductions. However, even with the imposition of BACT and a standard of 90 percent SO_2 removal, national SO_2 emissions will increase over the 1976 level as a result of added coal capacity and the continued utilization of existing plants covered by SIP regulations. If all SIPs that now allow SO_2 emission to exceed 2.0 lbs/10^6 Btu were changed to permit no

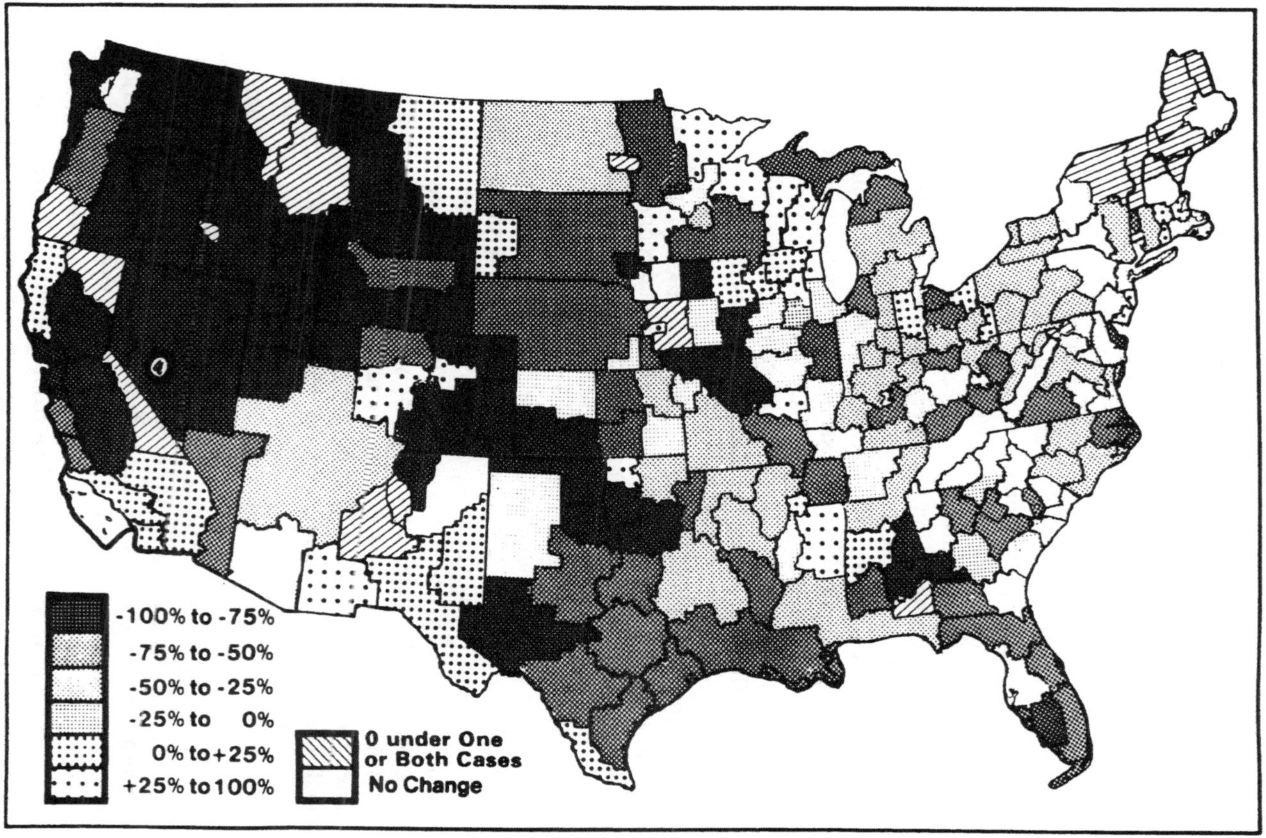

FIGURE 20–4. Percentage change in SO_2 emissions in 2000 (BACT with respect to current NSPS)

more than that amount, national SO_2 emissions in 2000 could be kept at roughly 1976 levels, as indicated by the lowest curve in Figure 20–3. Later we shall show that the imposition of tighter SIPs would have the most dramatic impact on SO_2 emissions in the eastern third of the nation.

As for particulates, assuming high growth of electricity demand, total emissions nationally under current standards will increase only slightly above the 1980 full-compliance level and will growth slightly in the 1990s. Revising the NSPS for particulates downward from 43 ng/J (0.10 lbs/10^6 Btu) to 12.9 ng/J (0.03 lbs/10^6 Btu) will reduce national aggregate emissions by 11 percent in 1990 and by 22 percent in the year 2000. Particulate emissions from units coming on line after 1982 will be reduced even more, which may have important local impacts. Finally, emissions of NO_x from electric power generation will increase substantially under current standards, even under an effective conservation program to curb electricity demand. Under high demand growth, NO_x will increase from 5.7 million metric tons in 1980 to 15.6 million metric tons in 2000; under moderate growth, NO_x will increase to 8.6 million metric tons in 2000.

20.3.1.2 Financial impacts of NSPS. Who will pay for the benefits of reduced emissions? NSPS revisions will have regional economic and financial impacts and will increase national pollution control costs. Between 1986 and 1995, assuming high growth in electricity demand, pollution control costs under the 90 percent SO_2 removal standard will be 41 percent higher than under the current standard. (Typical capital costs of lime flue gas desulfurization are about \$140/kW for a new 500 MW plant burning 3.5 percent sulfur coal.) However, since pollution control costs represent a relatively small fraction of electricity costs, the revised standard in 1995 will result in an electricity price increase of only about 5 percent. A detailed breakdown of yearly costs, balance sheets, and other financial statistics are calculated by state in the financial module of the Utility Simulation Model. National results for the baseline and the 90 percent removal standard are given in Table 20–3.

The relative regional price impacts of revising the NSPS to include 90 percent SO_2 removal and a lower particulate limit are shown in Table 20–4. These regional percentage price increases are influenced by the amount of anticipated coal capacity relative to current coal capacity, particularly in the West South Central states (now dependent on natural gas for electricity generation) and in the Mountain states (where coal resources are rapidly being developed). In New England, for example, the continued dependence on nuclear generation and the distance from coal supply sources will prevent substantial increases in coal-fired capacity and hence in the relative costs of stricter SO_2 controls.

TABLE 20–3. National economic impacts (1975 dollars) of revised NSPS, assuming high growth of electricity demand

	Baseline (Current Standard)	*Revised NSPS (90% SO_2 Removal)*	*Percentage Change*
1995 retail price (¢/kwh)	3.10	3.23	+4.2
1995 per capita cost	$685	+$27*	+3.9
Pollution control operating and maintenance costs (1986–1995, 10^9 $)	$ 40	+$16*	+41
Pollution control investment (1986–1995, 10^9 $)	$ 18	+$34*	+195
Total investment, excluding pollution control (1986–1995, 10^9 $)**	$519	+$5.5*	+1.1

*Change from Baseline.

**Includes capital and construction costs. Additional capacity is required to make up for capacity penalties and energy required by pollution controls.

TABLE 20–4. Relative regional price impacts of a proposed NSPS revision, assuming high growth of electricity demand

	*Percentage Increase in 1995 with Revision**
Nation	+ 4.2
Region	
West South Central	+12
North Mountain	+ 7.4
West North Central	+ 5.4
East North Central	+ 4.8
South Atlantic	+ 4.6
East South Central	+ 2.8
Mid Atlantic	+ 2.1
South Mountain	+ 1.7
Pacific	+ 1.0
New England	+ 0.2

*Mandatory FGD on all post-1982 plants; particulate limit reduced.

20.3.1.3 National and regional coal demand. Coal consumption will be significantly influenced by the growth rate in electricity demand after 1985. Figure 20–5 illustrates national coal consumption in metric tons under a high post-1985 growth rate of 5.5 percent per year and under a moderate post-1985 growth rate of 3.4 percent per year. The projection is based on currently announced utility plans for installing coal plants and on the operation of these plants projected by the USM. National Energy Plan goals for

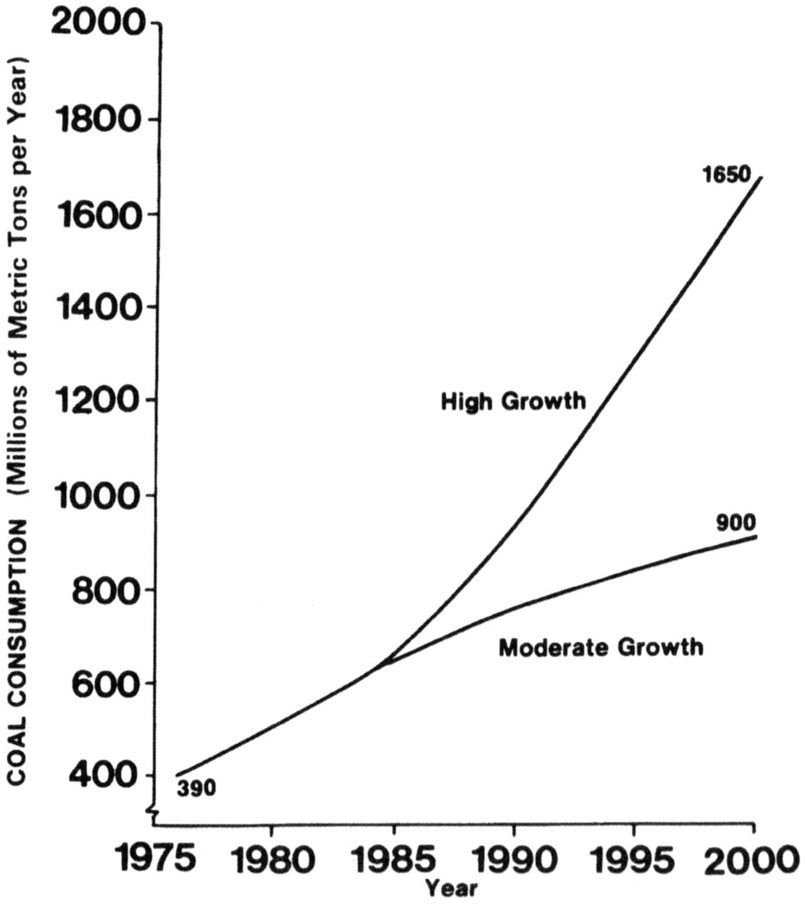

FIGURE 20–5. Projections of electric utility coal consumption under high vs. moderate growth in electricity demand

1985 coal consumption may be achieved by the electric utility sector, which now consumes two-thirds of the coal produced nationwide. It will be difficult, however, for the industrial use of coal to expand as rapidly.

Revised New Source Performance Standards will have a significant impact on the use of local coals and on the markets for western coals. Our analysis suggests that the consumption of Powder River Basin coal after 1985 may change substantially under a standard requiring 90 percent removal of SO_2 (see Figure 20-6).

20.3.1.4 Use of FGD (scrubbers) for SO_2 control. The USM projects the needed requirements for flue gas desulfurization (FGD) devices in order to

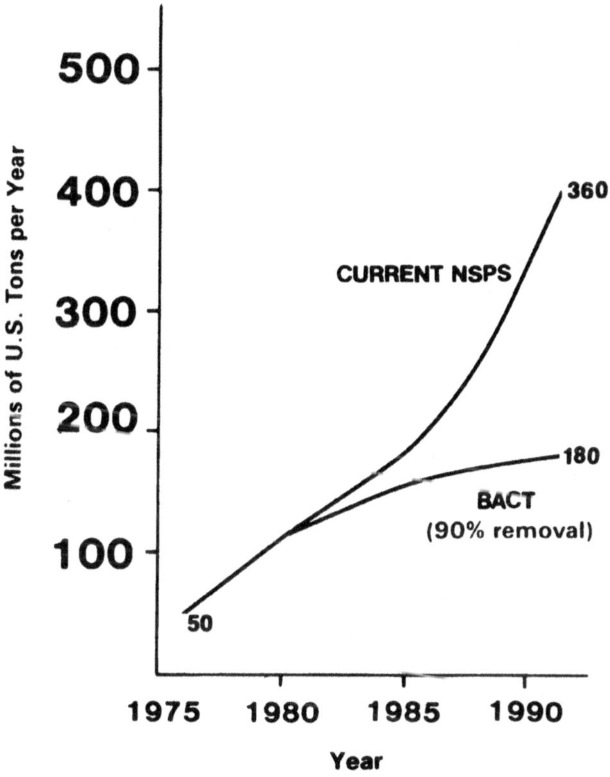

FIGURE 20-6. Consumption of Powder River Basin coal under the revised standard as compared with the current standard

meet specified emission limits. For the case of high growth in electricity demand, scrubbers will be used in 1995 for roughly 355 GW (gigga (i.e. 10^9) watts) of coal capacity under a standard requiring 90 percent post-combustion of SO_2 removal but for only about 80 GW under continuation of the current standard. The areas of the country with the highest installed scrubber capacities by 1995 under the revised standard will be the West South Central region (84 GW), the East North Central region (82 GW), and the South Atlantic region (76 GW). These three regions will contain 60 percent of the total installed FGD capacity in that year.

Table 20–5 shows the projected amounts of sludge produced and water consumed by FGD systems under the two SO_2 standards. Approximately 3.8 percent of the primary coal energy will be required to operate FGD scrubbers in 1995 under the 90 percent removal standard.

20.3.2 Identification of Air Quality Problem Areas

Results from the USM have been used in integrated assessments to identify the regional, subregional, and local areas that may have air quality problems in the future as a result of fossil steam plant emissions. By combining the model's county-by-county emission projections with exogenous meteorological and air quality data, we have identified future problem areas and possible integration strategies. Our air quality impact analyses cover five geographic scales: subnational (for example, the eastern United States); regional (the six-state Ohio River Basin area); subregional (the Lower Basin area); local (the portion of the Lower Basin between Louisville, Kentucky,

TABLE 20–5. Some national FGD impacts in 1995 under current and revised NSPS

	Baseline (Current Standard)	*Revised NSPS (90% SO_2 Removal)*
FGD sludge produced* (10^6 dry tonnes)	12	55
Cumulative disposal area	15	92
(km^2, 1990–2000)**	15	92
FGD water consumed (10^6 m^3)	110	607
FGD energy consumed (% total coal energy)	0.7%	3.8%

*Total coal ash production: 101 × 10^6 tonnes.

**Nine-meter depth.

and Cincinnati, Ohio); and site-specific (specific power plants). In this section we present some results of our local-scale analyses of the Lower Ohio River Basin. (In the following section, we discuss a regional-scale analysis.)

Our analysis has identified the Lower Ohio River Basin, particularly the area from Cincinnati to Louisville, as one of the most prominent air quality problem areas. Coincidentally, concerns of local citizen groups over the potential concentration of coal-fired power plants in this area have provided the impetus for another major EPA program, the Ohio River Basin Energy Study. In the Teknekron work performed in support of that study, the focus has been on determining the local and medium-range air quality impacts of clustered power plants and the additive long-range impacts of multiple clusters of plants. EPA is concerned that the operation of large new coal-fired plants may lead to further degradation of air quality in existing nonattainment areas or to consumption of the entire increment for SO_2 specified in regulations for the prevention of significant deterioration.

The clustering of power plants in the Lower Basin area near Louisville is shown in Figure 20–7. Also shown are the locations of air quality monitors indicating where SO_2 and particulate levels exceeded the ambient air quality standards in 1975. The four power plants near Louisville are associated with the exceeded standards. Moreover, the north-south line of these plants coincides with the direction of extremely persistent winds (winds blowing at ten to fifteen miles per hour, for periods of about six hours or more, in a sector less than 22.5° wide). These wind conditions occur at least several times each year. When the direction of persistent winds coincides with the location of power plants, additive pollutant concentrations can be transported downwind. High background levels of SO_2 or sulfates are frequently associated with these meteorological conditions. EPA's Point-Multiple Point (PTMTP) dispersion model has been used to estimate the additive ground-level SO_2 concentrations caused by the four power plants near Louisville (Figure 20–8). Under certain conditions, these concentrations may cause violations of the three-hour SO_2 air quality standard; and if the violations are of sufficient duration, even the twenty-four-hour standard may be exceeded.

These results have implications for the proposed power plants downwind along the Ohio River: the level of background emissions under persistent-wind conditions may be so high that the siting of new sources will be precluded by the regulations for the prevention of significant deterioration. Note the locations of the two proposed power plants in Figure 20–7. It is doubtful that these locations can be justified without a reduction in emissions from existing sources. Any judgment regarding the proposed plants should be backed up by ambient air quality data from additional monitors and by further air quality analyses.

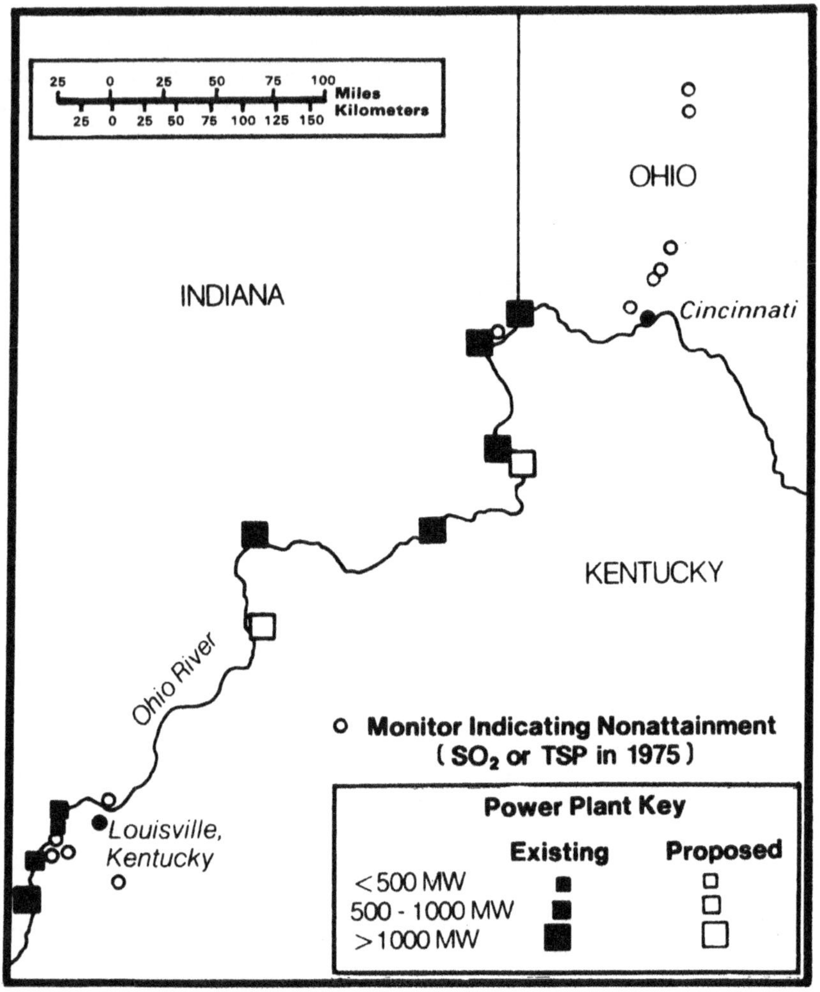

FIGURE 20–7. Fossil steam plants in the lower Ohio River Basin and the monitors indicating nonattainment

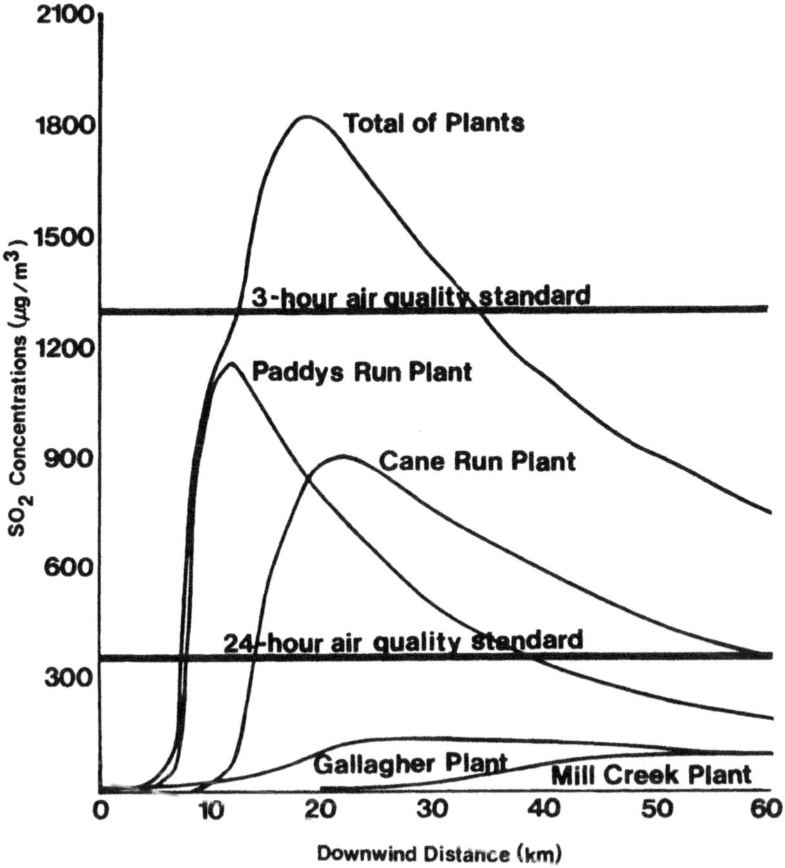

FIGURE 20–8. Ground-level SO_2 concentrations from four power plants along a north-south line near Louisville (from the EPA PTMTP model)

20.3.2.1 SO_2 emissions and SIP limits. Table 20–6 indicates that, under current or revised NSPS, the predominant sources of SO_2 emissions will be plants regulated by State Implementation Plans. More particularly, in all years, the predominant SO_2 emission sources will be post-1950 units subject to SIP emission limits. In the high growth case, up to 70 percent of SO_2 emissions in 2000 could be due to SIP-regulated plants (plants on line before 1977), and 23 percent to plants on line after 1982 (plants assumed to be subject to a revised NSPS). The predominance of SIP-regulated plants as

TABLE 20-6. Projected SO_2 emissions by coal plant regulatory category

	1985	*2000*
Percentage of Total Emissions		
SIP units	89%	70%
NSPS units	9%	7%
BACT units	2%	23%
Total emissions (10^6 tons)	16.0	19.5

emission sources suggests that SO_2 emission levels might be substantially reduced if existing SIP standards were made more stringent. In another study, in which the USM was used to investigate potential markets for physically cleaned coal, one scenario included changing all SO_2 SIP limits to allow no more than 2.0 lbs. $SO_2/10^6$ Btu. If that hypothetical policy were to be implemented uniformly, SO_2 emissions in 1985 would be reduced by 31 percent nationally. Regionally, there would be reductions of 51 percent in the West North Central region, 45 percent in the East South Central region, 30 percent in the South Atlantic region, 29 percent in the East North Central region, and 26 percent in the Mid Atlantic region. (Dramatic reductions would not be observed in the western United States, because SIP limits there are already more stringent than the upper limit postulated in this scenario.) The national emission reductions are illustrated by the lowest curve in Figure 20-3. Our integrated assessment results suggest that existing plants in specific subregional areas of the country will need to be controlled in order to permit future growth.

20.3.3 The Need for Regional Policies

Teknekron has recently used the USM's county-by-county emission results to help EPA evaluate the effects of the long-range transport of pollutants into the state of Pennsylvania. In 1976, EPA Region III notified Pennsylvania that every Air Quality Control Region in the State was a non-attainment area for particulates and that Pennsylvania should therefore revise its SIP. In the Fall of 1977, Dr. Maurice Goddard, secretary of the Pennsylvania Department of Environmental Resources, asked EPA Administrator Douglas Costle to investigate the degree to which SO_2 sources in upwind states were contributing to Pennsylvania's ambient concentrations of particulate matter. Dr. Goddard pointed out that preliminary results of Teknekron's integrated assessment and of studies performed at Carnegie-Mellon University indicated that a significant portion of Pennsylvania's nonattainment problem could not be addressed by revision of the Pennsylvania SIP but rather had to be dealt with by controlling SO_2 sources in the upwind states of Ohio and West Virginia. Dr. Goddard's petition was made in accordance with Section 110 of the Clean Air Act, as amended, which requires that SIP revisions in a given state not prevent or interfere with attainment or maintenance of air quality in other states. At issue here were the implications for Pennsylvania of Ohio's proposed SIP revision and of the proposed relaxation of SO_2 limits for two power plants in West Virginia.

Figure 20-9 conceptualizes the long-range-transport process, and Figure 20-10 shows the configuration of fossil steam plants in the three-state problem area. Under certain meteorological conditions, these power plants are upwind of Pennsylvania. In cooperation with EPA Regions III, IV, and I and EPA's Office of Air and Waste Management, Teknekron has conducted meteorological and air quality analyses to determine the contribution of these SO_2 sources in Ohio and West Virginia to particulate levels in western Pennsylvania.

Our study of five to ten years of conventional weather data from National Weather Service stations, as well as one to two years of special

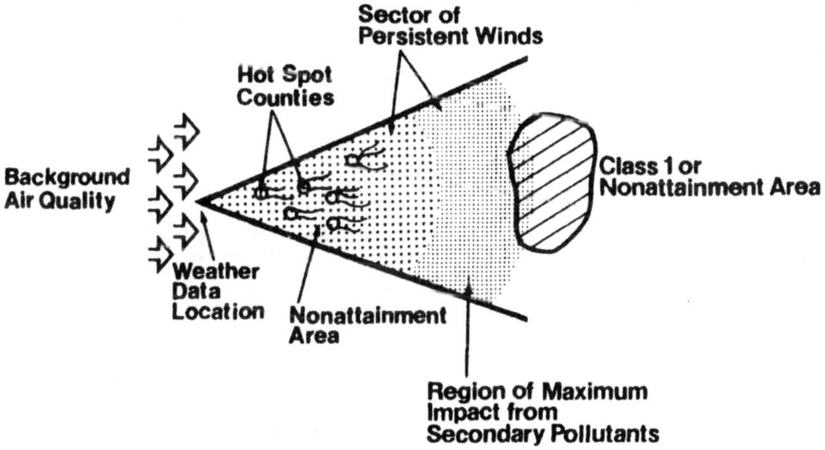

FIGURE 20-9. Long-range transport (approximately 180 miles, or 360 kilometers)

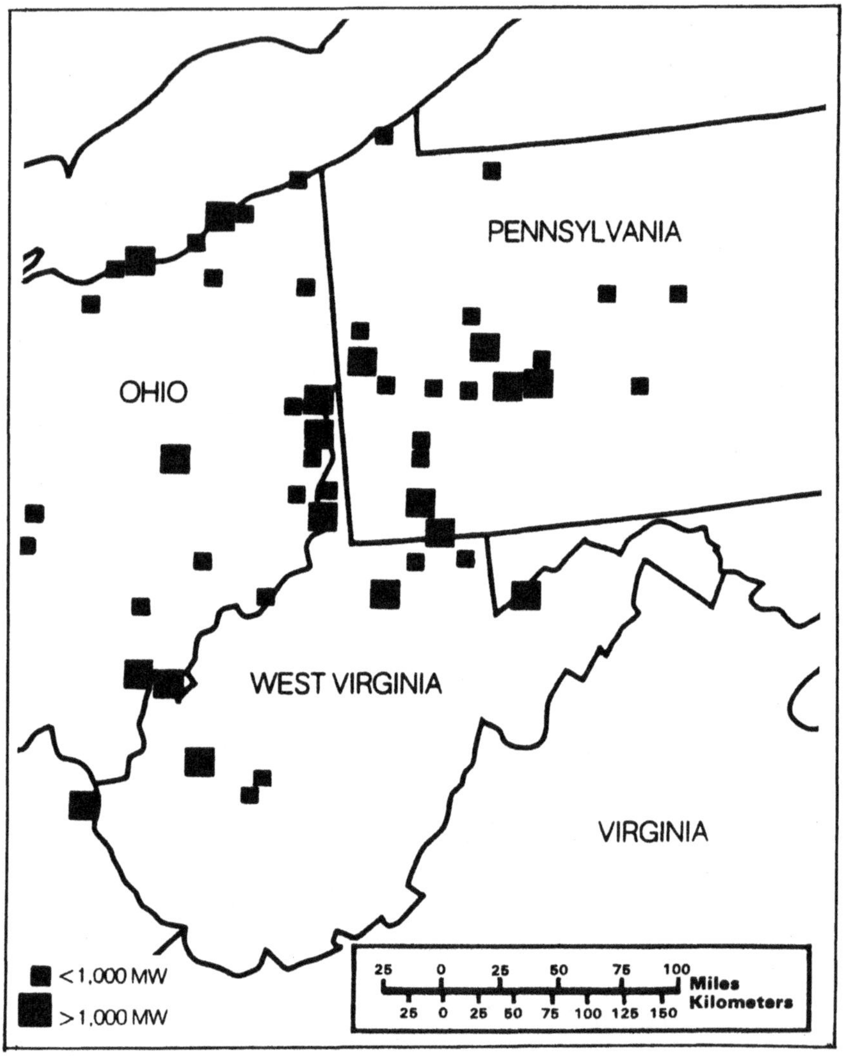

FIGURE 20-10. 1976 fossil steam power plants in Pennsylvania, Ohio, and West Virginia

meteorological tower data for a number of locations in the subregional problem area, has shown that the extremely persistent winds in this area blow most frequently toward western Pennsylvania from either Ohio or West Virginia. These conditions occur, on the average, at least thirty times a year. Our analysis of the spatial correlation of extremely persistent winds has revealed a source-receptor relationship in which pollutants from the Huntington, West Virginia area are transported over distances of 150 to 300 kilometers within a narrow sector downwind in the general direction of western Pennsylvania.

Teknekron's analysis of measured sulfate levels in Wheeling, West Virginia, from the Sulfate Regional Experiment (SURE) program shows that Wheeling's average sulfate levels exceeded the Pennsylvania sulfate standard (10 $\mu g/m^3$) in every month of the 1974–1975 period. Analysis of total suspended particulate levels in Pennsylvania suggests that, for days when long-range-transport conditions occurred, the sulfates coming from upwind sources provided the additional increment needed to push Pennsylvania's particulate levels over the secondary standard.

20.4 USEFULNESS OF THE INTEGRATED APPROACH TO MODELING

In evaluating the implications of environmental policies, one must always undertake some form of integrated assessment, whether or not such an approach is explicitly recognized. The analytical models developed by Teknekron have been designed for the examination of many energy and environmental issues. The aim of our model-based assessments has been to provide EPA and other decision-making bodies with a sound analytical framework and consistent quantitative results on which to base a comparison of alternative strategies and technical choices. The examples described here are leading to further refinement of Teknekron's energy and environmental models and to a better understanding of the probable results of future decisions.

REFERENCES

Niemann, B. L., and Mahan, A. L. 1978. *Impact of long-range transport of pollutants on air quality in the Commonwealth of Pennsylvania.* Report submitted to the U.S. Environmental Protection Agency, Office of Research and Development, Office of Energy, Minerals, and Industry, Teknekron, Inc., Berkeley, California.

Niemann, B. L.; Mills, M. M.; and Hall, B. R. 1978. Local and site-specific air quality impacts of power plants in the lower Ohio River Basin. Interim Report submitted to the U.S. Environmental Protection Agency, Office of Research and Development, Office of Energy, Minerals, and Industry, Teknekron, Inc., Berkeley, California.

Teknekron, Inc. 1978. *Review of new source performance standards for coal-fired utility boilers,* vol. I, *Emissions and non-air-quality environmental impacts.* Report submitted to the U.S. Environmental Protection Agency, Office of Air Quality Planning and Standards, Office of Energy, Minerals, and Industry, Teknekron, Inc., Berkeley, California.

Teknekron, Inc. 1978. *Review of new source performance standards for coal-fired utility boilers,* vol. II, *Economic and financial impacts.* Report submitted to the U.S. Environmental Protection Agency, Office of Planning and Evaluation, Teknekron, Inc., Berkeley, California.

21 SYSTEMS APPROACH TO ASSESSING ELECTRICITY CONSERVATION INITIATIVES

Bruce A. Smith, Tom L. Johnston, and Robert A. Meyer

This paper reports on an integrated model of electric utility systems designed to analyze potential impacts of introducing certain conservation initiatives. The Rate Simulation Model can be used to assess in an integrated manner the economic, financial, technical, and environmental consequences of a wide variety of policies and regulations affecting electric utilities. It is a flexible tool for policy analysis, enabling the investigator to ask a wide range of "what if?" questions about future utility developments. The principal application here is to economic and financial impacts. In particular the model has been used to examine the impacts of implementing time-of-day and flat rate structures on utilities in the United States. This study indicates that time-of-day rates can accomplish their intended purpose of flattening utility load curves. However, unless carefully designed, planned, and implemented, such rates can have several unintended consequences. They may shift a greater proportion of utility costs to residential customers, resulting in higher costs for equivalent service than under continuation of traditional pricing practices. Implementing time-of-day rates will require investment in new metering and billing equipment that will probably outweigh any savings in new generating capacity over the short run. Time-of-day rates may discourage conservation-oriented end-use technology such as solar (a finding also suggested by Asbury and Mueller (1977)) and may lead to increased energy use by some customers. Finally, time-of-use rates may encourage industrial establishments to adopt forms of self-generation that are less efficient than centralized generation provided by a utility.

21.1 INTRODUCTION

Many "reforms" or innovations in electricity pricing have been proposed in the last few years. At the same time, a number of "conservation" measures aimed at reducing electricity consumption have been advocated. These rate innovations and conservation measures have been championed by a number of parties, occasionally in explicit alliance. Direct interest has inspired some of the advocates — for example, price-conscious consumer groups — just as indirect interest has motivated others, including environmental organizations seeking to reduce new plant construction.

We have completed a simulation study designed to test the effects of several new rate-setting schemes. For this effort, it was necessary to create a demand-forecasting methodology that could take into account new end-use technologies with conservation potential. The framework of the study involved a coordinated, systemwide integrated approach.

Our results show how different "goods" may be in conflict, and how unintended consequences are likely to arise when innovations are adopted without considering systemwide effects. The state of the art of modeling the complex interactions of electric utility operations, and particularly of forecasting demand under radically new rate-settling schemes, does not permit any great degree of precision in our numerical results. We believe that the value of our study lies in the direction of the findings and in the interrelationships they reveal.

Since we were primarily interested in characterizing the kinds of impacts which may occur as the result of rate innovation, we used very simple, hypothetical, or "naive" rates. In detailed innovative proposals already put forward for specific utility systems, planners have attempted to foresee and avert adverse impacts through special measures. As rate-making authorities take up the task of deliberating and approving innovative rates, more complicated designs can be expected to emerge which may even be specific to particular systems, taking into account their local customer mix. The analysis of our "naive" rates may serve to define the problems which designers of detailed rate schemes will have to address and the uncertainties they will be working under.

21.2 THE RATE SIMULATION MODEL

The Rate Simulation Model consists of six modules (see Figure 21-1), and simulates future developments in the electric utility industry in response to selected pricing, energy, economic, and environmental alternatives. It was

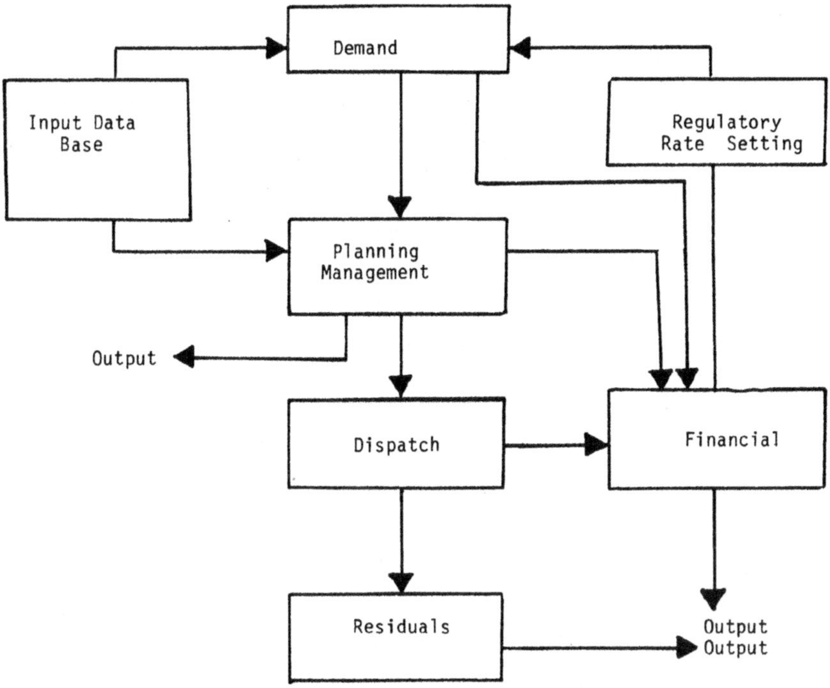

FIGURE 21-1. Utility rate simulation model

developed by Teknekron and adapted for the research reported here. Used in a number of technical studies of policy issues related to energy use (Teknekron, Inc., 1975, 1977, 1978), it was designed to take into account interrelated policy and technical issues of relevance in simulating electric utility performance. It was modified and restructured to study ratesetting and conservation issues.

It is an interactive supply-demand simulation model that addresses utility system impacts of alternative scenarios and generates integrated and consistent economic, financial, and environmental effects. It produces yearly state-by-state forecasts, as well as a national forecast. These modules are described briefly.

21.2.1 Demand Module

The economic/micro-engineering DEMAND module projects demand for electricity, specified as load curves for typical days, in response to rate levels, social and economic trends, technology available for electricity end use, and ability to modify applications or operations. Demand is projected on a state level to reflect regional variables. The DEMAND module is able to account for a variety of rate structures, end-use technologies, and customer responses. It forecasts electricity demand for each customer class under a variety of rate structures and their technical and economic consequences. The electricity demands are presented as inputs to the PLANNING-MANAGEMENT and FINANCIAL modules. The DEMAND module is described in greater detail later in this paper.

21.2.2 Planning-Management Module

Federal Power Commission data together with information from several other sources were compiled into data bases. These include files on: descriptors of each of the steam-electric generating units in the United States; all the steam units the utilities have announced will be added, with their currently projected dates for coming on line; financial data, by individual utility; and representative emission limits, by county. From these and other files, data for all utilities operating within each state were aggregated to form a simulated "state-firm."

The PLANNING-MANAGEMENT module projects the technical characteristics the state-firm must have in future years to meet forecasted electricity demands. In addition, it estimates construction requirements for generation, transmission, and distribution facilities; simulates fuel choice; and determines pollution-control needs in response to environmental regulations. Nonsteam-generating facilities are treated on an aggregated basis, reflecting both the paucity of data on individual units of this kind and their lesser environmental significance. In simulating the composition of the state systems, PLANNING-MANAGEMENT uses announced plans of the utilities through 1985, not only for new units but also for fuel conversions, retirements, and reratings.

After 1985 the module simulates system expansion including choice of generating units and transmission and distribution facilities. The capacity expansion algorithm used in the PLANNING-MANAGEMENT module is derived from that used by Joskow and Baughman (1976) and other investigators, which stems from developments of optimality relationships by Turvey (1968). The basic methodology is one of selection of amounts of capacity to be installed from among competing alternatives in order to meet electrical loads at least cost.

Impacts of air and water environmental regulations or system planning are accounted for and include hypothetical new levels of control as well as existing controls (that is, thermal and chemical controls on discharges to water as well as State Implementation Plan and New Source Performance Standard limits on emissions to air). In accordance with scenario specifications, compliance schedules can be adjusted and the various optional new controls may or may not be imposed. Fuels are selected from available alternatives by considering a trade-off between premium-priced clean fuels and the costs of controls necessary to use cheaper fuels and still comply with regulations. Pollution-control costs, determined in detail on a unit-by-unit basis include capital outlays, increased operating costs, and losses of capacity that make new construction necessary in order to maintain system performance.

21.2.3 Dispatch Module

The DISPATCH module allocates electricity production among the state-firm's various generating facilities. It forms this estimate for the hour-by-hour load for typical days on the basis of least marginal cost, subject to limitations on unit availability and on total energy output for the various types of facilities. Production expense is then determined from the cost of fuel and other variable operating costs.

21.2.4 Residuals Module

The RESIDUALS module takes the production levels from DISPATCH and associates them with individual units whose fuel choices and pollution-control methods are projected by PLANNING-MANAGEMENT. It then operates on this association to project levels of use of the different fuel resources and to estimate water consumption. It determines production levels of a wide range of air pollutants and solid wastes, estimating seasonal emissions on a unit-by-unit basis.

21.2.5 Financial Module

The FINANCIAL module integrates projected production expenses (from DISPATCH) with construction expenditures both for new generation facilities and for pollution control (from PLANNING-MANAGEMENT) and with projected sales and power-purchase levels (from DEMAND). Starting off with data on the state-firm's financial status in a base year, the module projects the state-firm's balance sheets, earnings statements, sources and uses of funds, and other financial statistics for each year of the simulation. The financial impact reports can provide forecasts aggregated nationally and regionally from state-by-state results.

21.2.6 Regulatory Rate-Setting Module

The REGULATORY RATE-SETTING module calculates the prices the utility must charge each customer class and subclass in order to meet its predicted revenue requirement. Rates are adjusted annually with revenue requirements, including a target return on equity, based on projecting last year's expenses forward to the coming year. The total revenue requirement is apportioned among subclasses and rate-schedule components (demand, energy, and customer charges), as appropriate for the rate structure being analyzed.

In estimating the impacts of innovative rate designs, the key modules are DEMAND, which must predict customer responses to the new rates and REGULATORY RATE-SETTING, which must project the actual price levels within the structures chosen for analysis. Of course, DISPATCH and PLANNING are also important in determining the future costs of meeting the new demand patterns; but in this limited space it seems best to focus on the principal assumptions, capabilities, and limitations of the DEMAND and REGULATORY RATE-SETTING modules.

21.3 CONCEPTS OF TECHNOLOGICAL MODELING

The task of forecasting electricity demand and load patterns is complicated because of the many economic, technical, and sociodemographic factors that influence the demand for electricity. Each of these factors must be addressed adequately — a task made more difficult when forecasts of key parameters are made with little or no empirical data. This was a major challenge facing us in developing this model framework and applying it to innovative rate structures.

A reliable electricity demand forecasting methodology must combine the perspectives and techniques of both economics and engineering. It should explicitly incorporate several considerations: (1) electricity demand should be recognized as a derived, not a final, demand; (2) the role of technology in influencing demand should be accounted for; and (3) the effects of electricity price levels and structure should be recognized. The demand for electricity stems from the consumer's wish to undertake productive work, not from his wish to "use" kilowatt-hours (kwh) or kilowatts (kw) themselves. The person who wants to cool his home, for example, is not actually demanding kwh, but air-conditioning. The use of kwh is derived from the demand for air conditioning, which requires electricity to power the compressor. Similarly, commercial and industrial demands for electricity are really demands for heating, cooling, lighting, and processing requirements.

An elementary technological demand model for a single user is basically a list of the appliances he owns. Electrical loads for these appliances are known, and the energy requirement of an average customer in this category can be estimated as the sum of loads for the appliances. These loads can be represented by formulas expressing weather dependence, regional factors, etc. In forecasting for the future, the effects of new price forms, new price levels, and new real income levels are reflected in new appliance mixes. That is, electricity pricing and conservation standards will affect appliance efficiency through replacement of old appliances and installations in new homes. Changes in customer volume in various appliance-mix categories, together with changes in efficiencies or load requirements, are determined by the model in a simulative manner.

A technological model for any class of customer — residential, commercial, or industrial — explicitly assumes that the demand for electricity is a derived demand. This means that the model accounts for different major end uses (e.g., cooling and heating) as identifiable, separable processes, rather than assuming that the kwh used for heating and other end uses are homogeneous, as many econometric forecasting models do. Central to such a methodology is the characterization of the different kinds of equipment that use electricity as an input. In order to account for long run and short run effects on electricity-using equipment and changes in the utilization patterns of existing stock. By accounting for such changes, the methodology models the consumers' actual decision process in using electricity.

Unlike the consumer of many other commodities, the electricity consumer does not face a single price. Rather, he may pay one of several different prices, depending on the amount of kwh he uses, or perhaps, the time of consumption. The DEMAND module, therefore, includes multiple prices. By representing the series of prices facing the customer rather than an average price, the model can account for changes in the structure as well as the level of electricity prices.

By viewing the demand for electricity as a derived demand, for end uses for electricity we explicitly model the electricity-using capital stock adjustment process. This approach allows flexibility in simulating the impact of different policy alternatives, such as conservation strategies. It can account for technical as well as economic changes affecting end use. Finally, it explicitly accounts for the actual process of decision-making in energy use. We now consider the structure of the model's projections and the structure of customer responses to rate innovations.

21.3.1 Structure of the Technological Demand Model

The model's basic mode of operation is to project the rate structure's impact on daily and seasonal load curves for a number of "typical customers" and to aggregate these curves, suitably weighted, into class and system load curves for each state. With these load curves for typical customers, it is also possible to determine revenue requirements under innovative rate structures, aggregating to levels of subclass and system.

Exogenous time series data reflecting projected social and economic trends, such as population growth and income projections, are incorporated in the demand estimates. Different typical customers are modeled to reflect technological differences in end use and other factors, such as size of establishment. The model is divided into four sectors corresponding to the four categories of customers for which relevant data and end uses are generically different. The sectors are: (1) Residential customers are differentiated by appliance stock for each state. Ten appliance categories are considered: space heaters, central air-conditioners, room air conditioners, water heaters, refrigerators, ranges, color TV sets, black and white TV sets, washers, and dryers; (2) Commercial customers are categorized by state as office buildings, schools, retail establishments, hospitals and nursing homes, and other; (3) Industrial customers are classified by major two-digit SIC Codes that account for the bulk of electricity use in manufacturing. The categories include: Food and Kindred Products (SIC 20), Paper and Allied Products (26), Chemicals and Allied Products (28), Petroleum Refining (29), Stone, Clay, and Glass Products (32), Primary Metals (33) and Other; and (4) Other customers include railroads, purchasers of street and highway lighting, government bodies not otherwise classified, interdepartmental purchasers, and miscellaneous customers. This method of forecasting electricity demand from an end-use perspective also accounts for each major end-use technology currently in operation and for prospective technologies that may be operable over the next fifteen years. After defining the stock of major electricity-using equipment and appliances for the residential, commercial, and industrial customer classes, the model forecasts responses to alternative rate structures and demographic trends to determine the changed patterns of electricity use. The response to altered rate structures and levels is based on the technological alternatives for each end use, their cost of acquisition, and their cost of operation.

21.3.2 The Model's Response Structure

Critically important in forecasting the impact of innovative rates structures is the calculation of customer responses. Although the empirical data on which to base this calculation are notably inadequate, we have been able to use such data as do exist to postulate a number of options that customers are likely to adopt in response to new rate structures. These include: use of passive and active solar, storage of energy, use of more efficient equipment and appliances, adoption of alternative space-conditioning technologies, adoption of industrial cogeneration, and alteration of industrial plant operations. These responses vary by the rate structure considered, depend on particular economic and technical parameters associated with the rate structure, and are specific to each major customer class.

The response structure developed for the demand model reflects the process of electricity using capital stock replacement in a manner that is sensitive to relative price effects. This structure employs a logit formulation of the replacement process. It is consistent with the end-use approach utilized and allows us to simulate the introduction and diffusion of new end-use technology responses to innovative rate structures as well as accounting for the interaction of responses to price sensitivity.

21.3.3 Modeling Electricity Rate Setting

The demand and supply segments of the Rate Simulation Model are interfaced through the REGULATORY RATE-SETTING module. This module calculates the prices at which revenues are in balance with projected costs, thus providing a kind of computer simulation of regulatory control. Strictly speaking, of course, it is impossible to render a computer simulation of the regulatory process. Computer simulation implies that prices can be determined from cost data by mathematical formulas, whereas the actual price judgments reached by regulatory commissions, while following a prescribed framework, are the result of deliberation on a case-by-case basis. However, a computer simulation does allow us to display the outcome of applying various hypothetical rules for regulatory procedures when these can be mathematically specified.

Two important assumptions are common to all our rate-setting scenarios: (1) Prices recover all costs and only costs. The rate-setting scenarios generate neither "excess" revenues nor subsidies from outside the system; and (2) A specified return on equity is included in the revenue requirement for each simulated year, thus return on equity is treated as a cost. One implication of the second assumption is that a cost increase (from any source) is reflected in prices rather than in losses to shareholders. Allowed earnings are partially offset by allowances for funds used during construction (AFDC) in the customary way. The first assumption is especially important for innovations such as time-of-day rates. It is common practice to say that such rates put a "high" price on electricity use in peak times. It is equally valid, under our assumption, to say they put a very "low" price on electricity use in off-peak times. The responses predicted by our DEMAND module are stimulated as much by the promise of very low off-peak prices as they are by the threat of very high on-peak prices. Similarly, in raising prices to any class of user (for example, large or industrial) to encourage a cutback, it is necessary to lower prices to other users, removing incentives to conserve.

As is true for any large, complex systems model, the scenario definitions are quite important. The rate-setting scenarios examined here and defined later address a broad range of "what if?" questions. The scenarios analyzed represent hypothetical rate structures that have been applied to utilities uniformly. They are not intended to portray actual rate schedules currently used or planned by U.S. utilities. The model, however, is easily able to examine such rate schedules when input into the REGULATORY RATE-SETTING module.

The selected rate structures illustrate a generic range of alternatives being considered by U.S. utilities and state regulatory agencies. In some sense these hypothetical rate structures can be characterized as simple, pure rates that are not very realistic. However, they include many of the characteristic qualities of innovative rate schedules now being implemented and evaluated in the United States. The assumptions regarding uniform implementation of these rate structures may represent a "worst case" forecast of their impacts on the utilities. To have relaxed the simplifying assumptions inherent in such scenarios, such as applying the rate structures selectively to only certain customer subclasses (e.g., large industrial customers) would have required additional computational algorithms and resources which were not available. Nevertheless, the results reported here provide interesting insights into the potential system effects of implementing the rate-structure scenarios defined now.

21.3.4 Baseline Scenario

For the baseline case (traditional declining block rate setting) we used the well-known excess demand method to partition the Demand requirement among customer classes in accordance with class load characteristics. We take no position with respect to preference of the excess demand method over the competing peak responsibility method. We used it for the baseline only because it appears to better represent common practice. The Energy requirement was partitioned in proportion to average class demand; and the Customer requirement, in proportion to customers. For commercial and industrial classes, the rate components included a peak-demand charge as well as an energy charge. Peak-demand charges were set to recover the "excess" demand requirements. All other revenue requirements were met from energy charges made on declining block rate schedules. The relative shape of the schedules was set for each state on the basis of an analysis of typical electricity bill data published by the FPC.

21.3.5 Time-of-Day Scenarios

For one of the two scenarios used for time-of-day rates, separate flat rates for peak and off-peak usage were calculated for each user class. Demand requirements were partitioned among classes in accordance with class peak and assigned to be recovered from peak charges. Other requirements were assigned to classes on the basis of average demand and number of customers and were then split between peak and off-peak charges in proportion to estimated average marginal production expense in those periods. The ratio of the resulting peak and off-peak rates varied from state to state, depending on characteristics of the systems in place. This scenario is labeled "Time-of-day Calculated" in the tables. For the other time-of-day scenario, revenue requirement was partitioned among classes as for the first scenario. Then peak and off-peak charges were set to recover total requirement with a prespecified ratio. The arbitrary peak/off-peak ratios used in the analysis was 8:1. As a point of information, the sixteen electric utility rate demonstration projects sponsored by the U.S. Department of Energy over the last several years have offered customers a wide range of experimental time-of-day rates. These rates have included peak/off-peak ratios between 2:1 and 10:1. On an average, our calculated rates were near 2:1, thus the 8:1 rates offered a contrast which may be representative of more highly capital intensive utilities.

21.3.6 Flat-Rate Scenario

The revenue allocation was extremely simple. The same price per kwh for all users at all levels of use was set so as to recover all required revenue. The common price was thus the average cost of production (where cost includes allowed return).

21.4 RESULTS OF APPLYING THE MODEL TO ALTERNATIVE RATE STRUCTURES

The Rate Simulation Model is a flexible tool for policy analysis, enabling the investigator to consider a wide range of "what if?" questions about future developments. It imposes no inherent limitations on such developments other than the fundamental one of beginning with systems as they now exist, including planned additions under way. All basic input prices to utility operations must be specified for a given scenario analysis. These include future fuel prices, future construction costs for possible new plants, labor rates, financial parameters associated with utility costs (such as future interest rates on debt, the rate of return needed to attract new equity, and tax credit policy), and environmental restrictions that will constrain future operations.

The analysis presented here uses only a single scenario for all input prices (e.g., fuel), financial parameters, etc. Only the rate structures vary. Implementation of the new rates is assumed to occur in 1985, with simulation carried out through 1990. Our supply scenario is highly optimistic. Hypothesized coal prices are low, as are costs for building new capacity. Furthermore, there are no regulatory constraints on adding new capacity given that the addition is cost justified. The expansion model is similar to that used by Joskow and Baughman (1976), with no limit on reserves nor any constraints other than lead time on building programs. Under this optimistic coal scenario, existing oil has a peaking role while coal capacity (much of it new) takes over the baseload and intermediate roles. These supply input parameters require the simulation of a massive building program with reserves exceeding 40 percent by 1990. This is the case despite the modification we made to the Joskow-Baughman expansion module that incorporates values of uncertainty about inputs and establishes confidence-level requirements reflecting a "conservative" tendency in expansion.

Despite these limitations, some of the results are of such a nature that they can be expected to hold for a wide range of supply scenarios. These are the results on the growth of electricity use, on the responses of different customers to new rate structures as these structures affect prices, and on the impacts the new rates will have on costs. The simulation also leads to observations on the sensitivity of the results.

21.4.1 Predicted Growth Patterns

The growth-rate levels predicted by our demand model are within the range of other published estimates but lower than most. Table 21-1 presents the forecasted growth rates for peak demand and energy requirement between 1985 and 1990 for the scenarios considered. In looking at these growth rates, bear in mind that all computations assumed normal weather patterns throughout the entire simulation period (although this is not an inherent limitation of the technological model, which has the capability of predicting response to changes in both average summer and winter temperatures). The evolution of growth rates exhibits a pattern of "tapering off," corresponding to the predictable effects of "technological maturity." We discuss this effect further in section 21.4.3.

The selection of 1985 as the year for implementing the new rates, although probably optimistic, reflects our judgment that planning, producing, and installing the new metering and billing equipment needed for time-of-day rates preclude this rate structure from being introduced universally

TABLE 21-1. Yearly growth rates under rate scenarios

	Baseline		*Time-of-Day Calculated*[1]		*Time-of-Day 8:1*		*Flat*	
Year	*En**	*Pk+*	*En**	*Pk+*	*En**	*Pk+*	*En**	*Pk+*
1985	3.6%	3.3%	0.6%	2.0%	0.7%	1.7%	2.7%	2.7%
1986	3.4	3.5	3.4	2.9	3.4	2.7	2.9	3.3
1987	3.3	3.3	3.4	2.7	3.3	2.6	2.8	3.1
1988	3.0	3.2	3.2	2.6	3.2	2.5	2.5	3.0
1989	3.1	3.1	3.1	2.6	3.1	2.6	2.6	3.0
1990	3.0	3.0	3.0	2.5	3.0	2.4	2.4	2.8

Definitions:
* = Energy requirement
\+ = Peak demand
[1] = For Scenario definitions, see text.

at any earlier date. Other new rate forms, such as flat rates, could theoretically be introduced in any year but were timed for 1985 to make comparisons clearer.

Table 21-1 shows that the hypothetical innovative rates succeed in meeting their primary goals. That is, time-of-day rates are effective in suppressing growth in peak demand relative to the energy requirement resulting in improved load factors, and flat rates suppress growth in energy requirement relative to peak demand, resulting in deteriorating load factors. As expected, the model projects greater suppression of peak demand for time-of-day rates. The longer-term pattern of development projected under time-of-day rates is thus shown to favor an improved load factor; that is, the trend is toward flatter loads as demonstrated by the reduction in the peak demand growth rate relative to the energy growth rate. However, there is a reverse effect in the first year: the load factor gets much worse before it gets better. This effect is considered further in section 21.4.3. The projection that the condition of "getting worse before getting better" will last only one year might change considerably with improved data or with different modeling of the customer's anticipation of the changeover. (The model assumes that the customer knows about a rate structure change five years in advance.)

The *reality* of the phenomenon is a different matter. It arises directly from an interaction between the responses of small users and the responses of large users. Large users (industrial, large commercial) have relatively flat loads. Small users (residential, small commercial) have low load factors. Therefore, any stimulus to reduce industrial and commercial usage more than residential will lead to a poorer load factor (improving as residential users switch to new end-use technology). Thus, a big move to cogeneration by industry will see the utility which formerly served the new cogenerators left with a load pattern that is technically less favorable and hence more expensive to serve. The customers remaining in the system, of course, will have to pick up the fixed costs that would otherwise have been borne by the departed customers, leading to higher prices (see section 21.4.2). Later we shall mention some potential technological developments that have not yet, we believe, been carefully assessed. These might permit large users to undertake self-supply economically or to reduce radically their peak loads while making heavy use of cheap off-peak energy. The experience of some European industrial customers may serve to document this potential response for U.S. industry. If these alternatives prove more applicable than our initial assessment indicated, the effect of "getting worse before getting better" could entirely disappear. But the projected price impacts of the changeover would not disappear; rather, they would be accentuated.

21.4.2 Prices and Costs

Table 21-2 indicates how average price to residential users and average system cost change from the baseline under innovative rates. Under our convention of having an appropriate return on equity included in costs, and under our assumption that revenue requirements are met, system average cost is identical to average price to all customers.

As shown in Table 21-2, the price increases to residential customers under time-of-day rates are about three times the rate of cost increases, so

TABLE 21-2. Price and cost effects of innovative rates

	Average Price to Residential (% Change)	*Average Price to All Customers (% Change)*
Time-of-Day Calculated[1]		
1985	11.1	3.4
1986	14.4	4.2
1987	13.7	3.9
1988	15.0	5.5
1989	13.6	3.6
1990	11.3	2.3
Time-of-Day 8:1		
1985	10.9	3.6
1986	14.9	4.5
1987	15.8	4.1
1988	14.0	4.0
1989	14.0	3.4
1990	10.5	1.7
Flat Rates		
1985	−12.0	0.2
1986	−11.4	0.7
1987	−10.9	0.6
1988	−11.0	0.8
1989	− 9.3	1.7
1990	− 9.7	1.1

Note: All entries represent percentage change from the baseline rate scenario.

[1]For Scenario definitions, see text.

that other customers get an average price decrease. The average cost increases are due to increased fixed costs associated with the metering and billing requirements. Table 21–3 shows how these requirements affect investment and financial needs. The price cut to residential users under flat rates (Table 21–2) results from shifting costs to other users. This pricing advantage exhibits steady erosion as the customers affected by price increases take steps to minimize their expenditures.

21.4.3 Sensitivity of Results

Although no extensive sensitivity analysis was conducted, our experience in the design and testing of key modules of the Rate Simulation Model provides some guidance on the likely sensitivity of results pertaining to the general growth pattern, the short-term impacts of time-of-day pricing on load factor, and the general direction of long-term response to rate innovations. Our baseline projection of growth rate shows a "tapering off" effect. Viewed against recent studies predicting eventual calamity under a prolonged exponential growth rate, this may seem an "optimistic" result. To other observers, it may seem a pessimistic harbinger of difficult times ahead for the utilities. For the short term under time-of-day pricing, considerable uncertainty surrounds the first-year effect of load factors deteriorating before improving. This uncertainty stems largely from what appears to be a lack of thorough study of industrial and commercial usage options under these rates. Most published articles on end-use options for exploiting cheap off-peak energy deal only with the residential sector. In contrast, for example, studies of cogeneration treat only the situation prevailing under current rates, where it makes no economic sense to provide capacity for less than all of an establishment's electricity needs. Under time-of-use rates, it may be cost effective to install peaking-type equipment, such as diesel-powered generators, to operate only during peak hours, purchasing cheap off-peak power at other times. If this option were to be widely adopted more quickly than our forecasts assume (we have estimated that full-scale cogeneration remains the dominant option), then loads could flatten more promptly while industrial users would provide even a smaller proportion of peak revenue requirements, thus raising prices further to residential and commercial customers.

Several studies have considered another technological option that could have the same impact as self-generation of peaking power. This is the shifting of electricity-intensive processes to off-peak hours, which might be accomplished without much change in the working hours of most of the labor

TABLE 21-3. Investment and financing needs to support innovative rate implementation

Time-of-Day Calculated[1]	*Change In Investment (%)*[2]	*Change In Financial Needs (%)*[3]
1982	15.0	24.5
1983	13.6	19.3
1984	13.1	18.8
1985	2.2	16.4
1986	− 1.4	− 3.3
1987	− 3.1	− 4.0
1988	− 3.1	− 7.4
1989	− 4.2	− 6.7
1990	− 5.5	− 8.4
Time-of-Day 8:1		
1982	15.0	24.5
1983	13.6	19.3
1984	13.1	18.8
1985	0.3	13.5
1986	− 2.4	− 5.2
1987	− 3.0	− 5.1
1988	− 4.8	− 8.2
1989	− 5.2	− 7.8
1990	− 5.2	− 7.8
Flat Rates		
1982	0.0	0.0
1983	0.0	0.0
1984	0.0	0.0
1985	− 3.2	− 4.2
1986	− 0.8	− 1.3
1987	− 1.0	− 1.1
1988	− 1.8	− 2.2
1989	− 1.9	− 2.7
1990	− 2.8	− 4.4

Note: All entries represent percentage change from the baseline rate scenario.

[1] For Scenario definitions, see text.

[2] The investment account includes construction expenditures plus related AFDC.

[3] The financial needs account includes total external financing requirements.

force. Electroplating is often cited as an example of such a process. However, the studies to date are not sufficient for a good appraisal of the potential of this kind of arrangement. What is needed is an inventory of the "shiftable" processes in the industries that make extensive use of electricity and an estimate of the investment requirement associated with the new arrangement, where the "batching" to replace continuous processing requires a capacity increase. Also to be considered are some highly critical, continuous processes that cannot be easily shifted, such as electrolytic reduction. Some of these warrant the installation of standby equipment to guard against electrical service interruption. Such standby equipment represents a potential source, already in place, of the peaking capability previously mentioned. Its viability as such a source should be determined through an investigation of the extent to which standby equipment now exists and its duty-cycle capability.

Finally, with regard to our projected long-term response to innovative rates, recall that we choose to model simple, "naive" rate forms. It is reasonable to suppose that rate-making bodies, in their role of protecting the public interest, will counter some of the tendencies shown in the specific, detailed provisions they will enact. There might be a ruling, for example, that any user should pay for at least as much peak usage as his off-peak electric energy. Such a ruling would inhibit peaking self-generation in the same way that high backup (standby) charges inhibit cogeneration. It would result, of course, in less flattening of electrical loads. Obtaining a more realistic picture of the long-term effects of innovative rate structures will require modeling the more complicated details of the new rate designs. Included in this additional analysis would be development of better load curves and installation costs for future appliances, refinement of the aggregation methods for each appliance load curve with regard to existing and new appliances, development of load priorities for industrial users for each state by SIC code, refinement of calculations for seasonal variations in industrial electricity use, and improvement in the calibration of system load curves to empirical data.

REFERENCES

Asbury, J. G., and Mueller, R. O. 1977. Solar and electric utilities: Should they be interfaced? *Science* 195:445–450.

Joskow, P. A., and Baughman, M. L. 1976. The future of the U.S. nuclear energy industry. *The Bell Journal of Economics* 7:3–32.

Teknekron, Inc. 1975. *Water pollution control for the steam electric power industry,* 3 vols. National Commission on Water Quality, Berkeley, Calif.

Teknekron, Inc. 1977. *An integrated technology assessment of electric utility energy systems.* Draft first-year report, 3 vols. EPA Contract 68-01-1921, Berkeley, Calif.

Teknekron, Inc. 1978. *Review of new source performance standards from coal-fired utility boilers,* 2 vols. EPA Contract 68-01-3970, Berkeley, Calif.

Turvey, R. 1968. *Optimal pricing and investment in electricity supply.* Cambridge, Mass.: MIT Press.

22 SAVING HALF OF CALIFORNIA'S ENERGY AND PEAK POWER IN BUILDINGS AND APPLIANCES*

Arthur H. Rosenfeld, David B. Goldstein,
Allen J. Lichtenberg, and Paul P. Craig

If energy and peak electric power were valued at their replacement costs, new buildings (including homes) and appliances would consume roughly half of what they do today, and old buildings would be retrofit so as to achieve similar reductions. We discuss the potentials for improved use of energy in refrigerators, homes, and stoves, and peak power shaving by storage of chilled water for air conditioning. We discuss long-range standards as a mechanism required to achieve these reductions.

*We wish to thank Dr. Eric Hirst of Oak Ridge National Laboratory and Dr. Jan Beyea of the Princeton University Center for Environmental Studies for their thoughtful comments. In addition, we express our appreciation for the critique from the staff of the California Energy Commission transmitted to us by Donald Watson, Acting Administrator of the Conservation Division. We have been able to incorporate some of their comments into this paper, and plan to address them more thoroughly in our research. Thanks are also due to T. Johnston and W. T. Ziemba for their comments and help in preparing the paper for this volume.

The results described here were partially supported by Conservation and Solar Applications (DOE) and by the California Policy Seminar. The first two authors also acknowledge support from the Department of Energy, Contract W07405-ENG-48 to the University of California for operation of the Lawrence Berkeley Laboratory with which they are associated.

22.1 OVERVIEW

Constraints on the use of energy are among the most complex and most important of all energy policies tools. Evidence developed over the past few years shows conclusively that, from a technical point of view, vigorous attention to energy conservation can have a profound impact in lowering energy requirements. The potential for saving energy and peak power in California is very large. We have studied many conservation measures that can be profitably implemented with commercially available equipment; their savings add up to 430×10^{12} Btu of gas (over 25 percent of the present use), 40×10^{9} kwh/year of electricity (over 25 percent of present use), and 12,500 mw of electric power capacity (about 50 percent of present peak capacity) (Goldstein and Rosenfeld, 1977a, 1977b). This can be done without sacrificing economic growth and with significant environmental advantages. New technologies can expand the options for cost-conservation even further.

When energy costs are a small part of total costs, lack of consumer information and institutional barriers prevent market forces from achieving minimum costs as predicted by classical economics. In California we have made progress toward overcoming these difficulties by establishing an energy commission with the power to mandate efficiency standards for major users of energy, such as buildings and appliances. The Warren-Alquist Bill (AB 1975, 1974), which founded the California Energy Resources Conservation and Development Commission (ERCDC, or Energy Commission), states that the Commission shall "prescribe standards for . . . efficiency . . . for all appliances. . . . Such [standards] shall be drawn so that they do not result in any added total cost *to the consumer* over the designed life of the appliance concerned" (emphasis added).

In practice there are two problems with the procedures by which the Energy Commission sets standards: (1) the long times needed for technological development, and (2) the fact that we presently price energy below its replacement cost.

22.1.1 Time Scale

The Energy Commission has, until now, used the following short-range criteria in setting standards.

1. Commission practice has been to require only efficiencies whose technical feasibility is self-evident. For example, the refrigerator standard is so lenient that many of the less efficient existing models already comply. In Table 22–1, we show that even though the 1979

TABLE 22–1. Peak power savings in California from refrigerator efficiency improvements after twenty years of sales

	Footnote Number	*Average Unit Monthly Use (kwh)*	*Average Unit Monthly Savings (kwh)*	*Average[1] Unit Peak Watts Saved*	*Units Sold After 20 Years*	*Statewide Peak Power Saved at Power Plant[2] (mw)*
Current weighted average	6	134	0	0	12.6 M	0
ERCDC 1979 standards	2	102	32	51	12.6 M	650
Choose most efficient model now on market	4	83	51	81	12.6 M	1100
Redesign for optimum efficiency	10	42	92	147	12.6 M	2000
Optimized freezers	11	40	77	105	3.7 M	2450

[1]Includes factor of 1.15 for increased refrigerator power demand during summer peak conditions.
[2]Includes 10 percent summer transmission losses.

standard will eventually save 600 mw, a long-range optimum standard would save 2500 mw, or about *twice* the output of the largest planned electric generation facilities. The projected cost of such facilities (e.g., nuclear plants) is about $3 billion; the improved appliances would cost consumers only about $0.75 billion.

2. The time-scale specified by the Commission for the regulations to take effect is usually one year. In cases that require changes in manufacturing plant, two or three years have been permitted, but no times longer than five years have been considered. In any case, the time-scale is so short that ERCDC standards are always based on existing technologies, and there is little pressure on manufacturers to innovate.

22.1.2 Energy Prices

Until recently energy prices were declining because new energy supplies were cheaper than existing supplies. Expansion of the energy system then reduced the average cost of energy. Now there has been a dramatic reversal as shown in Figure 22–1, with system expansion being so costly as to raise average

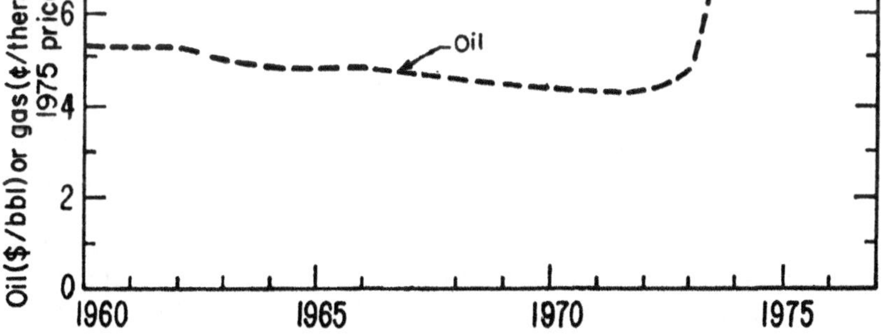

FIGURE 22–1. Prices of natural gas and oil, 1960–1975, for delivered fuels, in 1975 dollars

energy costs. In fact, the average cost of electricity from a new plant is almost twice the "average" cost at which it is sold to the typical consumer. And peak electric power costs are always higher than average costs. This low average cost to the consumer unrealistically discourages investment in energy and peak power conservation methods as opposed to new energy supplies.

Both of these problems can be attacked by use of long-range standards, that is, standards that consider both the long time scale of energy-using facilities and equipment, and those that allow a long time scale for implementation or compliance.

1. In terms of technical developments, industry can be presented with a strict requirement and given sufficient time for research, development, and retooling to meet the challenge.
2. In terms of the cost of energy projected through the life of a building that will last fifty to one hundred years, one can require many conservation measures that are cost-effective using energy costs integrated (and discounted) over the full life of the building but that are not yet cost-effective at today's prices.

In this paper we focus attention on the potential advantages that may accrue to Californians through legislative approaches to energy use based on long-range standards. Standards are just one of many approaches to energy conservation, but they offer many advantages. A comprehensive energy policy will, of course, necessarily consider a broad set of policy options, of which long-range standards would be only one. Indeed, equity considerations virtually mandate that any legislation emphasizing standards be coupled with other policy instruments.

Table 22-2 reviews the major features of long-range standards, and contrasts them with present California policy. The major features brought out are:

1. From a cost point of view, long-range standards would allow consideration of social costs (replacement cost and externalities such as environmental damage).
2. Long-range standards would allow regulatory bodies to take into account explicitly the likelihood of future energy price increases.
3. Long-range standards can be reviewed some years before they are to become effective, and can be changed should circumstances so warrant.

TABLE 22-2. Comparison of present versus proposed legislative mandates for achieving efficient use of energy

	Present	*Proposed*
Method of evaluating cost of energy	Average-cost pricing. (Utilities now charge the average cost of cheap old supply and expensive new supply.)	Replacement cost of new supply, including cost of externalities. (Replacement cost of new energy facilities and supplies is typically twice the average cost paid by the consumer.)
Time scale for evaluating cost of energy	Short-term.	Long-term. Takes into account energy cost escalation over life of appliance or building (which may be 50–100 years).
Legislative strategy	Standards based on present or near-future price.	Long-range standards based on anticipated energy costs and conservation costs. Supplementary incentives to minimize equity problems.
Technology	Present technology with unstructured development of new technology.	Technology development focussed on meeting long-range standards, e.g., 28 mile-per-gallon cars by 1985.
Key issues	Leads to unbalanced investment—supply favored over conservation. Relatively simple to implement.	Equity problems. Long-range standards require incentives (pricing and tax policy, etc.). Relieves stress on energy supply. Reduces environmental impact of energy. Increases security against interruption of energy supply.

4. Long-range standards explicitly incorporating replacement energy costs and future energy costs would probably be unacceptable to the public without a range of other governmental policies to make the standards coincide with the perceived lowest cost to the consumer.

Long-range standards are used at the federal level in a number of areas. Figure 22-2 shows the effect of federal automotive standards. As a result (at

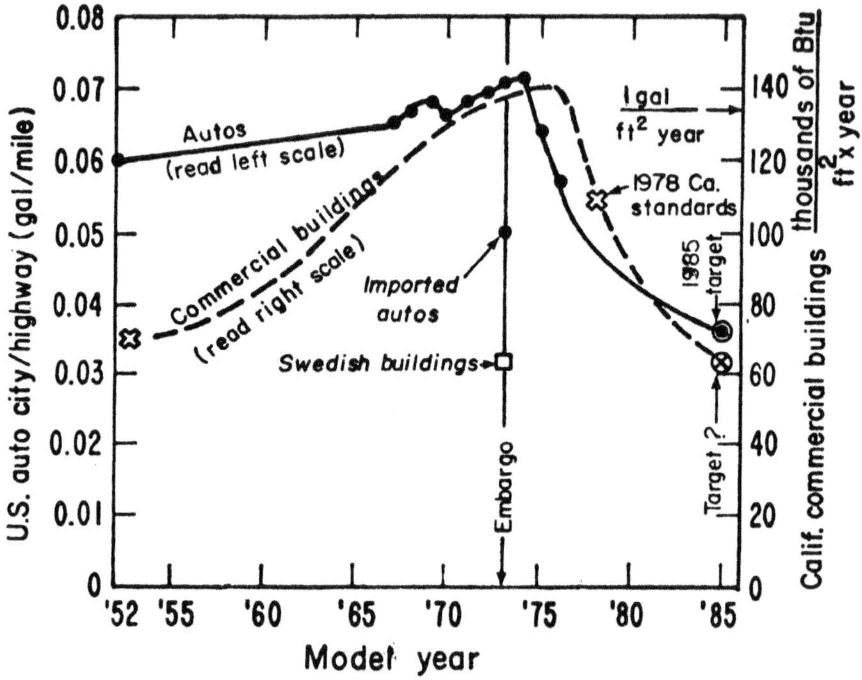

FIGURE 22-2. Trend of energy intensity for U.S. cars and commercial buildings over thirty-year period. The 1985 federal target for auto efficiency and 1978 California standard for commercial building performance are indicated. The fuel use for automobiles is in gallons per mile rather than the more usual miles per gallon in order to give energy intensity directly. A suggested commercial building target is also given.

least in part) of the legislative requirement that fuel economy must achieve 27.5 miles per gallon by 1985, the efficiency of U.S. automobiles has been improving rapidly. To show what might be accomplished with long-term building standards, the energy used by California commercial buildings is shown on the same curve. The present ERCDC standards are substantially less than could readily be achieved through economically justified long-term standards, as we demonstrate in the following example.

In order to provide some idea of the savings that may accrue to Californians through implementation of long range standards, we present an abbreviated discussion of one specific situation: improving the thermal integrity of homes. More extensive discussion is provided in a later section of this paper. Figures 22–3 and 22–4 summarize the results of extensive computer calculations of the costs and benefits of various levels of weatherproofing for typical homes in Oakland and Sacramento.

Figure 22–3 is an existing Oakland house. A number of retrofit conservation measures are illustrated, together with their costs. The energy used by the house is shown on the vertical scale. As increasingly stringent conservation measures are instituted (various thicknesses of wall and ceiling insulation, double glazing, etc.) the cumulative cost of weatherproofing increases, but energy consumed (and hence fuel cost) decreases. The optimal amount of weatherproofing is dictated by the cost of energy and the desired return on investment, after taking interest rates and inflation into account. We note that California at present has no retrofit standards (although certain cities do).

Suppose now that real energy prices (1975 dollars) continue to rise. Clearly, additional conservation measures will become justified. Figure 22–4 begins with the weatherproofing measures now required in a new home that are cost-effective at present prices and explores conservation measures going substantially beyond those considered in Figure 22–3 (more glazing, additional insulation, reduction of infiltration of outside air). Under the assumption of higher energy prices (60¢/therm is 2010, which is roughly halfway through the useful life of the house), these new conservation measures reduce space heating requirements to one-fourth and yield about a 20-percent annual return on investment assuming that inflation just cancels interest rates. If the real interest rate is different from zero the return on investment will be somewhat reduced but still substantial.

The primary conclusion to be drawn from this discussion is straightforward: *Under conditions of increasing energy prices, there are attractive weatherproofing measures that go substantially beyond the present ERCDC standards for new homes.* Under these circumstances, policies are justified that ensure conservation to the point where, from a societal point of view, no investments are made to expand energy supply when there are better investments to be had in conservation.

The question of what energy price to use in setting a standard is a particularly difficult one. In practice, administrative agencies make general statements about future replacement costs and about social and environmental costs, but then base standards on small extrapolations from present cost because these extrapolations are easiest to defend with existing data and research. But such a practice really involves making the heroic assumption that nothing will change substantially in the energy supply sector for twenty-five to fifty years.

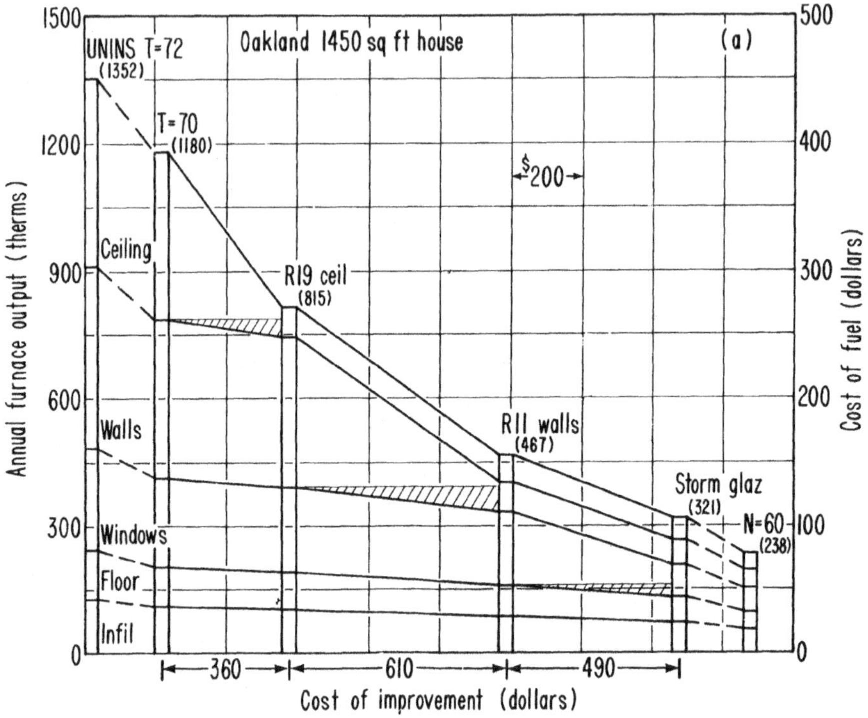

FIGURE 22–3. Energy savings possible in an uninsulated Oakland home as a result of various conservation measures. The calculations were performed on the LBL computer model TWO-ZONE. Fuel costs are shown assuming present-day gas prices to consumers (20¢/therm) divided by a furnace efficiency of 60 percent. Each vertical bar represents a different conservation "fix" of the house, and the "fixes" are cumulative, reading from left to right. The bar at the left represents a "pre-embargo" house kept at 72 °F night and day. The bar is divided into segments labeled "ceiling, walls" etc., to indicate what part of the house is responsible for that fraction of the heating energy. The second bar represents the same house kept at 70 °F instead of 72 °F. The third bar represents the same house with its ceiling insulated to R-19, a 1975 installed cost of $360, and still kept at 70 °F. The additional retrofits are wall insulation for $610, double glazing for $490, and finally night thermostat set back to 60° for $100 (for a clock thermostat). The reader should note that the year used to produce this figure was 25 percent colder than normal. Therefore, quantitative results for energy savings should be divided by 1.25 to simulate a typical year.

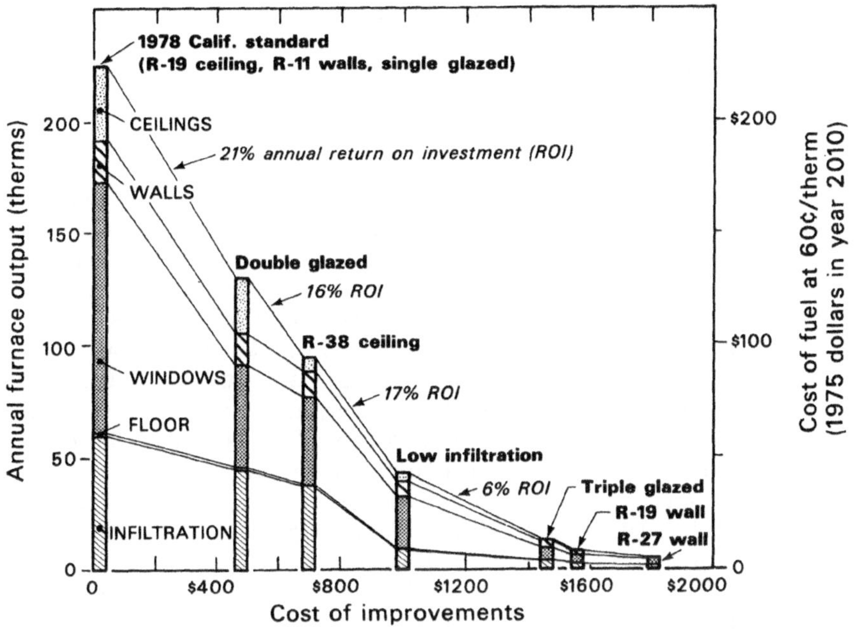

FIGURE 22-4. Heating energy use of a new Sacramento house under various "tightnesses" of insulation and infiltration. The base case bar at the left represents current California standards for new homes (R-19 ceilings, R-11 walls, single glazed). Double glazing will be required in a third of the state in 1979. The display follows the same format as Figure 22-3, and is again calculated with TWO-ZONE for the same size home of 1450 sq. ft. kept at 70° all winter. The right hand scale shows an energy cost in terms of a social cost (discounting and correcting for inflation) of 60¢ per therm of fuel, in 2010, which is nearly halfway through the useful life of a house built today.

A more prudent policy would have the legislature making a judgment on the value of future energy savings by using higher energy costs than those obtained from short-term projections. If the higher costs fail to materialize, the resulting total cost (conservation plus energy supply) will be somewhat higher than optimum. If policy is made based on lower energy cost, however, and the real cost is higher (or if availability of energy is restricted), the economic loss could be quite large.

22.2 CASE STUDIES: OPTIMIZED BUILDINGS AND APPLIANCES

22.2.1 Refrigerators

Some of the problems of encouraging energy conserving designs in appliances and buildings are illustrated in Figures 22-4 through 22-6. Figure 22-5 shows the cost effectiveness of several types of improvements in refrigerator design; it is a scatterplot of energy use (vertically) versus first cost (horizontally) for a number of real and hypothetical refrigerators.

Looking at the top of the figure, we see solid circles representing the refrigerators available to the consumer in California (Goldstein and Rosenfeld, 1977a, 1977b). Each solid circle describes an automatic defrost refrigerator in the size range 16.0-17.5 cubic feet. Note the two-to-one variation between the most efficient model on the market and the least efficient. This variation is typical of most classes of refrigerators (Berman, et al., 1976). Although the most efficient model happens to be one of the more expensive (in terms of first cost; it has the lowest life cycle costs), it can be seen that there is generally little correlation between first cost and energy consumption.

Encouraging the use of the most efficient refrigerators now on the market could have a large effect on power demand in California; we estimate that after twenty years it could save 1100 mw of peak electric power in the state[1] (Craig, et al., 1977) and thus defer the construction of more than $1 billion worth of new power plants and transmission lines (see Table 22-1). How can this potential be realized? One method (mandatory standards) has already been applied by the Energy Commission. As shown in the figure, the 1977 standard eliminates the most wasteful models on the market, while the 1979 standard forces manufacturers to approach the efficiencies of the best models on the market now, although the most efficient current model is still 25 kwh/mo better than the standard. (This 25 kwh/mo difference will

1. This number represents the long-run savings when the entire existing stock of refrigerators has been replaced. Such replacement will take over twenty-five years. As shown in Craig, et al. (1977, Table 3b), the adjustment will initially take place at a rate of 48 mw saved per year. When the adjustment is complete, there will be approximately 10.5 million households in the state, with about 1.2 refrigerators per household. (Refrigerators per household has been a slowly increasing function of time: there are presently about 1.15 refrigerators per household.) Thus the long-run potential savings are 78 watts per unit times 12.6 M units or 1000 mw statewide. To express the savings in peak load of the power plant, we must account for 10 percent summer peak transmission and distribution losses; thus total savings are 1100 mw.

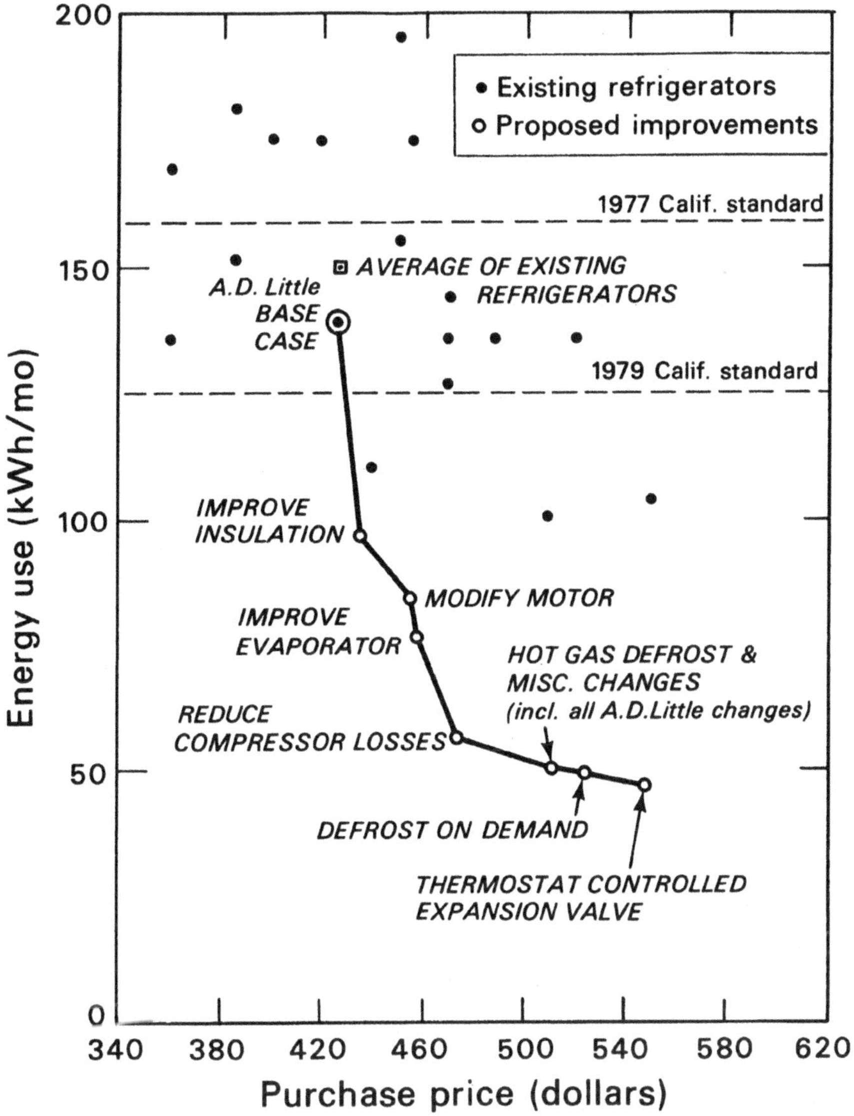

FIGURE 22–5. Energy use versus purchase price for a number of existing and proposed refrigerators. The closed circles in the upper half of the figure represent 16.0–17.5 cu. ft. top-freezer, frost-free refrigerators sold in California in 1976. The open circles in the lower half represent proposed redesigned refrigerators. California standards for maximum energy use allowable for refrigerators of this type are shown. Federal standards cannot be displayed because they involve weighted averages over all classes and sizes rather than class-specific maximum energy consumption.

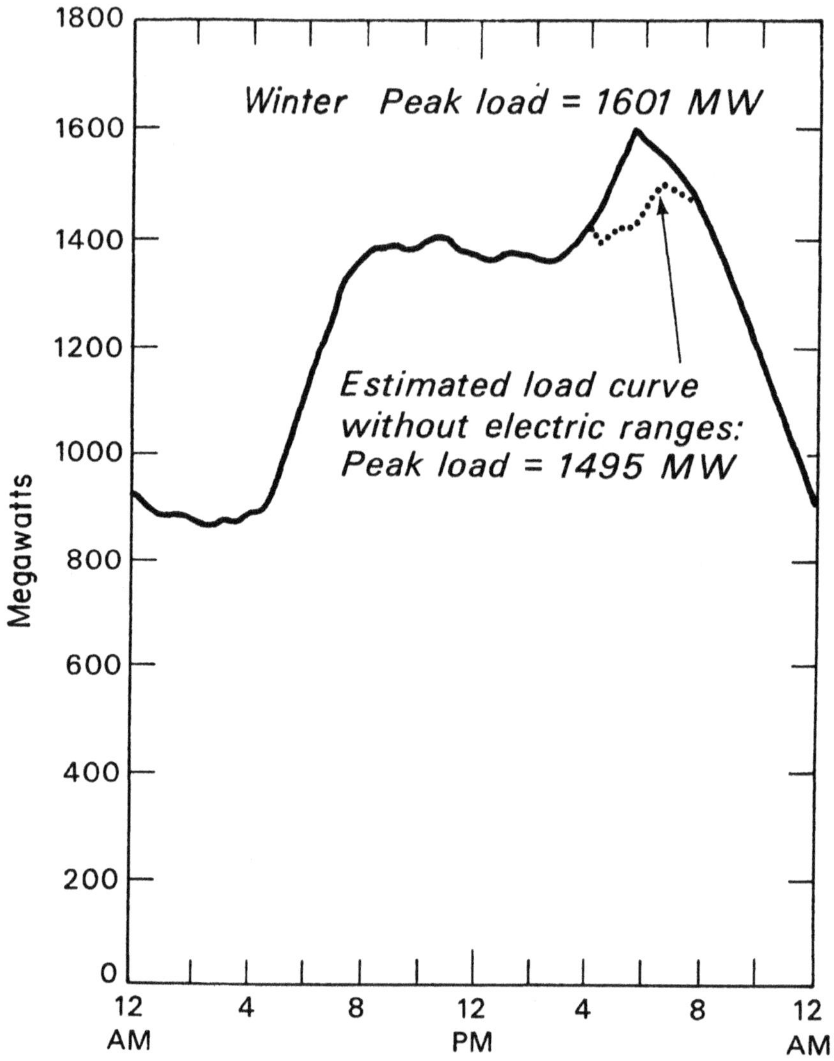

Figure 22-6. Load use for San Diego Gas and Electric Co. for the winter peak day in January 1975. The solid curve was observed; the dotted curve subtracts out the peak contribution of electric ranges.

be equivalent to about 550 mw of power statewide.[2]) So although the 1979 refrigerator standard is a big step toward effecting conservation (we estimate it will save[3] 650 mw), it still falls short of realizing the long-run potential.

How far short it falls is illustrated in Figure 22-5 by the open circles. These points represent the findings of a study done by A. D. Little (1977)[4] for the FEA on the cost, feasibility, and savings of future (e.g., 1980-1985) changes in refrigerator construction. The base case refrigerator (double circle) is a real 1972-style refrigerator "typical" of the market: as seen, it uses 137 kwh/mo compared to a California average in this class[5] (open square) of 148. We have assumed that it carries an average price tag of $425.

2. Multiply the 25 kwh/mo by 12.6 M units; convert to peak power by dividing by 720 hours per month and multiplying by 1.15 to account for higher power draw during the summer peak. (See Refrigerator Section of Appendix A of Berman, et al. (1976) for details.) Ten percent summer peak transmission losses raise the savings to 550 mw at the power plant.

3. Savings are hard to predict exactly, since the standard specifies a *maximum* energy consumption rather than an average. To estimate energy savings, we look at Goldstein and Rosenfeld (1977a, Figure 2b) to find the average energy use of the models currently sold that already better the 1979 standard. We do this by class and take a sales-weighted average as follows:

Energy Use In kwh/Month:

Class	*Sales %*	*Current*	*Post-Standard*
Manual	11.6%	58	55
Top freezer partial	17.4%	102	68
Top freezer auto	49%	148	112
Side by side	22%	167	132
Weighted average	—	134	102

Weighted average energy consumption (expressed on an *annual* basis) is about 1600 kwh for all existing models and about 1250 for those that pass the 1979 California standard. The difference: 350 kwh/yr, translates into 650 mw by the methods used in the previous two footnotes.

This calculation is only an approximation, since the "post-standards" energy consumptions were obtained from eyeballing the figure, and are not sales weighted. The "current-energy use" numbers were obtained from Berman, et al. (1976) and are more reliable; they are sales-weighted by class and size (to the extent permitted by the data).

4. For two earlier reports see Draper Laboratory (1972) and Hoskins and Hirst (1977). Points on the figure are taken from the data presented in Little (1977, Table 5.4) and from subsequent discussion. Note that Table 5.4 does not list all options in all orders; thus we cannot arrange the options on our figure in order of decreasing cost-effectiveness. Defrost-on-demand and automatic throttle valve options are calculated as a percentage savings from the previous case, since this paper only evaluates their savings in comparison to the base (137 kwh/mo) case.

5. The class average can be calculated in three ways; all give the same result. The first is to average the energy use for all top-freezer automatics in the 16-16.9 and 17-17.9 ft.^{3} range, using data from Berman, et al. (1976). The second is to perform a weighted average for the entire class (over all sizes.) The third is simply to take the unweighted average of all the points

(continued)

As shown in the figure, improvements that are cost-effective at yesterday's energy prices (e.g., 2¢ per kwh or less) will reduce energy use to 52 kwh/mo (42 percent of the 1979 standard). Further improvements that are just barely cost-effective (Little's more conservative cost calculations show them as losers) can lower energy use to 47.5 kwh/mo. The methodology of the study makes it seem probable that a number of lower cost-effectiveness options could be found that would cut energy use even further, but the success of the more basic measures resulted in the researchers concentrating on the biggest payouts.

Thus, we see a problem: how to encourage manufacturers to attack the long-range problem of developing a 50 kwh/mo refrigerator in seven years, rather than just meeting the 125 kwh/mo California standard[6] by 1980. The problem is serious because of the misplaced incentives involved. From the state's point of view, the potential savings of the 50 kwh/mo model (1350 mw more than the 1979 standard[7]) are tremendous. If we include similar savings for freezers, we can add another approximately 350 mw of savings.[8] Together this is 1700 mw or about 5 percent of total statewide electric power for all purposes.

---

on Figure 22-4, (except the energy-saving Philco's, which were not available when the A.D.L. base case refrigerator was sold (1972)). All three methods result in an average energy use of 148 ± 1 kwh/mo.

6. Since the ADL study (1977) concentrates on top-freezer automatic defrost refrigerators, and since this class accounts for about half of all refrigerators sold, our discussion uses numbers relevant to this class. Similarly large energy savings are possible in the other classes as well, according to ADL. Calculations of statewide energy savings are based on the correct model and class mix.

7. Savings are 60 percent of the 1979 standard for top freezer automatics. The calculations in Footnote 3 show a post-standards average energy consumption of 102 kwh/mo or 1250 kwh/yr. So the statewide average savings per unit are about 0.60×1250 kwh/yr or 750 kwh/yr. With 12.6 M refrigerators, this is an eventual savings of 1350 mw of peak power compared to the 1979 ERCDC standards, or 900 mw more than choosing the *most* efficient model in each size and features class.

8. The ADL study (1977) predicts a larger percentage savings in freezers; this is plausible because a larger fraction of the energy use of a freezer is consumed in removing the heat conducted through the walls. Better insulation will reduce this head load; so the reduction in overall energy use would be proportionally larger in freezers. Freezers currently use about 1400 kwh/yr or 117 kwh/mo. This energy use requires 160 peak watts (Berman, et al., 1976). We assume this will be reduced to 1200 kwh/yr (100 kwh/mo or 135 watts) by the new California standards. If we then take the same 60 percent improvement over the standards used in the refrigerator calculation, we get a new energy use of 480 kwh/yr and peak power use of 55 W for a savings of 105 W compared to current average. At present, one-third of California households use freezers. If we assume this eventually settles at 35 percent there will be 3.7 million freezers in the state. Statewide peak power savings are thus 350 mw more than the 1979 ERCDC standard or 450 mw compared to present practice.

The 1700 mw is also approximately the reliable output of the two proposed Sundesert nuclear plants, which together will cost $3 billion. The cost of the 16 million improved appliances is only $750 million, roughly one-quarter the cost of the plants. If, as refrigerators wear out, we replace them with improved models and defer power plants, the net gain to society will also include the entire avoided cost of operating the plants (including fuel) and any nuclear risk that has been deferred. Sundesert is chosen for this comparison only because it is currently in the news, not because we oppose nuclear plants as such. New electricity from nuclear, coal, or even hydro power is about equally expensive (in dollars plus ecological cost).

But from the manufacturer's point of view, the research and development costs of designing a reliable 50 kwh/mo refrigerator are very large, especially since there is no evidence that new designs will sell well. Note from the figure that consumers will apparently choose a 175 kwh/mo refrigerator as frequently as a 110 kwh/mo model with identical first cost; thus, a higher cost superefficient model may be a big money loser for its producer. So investing heavily in research and development is very risky for the manufacturer; even if the research is successful, there is no assurance that it will pay off. In addition, the modest level of the current state (and proposed federal) standards assures the manufacturers that a small retooling effort, as opposed to a major reengineering project, will suffice. If tighter standards or consumer resistance to energy-wasteful appliances should develop later, manufacturers can start their planning for redesign later (or they can drag their feet — note that AHAM (Association of Home Appliance Manufacturers) has sued California to prevent the enforcement of any appliance standard.[9]) So manufacturers presently lack any incentive to do the research necessary to make a 50 kwh/mo refrigerator. When and if they receive that incentive in the future, they will still have to go through a three- to seven-year process of engineering change, testing, receiving safety certifications, modifying assembly lines, etc.

This presents the consumer with the unfortunate situation of being unable to reduce refrigerator life-cycle energy costs much below $1000 without accepting a lifestyle change (e.g., manual defrost).[10]

9. The Association of Home Appliance Manufacturers (headquarters in Chicago, Illinois) sought an injunction against the state of California's attempts to enforce its refrigerator/freezer efficiency standards. The injunction was not issued, but AHAM has not withdrawn its lawsuit against the state. Amana, one of the major producers of refrigerators objected to the suit and withdrew from AHAM.

10. The lowest energy consumption automatic defrost unit uses 88 kwh/mo. At PG&E's nonlifeline rate of 4.8¢/kwh, this unit costs $47.50 a year, today, to operate, and a refrigerator has an average life of twenty years.

One approach to relieving this problem is an aggressive consumer education/energy extension program. When the manufacturers find that the most efficient models available (e.g, 90–100 kwh/mo) start to sell better than the 1980 barely-acceptable models (e.g., 124 kwh/mo) then they will tend to produce lower and lower energy units, finally approaching the 50 kwh/mo optimum.

A faster approach is to present the manufacturers with long-range targets for efficiency. A 1985 target of 50 kwh/mo, if recognized by them as inevitable, will spur the development effort necessary to make large changes in efficiency available on the market. They will see that the costs of this development are as necessary to compete in the large California market. The costs should also be recognizable as something that can be passed on to the consumer. (Perhaps at greater profit; A. D. Little estimates that a $1 cost increase to the manufacturer results in $2.50 in extra consumer costs. Much of the difference, $1.50, winds up as someone's increased profit.)

Long-range targets have the advantage of being adjustable. If electricity prices rise more slowly than now expected, or if it turns out to be more difficult to meet the standard than predicted, compliance can be delayed for a few years. But the manufacturers will have warning far enough in advance that they can comply in a reasonable fashion. (The imposition of stricter standards every three years is called "ratcheting" by the industry and can be disruptive if it requires frequent retooling or replanning to meet a moving target.)

22.2.2 New Homes

Figure 22–4 shows a different approach to long-range conservation planning. This figure shows the costs and savings of a variety of measures applicable to new houses in northern California.

We have already discussed (Figure 22–3) how insulation and double-glazing can reduce the energy use for heating an uninsulated Oakland home by up to three-quarters. The California State Department of Housing and Community Development issued standards in 1975 that ensure that new houses in California are insulated. This standard (applicable to the whole state), will save about 0.1×10^{15} Btu per year after twenty years of construction.[11] (Energy Units: A therm is defined at 10^5 Btu. 10^{15} (one quadril-

11. Previous construction practices allowed uninsulated walls but insulated the attic. Average energy use was about 600 therms for an average housing unit (average of 1/2 single family units and 1/2 multifamily). After the standards, average energy use is about 350 therms. After twenty years of construction; 225,000 units per year, the savings are $(600 - 350) \times 10^5$ Btu/yr $\times$ 20 yrs $\times$ 225 $\times$ 10^3 houses/yr = $.112 \times 10^{15}$ Btu/yr.

lion) Btu is often called one "Quad." California uses 5.2 Quads for all purposes; nearly 2 Quads are consumed in buildings.)

In 1976 the new Energy Commission strengthened this standard by requiring the use of efficient heating systems, restricting the installation of electric water heating, reducing allowable window area (except for passive-solar-collector windows) and required double-pane windows in northern California. Savings from the window requirements will be about 20×10^{12} Btu per year[12] after twenty years of construction. (Savings from efficient heating systems are harder to predict, since they depend on how many people would have installed inefficient systems without the standard, but they are on the order of 70×10^{12} Btu/year.)[13]

The Commission decided not to increase standards beyond this point because further insulation could not be justified on the basis of cost savings to the consumer. But Figure 22–4 shows that the heating energy needs of a northern California house can be reduced to one-quarter their current extent or less by higher levels of thermal tightness. If the state were to decide that a therm of gas was worth 60¢ for example, then the annual return on investment for increasing attic insulation from R–19 to R–38 would be 16 percent, rather than the present return of 6 percent to the consumer. Treating the house for low air leakage by sealing cracks and partition walls as well as envelope walls (Sinden, 1977) would have a return of 17 percent. Triple-glazing would yield only a 6 percent return (the payback would be low only because there was almost no heat left to save). The house would then use only 20 therms of heat annually, compared to the present average of 850 for northern California (existing houses not new ones).

(It is interesting to note that the entire insulation package — from no insulation to triple glazing — costs only $2000 and saves very nearly 100 percent of the heating bill.)

Similar figures would apply in southern California, except that the savings for each measure would be slightly lower and the heating bill would be reduced sooner to one-quarter or less. So we conclude that virtually the

12. Savings from double-glazing in northern California are approximately 150 therms per unit. If one-third of the new units are constructed in northern California, savings after twenty years are 150×10^5 Btu/yr $\times$ 20 yrs $\times$ ($1/3 \times 225 \times 10^3$ houses/yr) $-$ 22.5×10^{12} Btu/yr.

13. A typical electrically heated house used 500 kwh/yr (see Berman, et al. (1976)) at an efficiency about half that of a gas-heated house. Most electrically heated houses also have electric water heaters, which add 4000 kwh/yr. So the standard might save about $1/2 \times 9000$ kwh/yr. If we assume that 30 percent of the new housing stock would have used electric resistance heat, the savings after twenty years are about $1/2 \times 9000$ kwh/yr $\times$ 11,000 Btu/kwh $\times$ .3 $\times$ 225,000 houses/yr $\times$ 20 yrs = 66.8×10^{12} Btu/yr.

entire space-heat needs in California can be eliminated by forward-looking (that is, future-cost-based) standards. Statewide savings beyond those resulting from present insulation standards are about 0.18×10^{15} Btu/yr after twenty years.[14]

Increased insulation also makes home heating more resistant to interruption in energy supply. The superinsulated houses at the right of Figure 22–4 will stay relatively warm even when completely unheated (due to solar heat gain through the windows), in contrast to existing homes, which cool to below 55°F when unheated.

It is interesting to compare the results of insulation standards with those of the free market. Before wall insulation was required, in the early 1970s, walls of houses in California were almost never insulated. Yet the cost of insulating the walls of a typical 1500 ft^2 new house would have been about $125, and the annual savings (even at 1970 gas prices) would have been about $50 a year. Classical microeconomics would predict that wall insulation should have been routine, since the payback time was less than three years. However, walls were not, in fact, insulated until it was required by law.

22.2.3 Storing Coolth at Stanford — Shaving the Summer Peak

Until the 1960s, electric utilities experienced their peak loads in the winter, but the demand for air conditioning has moved the annual peak to summer. And now peak power has become expensive. To power a new two-ton residential air conditioner (which demands 3 kw at full load), a utility must now invest $1500 (i.e., $500/kw, including reserve equipment and transmission costs). From a societal point of view it is already cheaper in a large building to install thermal storage (to store water that is precooled off-peak) than it is to pay for peak power. If coolth storage were to take over and be extended to homes, the summer peak would drop below the winter peak, and it would pay to address winter peak shaving — a problem presently beyond the horizon of the Energy Commission.

To add a touch of realism, we summarize the remarkable economics of cold-water storage now being installed on the Stanford campus.

14. A single-glazed house in southern California and a double-glazed northern California house both use about 400 therms/yr. So 400×10^5 Btu/yr $\times$ 20 yrs $\times$ 225,000 house/yr = 180×10^{12} Btu/yr.

Stanford uses 5000 tons of peak air conditioning and foresees growth to 8000 tons in eight years. But the additional 3000 tons of new chillers and cooling towers would cost about $1.5 million. Instead Stanford finds that for the same price it can build a 4-million gallon insulated tank for cold-water storage, and connect it to the present chillers. Then it can meet its 8000-ton afternoon load by running its present capacity at night, saving *all* peak power charges, and saving energy because both electric plants and chilling systems are more efficient at night. Thus Stanford, at no increase in first cost, saves operating and peak power costs, and the utility sees a reduction in peak load. Under *marginal* peak power prices, the same economics apply to many commercial buildings (Rosenfeld and Dublin, 1977).

22.2.4 Fuel Substitution

Since most of the state's utilities are presently summer peaking, the Energy Commission's load management strategies have focused on reducing the summer peak. Over the long run, however, such strategies as storing coolth in commercial buildings, shading windows, and the commission's standards on air conditioner efficiency may be so effective as to shift the peak back to winter. (It should be noted that about 20 percent of the summer peak is caused by residential air conditioning (Goldstein and Rosenfeld, 1977a, 1977b).

If this is to be the case, a long run strategy would also look at winter peak loads. Some important contributors to winter peak loads are electric heating appliances, in particular, electric ranges. Besides being a peak load, electric ranges also use more energy resources than gas ranges. Since the efficiency of electric generation is about one-third, heat is supplied more efficiently by a gas flame than by electric resistance. Studies by RAND (Dole, 1975) and LBL (Berman, et al., 1976) confirm that gas ranges, clothes dryers, water heaters, and space heaters are more efficient than their electric counterparts, typically by a factor of two.[15]

15. Some might argue that the possibility of a gas shortage justifies the use of electric heating appliances even if they are less efficient. But such an argument ignores economics. If it is really preferable (to the state) to use electric ranges (1200 kwh/yr), rather than gas ranges (60 therms), then the value of the electricity used must be less than the value of the gas saved. The 1200 kwh costs $100 at marginal cost (approximately 8¢/kwh), so for electric ranges to be preferable to gas, it must be worth $100 to save 60 therms. But this value: $1.60/therm is more than five times what we currently pay for gas and more than twice the higher cost estimates for new supply schemes. For example, gas (from imported liquefied natural gas) is distributed to residents of Tokyo for less than 40¢/therm. A number of retrofit conservation measures with huge potential savings (e.g., wall insulation and storm windows in southern California) would

(continued)

The Energy Commission has added a section to the building standards to discourage electric resistance space heaters and water heaters in new construction. As we have discussed, this will result in substantial energy savings. However, it has ignored the fuel choice question for the other appliances. This is a serious omission. While electric ranges are only a moderately large *energy* user (accounting for about 20 percent of the electricity use of a typical California household) they are an immense contribution to the winter peak load.

The reason for this is intuitively clear; almost all range owners are cooking dinner from 5:00 to 6:00 P.M. Unfortunately, this is exactly the time when the rest of the electric system peaks, as workers come home and turn on lights and appliances, but before commercial buildings are turned off.

The average "diversified demand" of a range is about 800 watts from 5:00 to 6:00 P.M.; this figure was obtained from a PG&E load study,[16] which probably underestimates total range energy use: thus it is conservatively low. This demand has a very substantial impact on utility load curves. Figure 22-6 shows the winter peak-day load curve for San Diego Gas and Electric (a winter-peaking utility) with and without the peak-hour contribution of electric ranges. Note that the peak load without electric ranges is 6 percent lower (more than 100 mw) than the observed load. This 100 mw of extra peak load results from a "saturation" of 42 percent in electric ranges.[17] So, between the future scenarios of 10 percent saturation of electric ranges versus 90 percent saturation, there is a difference of about 12 percent of the total statewide winter peak load.

Thus, switching from electric to gas appliances could result in large peak power and energy savings. This switch is hard to implement on a consumer level, because most ranges are built into new houses, and the buyer has relatively little control over the built-ins the home builder provides (it is hard to imagine a family refusing to buy a new house because the range was electric instead of gas).

Mandatory standards are troublesome because there is some element of lifestyle change involved in the switch. Some people prefer electric to gas, irrespective of cost considerations. On the other hand, it could be argued that new home buyers are stuck with what the builder installed in any event, so

---

be cost effective at much less than $1.60 a therm, and the savings in gas from these measures would be far larger than that needed to fuel all the ranges, water heaters, and clothes dryers in the state. In the long run, producing gas from coal will be a less expensive way of heating than using electricity generated by burning coal in a new power plant.

16. See Berman, et al. (1976) for a discussion of the PG&E load study.

17. Saturation is defined as the ratio of the number of appliances used to the number of households. See Berman, et al. (1976).

that it might be better to shift the decision making from the contractor to the state, since the state has no entrepreneural interest.

In fact, there is evidence that a state move to mandate gas ranges would please most consumers. Despite the fact that most *new* ranges in the state are electric, almost all the ranges purchased directly by consumers are gas.[18] So the mandated use of gas ranges might represent an improvement in consumer satisfaction to most people, while saving on the order of 4000 mw, or $2 billion of utility investments. Switching to gas dryers, while having negligible effect on peak loads, would reduce electric energy use by 5×10^9 kwh per year, about 3 percent.[19]

REFERENCES

Berman, S. M.; Blumstein, C.; Goldstein, D.; et al. 1976. Electrical energy consumption in California: Data collection and analysis. Lawrence Berkeley Laboratory, UCID-3847. Appendix A, Refrigerator section (n.p.).

Craig, P. P.; Goldstein, D. B.; Kukulka, R.; Rosenfeld, A. H. 1977. Energy extension in California: Context and potential impact. Lawrence Berkeley Laboratory, LBL-5236.

Dole, S. H. 1975. Energy use and conservation in the residential sector: a regional analysis. The Rand Corporation, R-1641-NSF.

Draper Laboratory. 1972. Productivity of servicing consumer durable products. Massachusetts Institute of Technology.

Goldstein, D. B., and Rosenfeld, A. H. 1977a. Some potentials for energy and peak power conservation in California. Lawrence Berkeley Laboratory, LBL-5926.

Goldstein, D. B., and Rosenfeld, A. H. 1977b. Energy conservation in home appliances through comparison shopping. Lawrence Berkeley Laboratory, LBL-5910.

Hoskins, R. A., and Hirst, E. 1977. Energy and cost analysis of residential refrigerators. Oak Ridge National Laboratory Report ORNL-CON-6.

Arthur D. Little, Inc. 1977.

Arthur D. Little, Inc. 1977. Study of energy-saving options for refrigerators and water heaters, volume 1: Refrigerators. Cambridge, Massachusetts.

The Los Angeles Times. 1975. Continuing home audit. Los Angeles Times Marketing Research, Jan.-June.

Rosenfeld, A. H., and Dubin, F. S. 1977. Electric load leveling by chilled water storage. Lawrence Berkeley Laboratory, LBL-5909.

18. In *The Los Angeles Times,* it is shown that 91.5 percent of the ranges sold to consumers in the LA-Orange Country region in the first half of 1975 were gas. The percentage of gas ranges was 88.8 percent in 1974, 86.4 percent in 1973 and 90.0 percent in 1972.

19. Assuming a potential 50 percent saturation of electric dryers in 10.5×10^6 housing units. Electrical dryers use 1000 kwh/yr.

Sinden, F. 1977. A two-thirds reduction in energy consumption of a Princeton townhouse. Center for Environmental Studies, Princeton University, PU/CES 56.

Wall, L. W.; Dey, T.; Gadgil, A. J.; Lilly, A. B.; and Rosenfeld, A. H. 1976. Conservation options in residential energy use: Studies using the computer program TWOZONE. Lawrence Berkeley Laboratory, LBL-5271.

GPSR Compliance

The European Union's (EU) General Product Safety Regulation (GPSR) is a set of rules that requires consumer products to be safe and our obligations to ensure this.

If you have any concerns about our products, you can contact us on ProductSafety@springernature.com

In case Publisher is established outside the EU, the EU authorized representative is:

Springer Nature Customer Service Center GmbH
Europaplatz 3
69115 Heidelberg, Germany

Batch number: 10761588

Printed by Printforce, the Netherlands